Mayflower

NATHANIEL PHILBRICK

Mayflower

A Voyage to War

Harper*Press*

An Imprint of HarperCollinsPublishers

Harper*Press*
An imprint of HarperCollins*Publishers*
77–85 Fulham Palace Road,
Hammersmith, London w6 8jb
www.harpercollins.com

First published in Great Britain in 2006 by Harper*Press*

Maps by Jeffrey L. Ward

Originally published in the United States in 2006 by the Penguin Group

1

Nathaniel Philbrick asserts the moral right to
be identified as the author of this work

A catalogue record for this book
is available from the British Library

HB ISBN-13   978-0-00-715127-1
HB ISBN-10   0-00-715127-6

TPB ISBN-13   978-0-00-722861-4
TPB ISBN-10   0-00-722861-9

Set in Adobe Garamond

Printed and bound in Great Britain by Clays Ltd, St Ives plc

To Melissa

Contents

Part IV · *War*

List of Maps

Preface: The Two Voyages

WE ALL WANT TO KNOW how it was *in the beginning*. From the Big Bang to the Garden of Eden to the circumstances of our own births, we yearn to travel back to that distant time when everything was new and full of promise. Perhaps then, we tell ourselves, we can start to make sense of the complex mess we are in today.

But beginnings are rarely as clear-cut as we would like them to be. Take, for example, the event that most Americans associate with the start of the United States: the voyage of the *Mayflower*.

We've all heard at least some version of the story: how in 1620 the Pilgrims sailed to the New World in search of religious freedom; how after drawing up the Mayflower Compact, they landed at Plymouth Rock and befriended the local Wampanoags, who taught them how to plant corn and whose leader or sachem, Massasoit, helped them celebrate the First Thanksgiving. From this inspiring inception came the United States.

Like many Americans, I grew up taking this myth of national origins with a grain of salt. In their wide-brimmed hats and buckled shoes, the Pilgrims were the stuff of holiday parades and bad Victorian poetry. Nothing could be more removed from the ambiguities of modern-day America, I thought, than the Pilgrims and the *Mayflower*.

But, as I have since discovered, the story of the Pilgrims does not end with the First Thanksgiving. When we look to how the Pilgrims and their children maintained more than fifty years of peace with the Wampanoags and how that peace suddenly erupted into one of the deadliest wars ever fought on American soil, the history of Plymouth Colony becomes something altogether new, rich, troubling, and complex. Instead of the story we already know, it becomes the story we need to know.

In 1676, fifty-six years after the sailing of the *Mayflower,* a similarly named but far less famous ship, the *Seaflower,* departed from the shores of New England. Like the *Mayflower,* she carried a human cargo. But instead of 102 potential colonists, the *Seaflower* was bound for the Caribbean with 180 Native American slaves.

The governor of Plymouth Colony, Josiah Winslow—son of former *Mayflower* passengers Edward and Susanna Winslow—had provided the *Seaflower's* captain with the necessary documentation. In a certificate bearing his official seal, Winslow explained that these Native men, women, and children had joined in an uprising against the colony and were guilty of "many notorious and execrable murders, killings, and outrages." As a consequence, these "heathen malefactors" had been condemned to perpetual slavery.

The *Seaflower* was one of several New England vessels bound for the West Indies with Native slaves. But by 1676, plantation owners in Barbados and Jamaica had little interest in slaves who had already shown a willingness to revolt. No evidence exists as to what happened to the Indians aboard the *Seaflower,* but we do know that the captain of one American slave ship was forced to venture all the way to Africa before he finally disposed of his cargo. And so, over a half century after the sailing of the *Mayflower,* a vessel from New England completed a transatlantic passage of a different sort.

The rebellion referred to by Winslow in the *Seaflower's* certificate is known today as King Philip's War. Philip was the son of Massasoit, the Wampanoag leader who greeted the Pilgrims in 1621. Fifty-four years later, in 1675, Massasoit's son went to war. The fragile bonds that had held the Indians and English together in the decades since the sailing of the *Mayflower* had been irreparably broken.

King Philip's War lasted only fourteen months, but it changed the face of New England. After fifty-five years of peace, the lives of Native and English peoples had become so intimately intertwined that when fighting broke out, many of the region's Indians found themselves, in the words of a contemporary chronicler, "in a kind of maze, not knowing what to do." Some Indians chose to support Philip; others joined the colonial forces; still others attempted to stay out of the conflict altogether. Violence quickly spread until the entire region became a terrifying war zone. A third of the hundred or so towns in New England were burned and abandoned. There was even a proposal to build a barricade around the core settlements of Massachusetts and surrender the towns outside the perimeter to Philip and his allies.

The colonial forces ultimately triumphed, but at a horrifying cost. There were approximately seventy thousand people in New England at the outbreak of hostilities. By the end of the war, somewhere in the neighborhood of five thousand were dead, with more than three-quarters of those losses suffered by the Native Americans. In terms of percentage of population killed, King Philip's War was more than twice as bloody as the American Civil War and at least seven times more lethal than the American Revolution. Not counted in these statistics are the hundreds of Native Americans who, like the passengers aboard the *Seaflower,* ended the war as slaves. It had taken fifty-six years to unfold, but one people's quest for freedom had resulted in the conquest and enslavement of another.

It was Philip who led me to the Pilgrims. I was researching the history of my adopted home, Nantucket Island, when I encountered a reference to the Wampanoag leader in the town's records. In attempting to answer the question of why Philip, whose headquarters was in modern Bristol, Rhode Island, had traveled more than sixty-five miles across the water to Nantucket, I realized that I must begin with Philip's father, Massasoit, and the Pilgrims.

My initial impression of the period was bounded by two conflicting preconceptions: the time-honored tradition of how the Pilgrims came to symbolize all that is good about America and the now equally familiar modern tale of how the evil Europeans annihilated the innocent Native Americans. I soon learned that the real-life Indians and English of the seventeenth century were too smart, too generous, too greedy, too brave—in short, too human—to behave so predictably.

Without Massasoit's help, the Pilgrims would never have survived the first year, and they remained steadfast supporters of the sachem to the very end. For his part, Massasoit realized almost from the start that his own fortunes were linked to those of the English. In this respect, there is a surprising amount of truth in the tired, threadbare story of the First Thanksgiving.

But the Indians and English of Plymouth Colony did not live in a static idyll of mutual support. Instead, it was fifty-five years of struggle and compromise—a dynamic, often harrowing process of give and take. As long as both sides recognized that they needed each other, there was peace. The next generation, however, came to see things differently.

When Philip's warriors attacked in June of 1675, it was not because relentless and faceless forces had given the Indians no other choice. Those forces had existed from the very beginning. War came to New England because two leaders—Philip and his English counterpart, Josiah Winslow—allowed it to happen. For Indians and English alike, there was nothing inevitable about King Philip's War, and the outbreak of fighting caught almost everyone by surprise.

When violence and fear grip a society, there is an almost overpowering temptation to demonize the enemy. Given the unprecedented level of suffering and death during King Philip's War, the temptations were especially great, and it is not surprising that both Indians and English began to view their former neighbors as subhuman and evil. What *is* surprising is that even in the midst of one of the deadliest wars in American history, there were Englishmen who believed the Indians were not inherently malevolent and there were Indians who believed the same about the English. They were the ones whose rambunctious and intrinsically rebellious faith in humanity finally brought the war to an end, and they are the heroes of this story.

* * *

It would be left to subsequent generations of New Englanders to concoct the nostalgic and reassuring legends that have become the staple of annual Thanksgiving Day celebrations. As we shall see, the Pilgrims had more important things to worry about than who was the first to set foot on Plymouth Rock.

It is true that most of what we know about seventeenth-century New England comes from the English. In recent decades, however, archaeologists, anthropologists, and folklorists have significantly increased our understanding of the Native American culture of the time. This does not alter the fact that any account of the period must depend, for the most part, on contemporary narratives, histories, letters, documents, and poems written by English men and women.

I have focused on two people, one familiar, the other less so: Plymouth governor William Bradford and Benjamin Church, a carpenter turned Indian fighter whose maternal grandfather had sailed on the *Mayflower*. Bradford and Church could not have been more different—one was pious and stalwart, the other was audacious and proud—but both wrote revealingly about their lives in the New World. Together, they tell a fifty-six-year intergenerational saga of discovery, accommodation, community, and war—a pattern that was repeated time and time again as the United States worked its way west and, ultimately, out into the world.

It is a story that is at once fundamental and obscure, and it begins with a ship on a wide and blustery sea.

PART I

Discovery

CHAPTER ONE

They Knew They Were Pilgrims

*F*OR SIXTY-FIVE DAYS, the *Mayflower* had blundered her way through storms and headwinds, her bottom a shaggy pelt of seaweed and barnacles, her leaky decks spewing salt water onto her passengers' devoted heads. There were 102 of them—104 if you counted the two dogs: a spaniel and a giant, slobbery mastiff. Most of their provisions and equipment were beneath them in the hold, the primary storage area of the vessel. The passengers were in the between, or 'tween, decks—a dank, airless space about seventy-five feet long and not even five feet high that separated the hold from the upper deck. The 'tween decks was more of a crawlspace than a place to live, made even more claustrophobic by the passengers' attempts to provide themselves with some privacy. A series of thin-walled cabins had been built, creating a crowded warren of rooms that overflowed with people and their possessions: chests of clothing, casks of food, chairs, pillows, rugs, and omnipresent chamber pots. There was even a boat—cut into pieces for later assembly—doing temporary duty as a bed.

They were nearly ten weeks into a voyage that was supposed to have been completed during the balmy days of summer. But they had started late, and it was now November, and winter was coming on. They had long since run out of firewood, and they were reaching the slimy bottoms of their water casks. Of even greater concern, they were down to their last casks of beer. Due to the notoriously bad quality of the drinking water in seventeenth-century England, beer was considered essential to a healthy diet. And sure enough, with the rationing of their beer came the unmistakable signs of scurvy: bleeding gums, loosening teeth, and foul-smelling breath. So far only two had died—a sailor and a young servant—but if they didn't reach land soon many more would follow.

They had set sail with three pregnant mothers: Elizabeth Hopkins, Susanna White, and Mary Allerton. Elizabeth had given birth to a son, appropriately named Oceanus, and Susanna and Mary were both well along in their pregnancies.

It had been a miserable passage. In midocean, a fierce wave had exploded against the old ship's topsides, straining a structural timber until it had cracked like a chicken bone. The *Mayflower*'s master, Christopher Jones, had considered turning back to England. But Jones had to give his passengers their due. They knew next to nothing about the sea or the savage coast for which they were bound, but their resolve was unshakable. Despite all they had so far suffered—agonizing delays, seasickness, cold, and the scorn and ridicule of the sailors—they had done everything in their power to help the carpenter repair the fractured beam. They had brought a screw jack—a mechanical device used to lift heavy objects—to assist them in constructing houses in the New World. With the help of the screw jack, they lifted the beam into place, and once the carpenter had hammered in a post for support, the *Mayflower* was sound enough to continue on.

They were a most unusual group of colonists. Instead of noblemen, craftsmen, and servants—the types of people who had founded Jamestown in Virginia—these were, for the most part, families—men, women, and children who were willing to endure almost anything if it meant they could worship as they pleased. The motivating force behind the voyage had come from a congregation of approximately four hundred English Puritans living in Leiden, Holland. Like all Puritans, these English exiles believed that the Church of England must be purged of its many excesses and abuses. But these were Puritans with a vengeance. Instead of working for change within the established church, they had resolved to draw away from the Church of England— an illegal act in Jacobean England. Known as Separatists, they represented the radical fringe of the Puritan movement. In 1608, they had decided to do as several groups of English Separatists had done before them: emigrate to the more religiously tolerant country of Holland.

They had eventually settled in Leiden, a university town that could not have been more different from the rolling, sheep-dotted fields of their native England. Leiden was a redbrick labyrinth of building-packed streets and carefully engineered canals, a city overrun with refugees from all across Europe. Under the leadership of their charismatic minister, John Robinson, their congregation had more than tripled in size. But once again, it had become time for them to leave.

As foreigners in Holland, many of them had been forced to work menial, backbreaking jobs in the cloth industry, and their health had suffered. Despite the country's reputation for religious tolerance, a new and troubling era had come to Holland as a debate among the leading theologians of the day sparked civil unrest and, on occasion, violence. Just the year before, a member of their congregation had almost been killed by a rock-hurling crowd. Even worse, a Dutch treaty with Spain was about to expire, and it was feared Leiden might soon be subjected to the same kind of siege that had resulted in the deaths of half the city's residents during the previous century.

But their chief worry involved their children. Gradually and inevitably, they were becoming Dutch. The congregation had rejected the Church of England, but the vast majority of its members were still proudly, even defiantly, English. By sailing to the New World, they hoped to re-create the English village life they so dearly missed while remaining beyond the meddlesome reach of King James and his bishops.

It was a stunningly audacious proposition. With the exception of Jamestown, all other attempts to establish a permanent English settlement on the North American continent had so far failed. And Jamestown, founded in 1607, could hardly be counted a success. During the first year, 70 of 108 settlers had died. The following winter came the "starving time," when 440 of 500 settlers were buried in just six months. As it turned out, the most lethal days in Jamestown were yet to come. Between 1619 and 1622, the Virginia Company would send close to 3,600 settlers to the colony; over that three-year period, 3,000 would die.

In addition to starvation and disease, there was the threat of Indian attack. At the university library in Leiden were sensational accounts left by earlier explorers and settlers, telling how the Indians "delight to torment men in the most bloody manner that may be; flaying some alive with the shells of fishes, cutting off the members and joints of others by piecemeal and broiling on the coals." How could parents willingly subject their children to the risk of such a fate?

In the end, all arguments for and against emigrating to America ended with the conviction that God wanted them to go. The world, they believed, was on the verge of the millennium—the thousand-year rule of the saints predicted in the book of Revelation. In 1618, a comet appeared in the skies over Europe, signaling, many thought, the final, apocalyptic battle of good against evil. And, in fact, what became known as the Thirty Years' War would rage across the Continent as Protestant and Catholic forces reduced much of Europe to a burning, corpse-strewn battleground. So far, England had avoided this conflict, and as all God-fearing English Puritans knew, their country had been earmarked by the Lord to lead his forces in triumph. Instead of Europe, perhaps America, a continent previously dominated by the Catholic powers of Spain and France, was where God intended to bring the reformed Protestant Church to perfection. All Englishmen had heard of the atrocities the Spaniards' hateful hunt for gold had inflicted on the Indians of America. England, it had been predicted by Richard Hakluyt, the chronicler of British exploration, would do it differently. It was the Leideners' patriotic and spiritual duty to plant a godly English plantation in the New World. "We verily believe and trust the Lord is with us," they wrote, "and that He will graciously prosper our endeavors according to the simplicity of our hearts therein."

Their time in Leiden, they now realized, had been a mere rehearsal for the real adventure. "We are well weaned from the delicate milk of our mother country," they wrote, "and inured to the difficulties of a strange and hard land, which yet in a great part we have by patience overcome." Most important, however, they were "knit together as a body in a most strict and sacred bond."

They were weavers, wool carders, tailors, shoemakers, and printers, with almost no relevant experience when it came to carving a settlement out of the American wilderness. And yet, because of the extraordinary spiritual connection they had developed as exiles in Leiden and even before, they were prepared for whatever lay ahead. "[I]t is not with us as with other men," they confidently insisted, "whom small things can discourage, or small discontentments cause to wish themselves home again." Or, as one of their number, a thirty-year-old corduroy worker named William Bradford, later wrote, "they knew they were pilgrims."

Taking Bradford's lead, we refer to them today as the Pilgrims, a name that is as good as any to describe a people who were almost always on the move—even after they had supposedly found a home in America. If not for Bradford's steady, often forceful leadership, it is doubtful whether there ever would have been a colony. Without his *Of Plymouth Plantation,* certainly the greatest book written in seventeenth-century America, there would be almost no information about the voyage with which it all began. For William Bradford, however, the true voyage had begun close to twenty years before.

Bradford was born in the tiny farming town of Austerfield, Yorkshire, deep in northern England, where the closest thing to a wilderness was the famed Sherwood Forest to the south. The Great North Road from London to Edinburgh (actually more of a ribbon of mud than a proper road) passed nearby, but few from Austerfield had ever ventured far from home.

Although he came from a family of prosperous, land-rooted farmers, Bradford had experienced more than his share of dislocation and loss. By the time he turned twelve, he had lost not only his father, his mother, and a sister, but also the grandfather who had raised him. Soon after moving in with his two uncles, he was struck by a mysterious ailment that prevented him from working in the fields. Bradford later claimed that his "long sickness" had saved him from "the vanities of youth, and made him the fitter for what he was afterwards to undergo." Most important, his illness gave him the opportunity to read.

Lonely and intelligent, he looked to the Bible for consolation and guidance. For a boy in need of instruction, the Geneva Bible, translated in the previous century by a small team of English ministers and equipped with helpful notes and appendices, was just the thing. There was also John Foxe's *Book of Martyrs,* a compelling, tremendously popular account of the Protestants martyred by Queen Elizabeth's Catholic predecessor on the throne, "Bloody Mary." Foxe's insistence that England was, like Israel before it, God's chosen nation had a deep and lasting influence on Bradford, and as Foxe made horrifyingly clear, to be a godly Englishman sometimes required a person to make the ultimate sacrifice.

At issue at the turn of the seventeenth century—and long before— was the proper way for a Christian to gain access to the will of God. Catholics and more conservative Protestants believed that the traditions of the church contained valid, time-honored additions to what was found in the Bible. Given man's fallen condition, no individual could presume to question the ancient, ceremonial truths of the established church.

But for the Puritans, man's fallen nature was precisely the point. All one had to do was witness a typical Sunday service in England— in which parishioners stared dumbly at a minister mumbling incomprehensible phrases from the Book of Common Prayer—to recognize how far most people were from a true engagement with the word of God.

A Puritan believed it was necessary to venture back to the absolute beginning of Christianity, before the church had been corrupted by centuries of laxity and abuse, to locate divine truth. In lieu of time travel, there was the Bible, with the New Testament providing the only reliable account of Christ's time on earth while the Old Testament contained a rich storehouse of still vital truths. If something was not in the scriptures, it was a man-made distortion of what God intended. At once radical and deeply conservative, the Puritans had chosen to spurn thousands of years of accumulated tradition in favor of a text that gave them a direct and personal connection to God.

A Puritan had no use for the Church of England's Book of Common Prayer, since it tampered with the original meaning of the Bible and inhibited the spontaneity that they felt was essential to attaining a true and honest glimpse of the divine. Hymns were also judged to be a corruption of God's word—instead, a Puritan read directly from the Bible and sang scrupulously translated psalms whose meaning took precedence over the demands of rhyme and meter. As staunch "primitivists," Puritans refused to kneel while taking communion, since there was no evidence that the apostles had done so during the Last Supper. There was also no biblical precedent for making the sign of the cross when uttering Christ's name. Even more important, there was no precedent for the system of bishops that ran the Church of England. The only biblically sanctioned organizational unit was the individual congregation.

The Puritans believed that a congregation began with a covenant (a term they took from the Bible) between a group of believers and God. As a self-created and independent entity, the congregation elected a university-trained minister and, if the occasion should arise, voted him out. The Puritans also used the concept of a covenant to describe the individual's relationship with God. Ever since the Fall, when Adam had broken his covenant of works with God, man had been deserving of perpetual damnation. God had since made a covenant with Christ; upon the fulfillment of that covenant, God had offered a covenant of grace to just a small minority of people, known as the Saints.

The Puritans believed that the identity of the Saints had long since been determined by God. This meant that there was nothing a person could do to win salvation. But instead of being a reason to forsake all hope, what was known as predestination became a powerful goad to action. No one could be entirely sure as to who was one of the elect, and yet, if a person was saved, he or she naturally lived a godly life. As a result, the Puritans were constantly comparing their own actions to those of others, since their conduct might indicate whether or not they were saved. Underlying this compulsive quest for reassurance was a person's conscience, which one divine described as "the voice of God in man."

A Puritan was taught to recognize the stages by which he or she might experience a sureness of redemption. It began with a powerful response to the "preaching of the word," in which God revealed the heights to which a person must aspire if he or she was to achieve grace. This was followed by a profound sense of inadequacy and despair that eventually served as a prelude to, if a person was destined to be redeemed, "saving grace." From this rigorous program of divine discipline a Puritan developed the confidence that he or she was, in fact, one of the elect. For William Bradford, who had lost almost everyone he had ever loved, this emotionally charged quest for divinity would lead not only to the assurance of his own redemption but to the family he had never known.

Bradford was just twelve years old when he became uneasy with the way God was worshipped in Austerfield. Like just about every village in England, Austerfield possessed a small stone church built soon after the Norman Conquest in the eleventh century. But the Austerfield church, known as St. Helena's, was—and is—unusual. Over the door is a primitive stone carving from a much earlier era depicting an open-mouthed snake. One can only wonder whether this weird, almost runic figure first suggested to the young Bradford that the Puritans were right: the Church of England had been poisoned by "that old serpent Satan." He must seek out a congregation of like-minded believers and worship God as the Bible instructed.

In Scrooby, an even tinier town than Austerfield a few miles down the road in northern Nottinghamshire, he eventually found what he was looking for. In an old manor house, just a few decades from being demolished, lived the town's postmaster, William Brewster. It was here that a group of Separatists gathered every Sunday to worship in secret under the direction of two ministers, one of whom was the young John Robinson.

Taking their cue from Paul's admonition "come out among them, and be separate," the Separatists were Puritans who had determined that the Church of England was not a true church of Christ. If they

St. Helena's Church in Austerfield, Yorkshire

were to remain true to their faith, they must form a church of what were known as visible Saints: members of the elect who upheld each other in the proper worship of God. If members of the congregation strayed from the true path, they were admonished; if they failed to correct themselves, they were excommunicated. Purged of the ungodly, a Separatist congregation shared in an intense fellowship of righteousness that touched every facet of every communicant's life.

The Separatists believed in spiritual discipline, but they also believed in spontaneity. After the minister concluded his sermon, members of the congregation were encouraged to "prophesy." Instead of looking into the future, prophesying involved an inspired kind of improvisation: an extemporaneous attempt by the more knowledgeable members of the congregation to speak—sometimes briefly, sometimes at great length—about religious doctrine. By the end of the service, which lasted for several hours, the entire congregation had participated in a passionate search for divine truth.

Adding to the intensity of the spiritual bond shared by the Separatists in Scrooby was the fact that they were engaged in an illegal activity. During the previous century, several Separatists had been jailed and even executed for their beliefs, and since the coronation of King James in 1603, the pressure to conform to the Church of England had been mounting. From James's perspective, all Puritans were troublemakers who threatened the spiritual integrity of his realm, and at a gathering of religious leaders at his palace in Hampton Court, he angrily declared, "I shall harry them out of the land!" In the years since the Hampton Court Conference, increasing numbers of men and women had been prosecuted for their unorthodox religious beliefs. As Separatists, the congregation at Scrooby was in violation of both ecclesiastical and civil law, and all of them undoubtedly knew that it was only a matter of time before the authorities found them out.

Some time in 1607, the bishop of York became aware of the meetings at Brewster's manor house. Some members of the congregation were thrown in prison; others discovered that their houses were being watched. It was time to leave Scrooby. But if King James had vowed to "harry" the Puritans out of England, he was unwilling to provide them with a legal means of leaving the country. A person needed official permission to voyage to the Continent, something the authorities refused to grant religious nonconformists such as the Separatists from Scrooby. If they were to sail for Holland, they must do it secretly.

For a group of farmers and artisans most of whom had rarely, if ever, ventured beyond the Nottinghamshire-Yorkshire region, it was a most daunting prospect. But for seventeen-year-old Bradford, who would lose the people upon whom he had come to depend if he did not follow them to Holland, there was little choice in the matter. Despite the vehement protests of his friends and relatives, who must have pointed out that he was due to receive a comfortable inheritance at twenty-one, he decided to sail with John Robinson and William Brewster to a new land.

Their escape from England did not go well. The first captain they hired turned out to be a traitor and a thief who surrendered them to the authorities in the Lincolnshire town of Boston. After their leaders had spent several months in jail, they tried again. This time they secured the services of a trustworthy Dutch captain, who planned to meet them on the southern bank of the Humber River, just above the town of Grimsby. But they'd loaded no women and children and only a portion of the men onto the ship when the local militia appeared. Fearing capture, the captain determined to sail for Amsterdam, leaving the women and children weeping in despair as their husbands looked on from the deck of the departing ship. It was several months before they were all reunited in Holland.

Once in Amsterdam, the Separatists from Scrooby found themselves thrust into conflict and contention. As dissidents who had come to define themselves in opposition to an established authority, Separatists were often unprepared for the reality of being able to worship as they wanted in Holland. Relieved of all doctrinal restraint, the ministers of several English Separatist congregations began to advocate

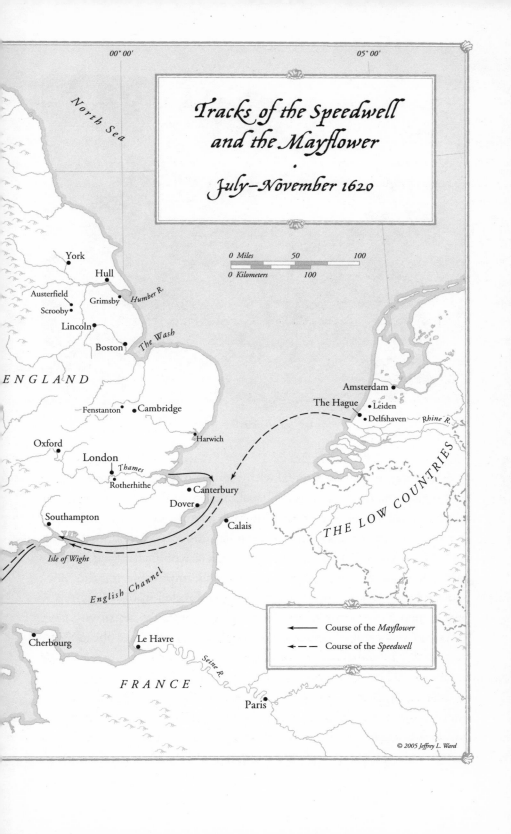

Tracks of the Speedwell
and the Mayflower

·

July–November 1620

0 *Miles* 50 100

0 *Kilometers* 100

North Sea

York
Hull
Austerfield
Scrooby• Grimsby• *Humber R.*
Lincoln•
Boston• *The Wash*

E N G L A N D

Fenstanton• •Cambridge
Harwich•

Oxford•
London
↓ *Thames*
Rotherhithe• •Canterbury
Dover•

Southampton•
Calais•

Isle of Wight

Amsterdam •
The Hague • • Leiden
• Delfshaven *Rhine R.*

THE LOW COUNTRIES

English Channel

Cherbourg•
Le Havre•
Seine R.

F R A N C E

Paris•

←—— Course of the *Mayflower*
←- - - Course of the *Speedwell*

© 2005 Jeffrey L. Ward

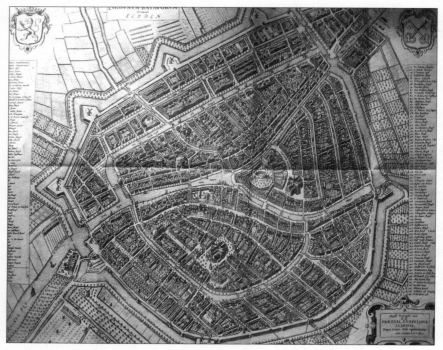

Leiden, Holland, in the early seventeenth century

positions that put them at odds with their own flocks. The minister of an English congregation from Gainsborough (only a few miles from Scrooby) had decided to reject infant baptism; another minister attempted to quell a messy series of personal scandals by claiming that he and his elders, or church officers, could dictate policy to their congregation. As fellow English Separatists, it was impossible for the newcomers from Scrooby to avoid becoming embroiled in these quarrels if they remained in Amsterdam. Showing the firmness, sensitivity, and judgment that came to characterize his ministry in the years ahead, John Robinson led the majority of the congregation to the neighboring city of Leiden, where they were free to establish themselves on their own terms.

In Leiden, Robinson secured a house not far from the Pieterskerk, one of the city's largest churches. In the garden behind Robinson's home, they created a miniature village of close to a dozen houses. Even though approximately half the congregation lived in houses elsewhere in the city, what was known as De Groene Poort, meaning the green lane or alley, came to represent the ideal of Christian fellowship they would aspire to for the rest of their lives.

William Bradford soon emerged as one of the leading members of the congregation. When he turned twenty-one in 1611, he sold the property he had inherited in Austerfield and used the proceeds to purchase a small house. A fustian, or corduroy worker, Bradford became a citizen of Leiden in 1612 in recognition of his high standing in the community. In 1613, he married Dorothy May, and four years later they had a son, John. But Bradford's life in Leiden was not without its setbacks. At one point, some poor business decisions resulted in the loss of a significant portion of his inheritance. In typical Puritan fashion, he interpreted this as a "correction bestowed by God . . . for certain decays of internal piety."

From the beginning, the Pilgrims exhibited all the strengths and weaknesses of a group held together by "a most strict and sacred bond." When circumstances turned against them, they demonstrated remarkable courage and resilience; indeed, adversity seemed to intensify their clannish commitment to one another. Once established in Leiden, they acquired a renewed sense of purpose—despite, or because of, the hardships of exile.

Leiden was a thriving city of forty thousand, but it was also a commercial center that required its inhabitants to work at a pace that must have come as a shock to farmers from Nottinghamshire and Yorkshire. A life of husbandry involved periods of intense labor, but its seasonal rhythms left long stretches of relative inactivity. In Leiden, on the other hand, men, women, and even children were expected to work from dawn to dusk, six days a week, with a bell sounding in the tower of the yarn market to announce when work was to begin and end. As the years of ceaseless labor began to mount and their children began to lose touch with their English ancestry, the Pilgrims decided it was time to start over again.

The members of Robinson's congregation knew each other wonderfully well, but when it came to the outside world they could sometimes run into trouble. They were too focused on their own inner lives to appreciate the subtleties of character that might have alerted them to the true motives of those who did not share in their beliefs. Time and time again during their preparations to sail for America, the Pilgrims demonstrated an extraordinary talent for getting duped.

It began badly when William Brewster ran afoul of the English government. In Leiden, he had established a printing press, which he ran with the help of the twenty-three-year-old Edward Winslow. In 1618 Brewster and Winslow published a religious tract critical of the English king and his bishops. James ordered Brewster's arrest, and when the king's agents in Holland came to seize the Pilgrim elder, Brewster was forced into hiding just as preparations to depart for America entered the most critical phase.

Brewster was the only Pilgrim with political and diplomatic experience. As a young man, he had served as an assistant to Queen Elizabeth's secretary of state, William Davison. Brewster's budding diplomatic career had been cut short when the queen had used Davison as her scapegoat for the execution of Mary Queen of Scots. With his mentor in prison, Brewster had been forced to return home to Scrooby, where he had taken over his father's position as postmaster.

In addition to having once been familiar with the highest levels of political power, Brewster possessed an unusually empathetic nature. "He was tenderhearted and compassionate of such as were in misery," Bradford wrote, "but especially of such as had been of good estate and rank and were fallen unto want and poverty." More than anyone else, with the possible exception of Pastor Robinson, Elder Brewster was the person upon whom the congregation depended for guidance and support. But as they wrestled with the myriad details of planning a voyage to America, Brewster was, at least for now, lost to them.

By the beginning of the seventeenth century, it had become apparent that the colonization of North America was essential to England's future prosperity. France, Holland, and especially Spain had already taken advantage of the seemingly limitless resources of the New World. But the British government lacked the financial wherewithal to fund a broad-based colonization effort of its own. Seeing it as an opportunity to add to their already considerable personal wealth, two groups of noblemen—one based in London, the other to the west in Plymouth—were eager to underwrite British settlements in America, and in 1606, James created the Virginia Company. But after the Plymouth group's attempts to found a colony in modern Maine failed miserably and Jamestown proved to be something less than a financial success, the two branches of the Virginia Company realized that they, too, lacked the resources required to colonize America. They then resolved to franchise future settlements by issuing subsidiary, or "particular," patents to those interested in beginning a plantation. These conditional patents gave the settlers the right to attempt to found a colony in five to seven years' time, after which they could apply for a new patent that gave them permanent title to the land.

With Brewster in hiding, the Pilgrims looked to their deacon John Carver, probably in his midthirties, and Robert Cushman, forty-one, to carry on negotiations with the appropriate officials in London. By June 1619, Carver and Cushman had succeeded in securing a patent from the Virginia Company. But the Pilgrims' plans were still far from complete. They had a patent but had not, as of yet, figured out how they were going to finance the endeavor. But William Bradford's faith in the undertaking was so strong that he sold his house in the spring of 1619.

Soon after, disturbing news came from London. Robert Cushman reported that a group very similar to their own had recently met with disaster on a voyage to America. Led by a Mr. Blackwell, 180 English Separatists from Emden, Holland, had sailed that winter for Virginia. By the time the ship reached America, 130 of the emigrants, including Blackwell, were dead. "[T]hey were packed together like herrings," Cushman wrote. "They had amongst them the flux, and also want of fresh water, so as it is here rather wondered at that so many are alive, than so many are dead." Still, the news was deeply troubling to those in Leiden, and many of them began to have second thoughts about sailing to America. Even Cushman had to admit that he, a grocer and wool-comber originally from Canterbury, felt overwhelmed by the challenges and responsibilities of organizing the voyage. "It doth often trouble me," he wrote, "to think that in this business we are all to learn and none to teach."

About this time some representatives from Holland, having heard of the Pilgrims' intention to relocate to America, "made them fair offers" concerning a possible settlement. But the Pilgrims declined. It would have been impossible to reassert their English identity in a Dutch colony. What they do not seem to have taken into account was the possible danger of spurning this particular overture. The Dutch, still several years from founding a colony at Manhattan, appear to have begun to work covertly to block the Pilgrims' subsequent attempts to settle in this strategic location.

Instead of looking to Holland, the Pilgrims threw in their lot with a smooth-talking merchant from London named Thomas Weston. Weston represented a group of investors known as the Merchant Adventurers—about seventy London merchants who viewed the colonization of America as both an investment opportunity and a way "to plant religion." Most of them appear to have shared Puritan spiritual leanings, although some were clearly wary of the radicalism of the Pilgrims' Separatist beliefs. Even though the Pilgrims had secured a patent the year before, the Merchant Adventurers obtained a patent of their own for a settlement in the northern portion of Virginia at the mouth of the Hudson River.

In the beginning, Weston seemed a godsend—a man sympathetic to their religious goals who also claimed to have the financial wherewithal to make their cherished dreams a reality. Weston proposed that they enter into a joint stock company. The Adventurers would put up most of the capital with the expectation that, once they were settled in America, the Pilgrims would quickly begin to generate considerable profits, primarily through codfishing and the fur trade. The Pilgrims would each be given a share in the company valued at ten pounds. For the next seven years they would work four days a week for the company and two days a week for themselves, with the Sabbath reserved for worship. At the end of the seven years, the capital and profits would be divided among all of them, with the Pilgrims owning their houses and home lots free and clear.

As the spring of 1620 approached, many had decided to wait until those in the "first brunt" had cleared the way for them; still others, such as Bradford, had already sold their homes and had long since been ready to depart. A census of the congregation revealed that only about 125 people (a third of their total number) would be departing for the New World, with the rest to follow soon after. Pastor Robinson, it was decided, would stay for now in Leiden with the majority of his flock, with Elder Brewster attending to the religious needs of those in America.

As the Pilgrims prepared to depart in the spring of 1620, Weston's true nature began to reveal itself. He now claimed that circumstances had changed, making it necessary to adjust the original agreement. He had hoped to secure a fishing monopoly for the settlement, but it was now clear that this was not possible. Many of his fellow Adventurers, he maintained, were inclined to back out. If the merchants in London were to come forward with the necessary funds, the Pilgrims must agree to dedicate all their time to working for the company. Instead of having two days a week for themselves, they must spend every minute laboring for the Adventurers. Robinson and the Pilgrims in Leiden vehemently objected, claiming that the new terms were "fitter for thieves and bondslaves than honest men." Making matters all the worse was that Robert Cushman had agreed to Weston's new terms without consulting the rest of them back in Leiden.

In June they discovered that, incredibly, Weston had not yet arranged any transportation to America. If they had any hope of reaching the mouth of the Hudson River before winter, they must depart as soon as possible. While Weston hunted up a ship in London, the Pilgrims decided to purchase a small sailing vessel of their own in Holland. Not only would it be used to transport some of them across the Atlantic, it would be useful for both fishing and exploring the coast once they were in America. And if the worst should happen, it would provide a means for the survivors to return to England.

Adding to the Pilgrims' growing sense of alarm was the fact that the

Departure of the Pilgrims from Delfshaven *by Adam Willaerts, 1620*

Adventurers had insisted on adding some non-Separatists from London to the mix. Some had strong ties to the group in Leiden, but others were completely unknown to them. How they would get along with these "Strangers" was of deep concern, especially since one of them, a man named Christopher Martin, was already proving to be a most difficult personality. The Adventurers designated Martin as a purchasing agent, and he, along with Cushman and Carver, began to secure supplies and provisions: beer, wine, hardtack, salted beef and pork, dried peas, fishing supplies, muskets, armor, clothing, tools, trade goods for the Indians, and the screw jack that would come in handy even before they reached America.

Martin, a haughty and willful man, refused to coordinate his efforts with Carver and Cushman. While the Pilgrim agents collected provisions in London and Canterbury, Martin proceeded to do as he pleased in Southampton, a major port in the south of England. Soon, no one really knew where matters stood when it came to provisions. "[W]e are readier to dispute than to set forward a voyage," Cushman lamented on June 10.

Despite the chaotic and acrimonious nature of the preparations in

England, the Pilgrims in Leiden forged ahead, purchasing a sixty-ton vessel named the *Speedwell.* Less than fifty feet in length, she was considered large enough for a voyage across the Atlantic; earlier expeditions had successfully completed the crossing in vessels that were less than half the *Speedwell*'s tonnage. The Pilgrims hired a master and crew who agreed to stay on for at least a year in America and who undoubtedly oversaw the fitting out of the vessel with two new and larger masts. The refitting of the *Speedwell* may have seemed like an insignificant matter at the time. As it turned out, however, this misnamed vessel and her master, known to us only as "Mr. Reynolds," would have a disastrous impact on the voyage ahead.

By the end of July, the Pilgrims, accompanied by a large number of family and friends, had made their way to Delfshaven, the small Dutch port where the *Speedwell* was waiting. The plan was to sail for Southampton, where they would rendezvous with whatever ship Weston had secured in London. "[T]hey went aboard and their friends with them," Bradford wrote, "where truly doleful was the sight of that sad and mournful parting, to see what sighs and sobs and prayers did sound amongst them, what tears did gush from every eye, and pithy speeches pierced each heart."

For Bradford and his wife, Dorothy, the parting in Delfshaven was particularly painful. They had decided to leave their three-year-old son, John, behind in Holland, perhaps with Dorothy's parents in Amsterdam. It was certainly safer for the child, but the emotional cost, especially for the boy's mother, would become increasingly difficult to bear. Whether he realized it or not, Bradford was inflicting his own childhood experience on his son: for a time, at least, John would be, for all intents and purposes, an orphan.

When the tide turned in their favor, it was time to depart. Pastor Robinson fell down to his knees on the *Speedwell*'s deck, as did everyone present, and "with watery cheeks commended them with most fervent prayers to the Lord and His blessing." It was a remarkable display of "such love as indeed is seldom found on earth." Years later, the residents of Delfshaven were still talking about the departure of the Pilgrims in July 1620.

* * *

By the time the Leideners departed from Delfshaven, Weston had hired an old and reliable ship named the *Mayflower,* which after taking aboard passengers in London sailed to Southampton to rendezvous with the *Speedwell.* Southampton was an ancient English port encircled by a medieval stone wall, and near the West Gate of Southampton, the Leiden contingent got their first glimpse of the ship that was to sail with them to America.

The *Mayflower* was a typical merchant vessel of her day: square-rigged and beak bowed, with high, castlelike superstructures fore and aft that protected her cargo and crew in the worst weather, but made beating against the wind a painfully inefficient endeavor. Rated at 180 tons (meaning that her hold was capable of accommodating 180 casks or tuns of wine), she was approximately three times the size of the *Speedwell* and about one hundred feet in length.

The *Mayflower's* commanding officer, known as the master, was Christopher Jones. About fifty years old, he was also a part owner of the ship. Records indicate that Jones had been master of the *Mayflower* for the last eleven years, sailing back and forth across the Channel with English woolens to France and returning to London with French wine. Wine ships such as the *Mayflower* were known as "sweet ships," since the inevitable spillage of the acidic wine helped to temper the stench of the bilge. In addition to wine and wool, Jones had transported hats, hemp, Spanish salt, hops, and vinegar to Norway and may even have taken the *Mayflower* on a whaling voyage to Greenland. He and his wife, Josian, had had five children, and although he had no way of knowing it at the time, Josian was pregnant with another son, who would be born at their home in Rotherhithe, just down the Thames from London, the following March.

Serving as Jones's mate and pilot was Robert Coppin, who, unlike Jones, had been to America before. Also serving as pilot was John Clark, forty-five, who'd delivered some cattle to Jamestown the previous year. Giles Heale was the ship's surgeon. In the days ahead, as sickness spread through the passengers and crew, he would become one of the most sought-after officers of the *Mayflower.* Another important position was that of the cooper, who was in charge of maintaining all barreled supplies and provisions. In Southampton, Jones secured the twenty-one-year-old cooper John Alden, who because of his youth and skills was already being encouraged by the Pilgrims to remain in America at the completion of the crossing. In addition, there were somewhere between twenty and thirty sailors, whose names have not survived.

In Southampton, the Leideners met up with the family and friends who had first boarded the *Mayflower* in London and would be continuing on with them to America. Most shared their religious beliefs and several of them were actual members of the Leiden congregation. The most notable of the group was Elder William Brewster, who had been hiding out in Holland and perhaps even England for the last year. The return of Brewster, the highest-ranking layperson of the congregation and their designated spiritual leader in the New World, must have been as emotionally charged as their departure from Leiden.

Also joining them in Southampton were Robert Cushman and John Carver, who was traveling with his wife, Katherine, and five servants. Although not a member of the congregation, Captain Miles Standish was well known to the Leideners. Standish, who was accompanied by his wife, Rose, and may or may not have come over on the *Speedwell,* had served as an English mercenary in Holland and would be handling the colony's military matters in America.

It was in Southampton that they met the so-called Strangers—passengers recruited by the Adventurers to take the places of those who had chosen to remain in Holland. Besides the domineering Christopher Martin, who had been designated the "governor" of the *Mayflower* by the Adventurers and was traveling with his wife and two servants, there were four additional families. Stephen Hopkins was making his second trip to America. Eleven years earlier in 1609 he had sailed on the *Sea Venture* for Virginia, only to become shipwrecked in Bermuda—an incident that became the basis for Shakespeare's *The Tempest.* While on Bermuda, Hopkins had been part of an attempted mutiny and been sentenced to hang, but pleading tearfully for his life, he was, at the last minute, given a reprieve. Hopkins spent two years in Jamestown before returning to England and was now accompanied by his pregnant wife, Elizabeth; his son, Giles; and daughters Constance and Damaris, along with two servants, Edward Doty and Edward Leister.

In addition to the Mullinses, Eatons, and Billingtons (whom Bradford later called "one of the profanest families amongst them"), there were four children from Shipton, Shropshire. Ellen, Jasper, Richard, and Mary More were the products of an adulterous relationship between their mother, Catherine More, and her longtime lover, Jacob Blakeway. When Catherine's husband, Samuel More, an aristocrat who spent most of his time in London, belatedly realized that his children were not his own (their resemblance to Blakeway, he insisted in court, was unmistakable), he divorced his wife and took custody of the children. More determined that it would be best for the children to begin a new life in America. They were sent to London and placed under the care of Weston, Cushman, and Carver, who assigned Ellen, eight, to Edward and Elizabeth Winslow; Jasper, seven, to the Carvers; and both Richard, five, and Mary, four, to William and Mary Brewster, who were accompanied by their evocatively named sons Love and Wrestling.

In the meantime, matters were coming to a head between the Leideners and Thomas Weston. Cushman had signed the revised agreement with the merchants in London, but the Leideners refused to honor it. Weston stalked off in a huff, insisting that "they must then look to stand on their own legs." As Cushman knew better than anyone, this was not in their best interests. They didn't have enough provisions to feed them all for a year, and yet they still owed many of their suppliers money. Without Weston to provide them with the necessary funds, they were forced to sell off some of their precious foodstuffs, including more than two tons of butter, before they could sail from Southampton.

Adding to the turmoil and confusion was the behavior of Christopher Martin. The *Mayflower*'s governor was, according to Cushman, a monster. "[H]e insulteth over our poor people, with such scorn and contempt," Cushman wrote, "as if they were not good enough to wipe his shoes. . . . If I speak to him, he flies in my face as mutinous, and

saith no complaints shall be heard or received but by himself." In a letter hastily written to a friend in London, Cushman saw only doom and
disaster ahead. "Friend, if ever we make a plantation God works a
miracle, especially considering how scant we shall be of victuals, and
most of all un-united amongst ourselves and devoid of good tutors and
regiment. Violence will break all. Where is the meek and humble spirit
of Moses?"

When it finally came time to leave Southampton, Cushman made
sure he was with his friends aboard the *Speedwell*. He was now free of
Martin but soon found that the *Speedwell* was anything but speedy.
"[S]he is as open and leaky as a sieve," he wrote. As they watched the
water spout through the gaps in the planking, he and his compatriots
from Leiden were reminded of the earthen dikes in Holland, claiming
that "the water came in as at a mole hole." Several days after clearing
the Isle of Wight off England's southern coast, it was decided they
must put in for repairs, and both vessels sailed for Dartmouth, a port
only seventy-five miles to the west of Southampton.

It was now August 17. The repairs were quickly completed, but this
time the wind refused to cooperate. They were stuck in Dartmouth, a
rock-rimmed harbor surrounded by high, sheltering hills, waiting for a
fair breeze. People were beginning to panic—and with good reason.
"Our victuals will be half eaten up, I think, before we go from the coast
of England," Cushman wrote. Many of the passengers decided it was
time to abandon the voyage. Even though they'd lose everything they
had so far invested, which for some of them amounted to everything
they possessed, they wanted out. But Martin refused to let them off the
Mayflower. "[H]e will not hear them, nor suffer them to go ashore,"
Cushman wrote from Dartmouth, "lest they should run away."

The months of unremitting tension had caught up with Cushman.
For the last two weeks he had felt a searing pain in his chest—"a bundle of lead as it were, crushing my heart." He was sure this would be his
last good-bye: "[A]lthough I do the actions of a living man yet I am but
as dead. . . . I pray you prepare for evil tidings of us every day. . . . I see
not in reason how we shall escape even the passing of hunger-starved
persons; but God can do much, and His will be done."

They departed from Dartmouth and were more than two hundred miles beyond the southwestern tip of England at Land's End when the *Speedwell* sprang another leak. It was now early September, and they had no choice but to give up on the *Speedwell*. It was a devastating turn of events. Not only had the vessel cost them a considerable amount of money, but she had been considered vital to the future success of the settlement.

They put in at Plymouth, about fifty miles to the west of Dartmouth. If they were to continue, they must crowd as many passengers as would fit into the *Mayflower* and sail on alone. To no one's surprise, Cushman elected to give up his place to someone else. And despite his fear of imminent death, he lived another five years.

It was later learned that the *Speedwell*'s master, Mr. Reynolds, had been secretly working against them. In Holland, the vessel had been fitted with new and larger masts—a fatal mistake that was probably done with Reynolds's approval, if not at his suggestion. As any mariner knew, a mast crowded with sail not only moved a ship through the water, it acted as a lever that applied torque to the hull. When a ship's masts were too tall, the excess strain opened up the seams between the planks, causing the hull to leak. By overmasting the *Speedwell,* Reynolds had provided himself with an easy way to deceive this fanatical group of landlubbers. He might shrug his shoulders and scratch his head when the vessel began to take on water, but all he had to do was reduce sail and the *Speedwell* would cease to leak. Soon after the *Mayflower* set out across the Atlantic, the *Speedwell* was sold, refitted, and, according to Bradford, "made many voyages . . . to the great profit of her owners."

Bradford later assumed that Reynolds's "cunning and deceit" had been motivated by a fear of starving to death in America. But the Pilgrims appear to have been the unknowing victims of a far more complex and sinister plot. Several decades later, Bradford's stepson Nathaniel Morton received information from Manhattan that indicated that the Dutch had worked to prevent the Pilgrims from settling in the Hudson River region "by [creating] delays, while they were in England." Morton claimed it was the *Mayflower*'s master, Christopher

Jones, who was responsible for the deception, but there is no evidence that Jones was anything but a loyal and steadfast friend to the Pilgrims. It was Reynolds, not Jones, who had kept them from sailing.

In early September, westerly gales begin to howl across the North Atlantic. The provisions, already low when they first set out from Southampton, had been eroded even further by more than a month of delays. The passengers, cooped up aboard ship for all this time, were in no shape for an extended passage. Jones was within his rights to declare that it was too late to depart on a voyage across the Atlantic.

But on September 6, 1620, the *Mayflower* set out from Plymouth with what Bradford called "a prosperous wind."

Robert Cushman had not been the only Leidener to abandon the voyage. His friend William Ring had also opted to remain in England, as had Thomas Blossom. By the time the *Mayflower* left Plymouth, the group from Leiden had been reduced by more than a quarter. The original plan had been to relocate the entire congregation to the New World. Now there were just 50 or so of them—less than a sixth of their total number, and only about half of the *Mayflower*'s 102 passengers.

John Robinson had no way of knowing their numbers would be so dramatically depleted by the time they left England for the last time, but the Pilgrims' minister had anticipated many of the difficulties that lay ahead. His selfless yet strong-willed insistence on probity would be dearly missed by the Pilgrims in the months ahead. At least for now, they had the wisdom of his words.

In a letter written on the eve of their departure from Holland, he urged his followers to do everything they could to avoid conflict with their new compatriots. Even if men such as Christopher Martin pushed them to the edge of their forbearance, they must quell any impulse to judge and condemn others. Robinson exhorted them to "[s]tore up . . . patience against that evil day, without which we take offense at the Lord Himself in His holy and just works." For the future welfare of the settlement, it was essential that all the colonists—Leideners and Strangers alike—learn to live together as best they could.

This nonjudgmental attitude did not come naturally to the Leiden-ers. As Separatists, they considered themselves godly exceptions to the vast, unredeemed majority of humankind. A sense of exclusivity was fundamental to how they perceived themselves in the world. And yet, there is evidence that Robinson's sense of his congregation as an au-tonomous enclave of righteousness had become considerably less rigid during his twelve years in Holland. By the time the Pilgrims departed for America, he had begun to allow members of his congregation to at-tend services outside their own church. Robinson's fierce quest for spiritual purity had been tempered by the realization that little was to be gained by arrogance and anger. "[F]or schism and division," Edward Winslow later wrote of Robinson, "there was nothing in the world more hateful to him." This softening of what had once been an inflexi-ble Separatism was essential to the later success of Plymouth Plantation.

In this regard, the loss of the *Speedwell* had been a good thing. Prior to their departure from Plymouth, the Leideners had naturally gravi-tated to their own vessel. But now, like it or not, they were all in the same boat.

When he later wrote about the voyage of the *Mayflower,* Bradford de-voted only a few paragraphs to describing a passage that lasted more than two months. The physical and psychological punishment endured by the passengers in the dark and dripping 'tween decks was com-pounded by the terrifying lack of information they possessed concern-ing their ultimate destination. All they knew for certain was that if they did somehow succeed in crossing this three-thousand-mile stretch of ocean, no one—except perhaps for some hostile Indians—would be there to greet them.

Soon after departing from Plymouth, the passengers began to suf-fer the effects of seasickness. As often happens at sea, the sailors took great delight in mocking the sufferings of their charges. There was one sailor in particular, "a proud and very profane young man," Bradford remembered, who "would always be contemning the poor people in their sickness and cursing them daily with grievous execrations." The sailor even had the audacity to say that "he hoped to help to cast half of them overboard before they came to their journey's end." As it turned out, however, this strong and arrogant sailor was the first to die. "But it pleased God," Bradford wrote, "before they came half seas over, to smite this young man with a grievous disease, of which he died in a desperate manner, and so was himself the first that was thrown overboard." Bradford claimed "it was an astonishment to all his fellows for they noted it to be the just hand of God upon him."

A succession of westerly gales required Master Jones to work his ship, as best he could, against the wind and waves. Several times during the passage, the conditions grew so severe that even though it meant he must lose many hard-won miles, Jones was forced to "lie ahull"—to furl the sails and without a stitch of canvas set, secure the helm to leeward and surrender his 180-ton ship to the elements.

In 1957, the crew members of the *Mayflower II*—a replica of the original vessel, built in Brixton, England—became the first mariners of the modern era to experience what it was like to ride out a gale in a Jacobean-era ship. Over the course of the first few weeks of the passage, they had discovered that the *Mayflower II*'s boxy hull shape took some getting used to. At times, the motion in the high aft poop cabin became so violent that Captain Alan Villiers—one of the most experienced blue-water sailors in the world—feared that he might be flung out of his bunk. What this ship would do in survival conditions was a matter of deep concern to Villiers and his men.

Toward the end of the voyage, a storm set in, forcing Villiers to do as Master Jones had done 337 years before. As the motion of the ship in the giant waves became intolerable, he decided he had no option but to lie ahull. The sails were furled, and everything on deck was tied down. Then, with considerable trepidation, Villiers ordered that the helm be secured to leeward. "This was the crucial test," Villiers wrote. "Would she lie that way, more or less quietly, with the windage of the high poop keeping her shoulder to the sea? Or would she just wallow hopelessly in the great troughs, threatening to roll her masts out? We didn't know. No one had tried the maneuver in a ship like that for maybe two centuries."

As soon as the ship's bow swung into the wind, a remarkable change came over the *Mayflower II*. Even though she was under bare poles in a howling gale, her slablike topsides functioned as a kind of wooden storm sail, magically steadying the ship's motion. Almost perfectly balanced, the *Mayflower II* sat like a contented duck amid the uproar of the storm. After being pounded unmercifully by the waves, the ship was finally at peace. "I reflected that the Pilgrim Fathers, who tossed through many such a wild night in Atlantic storms, at least knew tranquility in great gales," Villiers wrote.

In the fall of 1620, the *Mayflower*'s ability to steady herself in a gale produced a most deceptive tranquillity for a young indentured servant named John Howland. As the *Mayflower* lay ahull, Howland apparently grew restless down below. He saw no reason why he could not venture out of the fetid depths of the 'tween decks for just a moment. After more than a month as a passenger ship, the *Mayflower* was no longer a sweet ship, and Howland wanted some air. So he climbed a ladder to one of the hatches and stepped onto the deck.

Howland was from the inland town of Fenstanton, Huntingdonshire, and he quickly discovered that the deck of a tempest-tossed ship was no place for a landsman. Even if the ship had found her own still point, the gale continued to rage with astonishing violence around her. The shriek of the wind through the rope rigging was terrifying, as was the sight of all those towering, spume-flecked waves. The *Mayflower* lurched suddenly to leeward. Howland staggered to the ship's rail and tumbled into the sea.

That should have been the end of him. But dangling over the side and trailing behind the ship was the topsail halyard, the rope used to raise and lower the upper sail. Howland was in his midtwenties and strong, and when his hand found the halyard, he gripped the rope with such feral desperation that even though he was pulled down more than ten feet below the ocean's surface, he never let go. Several sailors took up the halyard and hauled Howland back in, finally snagging him with a boat hook and dragging him up onto the deck.

When Bradford wrote about this incident more than a decade later, John Howland was not only alive and well, but he and his wife, Elizabeth, were on their way to raising ten children, who would, in turn, produce an astounding *eighty-eight* grandchildren. A Puritan believed that everything happened for a reason. Whether it was the salvation of John Howland or the sudden death of the young sailor, it occurred because God had made it so. If something good happened to the Saints, it was inevitably interpreted as a sign of divine sanction. But if something bad happened, it didn't necessarily mean that God disapproved; it might mean that he was testing them for a higher purpose. And as they all knew, the true test was yet to come.

Unknown to Jones and any other mariner of the day was the presence of the Gulf Stream—a virtual river of warm water flowing up from the Caribbean along the North American coast, across the Atlantic, and past the British Isles. Bucking the Gulf Stream and westerly gales, the *Mayflower* had managed an average speed of just two miles an hour since leaving England back in September.

Jones had a cross-staff, a calibrated three-foot-long stick equipped with a sliding vane, that enabled him to calculate his latitude, or north–south position, within a few miles, but he had no reliable way of determining his longitude, or east–west position. This meant that after all the bad weather they'd encountered, he had only the vaguest idea of how far he was from land.

He knew the *Mayflower* was well north of her ultimate destination, the mouth of the Hudson River. But at this late stage in the voyage, with disease beginning to appear among the passengers and crew, he needed to find his way to the coast as quickly as possible. So he made a run for it, sailing west along a latitude that would lead him to the sandy peninsula known to most mariners of the time as Cape Cod. It was named Cape James in Captain John Smith's map of New England, but Jones didn't care what it was called. Reaching out to them like an upturned arm, the Cape was as good a target as any.

The *Mayflower* pushed on until they were within smelling distance of the continent. Seagulls began to appear in the sky, and the color of the water changed from deep blue to pale green. And then, at daybreak on Thursday, November 9, 1620, after sixty-five days at sea, they saw land.

CHAPTER TWO

Dangerous Shoals and Roaring Breakers

*I*T WAS A BEAUTIFUL late-fall morning—clear skies and light winds out of the northwest. There was a thin slice of moon overhead, gradually fading to nothingness as the sun rose behind them in the east. Up ahead to the west was what Jones believed to be the forearm of Cape Cod. Known to subsequent generations of mariners as the "back side" of the Cape, this almost thirty-mile stretch of barrier beach runs from north to south and is edged by dramatic hundred-foot-high cliffs of sand that must have been instantly recognizable to Jones's pilots if they had been in this region before. Stretching behind the cliffs were rolling, tree-covered hills.

The *Mayflower*'s passengers were, according to Bradford, "not a little joyful." The clarity of the atmosphere on a crisp autumn day in New England shrinks the distances and accentuates the colors, and the Pilgrims were "much comforted . . . [by] seeing so goodly a land, and wooded to the brink of the sea." Just to make certain, Jones tacked the *Mayflower* and stood in for shore. After an hour or so, all agreed that this was indeed Cape Cod.

Now they had a decision to make. Where should they go? They were well to the north of their intended destination near the mouth of the Hudson River. And yet there were reasons to consider the region around Cape Cod as a possible settlement site. In the final chaotic months before their departure from England, Weston and others had begun to insist that a more northern site in New England—which was the new name for what are now the states of Massachusetts, Connecticut, Rhode Island, Maine, New Hampshire, and Vermont—was a better place to settle. As Cape Cod's name indicated, this region was renowned for the large schools of cod that frequented these shores. Come spring, hundreds of codfishing vessels from England, France, Holland, and other European countries plied the waters of New England, particularly to the northeast off modern Maine. A colony established on Cape Cod would be well positioned to take advantage of this profitable fishery. But when the *Mayflower* had departed from England, it had been impossible to secure a patent for this region, since what came to be called the Council for New England had not yet been established by the king. If they were to settle where they had legally been granted land, they must sail south for the mouth of the Hudson River 220 miles away.

Master Jones had his own problems to consider. Given the poor health of his passengers and crew, his first priority was to get these people ashore as quickly as possible—regardless of what their patent dictated. If the wind had been out of the south, he could easily have sailed north to the tip of Cape Cod to what is known today as Provincetown Harbor. With a decent southerly breeze and a little help from the tide, they'd be there in a matter of hours. But the wind was from the north. Their only option was to run with it to the Hudson River. If the wind held, they'd be there in a couple of days. So Jones headed south.

Unfortunately, there was no reliable English chart of the waters between Cape Cod and the Hudson. Little had changed since 1614, when John Smith's experiences in the region had caused him to dismiss all existing charts as "so much waste paper, though they cost me more." Smith's own chart of New England only went as far south as the back side of the Cape—where the *Mayflower* had made landfall—and provided no help for a voyage south. Except for what knowledge his pilots might have of this coast—which appears to have been minimal—Jones was sailing blind.

The master of the *Mayflower* had no way of knowing about the specific hazards ahead, but he knew enough to make extensive use of his sounding leads, of which he had two: the deep-sea or "dipsy" lead, which weighed between forty and one hundred pounds and was equipped with 600 feet of line, and the smaller "hand-lead," just seven to fourteen pounds with 120 feet of line. As the *Mayflower* sailed south, the leadsman was in near-perpetual motion: heaving the lead, letting the line pay out, calling out the depth, then drawing in the line and heaving the lead again. The depth off Cape Cod hovers at about 120 feet—at the very limit of the hand-lead—until about three miles offshore, where the bottom plummets to more than 300 feet. Running roughly parallel to shore, this line of sudden drop-off is known as the Edge. As Jones made his way along the back side of the Cape, he more than likely followed the Edge as if it were an invisible lifeline south.

For the next five hours, the *Mayflower* slipped easily along. After sixty-five days of headwinds and storms, it must have been a wonderful respite for the passengers, who crowded the chilly, sun-drenched deck to drink in their first view of the New World. But for Master Jones, it was the beginning of the most tension-filled portion of the passage. Any captain would rather have hazarded the fiercest North Atlantic gale than risk the uncharted perils of an unknown coast. Until the *Mayflower* was quietly at anchor, Jones would get little sleep.

Jones stood perched on the aftmost deck of his ship—a narrow, razorback ridge of planking called the poop deck, just nine feet wide and about twenty-three feet above the water, with a taffrail adding another four feet of height. Here, two and a half stories up, with the expansive girth of the *Mayflower*—twenty or so feet at her widest—before him, Jones stared out nervously toward the shore to starboard, awaiting the latest word on the sea's depth.

The ship's helmsman was stationed in steerage, a tiny, suffocating space below and forward of the poop deck. Jones and his pilots could communicate with the helmsman through an open hatch above the helmsman's head. Peering down at him, they could see the ship's compass mounted in a candle-equipped binnacle, just forward of the helmsman and aft of the mizzenmast. Instead of a wheel, the helmsman steered the ship with a long vertical pole, called a whipstaff, that attached to the tiller through a hole in the steerage deck.

They sailed south on an easy reach, with the sandy shore of Cape Cod within sight, past the future locations of Wellfleet, Eastham, Orleans, and Chatham. Throughout the morning, the tide was in their favor, but around 1 p.m., it began to flow against them. Then the depth of the water dropped alarmingly, as did the wind. Suddenly, the *Mayflower* was in the midst of what has been called "one of the meanest stretches of shoal water on the American coast": Pollack Rip.

Pollack Rip is part of an intricate and ever-changing maze of shoals and sandbars stretching between the elbow of Cape Cod and the tip of Nantucket Island, fifteen or so miles to the south. The huge volume of water that moves back and forth between the ocean to the east and Nantucket Sound to the west rushes and swirls amid these shoals with a ferocity that is still, almost four hundred years later, terrifying to behold. It's been claimed that half the wrecks along the entire Atlantic and Gulf coasts of the United States have occurred in this area. In 1606, the French explorer Samuel Champlain attempted to navigate these waters in a small pinnace. This was Champlain's second visit to the Cape, and even though he took every precaution, his vessel fetched up on a shoal and was almost pounded to pieces before he somehow managed to float her free and sail into Nantucket Sound. Champlain's pinnace drew four feet; the deeply laden *Mayflower* drew twelve.

The placid heave of the sea had been transformed into a churning maelstrom as the outflowing tide cascaded over the shoals ahead. And with the wind dying to almost nothing, Jones had no way to extricate his ship from the danger, especially since what breeze remained was from the north, pinning the *Mayflower* against the rip. "[T]hey fell amongst dangerous shoals and roaring breakers," Bradford wrote, "and they were so far entangled therewith as they conceived themselves in great danger." It was approaching 3 p.m., with only another hour and a half of daylight left. If Jones hadn't done it already, he undoubtedly prepared an anchor for lowering—ordering the sailors to extract the hemp cable from below and to begin carefully coiling, or flaking, the thick rope on the forecastle head. If the wind completely deserted them, they might be forced to spend the night at the edge of the breakers. But anchoring beside Pollack Rip is never a good idea. If the ocean swell should rise or a storm should kick up from the north, any vessel anchored there would be driven fatally onto the shoals.

Eleven years earlier, Stephen Hopkins had been a passenger aboard the *Sea Venture*—a ship bound for Jamestown that wrecked on the coral-studded shore of Bermuda. As a nobleman wrote in a letter that subsequently became a source for Shakespeare's storm scene in *The Tempest,* the water pouring in through the leaking hull and decks was terrifying, but it was the screams of the "women and passengers not used to such hurly and discomforts" that none of them would ever forget. On the afternoon of November 9, 1620, with the breakers at Pollack Rip thundering in his ears, Hopkins must have begun to wonder whether he was about to hear those terrible cries again.

Just when it seemed they might never extricate themselves from the shoals, the wind began to change, gradually shifting in a clockwise direction to the south. This, combined with a fair tide, was all Master Jones needed. By sunset at 4:35 p.m., the *Mayflower* was well to the northwest of Pollack Rip.

With the wind building from the south, Jones made a historic decision. They weren't going to the Hudson River. They were going back around Cape Cod to New England.

By 5 p.m., it was almost completely dark. Not wanting to run into any more shoals, Jones elected to heave to—standard procedure on an unknown coast at night. With her main topsail aback, the *Mayflower* drifted with the tide, four or five miles off present-day Chatham, waiting for dawn.

In the meantime, all was bustle and commotion belowdecks. The news that they were headed to New England instead of the Hudson River put the passengers in an uproar. As they all knew, their patent did not technically apply to a settlement north of the Hudson. Some of the Strangers, no doubt led by Stephen Hopkins, who had unsuccessfully participated in an uprising eleven years before in Bermuda, made "discontented and mutinous speeches," insisting that "when they came ashore they would use their own liberty, for none had power to command them." It's likely that Hopkins was joined by John Billington, who subsequently established a reputation as the colony's leading malcontent and rabble-rouser.

No matter who were the agitators, it was now clear that the future of the settlement was, once again, in serious peril. The Strangers were about half the passengers, and unlike the Leideners, who were united by powerful and long-standing bonds, they had little holding them together except, in some cases, a growing reluctance to live in a community dominated by religious radicals. On the other hand, some of the Strangers, including the *Mayflower*'s governor, Christopher Martin, had strong ties to the Merchant Adventurers in London; in fact, passenger William Mullins was one of them. These Strangers recognized that the only way for the settlement to succeed financially was if everyone worked together. Although Martin had shown nothing but contempt for the Leideners at the beginning of the voyage, the disturbing developments off Cape Cod may have created an uneasy alliance between him and the passengers from Holland. Before they landed, it was essential that they all sign a formal and binding agreement of some sort. Over the course of the next day, they hammered out what has come to be known as the Mayflower Compact.

It is deeply ironic that the document many consider to mark the beginning of what would one day be called the United States came from a people who had more in common with a cult than a democratic society. It was true that Pastor Robinson had been elected by the congregation. But once he'd been chosen, Robinson's power and position had never been in doubt. More a benevolent dictator than a democratically elected official, Robinson had shrewdly and compassionately nurtured the spiritual well-being of his congregation. And yet, even though they had existed in a theocratic bubble of their own devising, the Pilgrims recognized the dangers of mixing temporal and spiritual authority. One of the reasons they had been forced to leave England was that King James had used the ecclesiastical courts to impose his own religious beliefs. In Holland, they had enjoyed the benefits of a society in which the division between church and state had been, for the most part, rigorously maintained. They could not help but absorb some decidedly Dutch ways of looking at the world. For example, marriage in Holland was a civil ceremony, and so it would be—much to the dismay of English authorities—in Plymouth Colony.

As had been true for more than a decade, it was Pastor John Robinson who pointed them in the direction they ultimately followed. In his farewell letter, Robinson had anticipated the need to create a government based on civil consent rather than divine decree. With so many Strangers in their midst, there was no other way. They must "become a body politic, using amongst yourselves civil government," i.e., they must all agree to submit to the laws drawn up by their duly elected officials. Just as a spiritual covenant had marked the beginning of their congregation in Leiden, a civil covenant would provide the basis for a secular government in America.

Written with a crystalline brevity, the Mayflower Compact bears the unmistakable signs of Robinson's influence, and it is worth quoting in full:

> Having undertaken, for the glory of God and advancement of the Christian faith and honor of our King and country, a voyage to plant the first colony in the northern parts of Virginia, do these present solemnly and mutually in the presence of God and one of another, covenant and combine ourselves together into a civil body politic, for our better ordering and preservation, and furtherance of the ends aforesaid; and by virtue hereof to enact, constitute and frame such just and equal laws, ordinances, acts, constitutions and offices, from time to time, as shall be thought most meet and convenient for the general good of the colony, unto which we promise all due submission and obedience.

Given the future course of New England and the United States, there is a temptation to make more out of the Mayflower Compact than there actually was. In truth, the compact made no attempt to propose that they now alter the form of local government that existed in any town back in England. What made the document truly extraordinary was that it applied to a group of people who were three thousand miles from their mother country. The physical reality of all that space—and all the terror, freedom, and insularity it fostered—informed everything that occurred in the days and years ahead.

In the end, the Mayflower Compact represented a remarkable act of coolheaded and pragmatic resolve. They were nearing the end of a long and frightening voyage. They were bound for a place about which they knew essentially nothing. It was almost winter. They were without sufficient supplies of food. Some of them were sick and two had already died. Still others were clamoring for a rebellion that would have meant the almost instantaneous collapse of their settlement and, most likely, their deaths. The Leideners might have looked to their military officer, Miles Standish, and ordered him to subdue the rebels. Instead, they put pen to paper and created a document that ranks with the Declaration of Independence and the United States Constitution as a seminal American text.

But there was one more critical decision to make. They must choose a leader. The Leideners were barely a majority, but they could be counted on to vote as a bloc, effectively guaranteeing that their leader would *not* be the *Mayflower's* governor, Christopher Martin. "[L]et your wisdom and godliness appear," Robinson had advised, "not only in choosing such persons as do entirely love and will promote the common good, but also in yielding unto them all due honor and obedience in their lawful administrations."

In lieu of Martin, the only other person aboard the *Mayflower* who had played a central role in organizing the voyage was John Carver. Unlike his fellow purchasing agent, Robert Cushman, Carver had managed to remain untainted by the controversy surrounding Weston's last-minute reconfiguration of the agreement with the Merchant Adventurers. Whereas Cushman was passionate and impulsive in temperament, Carver was, according to one account, "a gentleman of singular piety, rare humility, and great condescendency." He was also wealthy and had contributed much of his personal estate to the congregation in Leiden and to this voyage. He and his wife, Katherine, who had buried two children in Leiden, had brought five servants on the *Mayflower,* one of whom was the death-defying John Howland. John Carver, it was decided, would be their governor.

As the Pilgrims formulated their compact, Jones pointed the *Mayflower* north. With disease and dissension running rife among the passengers, Jones did everything he could to get every possible knot of speed out of his old ship. The *Mayflower* was equipped with six sails: five square sails, including a small spritsail off the bowsprit, and a lateen-rigged mizzen (a triangular sail set on a diagonal spar). The three lower sails—the mizzen, main course, and fore course—possessed additional sections of canvas called bonnets that were laced to the bottoms of the sails in moderate weather to gather more wind. With her bonnets laced tight, the *Mayflower* charged up the back side of Cape Cod.

By nightfall, the *Mayflower* was nearing the tip of Cape Cod. Master Jones once again hove to. They wanted to enter Provincetown Harbor, known to them as Cape Cod Harbor, as close as possible to sunrise so that they'd have most of the day for exploring the surrounding countryside. But before they could set foot on land, every man who was healthy enough to write his name or, if he couldn't write, scratch out an X, must sign the compact.

They awakened very early on the morning of November 11, 1620. Sunrise was at 6:55 a.m., and the passengers probably assembled in the *Mayflower's* great cabin—approximately thirteen by seventeen feet, with two windows in the stern and one on either side. Beginning with John Carver and ending with the servant Edward Leister, a total of forty-one men signed the compact. Only nine adult males did not sign the compact—some had been hired as seamen for only a year, while others were probably too sick to put pen to paper. In accordance with the cultural and legal norms of the times, no women signed the document. The ceremony ended with the official selection of a leader. Bradford informs us that "they chose or rather confirmed, Mr. John Carver (a man godly and well approved amongst them) their Governor for that year."

In the meantime, Master Jones guided the *Mayflower* into Provincetown Harbor, one of the largest and safest natural anchorages in New England. Tucked within the curled wrist of the Cape, the harbor is a vast watery amphitheater as many as four miles across in some sections. Jones estimated that it could accommodate at least a thousand ships.

But on the morning of November 11, they were the only vessel in the harbor. Jones found a deep spot with good holding ground hard up

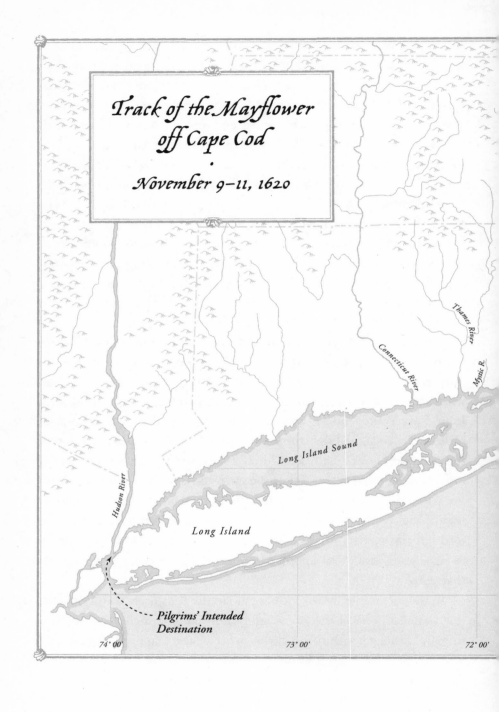

Track of the Mayflower
off Cape Cod
·
November 9–11, 1620

Thames River

Connecticut River

Mystic R.

Long Island Sound

Hudson River

Long Island

Pilgrims' Intended
Destination

74° 00'   73° 00'   72° 00'

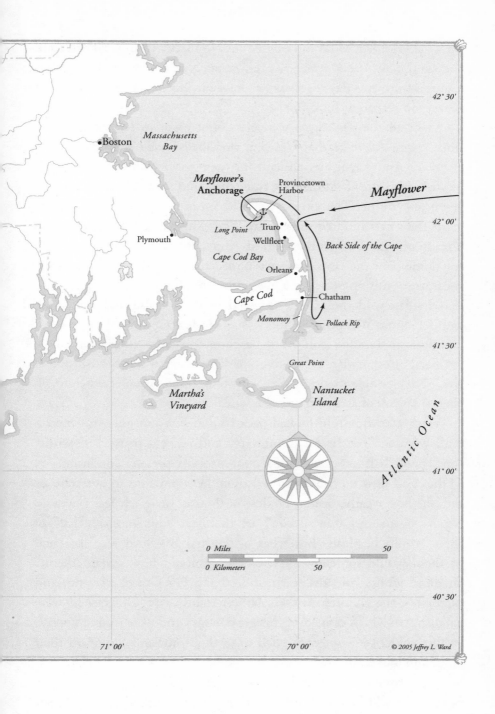

on what is known today as Long Point. No matter from what direction the wind blew, the *Mayflower* was now safely at anchor, and Jones, exhausted from two days of struggle along the New England coast, must have soon retired to his cabin.

Many of the passengers were no doubt eager to set foot on land once again. All were thankful that they had finally arrived safely in America. And yet, it was difficult for them to look to the future with anything but dread. There were three thousand miles of ocean between them and home. The closest English communities in America were more than five hundred miles away. They knew that Master Jones was already impatient to get them off his ship and head the *Mayflower* back for home. But the land that surrounded them was low and sandy—a most unpromising place for a plantation. Bradford called it "a hideous and desolate wilderness." They knew they had friends back in Holland, but if Thomas Weston's reaction was any indication, the Merchant Adventurers in London could not be counted on for much support— financial or otherwise. Of more immediate concern was the attitude of the Native people of this place, who they feared were "readier to fill their sides full of arrows than otherwise."

Years later, Bradford looked back to that first morning in America with wonder. "But here I cannot stay and make a pause," he wrote, "and stand half amazed at this poor people's present condition. . . . [T]hey had now no friends to welcome them nor inns to entertain or refresh their weatherbeaten bodies; no houses or much less towns to repair to, to seek for succor." In the next four months, half of them would be dead. But what astonished Bradford was that half of them would somehow survive. "What could now sustain them," Bradford wrote, "but the spirit of God and His Grace? May not and ought not the children of these fathers rightly say: 'Our fathers were Englishmen which came over this great ocean, and were ready to perish in this wilderness; but they cried unto the Lord, and He heard their voice and looked on their adversity.' "

It was time to venture ashore. They had brought with them an open boat that could be both rowed and sailed, known as a shallop. About thirty-five feet long, it had been cut up into four pieces and stored below—where it had been "much bruised and shattered" over the course of the voyage. It would take many days for the carpenter to assemble and rebuild it. For the time being, they had the smaller ship's boat. Loaded with sixteen well-armed men, the boat made its way to shore. It was only a narrow neck of land, but for these sea-weary men, it was enough. "[T]hey fell upon their knees," Bradford wrote, "and blessed the God of Heaven who had brought them over the vast and furious ocean, and delivered them from all the perils and miseries thereof, again to set their feet on the firm and stable earth, their proper element."

They wandered over hills of sand that reminded them of the Downs in Holland. Amid the hollows of the dunes they found growths of birch, holly, ash, and walnut trees. With darkness coming, they loaded their boat with red cedar. The freshly sawed wood "smelled very sweet and strong," and that night aboard the *Mayflower,* for the first time in perhaps weeks, they enjoyed the pleasures of a warm fire.

It had been, for the most part, a reassuring introduction to the New World. Despite the apparent sterility of the landscape, they had found more trees than they would have come across back in Holland and even coastal England. But there had been something missing: nowhere had they found any people.

CHAPTER THREE

Into the Void

*A*BOUT SIXTY MILES southwest of Provincetown Harbor, at the confluence of two rivers in the vicinity of modern Warren, Rhode Island, lived Massasoit, the most powerful Native leader, or sachem, in the region. He was in the prime of his life—about thirty-five, strong and imposing, with the quiet dignity that was expected of a sachem.

Despite his personal vigor and equanimity, Massasoit presided over a people who had been devastated by disease. During the three years that the Pilgrims had been organizing their voyage to America, the Indians of southern New England had been hit by what scientists refer to as a virgin soil epidemic—a contagion against which they had no antibodies. From 1616 to 1619, what may have been bubonic plague introduced by European fishermen in modern Maine spread south along the Atlantic seaboard to the eastern shore of Narragansett Bay, killing in some cases as many as 90 percent of the region's inhabitants.

So many died so quickly that there was no one left to bury the dead. Portions of coastal New England that had once been as densely populated as western Europe were suddenly empty of people, with only the whitened bones of the dead to indicate that a thriving community had once existed along these shores. In addition to disease, what were described as "civil dissensions and bloody wars" erupted throughout the region as Native groups that had been uneasy neighbors in the best of times struggled to create a new order amid the haunted vacancy of New England.

Massasoit's people, known as the Pokanokets for the area they occupied at the head of Narragansett Bay, had been particularly hard hit. Before the plague, they had numbered about twelve thousand, enabling Massasoit to muster three thousand fighting men. After three years of disease, his force had been reduced to a few hundred warriors. Making it even worse, from Massasoit's perspective, was that the plague had not affected the Pokanokets' neighboring enemies, the Narragansetts, who controlled the western portion of the bay and numbered about twenty thousand, with five thousand fighting men. Just recently, Massasoit and ten of his warriors had suffered the humiliation of being forced to do obeisance to the Narragansetts, whose sachem, Canonicus, now considered the Pokanokets his subjects.

Wasted by disease and now under the thumb of a powerful and proud enemy, the Pokanokets were in a desperate struggle to maintain their existence as a people. But Massasoit had his allies. The Massachusetts to the north and the Nausets on Cape Cod shared the Pokanokets' antipathy to the Narragansetts. Numerically the Pokanokets were at a decided disadvantage, but this did not prevent Massasoit from attempting to use his alliances with other tribes to neutralize the threat to the west. "A small bird is called sachem," the Englishman Roger Williams later observed, "because of its sachem or princelike courage and command over greater birds, that a man shall often see this small bird pursue and vanquish and put to flight the crow and other birds far bigger than itself." The Narragansetts might feel that they were now the Pokanokets' masters, but, as they would soon discover, Massasoit was the consummate small bird.

No one was sure how long ago it had occurred, but some of the Indians' oldest people told of what it had been like to see a European sailing vessel for the first time. "They took the first ship they saw for a walking island," the English settler William Wood recounted, "the mast to be a tree, the sail white clouds, and the discharging of ordnance for lightning and thunder, which did much trouble them, but this thunder being over and this moving-island steadied with an anchor, they manned out their canoes to go and pick strawberries there. But being saluted by the way with a [cannon's] broadside . . . , [they turned] back, not daring to approach till they were sent for."

As early as 1524, the Italian explorer Giovanni da Verrazano had put in at Narragansett Bay in the vicinity of modern Newport. There he encountered "two kings more beautiful in form and stature than can possibly be described. . . . The oldest had a deer's skin around his body, artificially wrought in damask figures, his head was without covering, his hair was tied back in various knots; around his neck he wore a large chain ornamented with many stones of different colors. The young man was similar in his general appearance. This is the finest looking tribe, the handsomest in their costumes, that we have found in our voyage." Almost a century before the arrival of the *Mayflower*, Verrazano may have met Massasoit's great-grandfather.

By 1602, when the English explorer Bartholomew Gosnold visited the region, European codfishing vessels had become an increasingly familiar sight along the New England coast. After giving Cape Cod its name, Gosnold ventured to the Elizabeth Islands at the southwestern corner of the Cape, where he built a small fort on the outermost island of Cuttyhunk. Gosnold began harvesting sassafras, the roots of which were used by Europeans to treat syphilis and rheumatism, with the intention of creating a small settlement.

A few days after his arrival, a delegation of fifty Indians in nine canoes arrived from the mainland for the purposes of trade. It was apparent to Gosnold that one of the Indians was looked to with great respect. This may have been Massasoit's father. It is possible that the sachem's son, who would have been in his early teens, was also present.

Gosnold presented the sachem with a pair of knives and a straw hat, which he placed experimentally on his head. Then the Indians "all sat down in manner like greyhounds upon their heels" and began to trade. With the exception of mustard ("whereat they made a sour face"), the Indians appeared to enjoy all the strange foods the English had to offer. For their part, Gosnold and his men took an immediate fancy to the Indians' tobacco, a dried green powder that when smoked in carefully crafted clay pipes proved addictively pleasant.

Gosnold was at a loss to understand the Natives' language, but the Indians proved to have an unnerving ability to mimic the Englishmen's speech. At one point, a sailor sat smoking beside an Indian and said, "How now, sir, are you so saucy with my tobacco?" The Indian proceeded to repeat the phrase word for word, "as if he had been a long scholar in the language."

But Gosnold's enchanting introduction to the area and its people turned as sour as his mustard. While foraging for food, two of his men were attacked by four Indians. No one was hurt (in part because one of the Englishmen had the presence of mind to cut the strings of the Natives' bows with his knife), but Gosnold decided to abandon his plan for establishing a year-round trading post and sailed for England.

It was a pattern that would be repeated over and over again in the years ahead. Soon after Gosnold returned to England with word of his discovery, the explorer Martin Pring sailed for Cape Cod and built a fort of his own in the vicinity of modern Truro. After a summer of harvesting sassafras, Pring also began to wear out his welcome with the local Natives. When an Indian-lit fire almost consumed his fort, Pring took the hint and sailed for home.

Beginning in 1605, the Frenchman Samuel Champlain began an extensive exploration of the Cape and produced detailed maps of several harbors and inlets. In 1611, the year that Shakespeare produced *The Tempest,* the English explorer Edward Harlow voyaged to the region. By the time he returned to London, he had abducted close to half a dozen Indians and killed at least as many in several brutal confrontations. One of his Indian captives was quite tall, and Harlow helped defray the cost of the voyage by showing him on the city streets "as a wonder."

The Indian's name was Epenow, and he soon realized that there was nothing the English valued more than gold. He told his captors that back on Martha's Vineyard, an island just to the south of Cape Cod, there was a gold mine that only he could lead them to. An expedition was promptly mounted, and as soon as the English ship came within swimming distance of the island, Epenow jumped over the side and escaped.

Around this time, in 1614, Captain John Smith of Pocahontas fame led a voyage of exploration to the region. There were several vessels in Smith's expedition, and one of the commanders, Thomas Hunt, decided to take as many Native captives as his ship could hold and sell them as slaves in Spain. As Smith later lamented, Hunt's actions grievously damaged Indian-English relations in New England for years to come.

The following year, a French ship wrecked on the north shore of Cape Cod, and the Indians decided to do to the French what the English had done to them. Indians from up and down the coast gathered together at the wreck site, and William Bradford later learned how they "never left dogging and waylaying [the French] till they took opportunities to kill all but three or four, which they kept as slaves, sending them up and down, to make sport with them from one sachem to another."

One of the Frenchmen was of a religious bent. He learned enough of the Natives' language to tell his captors that "God was angry with them for their wickedness, and would destroy them and give their country to another people." Scorning the prophecy, a sachem assembled his subjects around a nearby hill and, with the Frenchman beside him on the hilltop, demanded if "his God had so many people and [was] able to kill all those?" The Frenchman responded that he "surely would." In three years' time, everything the captive had predicted had come to pass.

In the spring of 1619, the English explorer Thomas Dermer sailed south from Maine in a small open boat. Accompanying Dermer was a Native guide who'd been abducted by Thomas Hunt in 1614. The Indian's name was Tisquantum, or Squanto, and after five long years in Spain, England, and Newfoundland, he was sailing toward his home at Patuxet, the site of modern Plymouth. In a letter written the following winter, Dermer described what they saw: "[We] passed along the coast where [we] found some ancient [Indian] plantations, not long since populous now utterly void; in other places a remnant remains, but not free of sickness. Their disease the plague, for we might perceive the sores of some that had escaped, who descried the spots of such as usually die. When [we] arrived at my savage's native country [we found] all dead." Squanto's reaction to the desolation of his homeland, where as many as two thousand people had once lived, can only be imagined. However, at some point after visiting Patuxet, he began to see the catastrophic consequences of the plague as a potential opportunity.

Upon Epenow's return to Martha's Vineyard, the former captive had become a sachem, and it seems that Squanto had similar, if not greater, ambitions. Squanto took Dermer to Nemasket, a settlement about fifteen miles inland from Patuxet, where Squanto learned that not everyone in his village had died. Several of his family members were alive and well. He may already have begun to think about reestablishing a community in Patuxet that was independent of Pokanoket control. In the wake of the plague, Massasoit was obviously vulnerable, and as Bradford later said of the former Indian captive, "Squanto sought his own ends and played his own game." But first he had to see for himself the condition of Massasoit and the Pokanokets, so he convinced Dermer that they must push on to the sachem's village.

It took about a day to walk from Nemasket to Pokanoket. There they met what Dermer described as "two kings," who were undoubtedly Massasoit and his brother Quadequina, and fifty warriors. In the immediate and stunning aftermath of the sickness, Massasoit was quite happy to see the Englishman and his Native guide. Dermer wrote that the sachem and his brother were "well satisfied with [what] my savage and I discoursed unto them [and] being desirous of novelty, gave me content in whatsoever I demanded." Massasoit still had one of the French captives in his possession and agreed to hand him over to Dermer. After redeeming yet another Frenchman and meeting Epenow on Martha's Vineyard, Dermer left Squanto with Native friends near Nemasket and headed south to spend the winter in Virginia.

When Thomas Dermer returned to the region the following summer, he discovered that the Pokanokets possessed a newfound and "inveterate malice to the English," and for good reason. That spring, an English ship had arrived at Narragansett Bay. The sailors invited a large number of Massasoit's people aboard the vessel, then proceeded to shoot them down in cold blood.

Almost everywhere Dermer went in the summer of 1620, he came under attack. He would certainly have been killed at Nemasket had not Squanto, who had spent the winter in the region, come to his rescue. But not even Squanto could save Dermer when he and his men arrived at Martha's Vineyard. Epenow and his warriors fell on Dermer's party, and only Dermer, who was badly wounded, and one other Englishman escaped, while Squanto was taken prisoner. Soon after reaching Virginia a few weeks later, Dermer was dead.

Epenow appears to have distrusted Squanto from the start. He more than anyone understood the temptations that went with an intimate understanding of a culture that was a wondrous and terrifying mystery to most Native Americans. If the English should ever achieve a foothold in this land, those such as Squanto and himself, who could speak the Englishmen's language, would possess a powerful and potentially dangerous advantage. They could claim to know what the English were saying, and no one would know whether or not they were telling the truth. For his part, Epenow had proven his loyalty to his people by attacking Dermer and his men. But Squanto's true motives were anyone's guess.

It wasn't just that Squanto had spent some time in England that set him apart. He also possessed a strong relationship with the Indians' spirit world. The cosmology of the Pokanokets included as many as thirty-eight gods and spirits, most of them linked to various aspects of the physical world—the sun, moon, sea, fire, and a wide range of animals. First and foremost in this pantheon was the god they regarded as their creator, Kietan, who, as Edward Winslow later wrote, "dwelleth above in the heavens, wither all good men go when they die, to see their friends, and have their fill of all things." Kietan was the one who had provided the Indians with their corn and beans, and sachems such as Massasoit called on him for support.

On the opposite end of the spectrum was the spirit known as Hobbamock or Cheepi. Unlike Kietan, who was benign and remote, Hobbamock was very much a part of this world: an ominous spirit of darkness who appeared at night and in swamps and assumed a variety of disturbing forms, from eels to snakes. The Pokanokets' spiritual leaders or shamans, known as powwows, looked to Hobbamock to cure the sick, cast a curse, or see into the future. And as it turned out, in addition to Hobbamock and Cheepi, there was a third name for the spirit Massasoit's people associated with death, the night, and the bitter northeast wind: Tisquantum, or Squanto for short. By assuming the spirit's name, Squanto was broadcasting his claim to an intimate relationship with an entity that the Pilgrims later equated with the devil.

Massasoit shared Epenow's distrust of Squanto, and by the fall of 1620, Squanto had been moved from the Vineyard to Pokanoket, where he remained a prisoner. When the *Mayflower* arrived at Provincetown Harbor in November, it was generally assumed by the Indians that the ship had been sent to avenge the attack on Dermer. In the weeks ahead, the Pilgrims would do little to change that assumption.

In the meantime, Squanto waited for his chance.

CHAPTER FOUR

Beaten with Their Own Rod

*T*HE *MAYFLOWER* HAD ARRIVED at Provincetown Harbor on Saturday, November 11. Since the next day was a Sunday, the Pilgrims remained aboard ship, worshipping God under the direction of Elder Brewster. As Puritans, they believed that the entire Sabbath must be devoted to worship—both a morning and an afternoon meeting along with personal and family prayers throughout the day. Work and especially play on a Sunday were forbidden.

On Monday, the four battered pieces of the shallop were taken ashore, where the carpenter and his assistants began to put the vessel back together. As the workers hammered and sawed, the passengers enjoyed their first day ashore. After more than two months at sea, there was what they termed a "great need" for washing, and the women found a small freshwater pond near the present site of Provincetown. For generations to come, Monday would be wash day in New England, a tradition that began with the women of the *Mayflower*.

At low tide, amid the barnacles and seaweed, they found abundant supplies of blue mussels—bivalves that grow up to four inches in length and attach themselves in clumps to shoreside rocks. Passengers and sailors alike enjoyed the first fresh food any of them had tasted in a very long time, only to fall victim to the vomiting and diarrhea associated with shellfish poisoning.

But there was other evidence of nature's bounty. The harbor contained untold numbers of ducks and geese—"the greatest store of fowl that ever we saw." But it was the whales that astounded them. "[E]very day we saw whales playing hard by us," they wrote. These were Atlantic right whales, huge, docile creatures that feed on plankton and other sea organisms by straining seawater between the large plates of baleen in their mouths. Jones and one of his mates, who had experience hunting whales in Greenland, claimed that if only they'd had some harpoons and lances they might have taken between three thousand and four thousand pounds' worth of whale oil and baleen.

For the Pilgrims, who were expected to provide the Merchant Adventurers with a regular supply of salable goods, it was frustrating in the extreme to be surrounded by all this potential wealth and yet have no way of capturing any of it. One day a whale, apparently enjoying the afternoon sun on her dark blubbery back, lay on the water's surface within only a few yards of the *Mayflower,* "as if she had been dead." It was just too much of a temptation. As a small crowd looked on, two muskets were loaded, but when the first was fired, the barrel burst into fragments. Amazingly, no one was injured, and the whale, after issuing "a snuff," swam leisurely away.

The shallop was proving to be a problem. Instead of days, it was going to be weeks before the boat was completed. Some of the passengers began to insist that they should launch an overland expedition. When the *Mayflower* first sailed into the harbor, the mouth of a river had been sighted several miles to the southeast. Some of them, probably headed by Captain Miles Standish, advocated that a small party be rowed to shore so that they could investigate this potential settlement site.

The risks of such a venture were considerable. So far they had seen no local inhabitants, but for all they knew, huge numbers of hostile Natives might be waiting just a few miles down the Cape. "The willingness of the persons was liked," Bradford wrote, "but the thing itself, in regard of the danger, was rather permitted than approved." Perhaps with an eye to reining in some of his military officer's obvious impatience for action, Carver provided Standish with "cautions, directions, and instructions." Standish's party comprised sixteen men, including Bradford, Stephen Hopkins (whose experience in Virginia might help them if they should encounter any Indians), and Edward Tilley. Each of them was equipped with a musket, sword, and corselet, a light form of body armor that included a metal breastplate.

On Wednesday, November 15, they were rowed ashore. Provincetown

John Smith's map of New England

Harbor, as well as much of the bay side of the lower Cape, is characterized by wide tidal flats. Even a small boat runs aground many yards out, requiring the passengers to wade through the shallows to shore. In November, with the temperature on the verge of freezing, it was a long, cold slog to the beach, especially weighted down with armor and weapons.

Standish soon had them marching single file along the shore. He was not a tall man—in the years ahead he won the sobriquet "Captain Shrimp"—but his courage and resolve were never questioned. Before leaving for America, the Pilgrims had contacted another potential candidate for the position of military leader: the redoubtable Captain John Smith. No one in England knew more about America than Smith. He had been at the founding of Jamestown in 1607; in 1614 he had led a voyage of exploration to what he named New England, creating the most detailed map of the region to date. (It had been Smith's associate on that voyage, Thomas Hunt, who had abducted Squanto.) When the Pilgrims approached him in London, Smith wanted desperately to return to America, particularly to "the country of the Massachusetts," which he described as "the paradise of those parts." But the Pilgrims decided that they wanted no part of him. Smith bitterly related how they had insisted that his "books and maps were better cheap to teach them than myself."

Smith's fatal flaw, as far as the Pilgrims were concerned, was that he knew too much. In the beginning of the settlement, they would have had no choice but to do as he said, and this could be dangerous. Smith possessed a strong personality, and a man of his worldly nature might come to dominate what they intended to be an inherently religious enclave. "[T]hey would not . . . have any knowledge by any but themselves," Smith wrote, "pretending only religion their governor and frugality their counsel, when indeed it was . . . because . . . they would have no superiors."

If the Pilgrims perceived Standish as a cheaper and more tractable alternative to Smith, they were now paying the price for their misjudgment. Standish was full of martial pugnacity, but he had no idea where he was leading them. If the Pilgrims did possess Smith's map of New England, they failed to make good use of it. Rivers were considered essential to a settlement site, and Smith's map clearly indicated that the nearest available navigable waterway was the Charles River, less than a day's sail to the northwest at present-day Boston. The Pilgrims, however, insisted on exploring the entire bay side of Cape Cod, even though there was no evidence on Smith's map of a river of any significance along this more than fifty-mile stretch of coastline.

As Smith later wrote, much of the suffering that lay ahead for the Pilgrims could easily have been avoided if they had seen fit to pay for his services or, at the very least, consult his map. "[S]uch humorists [i.e., fanatics] will never believe . . . ," he wrote, "till they be beaten with their own rod."

They had marched just a mile or so down the beach when up ahead they saw half a dozen people and a dog walking toward them. They initially assumed it was Master Jones and some of the sailors, who they knew were already ashore with the *Mayflower's* spaniel. But when the people started to run inland for the woods, they realized that these weren't sailors; they were the first Native people they had seen. One of the Indians paused to whistle for the dog, and the group disappeared into the trees.

They followed at a trot, hoping to make contact. But as soon as the Indians saw that they were being pursued, they made a run for it— setting out "with might and main" along the shore to the south. Standish and his party did their best to chase them, but it was slow going in the ankle-deep sand, and after several months aboard ship, they were in no shape for a long sprint across a beach. Even though they were quickly left behind, they followed the Indians' footprints in the sand. From the tracks they could tell that the Indians would bound up each hill and then pause to look back to see whether they were still being pursued. After what the Pilgrims judged to be ten miles of marching (but which was probably closer to seven), they stopped for the night. With three sentinels on guard at a time, they gathered around a large fire and tried to get some sleep.

The next morning Standish and his men once again set off in pursuit of the Indians. They followed the tracks past the head of a long tidal creek into a heavily wooded area, "which tore our armor in pieces." Finally, around ten in the morning, they emerged into a deep grassy valley, where they saw their first American deer. But it was water they truly needed. The only liquid they had brought with them was a bottle of aqua vitae (a strong liquor), and they were now suffering from violent thirst. They were also hungry, with just a ship's biscuit and some cheese to share among sixteen men. At last, at the foot of a small rise of land they found an upwelling of freshwater—called today Pilgrim

Spring. They claimed to have "drunk our first New England water with as much delight as ever we drunk drink in all our lives." From a group of lifelong beer and wine drinkers, this was high praise indeed.

Once they'd refreshed themselves, they marched to the shoreline, where they could see the *Mayflower* just four miles to the northwest across the arc of the bay. They made camp, and that night they built a large fire as part of a prearranged signal to let their friends and loved ones know that all was well.

The next morning, they found their first evidence of Native agriculture: stubbled fields that had been planted with corn in the last few years. Soon after, they found a small path that led to what appeared to be a grave site: mounds of sand covered with decayed reed mats. In one of the mounds they found a bow along with several badly rotted arrows. They were tempted to dig further, but deciding that "it would be odious unto [the Indians] to ransack their sepulchers," they returned the bow and arrows and covered them back up.

As they continued south, they came across evidence that they were not the first Europeans to have visited this place. First they found some sawed planks and an old iron ship's kettle—perhaps from the French shipwreck of 1615. Then, near the river mouth that they'd seen from the *Mayflower,* which was actually more of a two-pronged saltwater creek and known today as the Pamet River in Truro, they discovered the remnants of what must have been Martin Pring's seventeen-year-old fort. But it was evidence of a decidedly Native sort that soon commanded their attention.

On a high shoreside hill, they found an area where the sand had recently been patted smooth. This was clearly different from the grave site they had encountered earlier. As three of them dug, the others gathered around in a defensive ring with their muskets ready. Not far down they found a basket made of woven reeds filled with approximately four bushels of dried Indian corn—so much corn, in fact, that two men could barely lift it. Nearby they found a basket containing corn that was still on the cob, "some yellow and some red, and others mixed with blue." One of the more remarkable characteristics of Indian corn or maize is that, if kept dry, the kernels can be stored indefinitely.

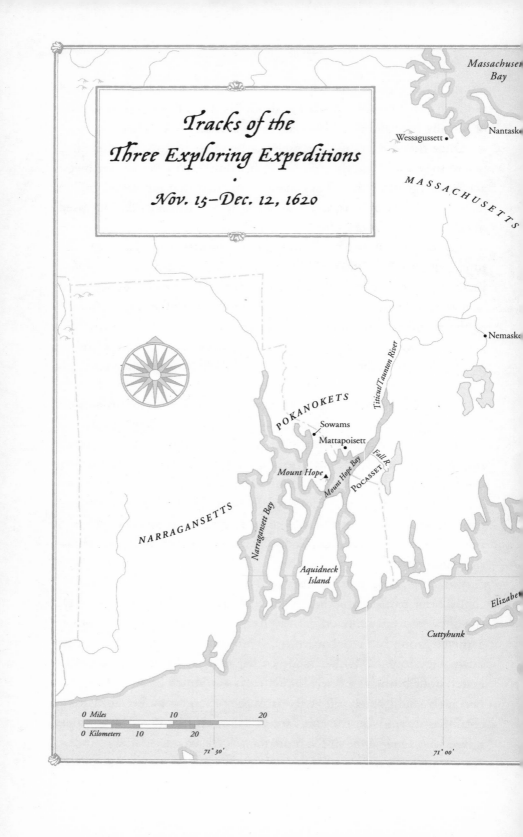

Tracks of the
Three Exploring Expeditions
·
Nov. 15–Dec. 12, 1620

Massachuset
Bay

Wessagussett ·

Nantask

MASSACHUSETTS

· Nemaske

POKANOKETS

Sowams

Mattapoisett

Titicut/Taunton River

Fall R.

Mount Hope ▲

Mount Hope Bay

POCASSET

NARRAGANSETTS

Narragansett Bay

Aquidneck
Island

Elizabe

Cuttyhunk

0 Miles   10   20
0 Kilometers   10   20

71° 30'   71° 00'

Route of exploring expedition, Nov. 15–17, 1620
Route of exploring expedition, Nov. 27–30, 1620
Route of exploring expedition of Dec. 6–12, 1620

Provincetown Harbor
Pilgrim Lake
Pilgrim Spring
Corn Hill
Mayflower's Anchorage
Clark Island
Gurnet
es R.
Patuxet/
ymouth
Manomet Bluff
Manomet
Cold Harbor
Pamet R.
Truro
Wellfleet
Cape Cod
Cape Cod Bay
Billingsgate
First Encounter
NAUSETS
Orleans
Manamoyick/
Pleasant Bay
Cummaquid/
Barnstable Harbor
Atlantic Ocean
uzzards
Bay
ds
Nantucket Sound
Great Point
Martha's Vineyard
Nantucket Island

42° 00'

41° 30'

70° 30'
70° 00'
© 2005 Jeffrey L. Ward

In Mexico, storage pits containing perfectly preserved corn have been unearthed that were at least a thousand years old.

The Pilgrims paused to discuss what they should do next. They had brought wheat, barley, and peas with them aboard the *Mayflower* for planting in the spring. Many, if not most, European settlers in a similar situation would have had enough faith in their own, supposedly superior, technology that they would have had no use for a buried bag of Native seed. But the Pilgrims were not usual European immigrants. For one thing, they were desperate. Due to the woeful state of their provisions, as well as the lateness of the season, they knew they were in a survival situation from the start. Without a plan—and the inevitable swagger a plan engenders—they were willing to try just about anything if it meant they might survive their first year. As a result, the Pilgrims proved to be more receptive to the new ways of the New World than nearly any English settlers before or since.

They were also experienced exiles. Their twelve years in Holland had given them a head start in the difficult process of acculturation. Going native—at least to a certain degree—was a necessary, if problematic, part of adapting to life in a strange and foreign land. If their European grains refused to grow in this new environment, their very survival might depend on having planted a significant amount of American corn. They decided they had no choice but to take the corn. The place where they found the buried seed is still called Corn Hill.

The decision to steal the corn was not without considerable risks. They were, after all, taking something of obvious value from a people who had done their best, so far, to avoid them. The Pilgrims might have opted to wait until they had the chance to speak with the Indians before they took the corn, but the last thing they possessed was time. They assured themselves that they would compensate the corn's owners as soon as they had the opportunity.

They poured as much corn as would fit into a kettle, which they suspended from a staff, and with two men shouldering the burden, they started back to the *Mayflower*. They planned to retrieve the rest of the corn once the shallop had been completed. They also hoped to explore the upper reaches of the two creeks. If some earlier European visitors had thought the location suitable for an outpost of some sort, perhaps it might serve their own needs.

By dusk it was raining. After a long wet night spent within a hastily constructed barricade of tree trunks and branches, they continued on to the north, only to become lost, once again, in the woods. Deep within a grove of trees, they came across a young sapling that had been bent down to the ground, where a Native-made rope encircled some acorns. Stephen Hopkins explained that this was an Indian deer trap similar to the ones he'd seen in Virginia. As they stood examining the ingenious device, William Bradford, who was taking up the rear, stumbled upon the trap. The sapling jerked up, and Bradford was snagged by the leg. Instead of being annoyed, Bradford could only marvel at this "very pretty device, made with a rope of their own making, and having a noose as artificially made as any roper in England can make." Adding the noose to what soon became a collection of specimens and artifacts, they continued on to the harbor, where they found a welcoming party on shore headed by Master Jones and Governor Carver. "And thus," Bradford wrote, "we came both weary and welcome home."

It took another few days for the carpenter to finish the shallop, and when it was done on Monday, November 27, yet another exploring expedition was launched, this time under the direction of Christopher Jones. As the master of the *Mayflower*, Jones was not required to assist the Pilgrims in their attempts to find a settlement site, but he obviously thought it in his best interests to see them on their way.

There were thirty-four of them, twenty-four passengers and ten sailors, aboard the open shallop, The wind was out of the northeast, and the shallop had a difficult time weathering the point within which the *Mayflower* was anchored. After being blown to the opposite side of the harbor, they spent the night tucked into an inlet that is now part of Pilgrim Lake. The tidal flats along the shore were becoming more than just a nuisance; as the temperatures dipped to well below freezing, their wet shoes and stockings began to freeze. "[S]ome of our people that are dead," Bradford wrote, "took the original of their death here."

Cape Cod is well to the south of England (indeed, the Cape is about the same latitude as Madrid, Spain), but so far they had experienced temperatures that were much colder than back home. As they soon discovered, New England has a very different climate from England. Weather along the eastern seaboard of North America usually comes from the continent to the west, while in England it comes from the Atlantic Ocean. Since land absorbs and releases heat much more quickly than water, New England tends to be colder in the winter and hotter in the summer than England.

Adding to the disparity between American and English winters is the Gulf Stream, which continually warms the British Isles. But in 1620 there was yet another factor at work. North America was in the midst of what climatologists have called the "little ice age"—a period of exceptional cold that persisted well into the eighteenth century. As a result, the Pilgrims were experiencing temperatures that were cold even by modern standards in New England, and they were more than a month away from finding a place to live.

By morning, there were six inches of snow on the ground. By the time they'd sailed south back to Pamet Harbor in modern Truro, they were so frostbitten and numb that they had no choice but to name the inlet Cold Harbor. Jones decided to explore the northern and largest of the two creeks by land. But after several hours of "marching up and down the steep hills, and deep valleys, which lay half a foot thick with snow," the master of the *Mayflower* had had enough. At fifty years old, he was most certainly the eldest of the group. Some of the Pilgrims—perhaps led by the recently demoted Standish—wanted to continue, but Jones insisted it was time to make camp under several large pine trees. That night they feasted on six ducks and three geese "with soldiers' stomachs for we had eaten little all that day."

Cold Harbor, it was decided, was too shallow to support a permanent settlement. Giving up on any further exploration of the two creeks, they went looking for Corn Hill the next morning. The snow made it difficult to find the stores of buried corn, but after brushing aside the drifts and hacking at the frozen topsoil with their cutlasses, they located not only the original bag of seed but an additional cache of ten bushels. For Master Jones, this was just the excuse he needed to return to the warmth of the *Mayflower's* cabin. He must get the corn, along with several men who were too sick to continue on, back to the ship. Once the corn and the invalids had been loaded aboard the shallop, he set sail for Provincetown Harbor. The boat would return the next day for the rest of them.

Standish was once again in charge. The next morning, he led the eighteen remaining men on a search for Indians. But after several hours of tramping through the woods and snow, they had found nothing. The Native Americans' seasonal settlement pattern—inland in the winter, near the water in the summer—meant that the Pilgrims, who were staying, for the most part, near the shore, were unlikely to encounter many Indians during their explorations of Cape Cod.

On their way back to the harbor, not far from where they had come across some burial sites the week before, Standish and his men found "a place like a grave, but it was much bigger and longer than any we had yet seen." Only the week before they'd decided it was wrong to violate the Indians' graves; this time they could not help themselves. There were boards positioned over the grave, suggesting that someone of importance had been buried here. They "resolved to dig it up."

They found several additional boards and a mat made of woven grass. One of the boards was "finely carved and painted, with three tines . . . on the top, like a crown." This may have been a carving of Poseidon's trident, suggesting that the board originally came from a ship—most probably the French ship that had wrecked on this coast in 1615. Farther down, they found a new mat wrapped around two bundles, one large and one small.

They opened the larger bundle first. The contents were covered with a fine, sweet-smelling reddish powder: red ocher used by the Indians as both a pigment and an embalmment. Along with some bones, they found the skull of a man with "fine yellow hair still on it, and some of the flesh unconsumed." With the skull was a sailor's canvas bag containing a knife and sewing needle. Then they turned to the smaller bundle. Inside were the skull and bones of a small child, along with a tiny wooden bow "and some other odd knacks."

Was this a castaway from the French ship and his Indian son? Had this particular sailor been embraced by the local Indians and died among them as a person "of some special note"? Or had the Indians killed and buried the sailor "in triumph over him"?

They had left Holland so that they could reclaim their English ancestry. But here was troubling evidence that America was no blank slate. There were others here who must be taken into account. Otherwise, they might share the fate of this yellow-haired sailor, whose bones and possessions had been left to molder in the sand.

Later that day, just a short distance from Cold Harbor, Standish and his men found some Indian houses whose occupants had clearly left in a great hurry. The description of what they found, recorded in a brief book about their first year in America cowritten by Bradford and Edward Winslow, is so detailed that it remains one of the best first-person accounts of an Indian wigwam, or wetu, that we have. Indeed, a modern anthropologist transported back to November 1620 would have a difficult time outdoing the report left by two cold, sick, and exhausted English émigrés who were far more familiar with the urban centers of Europe than the wilds of America.

> The houses were made with long young sapling trees, bended and both ends stuck into the ground; they were made round, like unto an arbor, and covered down to the ground with thick and well wrought mats, and the door was not over a yard high, made of a mat to open; the chimney was a wide open hole in the top, for which they had a mat to cover it close when they pleased; one might stand and go upright in them, in the midst of them were four little trunches [i.e., y-shaped stakes] knocked into the ground and small sticks laid over, on which they hung their pots . . . ; round about the fire they lay on mats, which are their beds. The

houses were double matted, for as they were matted without, so were they within, with newer & fairer mats.

Among the Indians' clay pots, wooden bowls, and reed baskets was an iron bucket from Europe that was missing a handle. There were several deer heads, one of which was still quite fresh, as well as a piece of broiled herring. As they had done with the graves of the blond-haired sailor and Indian child, the Pilgrims decided to take "some of the best things" with them.

Looting houses, graves, and storage pits was hardly the way to win the trust of the local inhabitants. To help offset the damage they'd already done, they resolved to leave behind some beads and other tokens for the Indians "in sign of peace." But it was getting dark. The shallop had returned, and they planned to spend the night back aboard the *Mayflower*. They must be going. In their haste to depart, they neglected to leave the beads and other trade goods. It would have been a meager gesture to be sure, but it would have marked their only unmistakable act of friendship since their arrival in the New World.

The explorers learned of some good tidings once back aboard the *Mayflower*. A son, named Peregrine, had been born to Susanna and William White. But a death was soon to follow the baby's birth. Edward Thompson, the Whites' servant, died on Monday, December 4.

Since Truro's Pamet Harbor was not going to serve their needs, they must find another settlement site. The pilot Robert Coppin had a rather hazy memory of a "good harbor" with a "great navigable river" about twenty-five miles across Cape Cod Bay. The reference to a large river suggests that Coppin was thinking of the future site of Boston. There was also talk of a place called Agawam, even farther to the north, known today as Ipswich.

After much discussion, it was decided to pick up where they had left off and follow the shoreline of the Cape west and eventually north. Under no circumstances were they to venture beyond the harbor described by Coppin, which he called Thievish Harbor, since an Indian had stolen one of his company's harpoons when he was there several years earlier. For the Pilgrims, who had so far stolen a good deal of corn and Native artifacts, Thievish Harbor might be just the place.

The shallop set out on Wednesday, December 6. The *Mayflower's* two pilots, Robert Coppin and John Clark, had replaced Master Jones and were accompanied by the master gunner and three sailors. The Pilgrims were represented by Bradford, Carver, Standish, Winslow, John Tilley and his brother Edward, John Howland, Richard Warren, Stephen Hopkins, and Hopkins's servant, Edward Doty—less than half the number of the previous expedition. Illness and freezing temperatures—it was now in the low twenties, if not colder—had already taken a considerable toll.

Almost as soon as they set sail, the salt spray froze on their coats— "as if they had been glazed," Bradford wrote. They sailed south into Wellfleet Bay, about fifteen miles beyond Truro. On the shore they saw a dozen or so Indians working around a large dark object that they later discovered was a pilot whale, a small, bulbous-headed black whale around twenty feet long. Also known as blackfish, pilot whales often become stranded on the tidal flats of the Cape. The Indians were cutting the whale's blubber into long strips when they saw the shallop approaching and fled, "running to and fro, as if they had been carrying something."

Once ashore, the Pilgrims built themselves a barricade and a large fire, and as night descended they noticed the smoke from another fire about four miles away. The next day was spent looking for a possible settlement site, with some of them taking to the shallop while others remained on land. Once again, they found plenty of graves and abandoned wigwams, but no people and no suitable anchorages. They determined to sail for Thievish Harbor the following day. Toward nightfall, the shore party rendezvoused with those in the shallop at a tidal creek known today as Herring River. As they had done the previous night, they built themselves a circular barricade of tree trunks and branches, with a small opening on the leeward side, where they stationed several sentinels.

Around midnight, the silence was broken by "a great hideous cry." The sentinels shouted out, "Arm! Arm!" Several muskets were fired, and all was silent once again. One of the sailors said he'd heard wolves make a similar noise in Newfoundland. This seemed to comfort them, and they went back to sleep.

About 5 a.m. they began to rouse themselves. Most of them were armed with matchlocks—muskets equipped with long burning wicks that were used to ignite the gun's priming powder. They were not the most reliable of weapons, particularly in the wet and cold, since it was difficult to keep the powder dry. Several men decided to fire off their guns, just to make sure they were still in operating order.

After prayer, they began to prepare themselves for breakfast and the long journey ahead. In the predawn twilight, some of the men carried their weapons and armor down to the shallop. Laying them beside the boat, they returned to the camp for breakfast. It was then they heard another "great and strange cry."

One of the men burst out of the trees and came running for the barricade, screaming, "They are men—Indians, Indians!" Suddenly the air was filled with arrows. Every man reached for his gun. Instead of a matchlock, Miles Standish possessed a snaplock, a predecessor to the flintlock, and immediately fired off a round. The others dipped their matches into the embers of the fire, and with their matches lit, began to blast away. Standish ordered them "not to shoot, till we could take aim." He didn't know how many Indians were out there in the woods, and they might need every shot.

In the meantime, those who had left their muskets beside the shallop sprinted back to retrieve them. The Indians soon had them trapped behind the boat. Standish and those guarding the entrance to the barricade called out to make sure they were unhurt. "Well, well, everyone," they shouted. "Be of good courage!" Three of them at the boat fired their muskets, but the others were without a way to light their matches and cried out for a firebrand. One of the men in the barricade picked up a burning log from the fire and ran with it to the shallop, an act of bravery that, according to Bradford, "did not a little discourage our enemies." For their part, the Indians' war cries were a particularly potent psychological weapon that the Pilgrims would never forget, later transcribing them as "Woath! Woach! Ha! Ha! Hach! Woach!"

They estimated that there were at least thirty Indians, "although some thought that they were many more yet in the dark of the morning." Backlit by the fire, the Pilgrims standing at the entrance of the barricade were easy targets, and the arrows came thick and fast. As the French explorer Samuel Champlain had discovered fourteen years earlier on the south coast of Cape Cod, the Indians' bows and arrows were fearsome weapons. Made from a five-and-a-half-foot piece of solid hickory, maple, ash, or witch hazel and strung with a three-stranded length of sinew, a Native bow was so powerful that one of Champlain's men was skewered by an arrow that had already passed through his dog—making, in effect, a gruesome shish kebab of the French sailor and his pet. The feathered arrows were over a yard long, and each warrior kept as many as fifty of them in a quiver made from dried rushes. With his quiver slung over his left shoulder and with the hair on the right side of his head cut short so as not to interfere with the bowstring, a Native warrior was capable of firing arrows much faster than a musket-equipped Englishman could fire bullets. Indeed, it was possible for a skilled bowman to have as many as five arrows in the air at once, and the Pilgrims were forced to take shelter as best they could.

There was one Indian in particular, "a lusty man and no whit less valiant, who was thought to be their captain." He stood behind a tree within "half a musket shot" of the barricade, peppering them with arrows as the Pilgrims did their best to blast him to bits. The Native leader dodged three different gunshots but, seeing one of the Englishman taking "full aim at him," wisely decided to retreat. As fragments of bark and wood flew around him, he let out "an extraordinary shriek" and disappeared with his men into the woods.

Some of the Pilgrims, led no doubt by Standish, followed for about a quarter of a mile, then stopped to shoot off their muskets. "This we did," Bradford wrote, "that they might see we were not afraid of them nor discouraged." The clothes they had left hanging on the barricade were riddled with arrows, but none of the men had suffered even a scratch. Before they departed in the shallop, they collected a total of eighteen arrows, "some . . . headed with brass, others with harts' horn, and others with eagles' claws," for eventual shipment back to England. "Thus it pleased God," Bradford wrote, "to vanquish our enemies and give us deliverance."

The approximate site of this exchange is still known as First Encounter Beach in Eastham. It could hardly be considered a victory. The Pilgrims knew they could not blast, fight, and kill their way to a permanent settlement in New England. But after the First Encounter, it was clear that goodwill was going to be difficult to find here on Cape Cod.

It was on to Thievish Harbor.

With the wind out of the southeast, they sailed along the southern edge of Cape Cod Bay. Then the weather began to deteriorate. The wind picked up, and with the temperature hovering around freezing, horizontal sleet combined with the salt spray to drench them to the bone. The rough seas made it difficult to steer this wide and heavy boat, and even though the carpenter had labored mightily in preparing the shallop, her rudder did not prove equal to the strain. They were somewhere off the whitish rise of Manomet Bluff when a wave wrenched the rudder off the transom, and the boat rounded up into the wind in a fury of luffing sails and blowing spray. It took two men standing in the stern, each clutching a long oak oar, to bring the shallop back around and start sailing, once again, along the coast.

The wind continued to build, and as night came on the boat became unmanageable in the waves. All seemed lost, when the pilot Robert Coppin cried out, "Be of good cheer, I see the harbor!" By now it was blowing a gale, and in the freezing rain, the visibility was terrible. But Coppin saw something—perhaps an inviting darkness between two wave-whitened shoals—that convinced him they were about to enter Thievish Harbor.

They were running before the wind, with their full mainsail set, bashing through the building seas, when their mast splintered into three pieces. Once they'd gathered up the broken mast and sodden sail and stowed them away, they took up the oars and started to row. The tide, at least, was with them.

But it quickly became evident that what they had taken to be their salvation was about to be their ruin. Instead of the entrance to a harbor, they were steering for a wave-pummeled beach. Coppin cried out, "Lord be merciful unto us, for my eyes never saw this place before!"

Just when all seemed lost, the sailor at the steering oar exhorted them to use their oars to round the boat up to windward, and with the waves bursting against the shallop's side, they attempted to row their way out of danger. "So he bid them be of good cheer," Bradford wrote, "and row lustily, for there was a fair sound before them, and he doubted not but they should find one place or other where they might ride in safety."

The shallop had nearly run into a shallow cove at the end of a thin, sandy peninsula called the Gurnet. The Gurnet terminates with a jog to the southwest known as Saquish Head. It was the beach between the Gurnet and Saquish Head that had almost claimed the Pilgrims. Once they rowed the shallop around the tip of Saquish, they found themselves in the lee of what they later discovered was an island.

In the deepening darkness of the windy night, they discussed what they should do next. Some insisted that they remain aboard the shallop in case of Indian attack. But most of them were more fearful of freezing to death, so they went ashore and built a large fire. When at midnight the wind shifted to the northwest and the temperature dropped till "it froze hard," all were glad that they had decided to come ashore.

The next day, a Saturday, proved to be "a fair, sunshining day." They now realized that they were on a heavily wooded island and, for the time being, safe from Indian attack. John Clark, one of the *Mayflower*'s pilots, had been the first to set foot on the island, and from that day forward it was known as Clark's Island.

They were on the western edge of a large, wonderfully sheltered bay that might prove to be exactly the anchorage they needed. Even though they had "so many motives for haste," they decided to spend the day on the island, "where they might dry their stuff, fix their pieces, and rest themselves." The shallop needed a mast, and they undoubtedly cut down as straight and sturdy a tree as they could find and fashioned it into a new spar. The following day was a Sunday, and as Bradford recorded, "on the Sabbath day we rested."

They spent Monday exploring what was to become their new home. They sounded the harbor and found it suitable for ships the size of the *Mayflower*. They ventured on land, but nowhere in either *Of Plymouth Plantation* or *Mourt's Relation,* the book Bradford and Winslow wrote after their first year in America, is there any mention of a Pilgrim stepping on a rock. Like Cape Cod to the southeast, the shore of Plymouth Bay is nondescript and sandy. But at the foot of a high hill, just to the north of a brook, was a rock that must have been impossible to miss. More than twice as big as the mangled chunk of stone that is revered today as Plymouth Rock, this two-hundred-ton granite boulder loomed above the low shoreline like a recumbent elephant. But did the Pilgrims use it as a landing place?

At half tide and above, a small boat could have sailed right up alongside the rock. For these explorers, who were suffering from chills and coughs after several weeks of wading up and down the frigid flats of Cape Cod, the ease of access offered by the rock must have been difficult to resist. But if they did use it as their first stepping-stone onto the banks of Plymouth Harbor, Bradford never made note of the historic event. That would be left to subsequent generations of mythmakers.

They marched across the shores of Plymouth "and found divers cornfields and little running brooks, a place (as they supposed) fit for situation." Best of all, despite the signs of cultivation, they found no evidence of any recent Indian settlements. The next day they boarded the shallop and sailed for the *Mayflower* with the good news.

It had been a long month of exploration. Later, when looking back on their trek across the wastes of Cape Cod, Bradford could not help but see their wintry walkabout in biblical terms. New World Israelites, they had, with God's help, finally found their Canaan. But back then, in the late afternoon of Tuesday, December 12, as the shallop approached the *Mayflower,* Bradford and his compatriots had little reason to believe they had found the Promised Land.

Plymouth Harbor was commodious, but much of it was so shallow that a ship the size of the *Mayflower*, which drew twelve feet, must anchor more than a mile from shore. The harbor was also without a navigable river to provide access to the country's interior. It was true that there were no Native settlements nearby, but that didn't mean they would be immune to attack. The Indians in the region had already surprised them once; it would probably happen again. Worst of all, they were approaching what Bradford called "the heart of winter," and many of them were sick; indeed, some were on the verge of death.

And then that evening, Bradford received what would have been, for many men, the final blow. He learned that five days before, Dorothy May Bradford, his wife of seven years and the mother of his three-year-old son, John, had slipped over the side of the *Mayflower* and drowned.

Bradford never wrote about the circumstances of his wife's death. Much later in the century, the Puritan historian Cotton Mather recorded that Dorothy Bradford had accidentally fallen overboard and "was drowned in the harbor." That she fell from a moored ship has caused some to wonder whether she committed suicide.

Dorothy certainly had ample reason to despair: She had not seen her son in more than four months; her husband had left the day before on his third dangerous trip away from her in as many weeks. On the same day the shallop had departed, seven-year-old Jasper More, one of the four children placed on the *Mayflower* by their cuckolded father, died in the care of the Brewster family. Two other More children would die in the months ahead. For Dorothy, whose own young son was on the other side of the Atlantic, the plight of these and the other children may have been especially difficult to witness.

We think of the Pilgrims as resilient adventurers upheld by unwavering religious faith, but they were also human beings in the midst of what was, and continues to be, one of the most difficult emotional challenges a person can face: immigration and exile. Less than a year later, another group of English settlers arrived at Provincetown Harbor and were so overwhelmed by this "naked and barren place" that they convinced themselves that the Pilgrims must all be dead. In fear of being forsaken by the ship's captain, the panicked settlers began to strip the sails from the yards "lest the ship should get away and leave them." If Dorothy experienced just a portion of the terror and sense of abandonment that gripped these settlers, she may have felt that suicide was her only choice.

Even if his wife's death had been unintentional, Bradford believed that God controlled what happened on earth. As a consequence, every occurrence *meant* something. John Howland had been rescued in the midst of a gale at sea, but Dorothy, his "dearest consort," had drowned in the placid waters of Provincetown Harbor.

The only clue Bradford left us about his own feelings is in a poem he wrote toward the end of his life.

> Faint not, poor soul, in God still trust,
> Fear not the things thou suffer must;
> For, whom he loves he doth chastise,
> And then all tears wipes from their eyes.

CHAPTER FIVE

The Heart of Winter

*T*HE *MAYFLOWER* LEFT Provincetown Harbor on Friday, December 15. Headwinds from the northwest prevented the ship from entering Plymouth Harbor until the following day. Both Plymouth Harbor and Duxbury Bay to the north are contained within two interlocking sickles of sand: the Gurnet, an extension of Duxbury Beach, to the north and Long Beach to the south. The *Mayflower* anchored just within Goose Point at the end of Long Beach, a mile and a half from Plymouth Rock.

Not until Wednesday, December 20, after three more days of exploration, did they decide where to begin building a permanent settlement. Some voted for Clark's Island, their refuge during the shallop's first night in the harbor, as the safest spot in case of Indian attack. Others thought a river almost directly across from the island was more suitable. Unfortunately Jones River, which they named for the *Mayflower*'s master, was not deep enough to handle a vessel of more than 30 tons (the *Mayflower* was 180 tons), and the settlement site (the current location of Kingston) would have been difficult to defend against the Indians. That left the area near the Rock.

The future site of Plymouth Plantation had much to recommend it. Rising up from shore was a 165-foot hill that provided a spectacular view of the surrounding coastline. On a clear day, it was even possible to see the tip of Cape Cod, almost thirty miles away. A stout, cannon-equipped fort on this hill would provide all the security they could ever hope for.

The presence of the Rock as a landing place was yet another plus. Even more important was the "very sweet brook" that flowed beside it, carving out a channel that allowed small vessels to sail not only to the Rock but up what they called Town Brook. Just inside the brook's entrance was a wide salt marsh where, Bradford wrote, "we may harbor our shallops and boats exceedingly well." There were also several freshwater springs along the high banks of the brook that bubbled with "as good water as can be drunk"—an increasingly important consideration now that they were forced to ration what remained of the beer.

The biggest advantage of the area was that it had already been cleared by the Indians. And yet nowhere could they find evidence of any recent Native settlements. The Pilgrims saw the eerie vacancy of this place as a miraculous gift from God. But if a miracle had indeed occurred at Plymouth, it had taken the form of a holocaust almost beyond human imagining.

Just three years before, even as the Pilgrims had begun preparations to settle in America, there had been between one thousand and two thousand people living along these shores. As a map drawn by Samuel Champlain in 1605 shows, the banks of the harbor had been dotted with wigwams, each with a curling plume of wood smoke rising from the hole in its roof and with fields of corn, beans, and squash growing nearby. Dugout canoes made from hollowed-out pine trees plied the waters, which in summer were choked with bluefish and striped bass. The lobsters were so numerous that the Indians plucked them from the shallows of the harbor. The mudflats were so thick with buried clams that it was impossible to walk across the shore without being drenched by squirting bivalves.

Then, from 1616 to 1619, disease brought this centuries-old community to an end. No witnesses recorded what happened along the shores of Plymouth, but in the following decade the epidemics returned, and Roger Williams told how entire villages became emptied of people. "I have seen a poor house left alone in the wild woods," Williams wrote, "all being fled, the living not able to bury the dead. So terrible is the apprehension of an infectious disease, that not only persons, but the houses and the whole town, take flight."

No Native dwellings remained in Plymouth in the winter of 1620, but gruesome evidence of the epidemic was scattered all around the

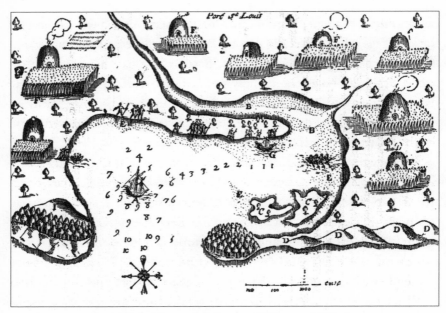

Samuel de Champlain's map of Plymouth Harbor

area. "[T]heir skulls and bones were found in many places lying still above the ground . . . ," Bradford wrote, "a very sad spectacle to behold." It was here, on the bone-whitened hills of Plymouth, that the Pilgrims hoped to begin a new life.

They decided to build their houses on what is called today Cole's Hill overlooking the salt marsh. Situated between the shore and the much higher hill, soon to be known as Fort Hill, Cole's Hill was flat enough to accommodate a small settlement and was easily accessible from the brook. That night twenty people remained on shore. They planned to begin building houses the next morning.

But Thursday, December 21, proved so stormy that the *Mayflower* was forced to set an additional anchor. The people on shore were without food, so despite the gale-force winds, the shallop set out from the *Mayflower* "with much ado with provisions." The terrible weather persisted throughout the following day, making it impossible to begin work on the houses. In the meantime, the wind-lashed *Mayflower* had become a grim hospital ship. In addition to colds, coughs, and fevers, scurvy tormented the passengers. James Chilton had died even before the *Mayflower* arrived in Plymouth Harbor. That Thursday, Richard Britteridge passed away, followed two days later by Christopher Martin's stepson Solomon Prower. On Friday morning Mary Allerton gave birth to a stillborn son.

Not until Saturday, December 23, were they able to transport a work party from the *Mayflower* to shore. With their axes and saws they felled trees and carried the timber to the building site. The fact that Monday, December 25, was Christmas Day meant little to the Pilgrims, who believed that religious celebrations of this sort were a profanation of the true word of Christ. Of more importance to them, December 25 was the day they erected the frame of their first house. "[N]o man rested that day," Bradford wrote. But toward sunset, the familiar cries of Indians erupted in the surrounding forest. The Pilgrims took up their muskets and stared tensely into the deepening darkness as the cries echoed briefly and died away.

Ahead of them was an unknown wilderness that they could not help but inhabit with all their fears. Behind them was the harbor and the distant *Mayflower,* lights beginning to twinkle through her cabin windows, a smudge of smoke rising up from the galley stove in the forecastle. What would have astounded a modern sensibility transported back to that Christmas Day in 1620 was the absolute quiet of the scene. Save for the gurgling of Town Brook, the lap of waves against the shore, and the wind in the bare winter branches, everything was silent as they listened and waited.

The Pilgrims' intensely felt spiritual lives did not prevent them from believing in witches and warlocks and living with the constant fear that Satan and his minions were *out there,* conspiring against them. It was a fear that must have been difficult to contain as they stared into the deepening gloom of the American night.

After waiting a few more tense minutes, they decided to send the shallop back to the *Mayflower,* leaving the usual number of twenty ashore. That night they were drenched by yet another rainstorm.

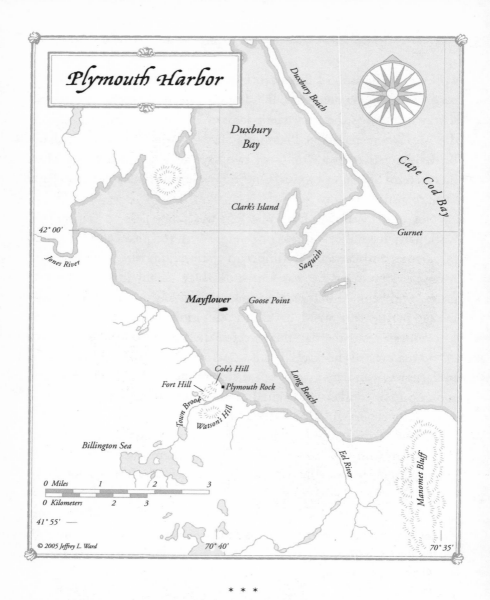

Plymouth Harbor

Duxbury Beach

Duxbury
Bay

Cape Cod Bay

Clark's Island

42° 00'

Gurnet

Jones River

Saquish

Mayflower   Goose Point

Cole's Hill

Fort Hill   ▪ Plymouth Rock

Town Brook

Long Beach

Watson's Hill

Billington Sea

Eel River

Manomet Bluff

0 Miles   1   2   3
0 Kilometers   2   3

41° 55' —

© 2005 Jeffrey L. Ward   70° 40'   70° 35'

* * *

It took them two more weeks to complete the first building, a twenty-foot-square "common house." It didn't have a proper foundation—there just wasn't the manpower or the time for such a luxury. Known as an earthfast house, the Pilgrims' first structure probably possessed walls of hewn tree trunks interwoven with branches and twigs that were cemented together with clay. This wattle-and-daub construction was typical of farmers' cottages in rural England, as was the building's thatched roof, which was made of cattails and reeds from the nearby

A steeple-crowned beaver hat attributed to Constance Hopkins

A cooking pot that may have come to America with Miles and Rose Standish

The wicker cradle reputed to have been brought to America by William and Susanna White

William Bradford's silver drinking cup, made in England in 1634

ABOVE: *A writing cabinet said to have been brought on the Mayflower by the White family in 1620*

RIGHT: *A chest reputed to have been brought aboard the Mayflower by William Brewster*

marsh. The house's tiny, barely translucent windows were made of linseed-coated parchment. The chimney—if, in fact, the house did have a chimney instead of a simple hole in the roof—was a primitive ductwork made of four soot-blackened boards that funneled the smoke from an open fire on the dirt floor. It was a most dark and smoky space, but for the first time, the Pilgrims had a real roof over their heads.

On the morning of Thursday, December 28, they turned their attention to the high hill, where they began to construct a wooden platform on which to mount the various cannons they had brought with them aboard the *Mayflower*. This was also the day they started to plan the organization of the settlement. But first they needed to decide how many houses to build. It was determined that "all single men that had no wives to join them" should find a family to live with, which brought the total number of houses down to nineteen. From the beginning, it was decided that "every man should build his own house, thinking by that course, men would make more haste than working in common."

Miles Standish appears to have had a hand in determining the layout of the town. At lectures on military engineering at the University of Leiden, soldiers could learn from the Dutch army's chief engineer that the most easily defended settlement pattern consisted of a street with parallel alleys and a cross street. The Pilgrims created a similar design that included two rows of houses "for safety." For the present, Plymouth was without a church and town green, the features that came to typify a New England town.

In the weeks ahead, the death toll required them to revise radically their initial plans. Instead of nineteen, only seven houses were built the first year, plus another four buildings for common use, including a small fortlike structure called a rendezvous. The houses were built along a street that ran from Fort Hill down to the sea. Known today as Leyden Street, it was crossed by a "highway" running from north to south down to Town Brook. Around this intersection, the town of Plymouth slowly came into being, even as death reduced the newcomers to half their original number.

* * *

Thursday, January 11, was "a fair day." Given the uncertainty of the weather, they knew they must make as much progress as possible on the houses—especially since, it was still assumed, the *Mayflower* would soon be returning to England.

The frantic pace of the last two months was beginning to tell on William Bradford. He had suffered through a month of exposure to the freezing cold on the exploratory missions, and the stiffness in his ankles made it difficult to walk. But there was more troubling him than physical discomfort. Dorothy's passing had opened the floodgates: death was everywhere. It pursued them in the form of illness, and it had been waiting for them here on the blighted shores of Plymouth. Now, in the midst of winter, he could only wonder if he would ever see his son again.

That day, as Bradford worked beside the others, he was "vehemently taken with a grief and pain" that pierced him to his hipbone. He collapsed and was carried to the common house. At first it was feared Bradford might not last the night. But "in time through God's mercy," he began to improve, even as illness continued to spread among them. The common house soon became as "full of beds as they could lie one by another." Like the Native Americans before them, they must struggle to survive on a hillside where death had become a way of life.

In the days ahead, so many fell ill that there were barely half a dozen left to tend the sick. Progress on the houses fell to a standstill as the healthy ones became full-time nurses—preparing meals, tending fires, washing the "loathsome clothes," and emptying chamber pots. Bradford later singled out William Brewster and Miles Standish as sources of indomitable strength:

And yet the Lord so upheld these persons as in this general calamity they were not at all infected either with sickness or lameness. And what I have said of these I may say of many others who died in this general visitation, and others yet living; that whilst they had health, yea or any strength continuing, they were not wanting to any that had need of them. And I doubt not that their recompense is with the Lord.

At one point, Bradford requested a small container of beer from the stores of the *Mayflower,* hoping that it might help in his recovery. With little left for the return voyage to England, the sailors responded that if Bradford "were their own father he should have none." Soon after, disease began to ravage the crew of the *Mayflower,* including many of their officers and "lustiest men." Unlike the Pilgrims, the sailors showed little interest in tending the sick. Early on, the boatswain, "a proud young man," according to Bradford, who would often "curse and scoff at the passengers," grew ill. Despite his treatment of them, several of the passengers attended to the young officer in his final hours. Bradford claimed the boatswain experienced a kind of deathbed conversion, crying out, "Oh, you, I now see, show your love like Christians indeed one to another, but we let one another die like dogs." Master Jones also appears to have undergone a change of heart. Soon after his own men began to fall ill, he let it be known that beer was now available to the Pilgrims, "though he drunk water homeward bound."

On Friday, January 12, John Goodman and Peter Brown were cutting thatch about a mile and a half from the settlement. They had with them the two dogs, a small spaniel and a huge mastiff bitch. English mastiffs were frequently used in bearbaitings—a savage spectator sport popular in London in which the two creatures fought each other to the death. Mastiffs were also favored by English noblemen, who used them to subdue poachers. The Pilgrims' mastiff appears to have been more of a guard dog brought to protect them against wild beasts and Indians.

That afternoon, Goodman and Brown paused from their labors for a midday snack, then took the two dogs for a short ramble in the woods. Near the banks of a pond they saw a large deer, and the dogs, no doubt led by the mastiff, took off in pursuit. By the time Goodman and Brown had caught up with the dogs, they were all thoroughly lost.

It began to rain, and by nightfall it was snowing. They had hoped to find an Indian wigwam for shelter but were forced, in Bradford's words, "to make the earth their bed, and the element their covering." Then they heard what they took to be "two lions roaring exceedingly for a long time together." These may have been eastern cougars, also known as mountain lions, a species that once ranged throughout most of North and South America. The cry of a cougar has been compared to the scream of a woman being murdered, and Goodman and Brown were now thoroughly terrified. They decided that if a lion should come after them, they would scramble into the limbs of a tree and leave the mastiff to do her best to defend them.

All that night they paced back and forth at the foot of a tree, trying to keep warm in the freezing darkness. They still had the sickles they had used to cut thatch, and with each wail of the cougars, they gripped their sickles a little tighter. The mastiff wanted desperately to chase whatever was out there in the woods, so they took turns restraining the huge dog by her collar. At daybreak, they once again set out in search of the settlement.

The terrain surrounding Plymouth was no primeval forest. For centuries, the Indians had been burning the landscape on a seasonal basis, a form of land management that created surprisingly open forests, where a person might easily walk or even ride a horse amid the trees. The constant burning created stands of huge white pine trees that commonly grew to over 100 feet tall, with some trees reaching 250 feet in height and as many as 5 feet in diameter. Black and red oaks were also common, as well as chestnuts, hickories, birches, and hemlocks. In swampy areas, where standing water protected the trees from fire, grew white oaks, alders, willows, and red maples. But there were also large portions of southern New England that were completely devoid of trees. After passing several streams and ponds, Goodman and Brown came upon a huge swath of open land that had recently been burned by the Indians. Come summer, this five-mile-wide section of blackened ground would resemble, to a remarkable degree, the wide and rolling fields of their native England.

Not until the afternoon did Goodman and Brown find a hill that gave them a view of the harbor. Now that they were able to orient themselves, they were soon on their way back home. When they arrived that night, they were, according to Bradford, "ready to faint with travail and want of victuals, and almost famished with cold." Goodman's frostbitten feet were so swollen that they had to cut away his shoes.

The final weeks of January were spent transporting goods from the *Mayflower* to shore. On Sunday, February 4, yet another storm lashed Plymouth Harbor. The rain was so fierce that it washed the clay daubing from the sides of the houses, while the *Mayflower,* which was riding much higher than usual after the removal of so much freight, wobbled precariously in the gusts.

On Friday, February 16, one of the Pilgrims was hidden in the reeds of a salt creek about a mile and a half from the plantation, hunting ducks. Throughout the last few weeks, there had been a growing concern about Indians. A few days earlier, Master Jones had reported seeing two of them watching the ship from Clark's Island. That afternoon, the duck hunter found himself closer to an Indian than any of them had so far come.

He was lying amid the cattails when a group of twelve Indians marched past him on the way to the settlement. In the woods behind him, he heard "the noise of many more." Once the Indians had safely passed, he sprang to his feet and ran for the plantation and sounded the alarm. Miles Standish and Francis Cook were working in the woods when they heard the signal. They dropped their tools, ran down the hill, and armed themselves, but once again, the Indians never came. Later that day, when Standish and Cook returned to retrieve their tools, they discovered that they'd disappeared. That night, they saw "a great fire" near where the duck hunter had first seen the Indians.

The next day, a meeting was called "for the establishing of military orders amongst ourselves." Not surprisingly, Miles Standish was officially designated their captain. A small man with a broad, powerful physique and reddish hair, Standish also had something of a chip on his shoulder. He seems to have been born on the Isle of Man off the west coast of England, and even though he was descended from "the house of Standish of Standish," his rightful claim to ancestral lands had been, according to his own account, "surreptitiously detained from me," forcing him to seek his fortune as a mercenary in Holland. Well educated and well read (he owned a copy of Homer's *The Iliad* and Caesar's *Commentaries*), he appears to have conducted himself with a haughty impulsiveness that did not endear him to some of the settlers, one of whom later claimed that the Plymouth captain "looks like a silly boy, and is in utter contempt." That first winter, John Billington took umbrage at Standish's attempts to whip the men of the settlement into a fighting force and responded to his orders "with opprobrious speeches."

Governor Carver's response was swift. Billington was sentenced to have his hands and feet tied together in a public display of humiliation. But Carver, whose dignified and normally gentle manner appears to have deeply influenced William Bradford, came to think better of the sentence. After listening to impassioned pleas from Billington's family, he granted him a reprieve, "it being his first offense."

But tensions among the Pilgrims remained high. With two, sometimes three people dying a day throughout the months of February and March, there might not be a plantation left to defend by the arrival of spring. Almost everyone had lost a loved one. Christopher Martin, the *Mayflower*'s governor, had died in early January, soon to be followed by his wife, Mary. Three other families—the Rigsdales, Tinkers, and Turners—were entirely wiped out, with more to follow. Thirteen-year-old Mary Chilton, whose father had died back in Provincetown Harbor, became an orphan when her mother passed away that winter. Other orphans included seventeen-year-old Joseph Rogers, twelve-year-old Samuel Fuller, eighteen-year-old John Crackston, seventeen-year-old Priscilla Mullins, and thirteen-year-old Elizabeth Tilley, who also lost her aunt and uncle, Edward and Ann. By the middle of March, there were four widowers: Bradford, Standish, Francis Eaton, and Isaac Allerton, who was left with three surviving children between the ages of four and eight. With the death of her husband, William, Susanna White, mother to the newborn Peregrine and five-year-old Resolved, became the plantation's only surviving widow. By the spring, 52 of the 102 who had originally arrived at Provincetown were dead.

And yet, amid all this tragedy, there were miraculous exceptions. The families of William Brewster, Francis Cook, Stephen Hopkins, and John Billington were left completely untouched by disease. It is tempting to speculate that John Billington's outburst against Standish may have been partly inspired by the fact that he and his fellow non-Leidener Stephen Hopkins had a total of six living children among them, accounting for more than a fifth of the young people in the entire plantation. The future of Plymouth was beginning to look less and less like a Separatist community of saints.

Even more pressing than the emotional and physical strain of all this death was the mounting fear of Indian attack. They knew that the Native inhabitants were watching them, but so far the Indians had refused to come forward. It was quite possible that they were simply waiting the Pilgrims out until there were not enough left to put up an effective resistance. It became imperative, therefore, to make the best possible show of strength.

Whenever the alarm was sounded, the sick were pulled from their beds and propped up against trees with muskets in their hands. They would do little good in case of an actual attack, but at least they were out there to be counted. The Pilgrims also tried to conceal the fact that so many of them had died. They did such a diligent job of hiding their loved ones' remains that it was not until more than a hundred years later, when the runoff from a violent rainstorm unearthed some human bones, that the location of these ancient, hastily dug graves was finally revealed.

On Saturday, February 17, in the midst of the Pilgrims' first official meeting about military matters, someone realized that two Indians were standing on the top of what became known as Watson's Hill on the other side of Town Brook, about a quarter mile to the south. The meeting was immediately adjourned, and the men hurried to get their muskets. When the Pilgrims reassembled under the direction of their newly designated captain, Miles Standish, the Indians were still standing on the hill.

The two groups stared at each other across the valley of Town Brook. The Indians gestured for them to approach. The Pilgrims, however, made it clear that they wanted the Indians to come to them. Finally, Standish and Stephen Hopkins, with only one musket between them, began to make their way across the brook. Before they started up the hill, they laid the musket down on the ground "in sign of peace." But "the savages," Bradford wrote, "would not tarry their coming." They ran off to the shouts of "a great many more" concealed on the other side of the hill. The Pilgrims feared an assault might be in the offing, "but no more came in fight." It was time, they decided, to mount "our great ordnances" on the hill.

On Wednesday of the following week, Christopher Jones supervised the transportation of the "great guns"—close to half a dozen iron cannons that ranged between four and eight feet in length and weighed as much as half a ton. With the installation of this firepower, capable of hurling iron balls as big as three and a half inches in diameter as far as 1,700 yards, what was once a ramshackle collection of highly combustible houses was on its way to becoming a well-defended fortress.

Jones had brought a freshly killed goose, crane, and mallard with him, and once the day's work was completed, they all sat down to an impromptu feast and were, in Bradford's words, "kindly and friendly together." Jones had originally intended to return to England as soon as the Pilgrims found a settlement site. But once disease began to ravage his crew, he realized that he must remain in Plymouth Harbor "till he saw his men begin to recover."

In early March, there were several days of unseasonably warm weather, and "birds sang in the woods most pleasantly." At precisely one o'clock on March 3, they heard their first rumble of American thunder. "It was strong and great claps," they wrote, "but short." They later realized that even though temperatures had been bitterly cold during their explorations along the Cape, the winter had been, for the most part, unusually mild—a respite that undoubtedly prevented even more of them from dying.

On Friday, March 16, they had yet another meeting about military matters. And as had happened the last time they had gathered for such a purpose, they were interrupted by the Indians. But this time there was only one of them atop Watson's Hill, and unlike the previous two Indians, this man appeared to be without hesitation or fear, especially when he began to walk toward them "very boldly." The alarm was sounded, and still the Indian continued striding purposefully down Watson's Hill and across the brook. Once he'd climbed the path to Cole's Hill, he walked past the row of houses toward the rendezvous, where the women and children had been assembled in case of attack. It was clear that if no one restrained him, the Indian was going to walk right into the entrance of the rendezvous. Finally, some of the men stepped into the Indian's path and indicated that he was not to go in. Apparently enjoying the fuss he had created, the Indian "saluted" them and with great enthusiasm spoke the now famous words, "Welcome, Englishmen!"

CHAPTER SIX

In a Dark and Dismal Swamp

*T*HEY COULD NOT HELP but stare in fascination. He was so different from themselves. For one thing, he towered over them. He stood before them "a tall straight man," having not labored at a loom or a cobbler's bench for much of his life. His hair was black, short in front and long in back, and his face was hairless. Interestingly, the Pilgrims made no mention of his skin color.

What impressed them the most was that he was "stark naked," with just a fringed strap of leather around his waist. When a cold gust of wind kicked up, one of the Pilgrims was moved to throw his coat over the Indian's bare shoulders.

He was armed with a bow and just two arrows, "the one headed, the other unheaded." The Pilgrims do not seem to have attached any special significance to them, but the arrows may have represented the alternatives of war and peace. In any event, they soon began to warm to their impetuous guest and offered him something to eat. He immediately requested beer.

With their supplies running short, they offered him some "strong water"—perhaps the aqua vitae they'd drunk during their first days on Cape Cod—as well as some biscuit, butter, cheese, pudding, and a slice of roasted duck, "all of which he liked well."

He introduced himself as Samoset—at least that was how the Pilgrims heard it—but he may actually have been telling them his English name, Somerset. He was not, he explained in broken English, from this part of New England. He was a sachem from Pemaquid Point in Maine, near Monhegan Island, a region frequented by English fishermen. It was from these fishermen, many of whom he named, that he'd learned to speak English. Despite occasional trouble understanding him, the Pilgrims hung on Samoset's every word as he told them about their new home.

He explained that the harbor's name was Patuxet, and that just about every person who had once lived there had "died of an extraordinary plague." The supreme leader of the region was named Massasoit, who lived in a place called Pokanoket about forty miles to the southwest at the head of Narragansett Bay. Samoset said that the Nausets controlled the part of Cape Cod where the Pilgrims had stolen the corn. The Nausets were "ill affected toward the English" after Hunt had abducted twenty or so of their men back in 1614. He also said that there was another Indian back in Pokanoket named Squanto, who spoke even better English than he did.

With darkness approaching, the Pilgrims were ready to see their voluble guest on his way. As a practical matter, they had nowhere for him to sleep; in addition, they were not yet sure whether they could trust him. But Samoset made it clear he wanted to spend the night. Perhaps because they assumed he'd fear abduction and quickly leave, they offered to take him out to the *Mayflower*. Samoset cheerfully called their bluff and climbed into the shallop. Claiming that high winds and low tides prevented them from leaving shore, the Pilgrims finally allowed him to spend the night with Stephen Hopkins and his family. Samoset left the next morning, promising to return in a few days with some of Massasoit's men.

All that winter, Massasoit had watched and waited. From the Nausets he had learned of the Pilgrims' journey along the bay side of Cape Cod and their eventual arrival at Patuxet. His own warriors had kept him updated as to the progress of their various building projects, and despite their secret burials, he undoubtedly knew that many of the English had died over the winter.

For as long as anyone could remember, European fishermen and explorers had been visiting New England, but these people were different. First of all, there were women and children—probably the first

European women and children the Indians had ever seen. They were also behaving unusually. Instead of attempting to trade with the Indians, they kept to themselves and seemed much more interested in building a settlement. These English people were here to stay.

Massasoit was unsure of what to do next. A little over a year before, the sailors aboard an English vessel had killed a large number of his people without provocation. As a consequence, Massasoit had felt compelled to attack the explorer Thomas Dermer when he arrived the following summer with Squanto at his side, and most of Dermer's men had been killed in skirmishes on Cape Cod and Martha's Vineyard. Squanto had been taken prisoner on the Vineyard, but now he was with Massasoit in Pokanoket. The former Patuxet resident had told him of his years in Europe, and once the *Mayflower* appeared at Provincetown Harbor and made its way to Plymouth, he had offered his services as an interpreter. But Massasoit was not yet sure whose side Squanto was on.

Over the winter, as the Pilgrims continued to bury their dead surreptitiously, Massasoit gathered together the region's powwows, or shamans, for a three-day meeting "in a dark and dismal swamp." Swamps were where the Indians went in time of war: they provided a natural shelter for the sick and old; they were also a highly spiritual landscape, where the unseen currents of the spirits intermingled with the hoots of owls.

Massasoit's first impulse was not to embrace the English but to curse them. Bradford later learned that the powwows had attempted to "execrate them with their conjurations." Powwows communed with the spirit world in an extremely physical manner, through what the English described as "horrible outcries, hollow bleatings, painful wrestlings, and smiting their own bodies." Massasoit's powwows were probably not the first and certainly not the last Native Americans to turn their magic on the English. To the north, at the mouth of the Merrimack River, lived Passaconaway, a sachem who was also a powwow—an unusual combination that endowed him with extraordinary powers. It was said he could "make the water burn, the rocks move, the trees dance, metamorphise himself into a flaming man." But not even

Passaconaway was able to injure the English. In 1660, he admitted to his people, "I was as much an enemy to the English at their first coming into these parts, as anyone whatsoever, and did try all ways and means possible to have destroyed them, at least to have prevented them sitting down here, but I could in no way effect it; . . . therefore I advise you never to contend with the English, nor make war with them." At some point, Massasoit's powwows appear to have made a similar recommendation.

The powwows were not the only ones who weighed in on the issue of what to do with the Pilgrims. There was also Squanto. Ever since the appearance of the *Mayflower,* the former captive had begun to work his own kind of magic on Massasoit, insisting that the worst thing he could do was to attack the Pilgrims. Not only did they have muskets and cannons; they possessed the seventeenth-century equivalent of a weapon of mass destruction: the plague. At some point, Squanto began to insist that the Pilgrims had the ability to unleash disease on their enemies. If Massasoit became an ally to the Pilgrims, he would suddenly be in a position to break the Narragansetts' stranglehold on the Pokanokets. "[E]nemies that were [now] too strong for him," Squanto promised, "would be constrained to bow to him."

It was a suggestion that played on Massasoit's worst fears. The last three years had been a nightmare of pain and loss; to revisit that experience was inconceivable. Reluctantly, Massasoit determined that he must "make friendship" with the English. To do so, he must have an interpreter, and Squanto—the only one fluent in both English and Massachusett, the language of the Pokanoket—assumed that he was the man for the job. Though he'd been swayed by Squanto's advice, Massasoit was loath to place his faith in the former captive, whom he regarded as a conniving cultural mongrel with dubious motives. So he first sent Samoset, a visiting sachem with only a rudimentary command of English, to the Pilgrim settlement.

But now it was time for Massasoit to visit the English himself. He must turn to Squanto.

* * *

On March 22, five days after his initial visit, Samoset returned to Plymouth with four other Indians, Squanto among them. The Patuxet Native spoke with an easy familiarity about places that now seemed a distant dream to the Pilgrims—besides spending time in Spain and Newfoundland, Squanto had lived in the Corn Hill section of London. The Indians had brought a few furs to trade, along with some fresh herring. But the real purpose of their visit was to inform the Pilgrims that Massasoit and his brother Quadequina were nearby. About an hour later, the sachem appeared on Watson's Hill with a large entourage of warriors.

The Pilgrims described him as "a very lusty [or strong] man, in his best years, an able body, grave of countenance, and spare of speech." Massasoit stood on the hill, his face painted dark red, his entire head glistening with bear grease. Draped around his neck was a wide necklace made of white shell beads and a long knife suspended from a string. His men's faces were also painted, "some black, some red, some yellow, and some white, some with crosses, and other antic works." Some of them had furs draped over their shoulders; others were naked. But every one of them possessed a stout bow and a quiver of arrows. These were unmistakably warriors: "all strong, tall, all men in appearance." Moreover, there were sixty of them.

For the Pilgrims, who could not have mustered more than twenty adult males and whose own military leader was not even five and a half feet tall, it must have been a most intimidating display of physical strength and power. Squanto ventured over to Watson's Hill and returned with the message that the Pilgrims should send someone to speak to Massasoit. Edward Winslow's wife, Elizabeth, was so sick that she would be dead in just two days, but he agreed to act as Governor Carver's messenger. Clad in armor and with a sword at his side, he went with Squanto to greet the sachem.

First he presented Massasoit and his brother with a pair of knives, some copper chains, some alcohol, and a few biscuits, "which were all willingly accepted." Then he delivered a brief speech. King James of England saluted the sachem "with words of love and peace," Winslow proclaimed, and looked to him as a friend and ally. He also said that Governor Carver wished to speak and trade with him and hoped to establish a formal peace. Winslow was under the impression that Squanto "did not well express it," but enough of his meaning was apparently communicated to please Massasoit. The sachem ate the biscuits and drank the liquor, then asked if Winslow was willing to sell his sword and armor. The Pilgrim messenger politely declined. It was decided that Winslow would remain with Quadequina as a hostage while Massasoit went with twenty of his men, minus their bows, to meet the governor.

The Pilgrims were men of God, but they also knew their diplomatic protocol. Undoubtedly drawing on his experiences as an assistant to the English secretary of state, William Brewster appears to have orchestrated a surprisingly formal and impressive reception of the dignitary they called the "Indian King." A Pilgrim delegation including Standish and half a dozen men armed with muskets greeted Massasoit at the brook. They exchanged salutations, and after seven of the warriors were designated hostages, Standish accompanied Massasoit to a house, still under construction, where a green rug and several cushions had been spread out on the dirt floor. On cue, a drummer and trumpeter began to play as Governor Carver and a small procession of musketeers made their way to the house.

Upon his arrival, Carver kissed Massasoit's hand; the sachem did the same to Carver's, and the two leaders sat down on the green rug. It was now time for Massasoit to share in yet another ceremonial drink of liquor. Carver took a swig of aqua vitae and passed the cup to Massasoit, who took a large gulp and broke into a sweat. The Pilgrims assumed the aqua vitae was what made him perspire, but anxiety may also have been a factor. As the proceedings continued, during which the two groups worked out a six-point agreement, Massasoit was observed to tremble "for fear."

Instead of Carver and the Pilgrims, it may have been Massasoit's interpreter who caused the sachem to shake with trepidation. Squanto later claimed that the English kept the plague in barrels buried beneath their storehouse. The barrels actually contained gunpowder, but the Pilgrims undoubtedly guarded the storehouse with a diligence that lent credence to Squanto's claims. If the interpreter chose to inform Massasoit of the deadly contents of the buried stores during the negotiations on March 22 (and what better way to ensure that the sachem came to a swift and satisfactory agreement with the English?), it is little wonder Massasoit was seen to tremble.

Bradford and Winslow recorded the agreement with the Pokanoket sachem as follows:

1. That neither he nor any of his should injure or do hurt to any of our people.
2. And if any of his did hurt to any of ours, he should send the offender, that we might punish him.
3. That if any of our tools were taken away when our people were at work, he should cause them to be restored, and if ours did any harm to any of his, we would do the like to him.
4. If any did unjustly war against him, we would aid him; if any did war against us, he should aid us.
5. He should send to his neighbor confederates, to certify them of this, that they might not wrong us, but might be likewise comprised in the conditions of peace.
6. That when their men came to us, they should leave their bows and arrows behind them, as we should do our pieces when we came to them.

Once the agreement had been completed, Massasoit was escorted from the settlement, and his brother was given a similar reception. Quadequina quickly noticed a disparity that his higher-ranking brother had not chosen to comment on. Even though the Indians had been required to lay down their bows, the Pilgrims continued to carry their muskets—a clear violation of the treaty they had just signed with

Massasoit. Quadequina "made signs of dislike, that [the guns] should be carried away." The English could not help but admit that the young Indian had a point, and the muskets were put aside.

Squanto and Samoset spent the night with the Pilgrims while Massasoit and his men, who had brought along their wives and children, slept in the woods, just a half mile away. Massasoit promised to return in a little more than a week to plant corn on the southern side of Town Brook. Squanto, it was agreed, would remain with the English. As a final gesture of friendship, the Pilgrims sent the sachem and his people a large kettle of English peas, "which pleased them well, and so they went their way."

After almost five months of uncertainty and fear, the Pilgrims had finally established diplomatic relations with the Native leader who, as far as they could tell, ruled this portion of New England. But as they were soon to find out, Massasoit's power was not as pervasive as they would have liked. The Pokanokets had decided to align themselves with the English, but many of Massasoit's allies had yet to be convinced that the Pilgrims were good for New England.

The next day, Squanto, who after a six-year hiatus was back to living on his native shore, left to fish for eels. At that time of year, the eels lay dormant in the mud, and after wading out into the cold water of a nearby tidal creek, he used his feet to "trod them out." That evening he returned with so many eels that he could barely lift them all with one hand.

Squanto had named himself for the Indian spirit of darkness, who often assumed the form of snakes and eels. It was no accident that he used eels to cement his bond with the Pilgrims. That night they ate them with relish, praising the eels as "fat and sweet," and Squanto was on his way to becoming the one person in New England they could not do without.

Two weeks later, on April 5, the *Mayflower,* her empty hold ballasted with stones from the Plymouth Harbor shore, set sail for England. Like the Pilgrims, the sailors had been decimated by disease. Jones had lost his boatswain, his gunner, three quartermasters, the cook, and more than a dozen sailors. He had also lost a cooper, but not to illness. John Alden had decided to stay in Plymouth.

The *Mayflower* made excellent time on her voyage back across the Atlantic. The same westerlies that had battered her the previous fall now pushed her along, and she arrived at her home port of Rotherhithe, just down the Thames from London, on May 6, 1621—less than half the time it had taken her to sail to America. Jones learned that his wife, Josian, had given birth to a son named John. Soon Jones and the *Mayflower* were on their way to France for a cargo of salt.

The voyage to America was to claim yet another life. Perhaps still suffering the effects of that desperate winter in Plymouth, Jones died after his return from France on March 5, 1622. For the next two years the *Mayflower* lay idle, not far from her captain's grave on the banks of the Thames. By 1624, just four years after her historic voyage to America, the ship had become a rotting hulk. Her owners, including Jones's widow Josian, ordered an appraisal. She was found to be worth just £128, less than a sixth her value back in 1609. Her subsequent fate is unknown, but she was probably broken up for scrap, the final casualty of a voyage that had cost her master everything he could give.

Soon after the *Mayflower* departed for England, the shallow waters of Town Brook became alive with fish. Two species of herring—alewives and bluebacks—returned to the fresh waters where they had been born, creating a roiling, silver-backed blanket of fish that occasionally burst through the river's surface as the herring worked their way up the brook to spawn.

Squanto explained that these fish were essential to planting a successful corn crop. The land surrounding Plymouth was so poor that it was necessary to fertilize the soil with dead herring. Although women were the ones who did the farming (with the sole exception of planting tobacco, which was considered men's work), Squanto knew enough of their techniques to give the Pilgrims a crash course in Indian agriculture.

The seed the Pilgrims had stolen on the Cape is known today as northern flint corn—eight-rowed with kernels of several colors—and was called weachimineash by the Indians. Using mattocks—hoes with stone heads and wooden handles—the Indians gathered mounds of earth about a yard wide, where several fish were included with the seeds of corn. Once the corn had sprouted, beans and squash were added to the mounds. The creepers from the beans and squash attached to the growing cornstalks, creating a blanket of shade that protected the plants' roots against the searing summer sun while also discouraging weeds. Thanks to Squanto, the Pilgrims' stolen corn thrived while their own barley and peas suffered in the alien soils of the New World.

In April, while laboring in the fields on an unusually hot day, Governor Carver began to complain about a pain in his head. He returned to his house to lie down and quickly lapsed into a coma. A few days later, he was dead.

After a winter of so many secret burials, they laid their governor to rest with as much pomp and circumstance as they could muster—"with some volleys of shot by all that bore arms." Carver's brokenhearted wife followed her husband to the grave five weeks later. Carver's one surviving male servant, John Howland, was left without a master; in addition to becoming a free man, Howland may have inherited at least a portion of Carver's estate. The humble servant who had been pulled from the watery abyss a few short months ago was on his way to becoming one of Plymouth's foremost citizens.

*A chair once owned by
William Bradford*

Carver's passing could not have come at a worse time. Just as the settlement was emerging from the horrors of the first winter, it had lost the man on whose judgment and counsel it had come to depend. The Pilgrims had hoped to load the *Mayflower* with goods, but that had been impossible given their sufferings that winter. With half the settlers dead and only a pile of ballast stones and a few Native artifacts to show for an outlay of thousands of pounds, the Merchant Adventurers might begin to doubt the profitability of the settlement and withdraw further financial support.

The new treaty with Massasoit had greatly reduced the threat of Indian attack, but there was still dissent inside the settlement. Billington had recently railed against Standish; there had been angry words from others throughout that terrible winter. In June, Stephen Hopkins's servants Edward Doty and Edward Leister injured each other in a duel and were sentenced to have their heads and feet tied together. There was a desperate and immediate need for strong and steady leadership.

Bradford was the natural choice, but he was still laid low by illness. With Isaac Allerton, a thirty-six-year-old widower and former Leidener, serving as his assistant, he agreed to take on the greatest challenge of his life. In addition to Allerton, he had William Brewster, Edward Winslow, and Miles Standish to look to for advice. But as governor, he inevitably came to know the loneliness of being Plymouth's ultimate decision maker. More than ever before, Bradford, who had left his son in Holland and lost his wife in Provincetown Harbor, was alone.

CHAPTER SEVEN

Thanksgiving

*A*FEW WEEKS AFTER Bradford's election to gover-
nor, Edward Winslow and Susanna White showed the rest of the settlement that it was indeed possible to start anew. Susanna had lost her
husband, William, on February 21; Edward had lost his wife, Elizabeth,
on March 24. Just a month and a half later, on May 12, Edward and Susanna became the first couple in Plymouth to marry. Six weeks may
seem too short a time to grieve, but in the seventeenth century, it was
quite normal for a widow or widower to remarry within three months
of his or her spouse's death. Children needed to be cared for; house-
holds needed to be maintained. And besides, these were exceptional
times. If all the deaths had failed to inure them to grief, it had certainly
alerted them to the wondrous necessity of life.

In accordance with "the laudable custom of the Low Countries,"
Edward and Susanna were married in a civil ceremony. Bradford, who
presided over the union, explained that "nowhere . . . in the Gospel"
did it say a minister should be involved in a wedding. In the decades to
come, marriages in Plymouth continued to be secular affairs, one of the
few vestiges of their time in Holland to persist in New England.

By the beginning of July, Bradford determined that they should send a
delegation to visit "their new friend Massasoit." They had not, as of
yet, had an opportunity to explore the interior of the surrounding
countryside, and it was time they made their presence known beyond
Plymouth and Cape Cod. They also needed to address an unexpected
problem. Ever since establishing diplomatic relations with Massasoit in

March, the Pilgrims had been beset by a continual stream of Indian visitors, particularly from the village of Nemasket just fifteen miles to the west in modern Middleborough. If they continued to entertain and feed all these guests, they would not have enough food to survive the next winter. They proposed an ingenious solution: They would present Massasoit with a copper chain; if the sachem had a messenger or friend he wanted the Pilgrims to entertain, he would give the person the chain, and the Pilgrims would happily provide him with food and fellowship. All others, however, would be denied.

On July 2, Edward Winslow and Stephen Hopkins left the settlement at around 9 a.m., with Squanto as their guide. Besides some gifts for Massasoit (the copper chain and a red cotton horseman's coat), they carried their muskets and a cooked partridge for sustenance. They might have a horseman's coat, but they did not, as of yet, have any horses. Like the Indians, they must walk the forty or so miles to Pokanoket.

They soon came upon a dozen men, women, and children, who were returning to Nemasket after gathering lobsters in Plymouth Harbor—one of countless seasonal rituals that kept the Indians constantly on the move. As they conversed with their new companions, the Englishmen learned that to walk across the land in southern New England was to travel in time. All along this narrow, hard-packed trail were circular foot-deep holes in the ground that had been dug where "any remarkable act" had occurred. It was each person's responsibility to maintain the holes and to inform fellow travelers of what had once happened at that particular place so that "many things of great antiquity are fresh in memory." Winslow and Hopkins began to see that they were traversing a mythic land, where a sense of community extended far into the distant past. "So that as a man travelleth . . . ," Winslow wrote, "his journey will be the less tedious, by reason of the many historical discourses [that] will be related unto him."

They also began to appreciate why these memory holes were more important than ever before to the Native inhabitants of the region. Everywhere they went, they were stunned by the emptiness and desolation of the place. "Thousands of men have lived there," Winslow wrote, "which died in a great plague not long since: and pity it was and is to see, so many goodly fields, and so well seated, without men to dress and manure the same." With so many dead, the Pokanokets' connection to the past was hanging by a thread—a connection that the memory holes, and the stories they inspired, helped to maintain.

At Nemasket, they enjoyed a meal of corn bread, herring roe, and boiled acorns. Squanto suggested that they push on another few miles before nightfall to give themselves enough time to reach Pokanoket the next day. Soon after leaving Nemasket, the path joined a narrow, twisting river called the Titicut. Known today as the Taunton River, this waterway flows southwest through modern Bridgewater, Raynham, and Taunton till it widens into a broad tidal estuary at the hilltop city of Fall River before emptying into the dramatic expanse of Mount Hope Bay. In 1621, the Titicut functioned as a kind of Native American highway. Whether by dugout canoe or by foot, the Indians followed the river between Pokanoket and Plymouth, and in the years ahead, the Titicut inexorably led the Pilgrims to several new settlement sites above Narragansett Bay.

But the Titicut was much more than a transportation system; it also provided the Indians with a seasonal source of herring and other fish. Around sunset, Winslow and Hopkins reached a spot on the river where the Indians had built a weir and were harvesting striped bass, and that night they "lodged in the open fields."

Six Indians decided to continue on with them the next morning. They followed the riverbank for about half a dozen miles until they came to a shallow area, where they were told to take off their breeches and wade across the river. They were midstream, with their possessions in their arms, when two Indians appeared on the opposite bank. In the aftermath of the plague, the Narragansetts had taken to raiding Pokanoket territory at will, and the two Indians feared that Winslow and Hopkins's group was the enemy. Winslow judged one of the Indians to be at least sixty years old, and despite their age, both men displayed great "valor and courage" as they ran "very swiftly and low in the grass to meet us at the bank" with their arrows drawn. On realizing that Winslow and Hopkins were accompanied by some of their Indian

Edward Winslow, painted in England, 1651

friends, the old warriors "welcomed us with such food as they had." Winslow later learned that these were the last two survivors of a once thriving village.

As the sun reached its height, the traveling became quite hot, and their companions cheerfully offered to carry their guns and extra clothing for them. The grassy fields and open forests were, in Winslow's words, "like many places in England." They came upon other Indians along the way, but all proved friendly, and before the day was over they reached Massasoit's village, known as Sowams. In the years to come, as the Pilgrims began to purchase land from the Pokanoket sachem, they spoke of Sowams as "the garden of the patent"—a fertile sweep of land with two rivers providing easy access to Narragansett Bay. As anyone could plainly see, Massasoit was positioned at a place that made Plymouth seem, by comparison, a remote and hilly wasteland.

The sachem invited them into his wigwam, where they presented him with the copper chain and horseman's coat. Winslow reported that once the sachem had "put the coat on his back and the chain about his neck, he was not a little proud to behold himself, and his men also to see their king so bravely attired." Indeed, the Pokanoket sachem appears to have been pleasantly surprised by Winslow's and Hopkins's appearance and readily agreed to all the Pilgrims' requests.

The sachem gathered his people around him and began to deliver a long and exuberant speech. "Was not he *Massasoit* commander of the country about him?" he proclaimed. He spoke of the many villages that paid him tribute and of how those villages would all trade with the Pilgrims. With the naming of each place, his men responded with a refrain about Massasoit's power over the village and how the village would be at peace with the English and provide them with furs. This went on until thirty or more settlements had been named. "[S]o that as it was delightful," Winslow wrote, "it was tedious unto us."

By this time, Winslow and Hopkins were desperate for something to eat. It had been more than a day since they'd had a decent meal, but the entire village of Sowams appeared to be without any food. Massasoit had only recently returned to the village after an extended time away, and his people had not yet had time to procure any fish or fowl. Unlike the Europeans, who relied on large stores of provisions, the Native Americans tended to follow the food wherever it might be seasonally available, whether it be a lobster-laden beach, an inland-river fishing weir, or, come fall, a forest full of deer. By arriving unannounced, Winslow and Hopkins had unintentionally placed Massasoit in a difficult and potentially embarrassing situation. He was happy, even ecstatic, to see them, but he had no food to offer.

Once he'd completed his speech, Massasoit lit his pipe and encouraged all of them to smoke as he "fell to discoursing of England." He said he was now "King James his man." As a consequence, the French were no longer welcome in Narragansett Bay. When he learned that the

English king had been a widower for more than a year, Massasoit expressed wonder that James had chosen to live "without a wife."

It was getting late, and it was now clear to the Pilgrims that there was nothing for them to eat. So they asked to go to bed. Much to their surprise, the sachem insisted that they share the wigwam's sleeping platform with himself and his wife, "they at the one end and we at the other." What's more, two of Massasoit's warriors crowded onto the platform with them.

That night, neither Winslow nor Hopkins slept a wink. Not only were they starving, they were kept awake by the Indians' habit of singing themselves to sleep. They also discovered that the dirt floor and reed mats of the wigwam were alive with lice and fleas even as voracious mosquitoes buzzed around their ears.

The next day, several minor sachems made their way to Sowams to see the two Englishmen. The increasingly crowded village took on a carnival atmosphere as the sachems and their men entertained themselves with various games of chance, in which painted stones and stiff reeds were used, much like dice and cards, to gamble for each other's furs and knives. Winslow and Hopkins challenged some of them to a shooting contest. Although the Indians declined, they requested that the English demonstrate the accuracy of their muskets. One of them fired a round of small shot at a target, and the Natives "wondered to see the mark so full of holes." Early that afternoon, Massasoit returned with two large striped bass. The fish were quickly boiled, but since there were more than forty mouths to feed, the bass did not go far. Meager as it was, it was the first meal Winslow and Hopkins had eaten in two nights and a day.

Their second night at Sowams proved to be as sleepless as the first. Even before sunrise, the two Englishmen decided that they best be on their way, "we much fearing," Winslow wrote, "that if we should stay any longer, we should not be able to recover home for want of strength."

Massasoit was "both grieved and ashamed that he could no better entertain" the Pilgrims, but that did not prevent the visit from ending on a most positive note. Squanto, it was decided, would remain at Pokanoket so that he could go from village to village to establish trading relations for the Pilgrims, who had brought necklaces, beads, and other trade goods to exchange with the Indians for furs and corn. It may have been that Massasoit also wanted the chance to speak with the interpreter alone. Until Squanto returned to Plymouth, Tokamahamon would serve as the Englishmen's guide.

Two days later, on the night of Saturday, July 7, after a solid day of rain, Winslow and Hopkins arrived back at Plymouth. They were wet, weary, footsore, and famished, but they had succeeded in strengthening their settlement's ties with Massasoit and the Indians to the west. It would be left to a boy—and a Billington at that—to do the same for the Indians to the east.

Back in January, fourteen-year-old Francis Billington had climbed into a tree near the top of Fort Hill. Looking inland to the west, he claimed he saw "a great sea." Like his father, the Billington boy had already developed a reputation as a troublemaker. When the *Mayflower* had still been at anchor in Provincetown Harbor, he had fired off a musket in his family's cabin that had nearly ignited a barrel of gunpowder that would have destroyed the ship and everyone aboard. Given the boy's past history, no one seemed to take his claim about a large inland sea very seriously. Eventually, however, someone agreed to accompany the teenager on an exploratory trip into the woods. About two miles in, they came upon a huge lake that was "full of fish and fowl." Even Bradford, who had no great love of the Billington family, had to admit that the lake would be "an excellent help to us in time," particularly since it was the source of Town Brook. To this day, the lake, which is close to five miles in circumference, is known as the Billington Sea.

In late March, Francis's father had berated Miles Standish and narrowly escaped public punishment. Toward the end of July, Francis's older brother John got into some trouble of his own. Not long after the return of Winslow and Hopkins, the sixteen-year-old lost his way in the woods somewhere south of the settlement. For five days, he wandered aimlessly, living on nuts, roots, and anything else he could find until he stumbled on the Indian village of Manomet, some twenty miles from Plymouth. Instead of returning the boy to the English, the Manomet sachem, Canacum, passed him to the Nausets of Cape Cod—the very people who had attacked the Pilgrims during the First Encounter back in December. The Nausets, led by sachem Aspinet, were also the ones whose corn pits and graves they had rifled.

Massasoit's influence in the region was apparently not as dominant as he had led Winslow and Hopkins to believe. The plagues that had decimated the Pokanokets appear to have had less of an impact on the Nausets. Even if sachem Aspinet was Massasoit's ally, he now commanded a larger number of warriors. By turning the Billington boy over to the Nausets instead of the Pokanokets, Canacum made a conscious effort to defer to a neighbor whose relative strength had increased dramatically since the plagues. It may also have been a way for Canacum to express his displeasure with Massasoit's decision to make peace with the Pilgrims. With the boy in their possession, the Nausets were able to send an unmistakable message to the English: "You stole something of ours; well, now we have something of yours."

It took a while for Bradford to discover what had happened to the boy. Eventually word filtered back from Massasoit that Billington was alive and well and living with the Nausets. The Pilgrims had no choice but to return to the scene of the crime.

Well aware that they were venturing back into potentially hostile territory, Bradford ordered a party of ten men—more than half the adult males in the settlement—to set out in the shallop with both Squanto, who had recently returned from his trading mission in the region, and Tokamahamon as guides. Not long after departing from Plymouth, they were socked by a tremendous thunderstorm that forced them to put in at Cummaquid, a shallow harbor near the base of Cape Cod known today as Barnstable.

At dawn the next morning they found themselves hard aground on the tidal flats. They could see several Indians collecting lobsters, and Squanto and Tokamahamon went to speak with them. The Pilgrims were soon introduced to the Indians' sachem, Iyanough. Still in his twenties, he impressed them as "very personable, courteous, and fair conditioned."

At Cummaquid they encountered disturbing evidence that all was not forgotten on Cape Cod when it came to past English injustices in the region. An ancient woman, whom they judged to be a hundred years old, made a point of seeking out the Pilgrims "because she never saw English." As soon as she set eyes on them, she burst into tears, "weeping and crying excessively." They learned that three of her sons had been captured seven years before by Thomas Hunt, and she still mourned their loss. "We told them we were sorry that any Englishman should give them that offense," Winslow wrote, "that Hunt was a bad man, and that all the English that heard of it condemned him for the same."

Iyanough and several others offered to accompany them to Nauset, about twenty miles to the east. Unlike the winter before, when the shores of Cape Cod had been empty of people, the Pilgrims found Indians almost everywhere they looked. They now realized why the Nausets had felt compelled to attack them; by setting up camp near First Encounter Beach, they had ventured into the very "midst of them."

They brought the shallop to within wading distance of shore and were soon approached by a huge number of Indians. Given their past history in this place, the Pilgrims ordered the crowd to back away from the boat. They could only hope that their alliance with Massasoit ensured their safety. Keeping their muskets ready, they insisted that only two Indians approach at a time. One of the first to come forward was the man whose corn they had stolen. The Pilgrims arranged to have him visit their settlement, where they promised to reimburse him for his loss.

It was growing dark by the time the Nauset sachem, Aspinet, arrived with more than a hundred men, many of whom had undoubtedly participated in the First Encounter back in December. Half the warriors remained on shore with their bows and arrows while the others waded out to the boat unarmed. One of Aspinet's men carried John Billington in his arms. Looking none the worse for his time in captivity, the teenager wore a string of shell beads around his neck. The Pilgrims presented Aspinet with a knife, and peace was declared between the two peoples. From the Pilgrims' perspective, it was a great relief to have finally righted the wrongs they'd committed during their first anxious and confusing weeks in America.

But Aspinet had some disturbing news. The Narragansetts were said to have killed several of Massasoit's men and taken their leader captive. "This struck some fear in us," Winslow wrote. If the Narragansetts should decide to attack their settlement, it would be a catastrophe: there were only about half a dozen men back at Plymouth. They must return as quickly as possible. If Massasoit had indeed been captured, they were, according to the terms of the treaty they had recently signed, at war with the most powerful tribe in the region.

Massasoit had indeed been taken, temporarily it turned out, by the Narragansetts. But they soon learned that the greatest threat was not from the Narragansetts but from the Pokanokets' supposed allies. For the lesser sachems who had opposed Massasoit's treaty with the Pilgrims, this was just the opportunity they had been looking for. One sachem in particular—Corbitant from the village of Mattapoisett just to the east of Massasoit's headquarters at Sowams—was attempting to use the sachem's troubles to break the Pokanoket-English alliance. Corbitant had arrived at the nearby village of Nemasket and was now attempting to "draw the hearts of Massasoit's subjects from him." Bradford decided to send Squanto and Tokamahamon to Nemasket to find out what Corbitant was up to.

The next day, one of Massasoit's men, a warrior named Hobbamock, arrived at Plymouth, gasping for breath and covered in sweat. He'd just run the fifteen miles from Nemasket, and he had terrible news. Squanto, he feared, was dead. When Hobbamock had last seen the interpreter, one of Corbitant's warriors had been holding a knife to his chest. Corbitant quite rightly viewed Squanto as the instigator of Massasoit's shift toward the Pilgrims. If Squanto was dead, Corbitant told the Indians at Nemasket, "the English had lost their tongue." Bradford immediately called a meeting of his advisers.

The Pilgrims were men of God, but this did not mean they were loath to use force. For more than a millennium and a half, Christians had looked to the Scriptures to sanction just about every conceivable act of violence. Moses had led the Jews to the Promised Land, but there had also been Joshua, a warrior king who had fought to uphold his people's claims. Undoubtedly counseling Bradford to take immediate and forceful action was the Pilgrims' Joshua, Miles Standish. This was their chance to show the Indians the consequences of challenging the English—either directly or indirectly through one of their emissaries. "[I]t was conceived not fit to be borne," Bradford wrote; "for if [the Pilgrims] should suffer their friends and messengers thus to be wronged, they should have none would cleave to them, or give them any intelligence, or do them service afterwards, but next they would fall upon themselves."

They decided to hit Corbitant quickly and to hit him hard. Standish volunteered to lead ten men on a mission to Nemasket. If Squanto had in fact been killed, they were to seize Corbitant. And since he'd been disloyal to Massasoit, he was to suffer the fate of all notorious traitors in Jacobean England. Standish was to cut off his head and bring it back to Plymouth for public display.

They left the next morning, Tuesday, August 14, with Hobbamock as their guide. Hobbamock was named for the same mysterious spirit of darkness as Squanto was. But unlike Squanto, Hobbamock was a pniese—a warrior of special abilities and stamina (it was said a pniese could not be killed in battle) who was responsible for collecting tribute for his sachem. From the start, Standish and Hobbamock had much in common, and the two warriors quickly became good friends.

Soon after they left Plymouth, it began to rain. About three miles from Nemasket, they ventured off the trail and waited for dark. In the summer rain, Standish briefed his men on his plan. Hobbamock was to lead them to Corbitant's wigwam around midnight. Once Standish had positioned them around the dwelling, he and Hobbamock would charge inside and take Corbitant. The men were instructed to shoot any Indians who attempted to escape. For those with no previous military experience, it was a terrifying prospect, and Standish did his best to instill some confidence in his ragtag commando unit. Soon "all men [were] encouraging one another to the utmost of their power."

After a last, quick meal, it was time for the assault. In the starless dark, Hobbamock directed them to the wigwam. The dwelling was probably larger than most, with a considerable number of men, women, and children inside, sleeping on the low platforms built along the interior walls. By this late hour, the central fire had dwindled to a few glowing embers. The drum of rain on the wigwam's reed mats masked the sounds of the Pilgrims taking their positions.

Standish burst in, shouting Corbitant's name. It was very dark inside, and with Hobbamock acting as his interpreter, the Pilgrim captain demanded to know where the petty sachem was. But the people inside the wigwam were too terror-stricken to speak. Some leaped off their sleeping platforms and attempted to force their way through the matted walls of the wigwam. Soon the guards outside were shooting off their muskets as the people inside screamed and wept. Several women clung to Hobbamock, calling him friend. What had been intended as a bold lightning strike against the enemy was threatening to become a chaotic exercise in futility.

Gradually they learned that Corbitant had been at Nemasket, but no one was sure where he was now. They also learned that Squanto was still alive. Hobbamock pulled himself up through the wigwam's smoke hole and, balancing himself on the roof, called out for the interpreter. Tokamahamon, it turned out, was also alive and well.

The next morning, they discovered that Corbitant and his men had fled, probably for their home at Mattapoisett. Standish delivered a message to the residents of Nemasket: "although Corbitant had now escaped us, yet there was no place should secure him and his from us if he continued his threatening us." A man and a woman had been wounded in the melee that night, and the Pilgrims offered to bring them back to Plymouth for medical attention. The following day the settlement's self-taught surgeon, Samuel Fuller, tended to the Indians' injuries, and they were free to return home.

Over the next few weeks, Bradford began to learn of the reaction to Standish's midnight raid. Just as his military officer had predicted, the show of force—no matter how confused—had won the Pilgrims some new respect. Several petty sachems sent their "gratulations" to Governor Bradford. Epenow, the Martha's Vineyard sachem who had attacked Dermer, made overtures of friendship. Even Corbitant let it be known that he now wanted to make peace. By this time, Massasoit was back in Sowams, and with the Pilgrims having proven themselves to be loyal and resolute supporters, "a much firmer peace" existed throughout the region.

On September 13, nine sachems—including Corbitant, Epenow, Massasoit's brother Quadequina, and Canacum, the sachem who had sent John Billington to the Nausets—journeyed to Plymouth to sign a treaty professing their loyalty to King James. About this time, Bradford determined that an exploratory expedition should be sent north to the land of the Massachusetts. Squanto had warned them that the Massachusetts, who lived in the vicinity of modern Boston, "had often threatened us." It was time to bring them into the fold as well.

They soon discovered where they *should* have settled. As they sailed their shallop across the island-speckled immensity of modern Boston Harbor, they were filled with envy. Instead of the shallow reaches of Plymouth Harbor, here was a place where ships of any size could venture right up to land. Instead of little Town Brook, there were three navigable rivers converging at an easily defensible neck of high ground known as Shawmet.

This was a place where an English settlement might blossom into a major port, with rivers providing access to the fur-rich interior of New England. Not surprisingly, the Indians in the region, who had been devastated by both disease and war with the rival tribes to the north, possessed many more furs than the Pilgrims had so far found among the Pokanokets.

But the thought of relocating themselves after so much loss and sacrifice was too much to bear. They decided to stay put. It would be left to others to transform this place into the "city on a hill" called Boston. The Pilgrims' ambitions were more modest. They were quite content with a village by a brook. The important thing was their spiritual life, and for that to flourish as it once had in Leiden, they needed their minister, John Robinson, and the rest of the congregation to join them there in the New World.

We do not know the exact date of the celebration we now call the First Thanksgiving, but it was probably in late September or early October, soon after their crop of corn, squash, beans, barley, and peas had been harvested. It was also a time during which Plymouth Harbor played host to a tremendous number of migrating birds, particularly ducks and geese, and Bradford ordered four men to go out "fowling." It took only a few hours for Plymouth's hunters to kill enough ducks and geese to feed the settlement for a week. Now that they had "gathered the fruit of our labors," Bradford declared it time to "rejoice together . . . after a more special manner."

The term Thanksgiving, first applied in the nineteenth century, was not used by the Pilgrims themselves. For the Pilgrims a thanksgiving was a time of spiritual devotion. Since just about everything the Pilgrims did had religious overtones, there was certainly much about the gathering in the fall of 1621 that would have made it a proper Puritan thanksgiving. But as Winslow's description makes clear, there was also much about the gathering that was similar to a traditional English harvest festival—a secular celebration that dated back to the Middle Ages in which villagers ate, drank, and played games.

Countless Victorian-era engravings notwithstanding, the Pilgrims did not spend the day sitting around a long table draped with a white linen cloth, clasping each other's hands in prayer as a few curious Indians looked on. Instead of an English affair, the First Thanksgiving soon became an overwhelmingly Native celebration when Massasoit and a hundred Pokanokets (more than twice the entire English population of Plymouth) arrived at the settlement with five freshly killed deer. Even if all the Pilgrims' furniture was brought out into the sunshine, most of the celebrants stood, squatted, or sat on the ground as they clustered around outdoor fires, where the deer and birds turned on wooden spits and where pottages—stews into which varieties of meats and vegetables were thrown—simmered invitingly.

In addition to ducks and deer, there was, according to Bradford, a "good store of wild turkeys" in the fall of 1621. Turkeys were by no means a novelty to the Pilgrims. When the conquistadors arrived in Mexico in the sixteenth century, they discovered that the Indians of Central America possessed domesticated turkeys as well as gold. The birds were imported to Spain as early as the 1520s, and by the 1540s they had reached England. By 1575, the domesticated Central American turkey had become a fixture at English Christmases. The wild turkeys of New England were bigger and much faster than the birds the Pilgrims had known in Europe and were often pursued in winter when they could be tracked in the snow.

The Pilgrims may have also added fish to their meal of birds and deer. In fall, striped bass, bluefish, and cod were abundant. Perhaps most important to the Pilgrims was that with a recently harvested barley crop, it was now possible to brew beer. Alas, the Pilgrims were without pumpkin pies or cranberry sauce. There were also no forks, which did not appear at Plymouth until the last decades of the seventeenth century. The Pilgrims ate with their fingers and their knives.

Neither Bradford nor Winslow mention it, but the First Thanksgiving coincided with what was, for the Pilgrims, a new and startling phenomenon: the turning of the green leaves of summer to the incandescent yellows, reds, and purples of a New England autumn. With the shortening of the days comes a diminshment in the amount of green chlorophyll in the tree leaves, which allows the other pigments contained within the leaves to emerge. In Britain, the cloudy fall days and warm nights cause the autumn colors to be muted and lackluster. In New England, on the other hand, the profusion of sunny fall days and cool but not freezing nights unleashes the colors latent within the tree leaves, with oaks turning red, brown, and russet; hickories golden brown; birches yellow; red maples scarlet; sugar maples orange; and black maples glowing yellow. It was a display that must have contributed to the enthusiasm with which the Pilgrims later wrote of the festivities that fall.

The First Thanksgiving marked the conclusion of a remarkable year. Eleven months earlier the Pilgrims had arrived at the tip of Cape Cod, fearful and uninformed. They had spent the next month alienating and angering every Native American they happened to come across. By all rights, none of the Pilgrims should have emerged from the first winter alive. Like the French sailors before them, they all might have been either killed or taken captive by the Indians.

That it had worked out differently was a testament not only to the Pilgrims' grit, resolve, and faith, but to their ability to take advantage of an extraordinary opportunity. During the winter of 1621, the survival of the English settlement had been in the balance. Massasoit's decision to offer them assistance had saved the Pilgrims' lives in the short term, but there had already been several instances in which the sachem's generosity could all have gone for naught. Placing their faith in God, the Pilgrims might have insisted on a policy of arrogant isolationism. But by becoming an active part of the diplomatic process in southern New England—by sending Winslow and Hopkins to Sowams; by compensating the Nausets for the corn; and most important, by making clear their loyalty to Massasoit at the "hurly-burly" in Nemasket—they had taken charge of their own destiny in the region.

In 1620, New England was far from being a paradise of abundance and peace. Indeed the New World was, in many ways, much like the Old—a place where the fertility of the soil was a constant concern, a place where disease and war were omnipresent threats. There were profound differences between the Pilgrims and Pokanokets to be sure—especially when it came to technology, culture, and spiritual beliefs—but in these early years, when the mutual challenge of survival dominated all other concerns, the two peoples had more in common than is generally appreciated today. For the Pilgrims, some of whom had slept in a wigwam and all of whom had enjoyed eating and drinking with the Indians during that First Thanksgiving, these were not a despicable pack of barbarians (even if some of their habits, such as their refusal to wear clothes, struck them as "savage"); these were human beings, much like themselves—"very trust[worth]y, quick of apprehension, ripe witted, just," according to Edward Winslow.

For his part, Massasoit had managed one of the more wondrous comebacks of all time. Scorned and humiliated by the Narragansetts, he had found a way to give his people, who were now just a fraction of the Narragansetts in terms of population, a kind of parity with the rival tribe. Massasoit had come to the Pilgrims' rescue when, as his son would remember fifty-four years later, the English were "as a little child." He could only hope that the Pilgrims would continue to honor their debt to the Pokanokets long after the English settlement had grown into maturity.

Amid all the bounty and goodwill of the First Thanksgiving, there was yet another person to consider. The Pilgrims had begun their voyage to the New World by refusing to trust John Smith; no Stranger, they decided, was going to tell them what to do. But instead of being led by an English soldier of fortune, they were now being controlled—whether they realized it or not—by a Native American named Squanto. For, unknown to both Bradford and Massasoit, the interpreter from Patuxet had already launched a plan to become the most powerful Indian leader in New England.

And first of y occasion, and Indusments ther unto; the which that I may truly unfould, I must begine at y very roote c rise of y same. The which I shall endeuor to manefest in a plaine stile; with singuler regard unto y simple trueth in all things, at least as near as my slender Iudgmente can attaine the same.

PART II

1. Chapter

It is well knowne unto y godly, and judicious; how euer since y first breaking out of y lighte of y gospell in our Honourable nation of England (which was y first of nations, whom y Lord adorned ther... couered c ouerspred y christian world) what warrs, c oppositions euer since satan hath raised, maintained, and continued against the saincts, from time, to time in one sorte, or other. Some times by bloody death c cruell torments; other whiles Imprisonments, banishments, c other hard vsages; As being loath his kingdom should goe downe, the trueth preuaile; and y churches of god reuerte to their anciente puritie; and recouer, their primative order, libertie c bewtie. But when he could not preuaile by these means, against the maine trueths of y gospell; but that they began to take rooting in many places; being watered with y blloud of y martires, and blesed from heauen with a gracious encrease. He then begane to take him to his anciente strategemes, vsed of old against the first christians. That when by y bloody, c barbarous persecutions of y Heathen Emperours, he could not stoppe c subuerte the course of y gospell; but that it speedily ouerspred, with a wounderfull celeritie, the then best known parts of y world. He then begane to sow errours, heresies, and wounderfull dissentions amongst y professours them selues (working vpon their pride, c ambition, with other corruxte pasions, Incidente to all mortall men; yea to y saincts them selues in some measure) By which wofull effects followed; as not only bitter contentions, c hartburnings, schismes, with other horrible confusions. But satan tooke occasion c aduantage therby to foyst in a number of vile ceremoneys, with many vnprofitable Cannons, c decrees which haue since been as snares, to many poore, c peaceable souls, euen to this day. So as in y anciente times, the persecuti

CHAPTER EIGHT

The Wall

*I*N MID-NOVEMBER, Bradford received word from the Indians on Cape Cod that a ship had appeared at Provincetown Harbor. It had been just eight months since the departure of the *Mayflower,* and the Pilgrims were not yet expecting a supply ship from the Merchant Adventurers. It was immediately feared that the ship was from France, a country that had already exhibited a jealous hostility toward earlier English attempts to colonize the New World. The vessel might be part of a French expeditionary force come from Canada to snuff out the rival settlement in its infancy.

For more than a week, the ship lingered inexplicably at the tip of Cape Cod. Then, at the end of November, a lookout atop Fort Hill sighted a sail making for Plymouth Harbor. Many of the men were out working in the surrounding countryside. They must be called back immediately. A cannon was fired, and the tiny settlement was filled with excitement as men rushed in from all directions and Standish assembled them into a fighting force. Soon, in the words of Edward Winslow, "every man, yea, boy that could handle a gun were ready, with full resolution, that if [the ship] were an enemy, we would stand in our just defense."

To their amazement and delight, it proved to be an English ship: the *Fortune,* about a third the size of the *Mayflower,* sent by the Merchant Adventurers with thirty-seven passengers aboard. In an instant, the size of the colony had almost doubled.

The Pilgrims learned that while they had been gripped by fear of the French, those aboard the *Fortune* had been paralyzed by fears of their own. Just as the Pilgrims had, almost exactly a year earlier, stared in shock and amazement at the barren coast of Provincetown Harbor, so had these sea-weary passengers been terrified by their first glimpse of the New World. The returning *Mayflower* had delivered word to London that the survivors of the first winter had managed to establish the beginnings of a viable settlement. But what the passengers aboard the *Fortune* saw gave them reason to think otherwise. It was difficult to believe that anyone could be still alive in this sterile and featureless land. Only after the ship's master had promised to take them to Virginia if the Plymouth settlement had met disaster did they leave Provincetown Harbor.

It was a tremendous relief for passengers and Pilgrims alike to discover that, for now at least, all seemed well. Everyone aboard the *Fortune* was in good health, and almost immediately after coming ashore, Martha Ford gave birth to a son, John. There were a large number of Strangers among the passengers, many of them single men who undoubtedly looked with distress at the noticeable lack of young women among the Pilgrims. With the arrival of the *Fortune,* there would be a total of sixty-six men in the colony and just sixteen women. For every eligible female, there were six eligible men. For young girls such as fifteen-year-old Elizabeth Tilley, nineteen-year-old Priscilla Mullins, and fourteen-year-old Mary Chilton (all of them orphans), the mounting pressure to marry must have been intense, especially since the new arrivals tended to be, in Bradford's words, "lusty young men, and many of them wild enough." Adding to the potential volatility of the mix was the fact there was no place to put them all. Bradford had no choice but to divide them up among the preexisting seven houses and four public buildings, some of which must have become virtual male dormitories.

But the biggest problem created by the arrival of the *Fortune* had to do with food. Weston had failed to provide the passengers aboard the *Fortune* with any provisions for the settlement. Instead of strengthening their situation, the addition of thirty-seven more mouths to feed at the onset of winter had put them in a difficult, if not disastrous, position. Bradford calculated that even if they cut their daily rations in half, their current store of corn would last only another six months. After a year of relentless toil and hardship, they faced yet another winter without enough food. "[B]ut they bore it patiently," Bradford wrote, "under hope of [future] supply."

There were some familiar faces aboard the *Fortune*. The Brewsters welcomed their eldest son, Jonathan, a thirty-seven-year-old ribbon weaver, whom they hadn't seen in almost a year and a half. Others from Leiden included Philip de la Noye, whose French surname was eventually anglicized to Delano and whose descendants included future U.S. president Franklin Delano Roosevelt. The newly remarried Edward Winslow greeted his twenty-four-year-old brother John. There was also Thomas Prence, the twenty-one-year-old son of a Gloucestershire carriage maker, who soon became one of the leading members of the settlement.

The most notable new arrival was Robert Cushman, whose chest pains aboard the ill-fated *Speedwell* had convinced him to remain in England during the summer of 1620. Cushman had negotiated the agreement with Thomas Weston and the Merchant Adventurers that Bradford and the others had refused to honor in Southampton. It was now time, Cushman told them, to sign the controversial agreement. "We . . . have been very chargeable to many of our loving friends . . . ," Cushman tactfully exhorted them in a sermon entitled "The Sin of Self-Love" delivered in the common house. "[B]efore we think of gathering riches," Cushman admonished, "we must even in conscience think of requiting their charge" by paying the Merchant Adventurers back in goods. Cushman also presented the Pilgrims with a new patent secured from the Council for New England.

Unfortunately, from Cushman's perspective, Weston had insisted on writing a letter. Addressed to the now deceased Governor Carver, the letter took the Pilgrims to task for not having loaded the *Mayflower* with goods. "I know your weakness was the cause of it," Weston wrote, "and I believe more weakness of judgment than weakness of hands. A quarter of the time you spent in discoursing, arguing and consulting would have done much more." Bradford was

justifiably outraged by Weston's accusation, apparently based on some
letters that had made their way back to England on the *Mayflower*.
Bradford acknowledged that the Merchant Adventurers had, so far,
nothing to show for their investment. But their potential losses were
only financial; Governor Carver had worked himself to death that
spring, and "the loss of his and many other industrious men's lives
cannot be valued at any price."

Despite his criticisms, Weston claimed to be one of the few financial backers the Pilgrims could still count on. "I promise you," he
wrote, "I will never quit the business, though all the other Adventurers
should." Only after Cushman assured them that Weston was a man to
be trusted did Bradford and the others reluctantly sign the agreement.

Over the next two weeks, they loaded the *Fortune* with beaver skins,
sassafras, and clapboards made of split oak (much smaller than modern
clapboards, they were used for making barrel staves instead of siding
houses). Valued at around £500, the cargo came close to cutting their
debt in half. Certainly this would go a long way toward restoring the
Merchant Adventurers' confidence in the financial viability of the
settlement.

On December 13, 1621, after a stay of just two weeks, the *Fortune*
was on her way back to London. Cushman returned with her, leaving
his fourteen-year-old son Thomas in Bradford's care. In addition to
Bradford's letter to Weston, Cushman was given a manuscript account
of the Pilgrims' first thirteen months in America that was published the
following year and is known today as *Mourt's* [an apparent corruption
of the editor George Morton's last name] *Relation*. Written by Bradford
and Edward Winslow, the small book ends with Winslow's rhapsodic
account of the First Thanksgiving and the abundance of the New
World. Just days after the *Fortune*'s departure, the Pilgrims had reason
to regret Winslow's overly optimistic view of life in Plymouth.

The Pilgrims soon began to realize that their alliance with the
Pokanokets had created serious problems with the far more powerful

Narragansetts. The previous summer, Bradford had exchanged what he felt were positive and hopeful messages with the Narragansett sachem, Canonicus. Since then, however, Canonicus had grown increasingly jealous of the Pokanoket-Plymouth alliance. The Narragansetts, it was rumored, were preparing to attack the English settlement.

Toward the end of November a Narragansett messenger arrived at the settlement, looking for Squanto. He had a mysterious object from Canonicus in his hands. When he learned that the interpreter was away, he "seemed rather to be glad than sorry," and hurriedly handed over what the Pilgrims soon realized was a bundle of arrows wrapped in the skin of a rattlesnake.

It was a most inauspicious offering to be sure, and when Squanto returned to Plymouth, he assured them that the arrows were "no better than a challenge." Bradford responded by pouring gunpowder and bullets into the snake skin and sending it back to Canonicus. This appeared to have the desired effect. "[I]t was no small terror to the savage king," Winslow reported, "insomuch as he would not once touch the powder and shot, or suffer it to stay in his house or country." The powder-stuffed snake skin was passed like a hot potato from village to village until it finally made its way back to Plymouth.

Despite their show of defiance, the Pilgrims were deeply troubled by the Narragansett threat. Their little village was, they realized, wide open to attack. Their cumbersome muskets took an agonizingly long time to reload. Their great guns might pose a threat to a ship attempting to enter Plymouth Harbor but were of little use in repelling a large number of Native warriors, especially if they attacked at night. Bradford, doubtless at Standish's urging, decided they must "impale" the town—build an eight-foot-high wall of wood around the entire settlement. If they were to include the cannon platform atop Fort Hill and their dozen or so houses on Cole's Hill below it, the wall had to be at least 2,700 feet—more than a half mile—in length. Hundreds, if not thousands, of trees must be felled, their trunks stripped of branches and chopped or sawed to the proper length, then set deep into the ground. The tree trunks, or pales, of the fort must be set so tightly together that a man could not possibly fit through the gaps between them. In addition, Standish insisted that they must construct three protruding gates, known as flankers, that would also serve as defensive shooting platforms.

By any measure, it was a gargantuan task, but for a workforce of fewer than fifty men living on starvation rations it was almost inconceivable. The vast majority of the new arrivals were Strangers, and even though they tended to be young and strong, they were less likely to answer to a leadership dominated by Separatists when called upon to help with such an awesome labor.

The differences between the newcomers and Leideners quickly came to a head on December 25. For the Pilgrims, Christmas was a day just like any other; for most of the Strangers from the *Fortune,* on the other hand, it was a religious holiday, and they informed Bradford that it was "against their consciences" to work on Christmas. Bradford be-grudgingly gave them the day off and led the rest of the men out for the usual day's work. But when they returned at noon, they found the once placid streets of Plymouth in a state of joyous bedlam. The Strangers were playing games, including stool ball, a cricketlike game popular in the west of England. This was typical of how most English-men spent Christmas, but this was not the way the members of a pious Puritan community were to conduct themselves. Bradford proceeded to confiscate the gamesters' balls and bats. It was not fair, he insisted, that some played while others worked. If they wanted to spend Christmas praying quietly at home, that was fine by him; "but there should be no gaming or reveling in the streets."

Writing about this confrontation years later, Bradford claimed it was "rather of mirth than of weight." And yet, for a young governor who must confront not only the challenges presented by a hostile Native nation but a growing divide among his own people, it was a crucial incident. It was now clear that no matter how it was done in England, Plymouth played by its own, God-ordained rules, and everyone—Separatist or Anglican—was expected to conform.

It seems never to have occurred to the Pilgrims that this was just the kind of intolerant attitude that had forced them to leave England. For them, it was not a question of liberty and freedom—those concepts, so near and dear to their descendants in the following century, were completely alien to their worldview—but rather a question of right and wrong. As far as they were concerned, King James and his bishops were wrong, and they were right, and as long as they had the ability to live as the Bible dictated, they would do so.

The Pilgrims had come to the New World to live and worship as they pleased. But with a growing contingent of Strangers in their midst, what had seemed like such a pure and straightforward goal when they were planning this endeavor back in Leiden had become more complicated.

For many of the new arrivals, it was all quite astonishing. Bradford had declared it illegal to follow the customs of their mother country. In the years ahead, the growing rift between Saints and Strangers led to the metamorphosis of the colony. For now they had more important things to worry about than whether or not it was right to play stool ball on Christmas Day. The Narragansetts were threatening, and they had a wall to build.

It took them a little more than a month to impale the town. The chopping and sawing was backbreaking, time-consuming work made all the more difficult by their equipment. Their English axes were quite different from the tools that evolved in America over the following century. Narrow and poorly balanced, an English felling ax wobbled with each stroke and required much more strength than the axes the Pilgrims' descendants came to know.

Without oxen to help them drag the tree trunks in from the forest, they were forced to lug the ten- to twelve-foot lengths of timber by hand. They dug a two- to three-foot-deep trench, first using picks to break through the frozen topsoil and then, in all likelihood, a large hoelike tool (similar to what was recently uncovered by archaeologists at Jamestown) to dig a trench that was deep and wide enough to accommodate the butt ends of the pales. Adding to their difficulties was the lack of food. Some of the laborers grew so faint with hunger that they were seen to stagger on their way back to the settlement after a day's work.

By March, it was complete: a massive, sap-dripping, bark-peeling boundary between them and the surrounding forest. A new sense of order and control had been willed upon the wilderness. Plymouth was now an entity, a circumscribed place, its streets and houses darkened by the shadows of its margins. It was quite shiplike in many ways. Plymouth was like a huge *Mayflower* run aground on the shores of New England, her bow resting atop Fort Hill, her stern edging toward the harbor and the outflow of Town Brook. By impaling the town, the Pilgrims had made it clear that they intended to remain there for a very long time.

Miles Standish developed a manpower plan to go with the new fortress. The men were divided into four companies, each with its own commander, and were assigned positions and duties in the event of an attack. There was also a plan in the event fire should break out. Most of the men would work to put out the conflagration, but a group was assigned to stand on guard in case the Indians attempted to use the fire as a diversion prior to an attack. Standish drilled the men regularly and set up contingency plans if he should be away from the settlement during an attack. They were now ready to reestablish contact with the rest of the world.

They had long since planned to visit the Massachusetts to the north to trade for furs. But as they prepared the shallop to depart, Hobbamock, the Pokanoket pniese who had led the midnight raid on Nemasket the summer before and who had been living with the Pilgrims throughout the winter, asked to speak with Bradford and Standish. Hobbamock had heard that the Massachusetts had joined in league with the Narragansetts and were planning to attack Standish and the trading party. With Standish eliminated, the Narragansetts would then fall upon the settlement. Even more disturbing, Hobbamock insisted that Squanto was in on the plot. According to Hobbamock, all that winter, while the Pilgrims had been preoccupied with their wall, Squanto had been meeting secretly with Indians throughout the region.

Without letting Squanto know of Hobbamock's claims, Standish and Bradford met with several other leading members of the community to discuss what to do next. As they all knew, they could not simply "mew up ourselves in our new-enclosed town." They were running out of food. If they were to trade for more corn, they must venture beyond their own settlement. Up until this point, they had, in Winslow's words, "ever manifested undaunted courage and resolution" when it came to their relations with the Indians. They must forge ahead, knowing, as always, that God was on their side. Standish must depart immediately for his trading mission with the Massachusetts and betray no signs of knowing about a possible Massachusett-Narragansett alliance.

Left unresolved was how to treat Hobbamock's accusations concerning Squanto. As had become obvious to all of them, a rift of jealousy had developed between the two Indians. It was quite possible that Hobbamock had misrepresented Squanto's involvement in the conspiracy, if indeed a conspiracy existed at all. Bradford and Squanto had developed a strong relationship over the last year, while Standish and Hobbamock—both warriors by inclination and training—had also become close. Rather than bring Squanto to task, it was decided to use the rivalry between the two Indians to their advantage. "[T]he governor seemed to countenance the one," Bradford wrote, "the Captain the other, by which they had better intelligence, and made them both more diligent."

Neither Bradford nor Winslow ever wrote about it, but by their second year in America they knew enough of the Indians' spiritual beliefs to realize that the two Indians they had come to rely on most closely, Squanto and Hobbamock, were both named for the Native spirit whom the Pilgrims equated with the devil. It was more than a little ironic. They had come to America to serve God as best they knew how, and they were now dependent on two Indians named Satan.

In April, Standish and ten men, accompanied by both Squanto and Hobbamock, departed in the shallop for Massachusetts. A few hours later, an Indian who was a member of Squanto's family appeared outside the gates of town. His face was bloody, and he had apparently been running for a long time. He kept looking behind him as if those who had been chasing him might appear at any moment. He shouted out that he had come from Nemasket and he had frightening news. The Narragansetts had teamed up with the Pokanokets for an assault on Plymouth. Being a member of Squanto's family, he had spoken in the Pilgrims' defense and had, as a consequence, received a blow to the head. The enemy might be on their doorstep at any moment.

It was a strange, alarming, and confusing performance. It was difficult to believe that Massasoit had joined with the Narragansetts against them. The circumstances of this Indian's arrival at Plymouth were suspiciously similar to Hobbamock's escape from Corbitant back in August, which had resulted in a raid on Nemasket. The timing was also suspect. The Indian had arrived just after Standish and company had left for Massachusetts. Without their military leader to protect them, the Pilgrims were especially vulnerable. Indeed, the Indian's sudden appearance seemed calculated to elicit a rash and possibly disastrous response on their part.

Given Hobbamock's recent claims concerning Squanto, there was ample reason to suspect that the interpreter was behind all this. But why was Squanto attempting to get them to attack Massasoit? Bradford immediately ordered that the cannons be fired as a warning signal. It was probably too late to recall Standish, but it was important that anyone working in the countryside return to the safety of town.

As it turned out, Standish *was* in earshot of the signal. Soon after the shallop rounded the Gurnet at the northern edge of the harbor mouth, the wind had deserted him and his men. When the cannons fired, they were anchored off the Gurnet, preparing to take down their mast and sails and start to row. Upon hearing the signal, they immediately turned back for town—something Squanto, who was in fact the central conspirator behind the unfolding drama, had never anticipated.

Upon returning to the settlement, Hobbamock angrily insisted that the claims of Squanto's relatives were all lies. Being a pniese, he was certain he would have been consulted by Massasoit if the sachem had been planning some kind of attack. Bradford "should do well," Hobbamock insisted, "to continue his affections" toward Massasoit. So as not to create any unnecessary suspicion, it was decided to send Hobbamock's wife to Pokanoket, where she could determine whether there was any truth to the claims of Squanto's relative.

As Hobbamock had predicted, all was peace at Pokanoket. Inevitably, Hobbamock's wife revealed the reason behind her visit to Massasoit, who was outraged to learn that Squanto had attempted to turn the Pilgrims against him. The sachem offered his assurances to Bradford that he would certainly warn him of any possible threats to Plymouth if they should ever arise.

Over the next few weeks, it became increasingly clear that Squanto had been laboring long and hard to overthrow Massasoit as the Pokanokets' supreme sachem. All winter he had been conducting a kind of covert psychological warfare on villages throughout the region. The Pilgrims, he claimed, possessed the plague, and they were about to unleash it at will. However, if a village sent him sufficient tribute, he assured them that he could convince the Pilgrims to relent. Gradually, more and more Indians began to look to Squanto rather than Massasoit for protection. Squanto had hoped the false alarm raised by his family member might prompt the Pilgrims to attack Massasoit. In the confusion that ensued, Squanto would emerge as New England's preeminent Native leader.

It was a bold, risky, and outrageous plan, but it was conduct perfectly becoming an aspiring sachem. Rather than accept the decimation of Patuxet as a fait accompli, he had secretly striven to resuscitate his and his family's fortunes by playing the English against the Pokanokets in a nervy game of brinksmanship. For Squanto, it had all been about honor, "which he loved as his life," Winslow wrote, "and preferred before his peace." In just a year, he had gone from being Massasoit's prisoner to being one of his chief rivals. But his ambitions, it now seemed, had gotten the better of him.

Under the terms of the treaty drawn up the previous year, Bradford must turn Squanto over to Massasoit for punishment. But Bradford could not bear the thought of being without his interpreter despite his clear treachery. His attachment to Squanto appears to have gone well beyond the need for an Indian who could speak both languages. Squanto had become part of the Plymouth community about the same time that Bradford had become governor. The two seem to have bonded in a deep, almost spiritual way, and Bradford was willing to risk the wrath of the supreme sachem of the Pokanokets if it meant keeping Squanto as his interpreter.

In May, Massasoit appeared at Plymouth and was "much offended and enraged" against Squanto. The traitor must die. Bradford attempted to pacify the sachem, but not long after he returned to Pokanoket, Massasoit sent a messenger insisting that Squanto be put to death immediately. While acknowledging that Squanto deserved to die, Bradford stubbornly insisted that his interpreter was vital to the welfare of the plantation and could therefore not be executed. Within a day of leaving for Pokanoket, Massasoit's messenger was back again, this time with several warriors. In keeping with their own customs, they had brought their sachem's knife and had been instructed to return to Pokanoket with Squanto's head and hands. They even offered to pay off the governor with some furs.

Bradford refused the payment, but did agree to send for Squanto. Even though he knew he was about to face his potential executioners, the interpreter valiantly appeared before Bradford and the emissaries from Pokanoket. None of this was his fault, he insisted. It was Hobbamock who was "the author and worker of his overthrow." In the end Squanto knew he had no choice but to submit to whatever the governor thought was right. Bradford seemed on the verge of turning him over to Massasoit's men when a boat appeared off the Gurnet. He would not surrender Squanto, the governor informed the Pokanokets, until he could determine the nationality of the boat. If it was French, they might be on the verge of attack.

But Massasoit's men refused to play along. "[B]eing mad with rage," Winslow reported, "and impatient at delay, they departed in great heat." Squanto had lived to see another day.

* * *

It was a shallop from an English fishing vessel hired by Thomas Weston, the Merchant Adventurer who had pledged his undying loyalty to the Pilgrim cause in an earlier letter. In the months ahead, Bradford learned that all those promises were "but wind." Not only had Weston abandoned them, he was now their competitor. Weston had secured a patent for his own settlement and had the temerity to expect the Pilgrims to host his sixty or so settlers as their leaders searched for a settlement site. He communicated this information in a series of "tedious and impertinent" letters that Bradford concealed from everyone but his most trusted associates.

Even though Weston had betrayed them, Bradford felt compelled to offer his men the requested hospitality. They proved to be young ruffians who made the already unstable mix of Leideners and Strangers even more combustible. The settlement had been on half rations before the addition of all these men; now it was on the edge of starvation. With the arrival of spring, fish became plentiful, but the Pilgrims were farmers not fishermen, and though the surrounding waters seethed with cod, bluefish, and striped bass, they were unable to catch enough to feed themselves. In desperation, they sought shellfish in the mudflats of Plymouth Harbor and planted their corn. But as the young plants began to grow, Weston's men, who pretended to assist them in the fields, took to gobbling up the immature cornstalks and ruined the crop.

As if this wasn't bad enough, Bradford learned that the *Fortune,* the ship they had loaded with clapboards in the fall, had been seized by the French just before she arrived in England. They had lost everything. The voyage that was to have turned a significant profit had put them even deeper in the hole. "I pray you be not discouraged," Robert Cushman wrote, "but gather up yourself, to go through these difficulties cheerfully and with courage in that place wherein God hath set you, until the day of refreshing come."

Then they received a different sort of letter. To the northeast, off the coast of modern Maine, the codfishing season was in full swing. Between three hundred and four hundred vessels were gathered off that rocky, fogbound coast, and a master of one of the ships had taken it upon himself to write the Pilgrims concerning some disturbing developments at Jamestown. That spring, the Indians had massacred 347 English colonists—more than four times the total population of Plymouth. "Happy is he," the codfisherman wrote, "whom other men's harms doth make to beware."

As it so happened, the Pilgrims' relations with the Indians were at a new low. Thanks to Squanto's machinations and Bradford's reluctance to punish his interpreter, they could no longer count on the support of their former allies the Pokanokets. Recognizing that the English were newly vulnerable, the Massachusetts and Narragansetts were said to be planning an assault on Plymouth.

Bradford decided that the wall was not enough. If they should become the victims of a Jamestown-like attack, they needed a heavily reinforced structure that was large enough to accommodate all of them. They needed a fort. Perched atop the hill overlooking the town, it might very well provide the means of their deliverance. Even though food supplies were still low, the inhabitants launched into the work with a will. It was hoped that the mere presence of this imposing, well-defended structure would be enough to discourage future Indian attacks.

But as the work progressed, many of the settlers began to lose their enthusiasm for the project. Given the nebulousness of the Indian threat, it was difficult to justify the expenditure of so much time and effort—especially given their lack of food. The question of how much of a society's resources should be dedicated to security persists to this day. What amazed Edward Winslow during the summer and fall of 1622 was how "reasonable men [will be led] to reason against their own safety."

If they were to have any hope of completing the fort, they needed more provisions. Even though they lived on the edge of one of the world's great fishing grounds, the Pilgrims were without the skills and the equipment required to take advantage of it. They could, however, look to the fishermen assembled to the east as a possible provisioning source. Winslow headed out in the shallop on an emergency mission to Maine, where he succeeded in securing some desperately needed food.

With the approach of winter, the fort was nearing completion, and Weston's men had settled at Wessagussett, about twenty-two miles to the north in modern Weymouth. Taking their cue from the Pilgrims, the men at Wessagussett immediately began building a fort of their own. Due to the depredations of Weston's crew, the Pilgrims' corn crop had been disastrously insufficient. Wessagussett was in even more desperate need of food. That fall, it was decided, the two settlements would band together in search of provisions and take Wessagussett's thirty-ton vessel, the *Swan,* on a trading voyage to the south of Cape Cod.

Standish was to lead the expedition, but in November the normally vigorous captain was struck by a debilitating fever. Bradford decided to go in his stead with Squanto as his guide and interpreter. Since his downfall in May, Squanto had done his best to win back the confidence of both Bradford and Massasoit. Winslow claimed that by the time the *Swan* departed from Plymouth, he had secured a "peace" with the Pokanoket sachem. It is difficult to imagine the circumstances under which the disgraced interpreter could have regained Massasoit's trust. But whatever the sachem's true disposition toward him may have been, Squanto, at least, was under the impression that all was once again right with the world. It was now safe for him to venture beyond Plymouth.

In order to sail to the south of Cape Cod, they must negotiate the same shoals that had almost wrecked the *Mayflower* two years before. Squanto claimed that he had done just that not once but twice—with the Englishman Thomas Dermer and a Frenchman. But once in the waters off modern Chatham, Bradford was gripped by a sickening sense of déjà vu. They were surrounded by breakers, and the *Swan's* master "saw no hope of passage." They bore up and headed for shore, toward what is called today Pleasant Bay but was then known as Manamoyick, where Squanto said they might spend the night. Using their shallop to scout ahead of them, they followed a narrow and crooked channel and soon had the *Swan* safely anchored in the harbor.

That evening Bradford and Squanto went ashore to speak with the local Indians. Only after the Manamoyicks had hidden away most of their goods and provisions were they willing to entertain the two in their wigwams. It took some convincing, but eventually they agreed to trade. Over the next few days, with Squanto's help, Bradford secured eight hogsheads of corn and beans.

Just before they were about to leave for a second attempt at crossing the breakers, Squanto suddenly fell ill. Bradford described it as an "Indian fever, bleeding much at the nose (which the Indians take for a symptom of death)." Within a few days, Squanto—the Indian whom Bradford valued so highly that he had put the entire plantation at risk rather than see him killed—was dead. Bradford claimed Squanto asked him "to pray for him that he might go to the Englishmen's God in Heaven; and bequeathed sundry of his things to sundry of his English friends as remembrances of his love." For Bradford, it was yet another terrible personal and professional loss. With Dorothy, Governor Carver, and now Squanto dead, he must once again regroup and find a way to continue on.

Bradford assumed that his trusted interpreter had died of natural causes. But he may have been the victim of an assassination plot masterminded by Massasoit. Although difficult to document, there were several suspected poisonings of high-ranking Indians in New England during the seventeenth century. That Squanto, who had survived the infectious streets of London, should suddenly fall prey to disease on Cape Cod is highly unlikely. Massasoit's supposed reconciliation with the interpreter may have been only a ruse. Years later, his son was accused of ordering the secret execution of yet another Indian interpreter.

Squanto might have been guilty of clandestinely following his own agenda, but he had the diplomatic instincts of a leader. Sachem-like, he had attempted to outwit and outmaneuver his more powerful rivals. He had put Bradford in a most difficult and dangerous position, and yet to the end, the Plymouth governor insisted that the interpreter had been "a special instrument sent of God for their good beyond their expectation."

It remained to be seen whether Massasoit still held Squanto's machinations against the Pilgrims. A year ago, there had been nothing but trust and friendship between Plymouth and the Pokanokets. Now there was uncertainty and lingering bitterness.

Without Squanto to guide them, the Pilgrims must look to Hobbamock—a warrior of unfailing loyalty to both Massasoit and Miles Standish. Negotiation and cunning had had their day. In the perilous months ahead, a brutal darkness would fall across New England.

CHAPTER NINE

A Ruffling Course

*P*LYMOUTH BY THE WINTER OF 1623 was a place of exceptional discipline, a community where shared religious beliefs and family ties had united the Leideners from the start and where two years of strong leadership on the part of William Bradford had convinced even the Strangers that it was in their best interests to work together. Some twenty miles to the north, at Wessagussett, an entirely different community had come into being.

Wessagussett was more like early Jamestown—a group of unattached men with relatively little in common. In the beginning, their energies were directed toward building a fort. But once that was completed, they were unprepared to face the rigors of a hard New England winter. As in Jamestown, a state of almost unaccountable languor quickly descended on the inhabitants. Suffering from a deadly combination of malnutrition and despair, the colonists appeared powerless to adapt to the demands of the New World.

It was quite possible, the Pilgrims insisted, for Weston's men to survive. Even without corn and migratory birds, there were still shellfish (including oysters, which were not available at Plymouth) along the water's edge at Wessagussett. There were also groundnuts, fleshy potatolike tubers that grew in clusters beneath the ground. Rather than give up, they must strive to feed themselves.

But to seek food required them to leave the safety of their fortress, and unlike Plymouth, where the closest Indian village was fifteen miles away, Wessagussett was set right beside a Massachusett settlement. Not only was the threat of attack greater, but there was also an even more powerful form of temptation. The Indians possessed stores of corn that they were saving for the spring. Why spend the day rooting for clams in the cold mud when there was so much corn for the taking?

In February, John Sanders, the settlement's leader, wrote to Governor Bradford, asking if it was right to steal a few hogsheads of corn, especially if they promised to reimburse the Indians once they'd grown their own corn in the summer. This was, of course, almost exactly what the Pilgrims had done two years before, but Bradford urged them to leave the corn alone, "for it might so exasperate the Indians . . . [that] all of us might smart for it."

In desperation, Sanders sailed to the east in hopes of securing some provisions from a fishing outpost on the island of Monhegan. He left his plantation in a state of misery and disorder. One morning they found a man dead in the tidal flats, waist deep in muck and apparently too feeble to extract himself. As the sufferings of Weston's men increased, the Indians, who were already resentful of the English interlopers, began to harass them unmercifully. They scoffed at their weakness and even snatched from their hands what few clams and groundnuts they had been able to gather. Some of the English resorted to trading their clothes for food until they were reduced to naked, trembling skeletons of wretchedness; others contracted themselves out as servants to the Indians; one man, according to Winslow, willingly *became* an Indian.

About this time, Miles Standish traveled to Manomet, just fifteen miles to the south of Plymouth, to pick up some of the corn Bradford had secured during his trading voyage with Squanto. Standish was being entertained by sachem Canacum when two Massachusett Indians arrived with word from sachem Obtakiest at Wessagussett.

One of the Indians was a warrior of immense pride named Wituwamat, who bragged of having once killed several French sailors. Wituwamat possessed an ornately carved knife that he had taken from one of his victims. Soon after his arrival, he presented the knife to Canacum and began "a long speech in an audacious manner." Without the assistance of an interpreter, Standish was not sure what Wituwamat was saying, but he did know that once the Indian had completed his speech, he—not Standish—became Canacum's favored guest and Wituwamat's "entertainment much exceeded the captain's."

Standish was not the sort to overlook a social slight. Where Bradford was willing to give even a potential traitor the benefit of the doubt, Standish was quick to take offense. He objected vehemently to his treatment by Canacum and chastised the two Massachusett Indians for their refusal to pay him the proper respect.

In an attempt to pacify the captain, Canacum insisted that Standish invite his three English compatriots, who were then loading the shallop with corn, to join them beside the fire. But Standish would have none of it. He stormed out of the wigwam and resolved to spend the night with his men at the temporary rendezvous they had built beside the shallop.

Standish's indignant furor appears to have blinded him to the fact that something of far more consequence than a social rebuff had occurred at Manomet. Only in hindsight did Standish see the interchange between Wituwamat and Canacum as the first indication that the Indians in the region were conspiring against them. For, as it turned out, he and Wituwamat were destined to meet again.

While Standish was at Manomet, word reached Plymouth that Massasoit was gravely ill. Bradford decided he must send an emissary—not only to attend to Massasoit, but to make contact with the crew of a Dutch vessel that had reportedly been driven ashore, almost to the door of the sachem's wigwam. Since Winslow had already visited Massasoit and could speak Dutch, he was chosen for the expedition to Pokanoket.

Winslow was accompanied by Hobbamock and John Hamden, a gentleman from London who was wintering with the Pilgrims, and about midway in their forty-mile journey, they received word from some Indians that Massasoit was dead. "This news struck us blank," Winslow wrote. The Indians also said that the Dutch had succeeded in refloating their vessel and had already left Pokanoket.

Hobbamock was the most profoundly affected by the unsubstantiated news of the sachem's passing, and he insisted that they return immediately to Plymouth. But Winslow was not so sure. If Massasoit was
dead, then Corbitant, who lived just to the east of Pokanoket, would in
all likelihood succeed him. Even though he was, in Winslow's words, "a
most hollowhearted friend toward us," it might be in their best interests to stop at Corbitant's village and pay their respects. Given that less
than a year ago both Winslow and Hobbamock had been part of an
expedition sent to kill Corbitant (who had reportedly murdered
Squanto), it was an extremely hazardous proposition. But after some
reflection, all of them thought it worth the risk.

As they made their way to Corbitant's village, Hobbamock could
not contain his sorrow over the loss of Massasoit. "My loving sachem,
my loving sachem!" he cried. "Many have I known, but never any like
thee." He said that with Massasoit's death he feared Plymouth "had not
a faithful friend left among the Indians." He then proceeded to deliver
a eulogy that still stands as a remarkably timeless description of an ideal
leader:

[H]e was no liar, he was not bloody and cruel . . . ; in anger and
passion he was soon reclaimed; easy to be reconciled towards such
as had offended him; [he] ruled by reason in such measure as he
would not scorn the advice of mean men; and . . . he governed his
men better with few strokes, than others did with many; truly loving where he loved.

Corbitant, they soon discovered, was not at home. He was still at
Pokanoket, his wife said; she wasn't sure whether or not Massasoit was
still alive. Winslow hired a runner to go to Pokanoket to get the latest
news. Just a half hour before sunset, the messenger returned with word
that the sachem "was not yet dead, though there was no hope we
should find him living." Winslow resolved to set out immediately for
Pokanoket.

* * *

It was still dark when they arrived at Massasoit's village. His wigwam was so jammed with people that they had difficulty making their way to the sachem's side. Several powwows hovered over him, "making such a hellish noise, as it distempered us that were well," Winslow wrote. Massasoit's arms, legs, and thighs were being worked over by half a dozen women, who chafed his skin "to keep heat in him." During a lull, Winslow requested that Massasoit be informed that "his friends, the English, were come to see him."

The sachem was unable to see, but he could still hear. He weakly asked which one of the English was present. The Indians said Winslow's name as "Winsnow," and Massasoit responded, "Keen Winsnow?" or "Are you Winslow?" The Pilgrim answered, "Ahhee," or yes. Massasoit's response: "Matta neen wonckanet namen, Winsnow!" or "O Winslow, I shall never see thee again."

Winslow explained that Governor Bradford had wished he could be there but pressing business had required him to remain at Plymouth. In his stead, he had come with some medicines and foods "most likely to do [the sachem] good in this his extremity." Massasoit had eaten nothing in a very long time, and Winslow attempted to feed him some fruit preserves, administered on the tip of a knife. Once the sweetened fruit had dissolved in Massasoit's mouth, he swallowed—for the first time in two days.

Winslow began to examine the interior of the sachem's mouth. It was "exceedingly furred," and his tongue was so swollen that it was little wonder he had been unable to eat anything. After scraping the "corruption" from his mouth and tongue, Winslow fed him more of the preserves.

Massasoit may have been suffering from typhus, probably brought to the village by the recently departed Dutch traders. Spread by infected lice, typhus was known as "pestilential fever" in the seventeenth century and was most common in winter and spring. Typhus thrived in the crowded, unsanitary conditions typical of an Indian or, for that matter, English village of the time, and there were also several other Pokanokets suffering from the disease. According to a modern description of typhus, symptoms include "fever and chills, vomiting, constipation or diarrhea, muscle ache and delirium or stupor. The tongue is first coated with a white fur, which then turns brown. The body develops small red eruptions which may bleed." In severe cases, the mortality rate can reach 70 percent.

Within a half hour of receiving his first taste of Winslow's fruit preserves, Massasoit had improved to the extent that his sight had begun to return. Winslow had brought several bottles of medicines, but they had broken along the way. He asked Massasoit if he could send a messenger to get some more from the surgeon back in Plymouth, as well as a couple of chickens, so that he might cook up a broth. This was readily agreed to, and by 2 a.m. a runner was on his way with a letter from Winslow.

The next day, Massasoit was well enough to ask Winslow to shoot a duck and make an English pottage similar to what he had sampled at Plymouth. Fearing that his stomach was not yet ready for meat, Winslow insisted that he first try a more easily digested pottage of greens and herbs. Neither Winslow nor John Hamden had any experience in making such a concoction, however, and after much hunting about they were able to find only a few strawberry leaves and a sassafras root. They boiled the two together, and after straining the results through Winslow's handkerchief and combining it with some roasted corn, they fed the mixture to Massasoit. He drank at least a pint of the broth and soon had his first bowel movement in five days.

Before fading off to sleep, the sachem asked Winslow to wash out the mouths of all the others who were sick in the village, "saying they were good folk." Reluctantly the Pilgrim envoy went about the work of scraping the mouths of all who desired it, a duty he admitted to finding "much offensive to me, not being accustomed with such poisonous savors." This was a form of diplomacy that went far beyond the usual exchange of pleasantries and gifts.

That afternoon Winslow shot a duck and prepared to feed Massasoit the promised pottage. By this time, the sachem had improved remarkably. "Never did I see a man so low . . . recover in that measure in so short a time," Winslow wrote. The duck's meat was quite fatty, and Winslow said it was important to skim the grease from the top of the broth, but Massasoit was now ravenous and insisted on making "a gross meal of it"—gobbling down the duck, fat and all. An hour later, he was vomiting so violently that he began to bleed from the nose.

For the next four hours the blood poured from his nose, and Winslow began to fear that this might be the end. But eventually the bleeding stopped, and the sachem slept for close to eight hours. When he awoke, he was feeling so much better that he asked that the two chickens, which had just arrived from Plymouth, be kept as breeding stock rather than cooked for his benefit.

All the while, Indians from as many as a hundred miles away continued to arrive at Pokanoket. Before Winslow's appearance, many of those in attendance had commented on the absence of the English and suggested that they cared little about Massasoit's welfare. With this remarkable recovery, everything had changed. "Now I see the English are my friends and love me," Massasoit announced to the assembled multitude; "and whilst I live, I will never forget this kindness they have showed me."

Before their departure, Massasoit took Hobbamock aside and had some words with the trusted pniese. Not until the following day, after they had spent the night with Corbitant, who now declared himself to be one of the Pilgrims' staunchest allies, did Hobbamock reveal the subject of his conversation with Massasoit.

Plymouth, the sachem claimed, was in great danger. Pushed to the limit of their endurance by Weston's men at Wessagussett, the Massachusetts had decided they must wipe out the settlement. But to attack Wessagussett would surely incite the wrath of the Pilgrims, who would feel compelled to revenge the deaths of their countrymen. The only solution, the Massachusetts had determined, was to launch raids on both English settlements. But the Massachusetts had just forty warriors; if they were to attack Wessagussett and Plymouth simultaneously, they needed help. Massasoit claimed that they had succeeded in gaining the support of half a dozen villages on Cape Cod as well as the Indians at Manomet and Martha's Vineyard. An assault was imminent, Massasoit insisted, and the only option the Pilgrims had was "to kill the men of Massachusetts, who were the authors of this intended mischief." If the

Pilgrims waited until after the Indians had attacked Wessagussett, it would be too late. By then the regionwide Native force would have been assembled, and the "multitude of adversaries" would overwhelm them. They must act "without delay to take away the principals, and then the plot would cease."

It was terrifying to learn that they were, in Winslow's words, "at the pit's brim, and yet feared nor knew not that we were in danger." They must return to Plymouth as soon as possible and inform Governor Bradford. After more than two years of threatened violence, it now appeared that the Pilgrims might have no choice but to go to war.

As Winslow, Hobbamock, and John Hamden were hurrying back to Plymouth, Phineas Pratt, a thirty-year-old joiner who had become, by default, one of the leaders of the sorry settlement of Wessagussett, was beginning to think it was time to escape this hellhole and find his way to Plymouth.

Their sufferings had become unendurable. They had nothing to eat, and the Indians were becoming increasingly belligerent. The warriors, led by a pniese named Pecksuot, gathered outside the wall of the Wessagussett fort. "Machit pesconk!" they shouted, which Pratt translated as "Naughty guns." An attack seemed at hand, so the English increased the number of men on watch. But without food, the guards began to die at their posts. One bitterly cold night, Pratt reported for guard duty. "I [saw] one man dead before me," he remembered, "and another [man dead] at my right hand and another at my left for want of food."

Word reached the settlement from an Englishman living with the Indians that the Massachusetts planned to attack both Wessagussett and Plymouth. Sachem Obtakiest was waiting for the snow to melt so that his warriors' footprints could not be tracked when they left for the other settlement. "[T]heir plot was to kill all the English people in one day," Pratt wrote. He decided he must leave as soon as possible for Plymouth. "[I]f [the] Plymouth men know not of this treacherous plot," he told his compatriots, "they and we are all dead men."

With a small pack draped across his back, he walked out of the settlement as casually as he could manage with a hoe in his hand. He began to dig at the edge of a large swamp, pretending to search for groundnuts. He looked to his right and to his left and, seeing no Indians, disappeared into the swamp.

He ran till about three o'clock in the afternoon. There were patches of snow everywhere, and he feared the Indians had followed his footprints and would soon be upon him. Clouds moved in, making it difficult to determine the position of the sun and the direction in which he was traveling. "I wandered," he wrote, "not knowing my way." But at sunset, the western sky became tinged with red, providing him with the orientation he needed.

As darkness overtook him, he heard "a great howling of wolves." He came to a river and, skittering over the rocks, drenched himself in the chilly water. He was tired, hungry, and cold, but he feared to light a fire, since it might be seen by the Indians. He came to a deep gorge into which several trees had fallen. "Then I said in my thoughts," he wrote, "this is God's providence that here I may make a fire." As he attempted to warm himself beside the feeble blaze, the sky above miraculously cleared, and he stared up at the stars. Recognizing Ursa Major, he was able to determine the direction he should go the next morning.

By three in the afternoon he had reached the site of what would become the village of Duxbury, just to the north of Plymouth. As he ran across the shallows of the Jones River, haunted by the fear that the Indians were about to catch up to him, he said to himself, "[N]ow am I a deer chased [by] wolves." He found a well-worn path. He was bounding down a hill when up ahead he saw an Englishman walking toward him. It was John Hamden, the gentleman from London who had recently returned from Pokanoket with Edward Winslow. Suddenly overcome by exhaustion, Pratt collapsed onto the trunk of a fallen tree. "Mr. Hamden," he called out, "I am glad to see you alive."

Hamden explained that Massasoit had told them of the plot against Plymouth and Wessagussett and that Governor Bradford had recently convened a public meeting to discuss how the plantation should proceed.

It was irritating in the extreme to know that they had been put into this mess not by anything *they* had done but by the irresponsible actions of Weston's men. The one encouraging bit of news was that thanks to Winslow's efforts at Pokanoket, Massasoit was once again on their side. There was little doubt what the sachem expected of them: they were to launch a preemptive strike against the Massachusetts and snuff out the conspiracy at its source.

The fact remained, however, that thus far no Indians had even threatened them. If they were to initiate an attack, it would be based on hearsay—and they all knew from experience how misleading and convoluted the rumors could be. Then again, with a sachem as trustworthy and powerful as Massasoit telling them to act, what more justification did they need? Yes, they decided, their future safety depended on a swift and daring assault.

Edward Winslow later claimed that "it much grieved us to shed the blood of those whose good we ever intended." In truth, however, there were some Pilgrims who felt no such misgivings. Miles Standish had been itching to settle a score with Wituwamat ever since the Massachusett warrior had snubbed him at Manomet. For the captain, the matter was personal rather than diplomatic, and he was going to make the most of it. Bradford, normally careful to restrain his combative military officer, appears to have given Standish free rein. It was agreed that the captain should make an example of "that bloody and bold villain" and bring back Wituwamat's head to Plymouth, "that he might be a warning and terror to all of that disposition."

Standish put together a force that included Hobbamock and seven Englishmen; any more and the Massachusetts might suspect what the English were about. They would sail for Wessagussett pretending to be on a trading mission. Instead of launching a full-scale attack, they would, after secretly warning Weston's men, "take [the Indians] in such traps as they lay for others."

They were scheduled to leave the same day Pratt staggered out of the forest. Standish postponed their departure so that he could extract as much information as possible from the young man. The Pilgrims found Pratt's story "good encouragement to proceed in our intendments," and with the help of a fair wind, Standish and his men left the next day for Wessagussett.

Before landing, they stopped at the *Swan,* anchored just offshore. The little vessel was deserted, but after Standish's men fired off a musket, the ship's master and several other men from Wessagussett walked down to the water's edge. They had been gathering groundnuts and seemed distressingly nonchalant given what the Pilgrims had been led to believe. Standish asked why they had left the ship without anyone on guard. "[L]ike men senseless of their own misery," they replied that they had no fear of the Indians. In fact, many of them were living with the Massachusetts in their wigwams. If this was indeed the case, then why was Standish about to launch an attack? Had Pratt simply told the Pilgrims what they wanted to hear?

Standish was not about to allow anything—not even evidence that all was peace at Wessagussett—dissuade him from his plan. He marched to the fort and demanded to speak to whoever was in charge. Once he'd done his best to quell the Indians' suspicions, he explained, he was going to kill as many of them as he could. With the completion of the mission, the settlers could either return with him to Plymouth or take the *Swan* up to Maine. Standish had even brought along some corn to sustain them during their voyage east.

It was their hunger, not their fear of the Indians, that was the chief concern of Weston's men. It was not surprising, then, that they quickly embraced Standish's plan, since it meant they would soon have something to eat. Swearing all to secrecy, the captain instructed them to tell those who were living outside the settlement to return as soon as possible to the safety of the fort. Unfortunately, the weather had deteriorated, and the rain and wind prompted several of the English to remain in the warmth of the Indians' wigwams.

In the meantime, a warrior approached the fort under the pretense of trading furs with Standish. The fiery military officer tried to appear welcoming and calm, but it was clear to the Indian that Standish was up to no good. Once back among his friends, he reported that "he saw by his eyes that [the captain] was angry in his heart."

This prompted the Massachusett pniese Pecksuot to approach Hobbamock. He told the Pokanoket warrior that he knew exactly what Standish was up to and that he and Wituwamat were unafraid of him. "[L]et him begin when he dare," he told Hobbamock; "he shall not take us unawares."

Later that day, both Pecksuot and Wituwamat brashly walked up to Standish. Pecksuot was a tall man, and he made a point of looking disdainfully down on the Pilgrim military officer. "You are a great captain," he said, "yet you are but a little man. Though I be no sachem, yet I am of great strength and courage."

For his part, Wituwamat continued to whet and sharpen the same knife he had so ostentatiously flourished in Standish's presence several weeks before at Manomet. On the knife's handle was the carved outline of a woman's face. "I have another at home," he told Standish, "wherewith I have killed both French and English, and that has a man's face on it; by and by these two must marry."

"These things the captain observed," Winslow wrote, "yet bore with patience for the present."

The next day, Standish lured both Wituwamat and Pecksuot into one of the settlement's houses for a meal. In addition to corn, he had brought along some pork. The two Massachusett pnieses were wary of the Plymouth captain, but they were also very hungry, and, as Standish had anticipated, pork was a delicacy that the Indians found almost impossible to resist. Wituwamat and Pecksuot were accompanied by Wituwamat's brother and a friend, along with several women. Besides Standish, there were three other Pilgrims and Hobbamock in the room.

Once they had all sat down and begun to eat, the captain signaled for the door to be shut. He turned to Pecksuot and grabbed the knife from the string around the pniese's neck. Before the Indian had a chance to respond, Standish had begun stabbing him with his own weapon. The point was needle sharp, and Pecksuot's chest was soon riddled with blood-spurting wounds. As Standish and Pecksuot struggled, the other Pilgrims assaulted Wituwamat and his companion. "[I]t is incredible," Winslow wrote, "how many wounds these two pnieses received before they died, not making any fearful noise, but catching at their weapons and striving to the last."

All the while, Hobbamock stood by and watched. Soon the three Indians were dead, and Wituwamat's teenage brother had been taken captive. A smile broke out across Hobbamock's face, and he said, "Yesterday, Pecksuot, bragging of his own strength and stature, said though you were a great captain, yet you were but a little man. Today I see you are big enough to lay him on the ground."

But the killing had just begun. Wituwamat's brother was quickly hanged. There was another company of Pilgrims elsewhere in the settlement, and Standish sent word to them to kill any Indians who happened to be with them. As a result, two more were put to death. In the meantime, Standish and his cohorts found another Indian and killed him.

With Hobbamock and some of Weston's men in tow, Standish headed out in search of more Indians. They soon came across sachem Obtakiest and a group of Massachusett warriors. Situated between the English and the Indians was a rise of land that would afford a strategic advantage, and both groups began to run for it. Standish reached it first, and the Indians quickly scattered along the edge of the nearby forest, each man hiding behind a tree. Arrows were soon whizzing through the brisk afternoon air, most of them aimed at Standish and Hobbamock. Being a pniese, and therefore supposedly invulnerable, Hobbamock looked scornfully at the Indians behind the trees. Throwing off his coat, he began to chase after them, and most of them fled so quickly that none of the English could keep up with them.

There was a powwow who stood his ground and aimed an arrow at Standish. They later learned that he had been one of the original instigators of the plot against them. The captain and another Englishman fired simultaneously at the powwow, and the bullets broke his arm. With that, the remaining Indians, which included sachem Obtakiest, ran for the shelter of a nearby swamp, where they paused to hurl taunts and expletives at the Plymouth captain. Standish challenged the sachem to fight him man-to-man, but after a final exchange of insults, Obtakiest and the others disappeared into the swamp.

Several women had been captured during the scuffle with Pecksuot and Wituwamat. Now that the killing spree had finally come to an end, Standish decided to release the women, even though he knew there were at least three of Weston's men still living with the Indians. If he had kept these women as hostages, Standish could easily have bargained for the Englishmen's lives. But killing Indians, not saving lives, appears to have been the captain's chief priority at Wessagussett, and all three Englishmen were later executed.

Now that Standish's terrifying whirlwind of violence had come to an apparent end, the vast majority of the Wessagussett survivors decided to sail for Monhegan. The Pilgrims waited until the *Swan* had cleared Massachusetts Bay, then turned their shallop south for Plymouth, with the head of Wituwamat wrapped in a piece of white linen.

Standish arrived at Plymouth to a hero's welcome. After being "received with joy," the captain and his men marched up to the newly completed fort, where Wituwamat's head was planted on a pole on the fort's roof. As it turned out, the fort contained its first prisoner: an Indian who had been sent in pursuit of Phineas Pratt. Unable to find Pratt, who had saved his own life by becoming so hopelessly lost, the Indian had continued past Plymouth to Manomet, then backtracked to the English settlement in hopes of obtaining some information about the Pilgrims. By this time, Standish had already departed for Wessagussett, and suspicious of the Indian's motives, Bradford had thrown him in irons until the captain's return.

The Indian was released from his shackles and brought out for examination. After looking "piteously on the head" of Wituwamat, the captive confessed everything. The plot had not originally been sachem Obtakiest's idea. There were five—Wituwamat, Peksuot, and three powwows, including the one Standish had injured at Wessagussett—who had convinced their sachem to launch an attack against the Pilgrims.

Bradford released the prisoner on the condition that he carry a message to Obtakiest: If the sachem dared to continue in "the like courses," Bradford vowed, "he would never suffer him or his to rest in peace, till he had utterly consumed them."

It took many days for the Pilgrims to receive an answer. Finally a Massachusett woman appeared at Plymouth with Obtakiest's response. She explained that her sachem was eager to make peace with the Pilgrims, but none of his men were willing to approach the settlement. Ever since the massacre at Wessagussett, Obtakiest had kept on the move, fearful that Standish might return and "take further vengeance on him."

The Massachusetts were not the only Indians in the region to have taken flight into the wilderness. All throughout Cape Cod—from Manomet to Nauset to Pamet—the Native inhabitants had fled in panic, convinced that Standish and his thugs were about to descend on their villages and kill every Indian in sight. "[T]his sudden and unexpected execution . . . ," Edward Winslow wrote, "hath so terrified and amazed them, as in like manner they forsook their houses, running to and fro like men distracted, living in swamps and other desert places, and so brought manifold diseases amongst themselves, whereof very many are dead."

Huddled in swamps and on remote islands, fearful that to venture back to their villages meant certain death, Indians throughout the region were unable to plant the crops on which their lives depended. By summer, they had begun to die at a startling rate. "[C]ertainly it is strange to hear how many of late have, and still daily die amongst them," Winslow wrote. Just about every notable sachem on the Cape died in the months ahead, including Canacum at Manomet, Aspinet at Nauset, and the "personable, courteous, and fair conditioned" Iyanough at Cummaquid. Word reached Plymouth that before he died, the handsome young sachem had "in the midst of these distractions, said the God of the English was offended with them, and would destroy them in his anger." One village decided to send some gifts to the Pilgrims in hopes of establishing peace, but the Indians' canoe capsized almost within sight of the plantation, and three of them drowned. Since that incident, not a single Indian from Cape Cod had dared to approach the settlement. Among the Massachusetts, the Pilgrims had earned a new name: wotawquenange—cutthroats.

Standish's raid had irreparably damaged the human ecology of the region. Not only had the Pilgrims proved unexpectedly violent and vindictive, but Massasoit had betrayed his former confederates. By siding with the Pilgrims against the Indians of Massachusetts and Cape Cod, the Pokanoket sachem had initiated a new and terrifying era in New England. It was no longer a question of Indian versus English; it was now possible for alliances and feuds to reach across racial lines in a confusing amalgam of cultures.

It took some time before a new equilibrium came to the region. In the immediate aftermath of the Wessagussett raid, the Pilgrims were astonished to discover that they had, at least temporarily, ruined their ability to trade with the Indians. "[W]e have been much damaged in our trade," Bradford wrote to the Merchant Adventurers, "for there where we had [the] most skins the Indians are run away from their habitations, and set no corn, so as we can by no means as yet come to speak with them." Without furs as a potential source of income, the Pilgrims looked to codfishing—with the usual disastrous results.

The people who *had* been helped by the attack were the Pokanokets. With the death of the most influential sachems on Cape Cod, a huge power vacuum had been created in the region. Prior to Wessagussett, Aspinet, sachem of the Nausets, had commanded more warriors than Massasoit. But now Aspinet was dead, and his people had fled in panic. Over the next few years, Massasoit established the Indian nation we now refer to as the Wampanoag—an entity that may not even have existed before this crucial watershed.

It was exactly the scenario Squanto had envisioned for himself the year before. But it had been Massasoit who had pulled it off. Just a few words, delivered from what had almost been his deathbed, had unleashed a chain of events that had completely reinvented the region in his own image. The English had served him well.

* * *

The Pilgrims knew that there were those back in England who would criticize them for launching what was, in essence, an unprovoked attack on sachem Obtakiest and the Massachusetts. In the months ahead, Edward Winslow wrote *Good Newes from New England*. As the title suggests, Winslow's account puts the Wessagussett raid in the best possible light. The Pilgrims, Winslow points out, had been operating in a climate of intense fear since learning about the massacres in Virginia the previous spring. Given the dramatic and apparently irrefutable nature of Massasoit's disclosure of the plot against them, there was little else they could have been expected to do.

There was one man, however, who refused to forgive the Pilgrims for "the killing of those poor Indians." When he heard about the incident back in Leiden, Pastor John Robinson sent Governor Bradford a letter. "Oh, how happy a thing had it been," he wrote, "if you had converted some before you had killed any! Besides, where blood is once begun to be shed, it is seldom staunched of a long time after. You say they deserved it. I grant it; but upon what provocations and invitements by those heathenish Christians [at Wessagussett]?"

The real problem, as far as Robinson saw it, was Bradford's willingness to trust Standish, a man the minister had come to know when he was in Leiden. The captain lacked "that tenderness of the life of man (made after God's image) which is meet," Robinson wrote, and the orgiastic violence of the assault was contrary to "the approved rule, The punishment to a few, and the fear to many."

Robinson concluded his letter to Bradford with words that proved ominously prophetic given the ultimate course of New England's history: "It is . . . a thing more glorious, in men's eyes, than pleasing in God's or convenient for Christians, to be a terror to poor barbarous people. And indeed I am afraid lest, by these occasions, others should be drawn to affect a kind of ruffling course in the world."

That summer the supply ship *Anne* arrived with sixty passengers, including the widow Alice Southworth. The Southworths and Bradfords had known each other in Leiden, and just a few weeks after the *Anne*'s arrival, William and Alice were married on August 14, 1623.

The festivities that followed were much more than the celebration of a marriage. A new order had come to New England, and there to commemorate the governor's nuptials was Massasoit, with a black wolf skin draped over his shoulder and, for propriety's sake, with just one of his five wives by his side. Also attending were about 120 of his warriors (about twice as many men as he had been able to muster a little more than a year ago), who danced "with such a noise," one witness reported, "that you would wonder."

As Indians on Cape Cod to the east and in Massachusetts to the north continued to be gripped by fear and confusion, a supreme confidence had come to the Pokanokets. Massasoit was now firmly in control, and it had been Standish's assault at Wessagussett that had made it possible. Serving as a grim reminder of the fearful power of the Pokanoket-Pilgrim alliance was the flesh-blackened skull of Wituwamat, still planted on a pole above the fort roof.

It was only appropriate that a new flag be raised for Massasoit's benefit. Instead of the standard of England and its red St. George's cross, the Pilgrims unfurled a blood-soaked piece of linen. It was the same cloth that had once swaddled Wituwamat's head, and it now flew bravely above the fort: a reddish brown smear against the blue summer sky.

PART III

Community

CHAPTER TEN

One Small Candle

*U*P UNTIL 1630, Plymouth was the only significant English settlement in the region. That year, an armada of seventeen ships arrived off the New England coast. In a matter of months, approximately a thousand English men, women, and children—more than three times the entire population of Plymouth—had been delivered to the vicinity of Boston. In the years ahead, the Puritan colony of Massachusetts Bay grew to include modern New Hampshire and Maine, while other Puritan settlers headed south to found Connecticut. Adding to the mix was the Massachusetts exile Roger Williams, who in 1636 founded what became the religiously tolerant colony of Rhode Island, a haven for Baptists, Quakers, and other non-Puritans. With Plymouth serving as the great original, New England had become exactly what its name suggested, a *New* England composed of autonomous colonies. But for William Bradford, who had come to America to re-create the community of fellow worshippers he had known in Scrooby and in Leiden, there would always be something missing.

In 1625, Bradford received the stunning news that the congregation's minister, John Robinson, had died in Leiden. Robinson was irreplaceable, and a profound sense of sadness and inadequacy settled over the Plymouth church. For all they had suffered during those first terrible winters in America, their best years were behind them, in Leiden. Never again would they know that same rapturous sense of divine fellowship that had first launched them on this quest. Elder William Brewster soldiered on as their spiritual leader, but the Plymouth congregation never warmed to another minister throughout the first half of the century.

Without Robinson, the Pilgrims could not help but fear that their original purpose in coming to America was in constant danger of being subverted if not entirely destroyed. As a consequence, the passion and fervor that had enabled them to survive those first grim years threatened to darken into a mean-spirited fanaticism. Even before Robinson's death, John Lyford, a minister sent over by the Merchant Adventurers, was cast out of the settlement for secretly meeting with disgruntled settlers who wished to worship as they had back in England. One of Lyford's supporters, John Oldham, was forced to run through a gauntlet of musket-wielding Pilgrims who beat him with the butt ends of their weapons. When Edward Winslow, just back from a voyage to England, arrived on the scene, he urged his comrades "not [to] spare" Oldham.

In his correspondence and his history of the colony, Bradford did his best to claim that Lyford and Oldham richly deserved their punishments. The Merchant Adventurers, however, remained unconvinced and chastised the Pilgrims for being "contentious, cruel and hard hearted, among your neighbors, and towards such as in all points both civil and religious, jump not with you." In the years just before and after Robinson's death, Plymouth lost approximately a quarter of its residents as disaffected Strangers either returned to England or moved to Virginia. Some, such as Oldham and a salter named Roger Conant, found refuge amid the isolated fishing and trading outposts that had sprouted up along the New England coast at places like Nantasket and Cape Ann.

We can only wonder how different the early years of Plymouth might have been if Robinson had made it to the New World. If his letters to Bradford and the others are any indication, he might have insisted on a policy of moderation and restraint—not only with the Indians but also with the Strangers in the settlement. Despite Robinson's warnings about Miles Standish, Bradford continued to depend on his military officer to push forward the often brutal agenda of what was becoming the Pilgrim way in New England.

About the same time as Robinson's passing, a new settlement was started just to the north of Wessagussett in modern Braintree. The settlement's founder was, according to Bradford, "a man of pretty parts," who quickly decided to relocate to Virginia. One of his fellow investors, a jolly down-on-his-luck lawyer from London named Thomas Morton, opted to remain in New England with a handful of servants, and Morton subsequently dubbed the new venture Merrymount.

As the name of his settlement might suggest, Morton represented everything the Pilgrims had come to America to escape. In addition to being, in Bradford's words, "a pettifogger [of] more craft than honesty," Morton was an Anglican who enjoyed reading the Greek and Latin classics and composing his own ribald verse. For Morton, a Sunday was best spent not in prayer but in hunting with his falcon or, better yet, sharing a drink with the local Indians. Instead of building a wall around Merrymount, Morton erected an eighty-foot-high maypole— a gleeful and decidedly pagan proclamation that God was not to be taken overly seriously, at least in Morton's neck of New England.

Lubricated by plenty of alcohol, he and his men danced around the maypole with their Native neighbors, making a mockery of the solemn exclusivity of the Plymouth settlement. What was worse, Morton's intimacy with the Indians quickly made him the favored trading partner in the region. He even dared to equip them with guns, since this enabled the Indians to procure more furs.

The Pilgrims had come face-to-face with a figure from a future America: the frontiersman who happily thumbed his nose at authority while embracing the wilderness. One of Plymouth's residents—Richard and Elizabeth Warren's ten-year-old daughter Elizabeth—would one day give birth to a son named Benjamin Church, who would have a decidedly Morton-like love of the wilderness and play a significant role in the emerging American frontier. But that was decades in the future. For now, the Pilgrims had no use for anyone who dared to favor the heathen over the godly. Bradford decided to send Standish on yet another raid to the north—not to kill any Indians but to seize this "Lord of Misrule."

Morton quickly discovered what the Pilgrims had become in the years since Wessagussett. He had already learned from the Massachusett Indians of the viciousness of Standish's earlier attack and the fear it had unleashed in the region. After being taken by Standish and his men, who "fell upon him as if they would have eaten him," Morton began to question who were now the true savages in this land. "But I have found the Massachusetts Indians more full of humanity than the Christians," he wrote, "and have had much better quarter with them."

Morton wasn't the only Englishman to be astonished by the vindictiveness of the Pilgrims. In 1625, the former Plymouth resident Roger Conant was forced to intercede in an altercation between Standish and some fishermen on Cape Ann. Conant was so appalled by the violence of the Plymouth captain's manner that he later described the incident in great detail to the Puritan historian William Hubbard. Echoing Robinson's earlier concerns, Hubbard wrote, "Capt. Standish . . . never entered the school of our Savior Christ . . . or, if he was ever there, had forgot his first lessons, to offer violence to no man." As Morton and Pecksuot had observed, it was almost comical to see this sort of fury in a soldier who had been forced to shorten his rapier by six inches—otherwise the tip of his sword's scabbard would have dragged along the ground when he slung it from his waist. "A little chimney is soon fired," Hubbard wrote; "so was the Plymouth captain, a man of very little stature, yet of a very hot and angry temper."

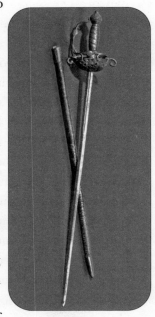

A German-made rapier attributed to Miles Standish

In 1624, Holland purchased Manhattan from the Indians and established the colony of New Netherland. Since many of the Pilgrims knew the language, it was perhaps inevitable that Plymouth established a strong relationship with the Dutch colony. In 1627, the Dutch trading agent Isaack de Rasiere visited Plymouth, and his description of the English community on a typical Sunday provides fascinating evidence of just how strong Standish's influence continued to be:

They assembled by beat of drum, each with his musket or fire-lock, in front of the captain's door; they have their cloaks on, and place themselves in order, three abreast, and are led by a sergeant without beat of drum. Behind comes the Governor, in a long robe; beside him on the right hand, comes the preacher with his cloak on, and on the left hand, the captain with his side-arms and cloak on, and with a small cane in his hand; and so they march in good order, and each sets his arms down near him. Thus they are constantly on their guard night and day.

Seven years after the *Mayflower* had sailed, Plymouth Plantation was still an armed fortress where each male communicant worshipped with a gun at his side.

The fall of 1623 marked the end of Plymouth's debilitating food shortages. For the last two planting seasons, the Pilgrims had grown crops communally—the approach first used at Jamestown and other English settlements. But as the disastrous harvest of the previous fall had shown, something drastic needed to be done to increase the annual yield.

In April, Bradford had decided that each household should be assigned its own plot to cultivate, with the understanding that each family kept whatever it grew. The change in attitude was stunning. Families were now willing to work much harder than they had ever worked before. In previous years, the men had tended the fields while the women tended the children at home. "The women now went willingly into the field," Bradford wrote, "and took their little ones with them to set corn." The Pilgrims had stumbled on the power of capitalism. Although the fortunes of the colony still teetered precariously in the years ahead, the inhabitants never again starved.

By 1623, the Pilgrims had goats, pigs, and chickens; that year Winslow sailed for England and returned with some cows; soon to follow were more cattle and some horses. Despite Winslow's claim that

New England
·
1625–1674

Connecticut River

Merrimack River

Portsmouth

Newbury

Cape A

Wamesit †

Gloucer

Salem •
Marblehead

Northfield •

Nashobah
†

Deerfield •

Lancaster •
Concord •

NIPMUCKS

Sudbury
Cambridge

Massachus
Bay

Hatfield •
Marlborough

Boston •
Hull •

Hadley •

Natick †

Northampton

Makunkokoag

Merrymount •

Brookfield •

Hassanamesitt †

Scituate •

Quabaug

Medfield •

Springfield •

Mendon •

†Punkapaug

Marshfiel

Monponsett Pond

Duxb

Bridgewater •

Plym

Taunton •

Middleborough •

Providence •

Rehoboth •

Assawompsett Po

Matianuck ○

Wannamoisett •
Swansea •

Aptucxet ○

Sowams ○

San

Hartford •

Pocasset •

Mount Hope •

Mash

CONNECTICUT

MOHEGANS

Thames River

PEQUOTS

NARRAGANSETTS

RHODE
ISLAND

POCASSETS

Dartmouth •

Connecticut River

Newport •

Mystic R.

New London •

NIANTICS

Sakonnet •

New Haven •

Aquinnah/Gay Head •

Marth
Vineya

73° 00'

72° 00'

71° 00'

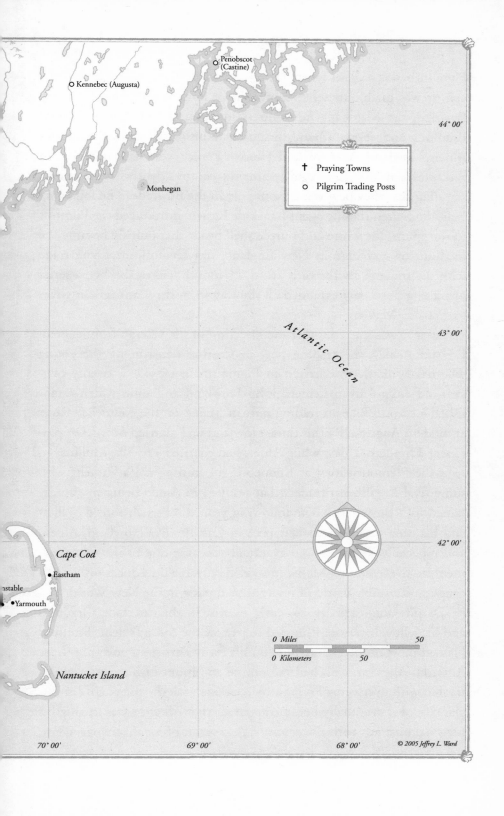

Penobscot
(Castine)

Kennebec (Augusta)

44° 00'

† Praying Towns

○ Pilgrim Trading Posts

Monhegan

Atlantic Ocean

43° 00'

42° 00'

Cape Cod

Eastham

nstable

Yarmouth

0 Miles   50

0 Kilometers   50

Nantucket Island

70° 00'   69° 00'   68° 00'   © 2005 Jeffrey L. Ward

Plymouth was a place where "religion and profit jump together," the colony was unable to achieve any sort of long-term financial success. By 1626, the Merchant Adventurers in London had disbanded, and Bradford and seven others, including Winslow, Brewster, Standish, Alden, Howland, Allerton, and Thomas Prence, who had come over in the *Fortune* in 1621, agreed to assume the colony's debt with the understanding that they be given a monopoly in the fur trade. The following year, the Dutch trading agent Isaack de Rasiere introduced the Pilgrims to wampum, the white and purple shell beads that quickly became the medium of exchange in New England and revolutionized the trade with the Indians. By the early 1630s, Plymouth had established a series of trading posts that extended all the way from the Connecticut River to Castine, Maine.

After it was started under the direction of the veteran frontiersman Edward Ashley, the trading post in Castine was run by the young Thomas Willett, who arrived in Plymouth in 1629 as a twenty-two-year-old émigré from Leiden. John Howland and John Alden established a second Pilgrim trading post in Maine on the Kennebec River at modern Augusta. By this time, Howland had married *Mayflower* passenger Elizabeth Tilley, while Alden had married Priscilla Mullins. In 1634 the Plymouth men at Kennebec got into a fatal argument with some rival English fur traders that resulted in Alden being briefly detained in a Boston jail. The following year, the French forced Willett and his men to abandon their post in Castine. For Howland, Alden, and especially Willett—who eventually became one of the wealthiest men in the colony—Maine provided a valuable education in the rough-and-tumble world of international trade in the New World.

Despite some remarkable early returns in the fur trade, Bradford and his fellow investors struggled to pay off the colony's debt. Bradford blamed most of their difficulties on his former assistant governor, Isaac Allerton. Allerton, who had mercantile ambitions of his own, was entrusted with overseeing Plymouth's relations with the merchants in England, and it eventually became apparent that Allerton was mixing his personal business with the colony's. As a result of his mismanagement, if not outright fraud, Plymouth's debts only increased even though the Pilgrims had sent significant quantities of furs back to England.

In truth, it was not all Isaac Allerton's fault. Bradford, who'd suffered reversals of his own back in Leiden, never had a talent for financial matters, and the colony continued to have trouble with the merchants in London long after Allerton ceased representing them in 1630. According to Bradford's calculations, between 1631 and 1636, they shipped £10,000 in beaver and otter pelts (worth almost 2 million in today's dollars) yet saw no significant reduction in their debt of approximately £6,000.

Not only were the Pilgrims poor judges of character, they were forced to struggle with the logistical difficulties of sending goods back and forth across three thousand miles of ocean. Plymouth was an inadequate port to begin with, and financial stability only came to the colony when their principal market shifted from London to Boston, which later emerged as New England's primary port. Not until 1648, after they had been forced to sell off some of their own land, did Bradford and the other Plymouth investors finally settle their accounts with the merchants in England. It would be left to others to hit upon a way to wealth in the New World.

As Pastor Robinson had suggested, the Pilgrims had lost more than a little of their collective soul at Wessagussett. But so had the Pokanokets. Massasoit had entered into a devil's bargain with the English. By selling out his Native neighbors in Massachusetts and Cape Cod, he had cast his lot with a culture and technology on which his own people increasingly came to depend. Whether it was iron hoes and kettles, blankets, liquor, or guns, the English had what the Pokanokets wanted. There would be some good years ahead as the Pilgrims eagerly traded with them for furs. But as the beavers and other fur-bearing animals grew scarce, the only thing the Indians had to sell to the English was their land.

It had begun innocently enough in 1621, when Massasoit had given

Patuxet to the Pilgrims as a gift. Back then it had been difficult to imagine a time when land would be anything but a boundless resource. The Pilgrims believed that since no Indians were presently living on the land, it was legally theirs. "[I]t is lawful now to take a land which none useth," Robert Cushman wrote, "and make use of it." By the 1630s, however, the Pilgrims had begun to take a different view—a change in attitude that may have been in response to the radical beliefs of a new minister.

Roger Williams had already upset the authorities in Massachusetts Bay by the time he moved from Boston to Plymouth in 1633. In addition to what Bradford described as some "strange opinions" regarding spiritual matters, Williams insisted that the Indians were the legal owners of their lands. If the English were to take title, Williams argued, they must first purchase the land from its previous owners. Williams's unusual religious convictions soon got him into trouble in Plymouth, forcing him to move back to Massachusetts Bay. (By 1635, his "unsettled judgment" resulted in his banishment from the colony, and he soon after founded Rhode Island.) Despite the brief and tumultuous nature of Williams's time in Plymouth, he appears to have had a lasting influence on the colony. Soon after his departure, the Pilgrims began recording their purchases of Indian land.

It's true that the English concept of land ownership was initially unfamiliar to the Indians. Instead of a title and deed, the Indians' relationship to the land was based on a complex mixture of cultural factors, with the sachem possessing the right to distribute land in his own territory. But whatever misunderstandings existed in the beginning between the Indians and English, by the second decade of Plymouth Colony, with towns springing up across the region, there was little doubt among the Indians as to what the Pilgrims meant by the purchase and sale of land.

From the start, Plymouth authorities insisted that all Native land purchases must have prior court approval. By maintaining control over the buying and selling of Indian land, the colony hoped to ensure clear titles while protecting the Natives from unscrupulous individuals who might use alcohol and even violence to part them from their property. In 1639,

Massasoit and his son Wamsutta confirmed their original treaty with the colony and promised that "they shall not give, sell, or convey any of his or their lands . . . without the . . . consent of this government."

Initially, it appears, the transactions were quite informal—at least when it came to determining the price the English paid for the land. In November 1642 Massasoit agreed to sell a portion of what became the township of Rehoboth. The deed reports that the sachem "chose out ten fathom of beads . . . and put them in a basket, and affirmed that he was full satisfied for his lands . . . , but he stood upon it that he would have a coat more." In 1650, he sold 196 square miles of what became modern Bridgewater for seven coats, nine hatchets, eight hoes, twenty-nine knives, four moose skins, and ten and a half yards of cotton. In 1652, he and Wamsutta sold the future site of Dartmouth for thirty yards of cloth, eight moose skins, fifteen axes, fifteen hoes, fifteen pairs of shoes, one iron pot, and ten shillings' worth of assorted goods. The following year they sold lands in the vicinity of the Pokanokets' ancestral village of Sowams for £35, currently worth somewhere in the neighborhood of $7,000.

Today, the sums paid for Massasoit's lands seem criminally insignificant. However, given the high cost of clearing Native land and the high value the Indians attached to English goods, the prices are almost justifiable. Certainly, the Pilgrims *felt* they were paying a fair price, and their descendants later insisted that they "did not possess one foot of land in this colony but what was fairly obtained by honest purchase of the Indian proprietors."

This may have been true as far as it went, but in at least one instance, lands bought from the Indians were subsequently resold at a 500 percent profit. In reality, the system cut the Indians out of the emerging New England real estate market. By monopolizing the purchase of Indian lands, Plymouth officials kept the prices they paid artificially low. Instead of selling to the highest bidder, Massasoit was forced to sell his land to the colonial government—and thus was unable to establish what we would call today a fair market price for the one Native commodity, besides the ever dwindling supply of furs, that the English valued.

We have been taught to think of Massasoit as a benevolent and wise leader who maintained a half century of peace in New England. This is, of course, how the English saw it. But many of the Indians who lived in the region undoubtedly had a very different attitude toward a leader whose personal prosperity depended on the systematic dismantling of their homeland.

As their land dwindled, the Pokanokets continued to be afflicted by disease. In 1634, smallpox and influenza ravaged both the Indians and the English in the region. William Brewster, whose family had managed to survive the first terrible winter unscathed, lost two daughters, Love and Patience, now married to Isaac Allerton and Thomas Prence, respectively. For the Native Americans, the smallpox epidemic was, in many ways, worse than the plague of 1616–19. Their skin became so consumed with sores that their flesh adhered to the mats on which they slept. "When they turn them," Bradford wrote, "a whole side will flay off at once as it were, and they will be all of a gore blood, most fearful to behold. . . . [T]hey die like rotten sheep."

And yet, from Massasoit's perspective, his alliance with the English continued to serve him well. In 1632, the Pokanokets' old enemies, the Narragansetts, attacked Sowams. The Pilgrims had recently built a trading post near the village, and Massasoit took refuge in the English structure. Standish rallied to the sachem's defense, and the Pokanokets were soon free to return to their village. The incident at the Sowams trading post appears to have been a pivotal event for Massasoit. As Native Americans customarily did after undergoing a life-altering experience, he changed his name, calling himself Usamequin, meaning yellow feather.

Massasoit had promised on his sickbed always to remember the debt he owed the Pilgrims—particularly to Edward Winslow. And yet, in true sachem fashion, Massasoit never ceased manipulating those around him. In 1634, the year that smallpox swept away so many Indians, he and Winslow were walking together from Sowams to Plymouth. Unbeknownst to his companion, the sachem sent word ahead that Winslow was dead. Massasoit even instructed the messenger to show the residents of Plymouth "how and where [Winslow] was killed."

By this point, Edward and Susanna Winslow had had five children, including seven-year-old Josiah, the future governor of the colony. Needless to say, the Indian messenger's news created great grief in Plymouth. The following day, Massasoit appeared in Plymouth with Winslow by his side. When asked why he had played such a cruel trick on the inhabitants, the sachem replied "that it was their manner to do so, that they might be more welcome when they came home." Winslow may once have saved his life, but that had not prevented the sachem from reminding the Pilgrims that death stalked them all.

Over the course of the next decade, as King Charles and Archbishop Laud made life increasingly difficult for nonconformists in England, an estimated twenty-one thousand Puritan immigrants flooded across New England. With larger, more economically successful colonies flourishing to the north, south, and west, Plymouth had become a backwater.

But if they were now outnumbered, the Pilgrims could take consolation in the fact that the new arrivals shared their belief in a reformed Protestant Church. For the last ten years, the Pilgrims had conducted a virtual laboratory experiment in how an individual congregation, removed from the intrusions of the Church of England, might conduct itself. How much real influence the Pilgrims had on the development of what eventually became the Congregational Church is still subject to debate, but Bradford quite rightly took pride in how he and his little community of believers had laid the groundwork for things to come. "Thus out of small beginnings," he wrote, "greater things have been produced by His hand that made all things of nothing, and gives being to all things that are; and, as one small candle may light a thousand, so the light here kindled hath shone unto many, yea in some sort to our whole nation; let the glorious name of Jehovah have all the praise."

The Puritans staunchly denied it, but their immigration to America

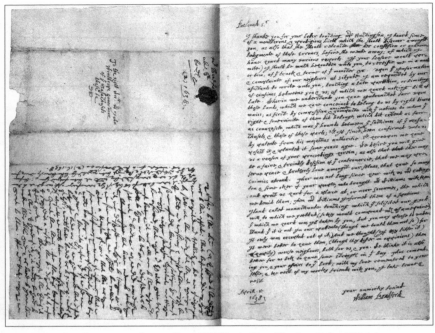

An April 11, 1638, letter from William Bradford to John Winthrop,
with a draft of Winthrop's response on the lower left

had turned them, like the Pilgrims before them, into Separatists. They
might claim to be still working within the Church of England, but as a
practical matter, with no bishops in New England, they were free to
worship as they saw fit. With a clutch of Cambridge-educated divines
scripting their every move, the Puritans of Massachusetts Bay developed a more rigorous set of requirements for church membership than
had been used at Plymouth, where it had been assumed since the days
of John Robinson that only God ultimately knew whether a person was
or was not a Saint. In the years since Robinson's death, the members of
the congregation at Plymouth had resigned themselves to going their
own, often ministerless way in the New World, and in the process they
had become considerably less jealous about guarding their divine
legacy. Now, with the arrival of the Puritans in Massachusetts Bay, it
was up to others to become the spiritual arbiters of New England.

Minimal from the beginning, the religious distinction between the "Pilgrims" and "Puritans" quickly became inconsequential, especially when in 1667 John Cotton, a Harvard-trained minister from Massachusetts Bay, became the pastor at Plymouth. Instead of serving as religious designations, the terms "Puritan" and "Pilgrim" came to signify two different groups of settlers, with the perpetually underfunded Pilgrims and their associates arriving in Plymouth between 1620 and 1630, and the more well-to-do and ambitious Puritans arriving in Massachusetts Bay and Connecticut after 1629.

The influx of Puritan immigrants prompted the Pilgrims to rethink how the government of their settlement was organized, and once again, Plymouth and Massachusetts Bay followed a similar course. By the 1630s, each colony was ruled by its own General Court, which included the governor and his assistants and, after 1638 in the case of Plymouth, deputies from the various towns. In addition to passing laws, levying taxes, and distributing land, the General Court probated wills and heard criminal trials. As it so happened, Plymouth magistrates found themselves presiding over the colony's first murder trial just as the Puritans began to arrive at Boston Harbor.

In the summer of 1630, the profane John Billington fell into an argument with his English neighbor John Newcomen. A few days later, while hunting for deer, Billington happened upon Newcomen and shot him down in cold blood.

Billington had believed, the historian William Hubbard later reported, "that either for want of power to execute for capital offenses, or for want of people to increase the plantation, he should have his life spared." But with the appearance of the Puritans, the dynamics of the region had changed. By the fall, Bradford had already established a rapport with Massachusetts Bay governor John Winthrop, and after consulting with him, Bradford determined that Billington "ought to die, and the land to be purged from blood," and he was executed in September 1630.

That year, the infamous ne'er-do-well Thomas Morton made his way back to Merrymount. Since the settlement was technically in his

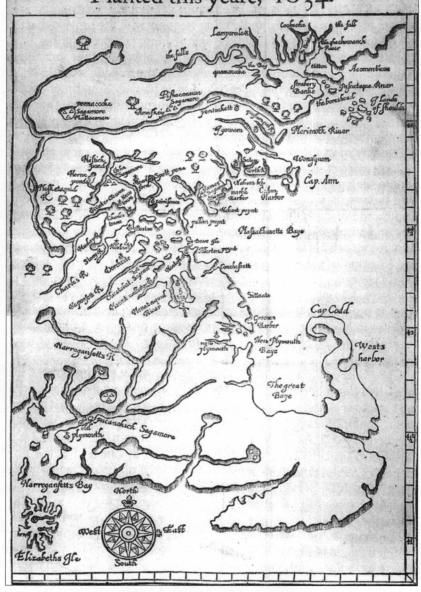

A 1634 map of New England

territory, Winthrop offered to kill two birds with one stone. The Puritans not only arrested Morton, they burned his house to the ground. Evidently, Plymouth and Massachusetts Bay had much in common.

Convinced that they had God on their side, magistrates from both colonies showed no qualms about clamping down on dissent of any kind. In the years ahead, Roger Williams and Anne Hutchinson were cast out of Massachusetts Bay for espousing unorthodox views, and in 1645 Bradford angrily opposed an attempt to institute religious tolerance in Plymouth. Soon after, the Quakers, who began arriving in New England in 1655, were persecuted with a vehemence that climaxed with the hanging of four men and women on Boston Common between 1659 and 1661.

It was the Puritans who led the way in persecuting the Quakers, but the Pilgrims were more than willing to follow along. As a Quaker sympathizer acidly wrote, the "Plymouth-saddle is on the Bay horse," and in 1660 Isaac Robinson, son of the late pastor John Robinson, was disenfranchised for advocating a policy of moderation to the Quakers.

In the beginning, the Puritan settlement to the north proved a financial windfall for the Pilgrims. What the new arrivals wanted more than anything else were cattle and hogs, which the Pilgrims now had in surplus. Over the course of the next decade Plymouth experienced an economic boom fueled, in large part, by the rising price of livestock. Inevitably, however, the grandees of Massachusetts Bay began to cast what Bradford felt was "a covetous eye" on the profitable trading posts Plymouth had established in Maine and Connecticut. As Massachusetts moved into the region with outposts of its own, tensions rose between the Pilgrims and Puritans. But as became increasingly clear, the sheer size of what is now known as the Great Migration meant that Plymouth had no choice but to be shunted aside as it watched dozens of Puritan settlements spring up to the north and south.

It was only a matter of time before Massachusetts Bay's economic ambitions brought the Puritans into conflict with the region's other occupants, the Native Americans. In the lower portion of the Connecticut

River valley lived the Pequots, a tribe whose economic might more than equaled that of the Puritans. When the captains of several English trading vessels were killed by Indians in the region, Massachusetts Bay seized upon the murders as a pretext for launching an attack on the Pequots. In many ways, the Pequot War of 1637 was the Puritans' Wessagussett: a terrifyingly brutal assault that redefined the balance of power in the region for decades to come.

Much as Massasoit had done more than a decade before, a local sachem used the conflict between the Indians and English as an opportunity to advance his own tribe. Prior to the Pequot War, Uncas, sachem of the Mohegans, was a minor player in the region, but after pledging his loyalty to the Puritans, he and his people were on their way to overtaking the Pequots as the most powerful tribe in Connecticut.

The Narragansetts, on the other hand, were less enthusiastic in their support of the English. The Pequots were their traditional enemies, but they were reluctant to join forces with Uncas and the Mohegans. Only after Roger Williams, the new founder of Providence, had personally interceded on Massachusetts Bay's behalf did Narragansett sachem Miantonomi agree to assist the Puritans in a strike against the Pequots.

Led by several veterans of the Thirty Years' War in Europe, the Puritans fell upon a Pequot fortress on the Mystic River. After setting the Indians' wigwams ablaze, the soldiers proceeded to shoot and hack to pieces anyone who attempted to escape the inferno. By the end of the day, approximately four hundred Pequot men, women, and children were dead. "It was a fearful sight to see them thus frying in the fire and the streams of blood quenching the same," Bradford wrote, "and horrible was the stink and scent thereof; but the victory seemed a sweet sacrifice, and they gave the praise thereof to God."

Bradford saw the devastation as the work of the Lord. The Narragansetts, however, saw nothing divine in the slaughter. As Roger Williams observed, Native American warfare was more about the bravery and honor of the combatants than the body count, and usually only a handful of warriors were killed in battle. Prior to the attack on the Pequot fort in Mystic, sachem Miantonomi had attempted to get assurances from Williams that no women and children would be killed.

Unfortunately, Williams, who had been cast out of Massachusetts Bay just two years before, had been unable to extract any concessions from the Puritans. As the flames devoured every living thing in the fortified village, the Narragansetts angrily protested the slaughter, claiming "it is too furious, and slays too many men." With the Pequot War, New England was introduced to the horrors of European-style genocide.

Before the massacre, the Pequots had urged the Narragansetts to join them against the Puritans, claiming that the English would soon "overspread their country" and force them off their own lands. In the years ahead, sachem Miantonomi came to realize that the Pequots had been right. By the late 1630s, when he saw that there were more Puritans in Massachusetts Bay than Native Americans in all of New England, he decided to eliminate the English threat before the Narragansetts suffered the same fate as the Pequots.

In 1642, he traveled to the Montauks on Long Island in hopes of persuading them to join the Narragansetts against the English. To accomplish this, he proposed a truly visionary strategy of pan-Indian cooperation. By laying aside their ancient differences, which the English had exploited so effectively during the Pequot War, the Indians might retake New England. Miantonomi's speech to the Montauks included an insightful account of the ecological endgame that had come to New England: "You know our fathers had plenty of deer and skins, our plains were full of deer, as also our woods, and of turkeys, and our coves full of fish and fowl. But these English having gotten our land, they with scythes cut down the grass, and with axes fell the trees; their cows and horses eat the grass, and their hogs spoil our clam banks, and we shall all be starved." Miantonomi knew from experience that to pick a fight with the Puritans was to fight to the death. He proposed that they employ guerrilla tactics to "kill men, women, and children, but no cows," since the Indians would need the English livestock for food until the deer had increased to precontact levels.

In the end, Miantonomi was unable to follow his own advice. Instead of attacking the English, he attacked Uncas and the Mohegans.

Like Massasoit before him, Uncas had parlayed his allegiance to the English into a sudden and, from the Narragansetts' perspective, most annoying increase in power and influence. Uncas also did his best to undermine rival tribes, and the rumors he spread of Narragansett intrigue did much to worsen the tribe's relations with the English.

By 1643, Miantonomi had had enough of the Mohegans and their upstart sachem. After an assassination plot against Uncas failed, Miantonomi and a thousand of his warriors launched an assault on the Mohegans. Prior to the attack, Miantonomi donned a protective iron corselet. But instead of saving his life, the English armor proved his death sentence. When the fighting turned against the Narragansetts and the sachem was forced to flee, he staggered under the weight of the metal breastplate and was easily taken by the enemy. Uncas might have executed Miantonomi on the spot. But the crafty sachem, who was destined to outlive all of the Native leaders of his generation, recognized an opportunity to ingratiate himself even further with the English.

By 1643, it had become apparent to several prominent New Englanders that Indian-English relations throughout the region needed to be managed in a more coordinated manner. With the rise of Native leaders such as Miantonomi and especially Uncas, who had learned to exploit the needs and fears of both the English and the Indians with Machiavellian sophistication, it was important that the English colonies attempt to act as a unified body. Since the boundaries of the colonies had been in dispute from the beginning, cooperation did not necessarily come naturally to the English. But in 1643, with the troubles between the Mohegans and Narragansetts threatening to spread across the region, the United Colonies of New England came into being. The union included Plymouth, Massachusetts Bay, Connecticut, and New Haven, which would later be absorbed by Connecticut. Each colony sent its own delegation of commissioners to act on its behalf, but only with approval of the individual colonies' General Courts. Noticeably missing from the confederation was Roger Williams's Rhode Island—the only non-Puritan colony in New England.

Edward Winslow appears to have had an important role in creating the United Colonies, a combination for which it is difficult to find an

The seals of Plymouth (left), Massachusetts (below left), and Connecticut (below)

English precedent. In Holland, however, there had been a similar confederation of independent states since 1579, and the Pilgrims may have introduced the concept to their Puritan counterparts from Massachusetts, Connecticut, and New Haven. According to John Quincy Adams, the United Colonies of 1643 was "the model and prototype of the North American Confederacy of 1774," which, in turn, became the basis of the United States. More than a hundred years before the colonies' growing tensions with England provided the impetus to create a confederation, the United Colonies of New England demonstrated the importance of looking beyond local concerns and prejudices. If Miantonomi had succeeded in accomplishing the same kind of combination for the Native Americans of the region, the history of New England might have been very different.

Miantonomi was still in Uncas's custody when the commissioners of the United Colonies met for the first time in Hartford, Connecticut, on September 7, 1643, and Uncas asked the commissioners what he should do with the Narragansett sachem. By appealing to what was for all intents and purposes the Puritan Nation of New England, Uncas had given the Mohegans truly regionwide exposure and influence. After extensive deliberations, the commissioners decided to let Uncas do what he wanted with Miantonomi.

There is evidence that the Narragansett sachem attempted one last bid to unite the Native peoples of New England by proposing that he marry one of Uncas's sisters. It was, however, too late for a reconciliation, and on the path between Hartford and Windsor, Connecticut, Uncas's brother walked up behind Miantonomi and "clave his head with a hatchet." For the time being, the threat of a united Native assault against Puritan and Pilgrim New England had been laid to rest.

CHAPTER ELEVEN

The Ancient Mother

*B*Y THE EARLY 1640s, the Great Migration had come to an end as England was torn apart by civil war. Many settlers returned to England to join in Parliament's efforts to overthrow King Charles's repressive regime. With the king's execution in 1649, England became a Puritan state—unimaginable just a decade before. Bradford felt compelled to turn to an early page in his history of Plymouth and write, "Full little did I think, that the downfall of the bishops, with their courts, canons, and ceremonies, etc. had been so near, when I first began these scribbled writings . . . or that I should have lived to have seen, or hear of the same; but it is the Lord's doing, and ought to be marvelous in our eyes!"

Until this spectacular turn of events, it had been possible for a Puritan to believe that America was where God planned the apocalyptic series of events that would anticipate the millennium. Now it seemed that England was the true center stage, and those who had ventured to the New World were in danger of being left out of the most critical events of their time. In addition to putting Puritan New England's raison d'être into question, the civil war endangered the region's economy. Pilgrims who had watched the prices of their cattle and crops skyrocket over the last decade were suddenly left with a surplus that was worth barely a quarter of what it had commanded in the 1630s. More than a few New Englanders decided that it was time to return to the mother country, and one of those was Edward Winslow.

From the very beginning Winslow had shown a talent for getting what he wanted, whether it was the hand of the widow Susanna White just a few weeks after the death of his own wife or winning back the loyalty of Massasoit. For two and a half decades, he had conducted a kind of shuttle diplomacy between America and England as he spearheaded negotiations with merchants and government officials in London. He was also valued by Massachusetts Bay for his diplomatic savvy, even if some found the peripatetic Pilgrim a little too glib for his own good. Samuel Maverick was an Anglican who had once lived on an island in Boston Harbor, and he later remembered the Pilgrim diplomat as "a smooth tongued cunning fellow."

In 1646, Winslow sailed for England on yet another diplomatic mission. His talents came to the notice of the Puritan regime of Oliver Cromwell, and as happened to Benjamin Franklin in the following century, the Pilgrim diplomat kept postponing his return to America as he became caught up in the historical destiny of his country. To Bradford's bitter regret, Winslow never returned to Plymouth. In 1654, he was named commissioner of a British naval effort against the Spanish in the West Indies; a year later, he succumbed to yellow fever off the island of Jamaica and was buried at sea with full honors. Winslow undoubtedly looked to his final decade in England as his shining hour as a diplomat, but his most significant contribution to British and American history had actually occurred more than thirty years earlier when he became the Englishman Massasoit trusted above all others.

By the time Bradford received word of Winslow's passing, Elder William Brewster had been dead for more than a decade. A year later, in 1656, Miles Standish died in his home in Duxbury.

In 1656, Bradford was sixty-eight years old. According to the patent issued by the Council for New England, he might have become the sole proprietor of the colony back in 1630. Instead, he had shared his rights with those who had come to America during the first years of the colony. Ten years later, in 1640, Bradford and the other "Old Comers" turned the patent over to the colony's freemen.

He had come to America not to establish a great and powerful colony, but to create a tightly knit and godly community. For that to happen, everyone must live together and worship in the same church.

But by the early 1630s it had become apparent that the soil around the original settlement was not the best; many inhabitants, moreover, claimed they needed more land to accommodate the growing herds of cattle. To the governor's dismay, many of his closest associates, including Brewster, Winslow, Standish, and John Alden, left Plymouth to found communities to the north in Duxbury and Marshfield. Thomas Prence, one of the colony's rising stars and who first served as governor in 1634, also moved to Duxbury, then helped found the town of Eastham on Cape Cod. Although he didn't arrive in New England until the 1630s, John Brown was one of the colony's wealthier inhabitants. He would probably have joined the Puritans in Massachusetts Bay had not a meeting with John Robinson in Leiden in the 1620s caused him to choose Plymouth instead. In 1640, Brown helped found the town of Taunton; by 1645 he had moved to Wannamoisett (in the vicinity of modern Barrington, Rhode Island), which became a part of Swansea in 1667. By that time Brown had long since been joined by his son James and his son-in-law Thomas Willett, who established a prosperous trade with the Dutch in Manhattan.

At the root of this trend toward town building was, Governor Bradford insisted, a growing hunger for land. For Bradford, land had been a way to create a community of Saints. For an increasing number of Pilgrims and especially for their children, land was a way to get rich. Bradford claimed that the formation of new towns was "not for want or necessity," but "for the enriching of themselves," and he predicted it would be "the ruin of New England." Even Roger Williams, whose vision of an ideal community was very different from Bradford's, shared his concern about land. Williams railed against the rise of "God Land" in New England and feared that it would become "as great with us English as God Gold was with the Spaniards."

It was difficult for Bradford not to take the exodus of Winslow, Brewster, and the others as a personal affront. For as the new towns prospered and grew, Plymouth, the village with which it had all begun, fell on hard times. "And thus was this poor church left," Bradford wrote, "like an ancient mother grown old and forsaken of her children. . . . Thus, she that had made many rich became herself poor."

Despite Bradford's lament, his vision of a compact, self-contained community of fellow worshippers remained the organizing principle behind each of the colony's new towns. In 1652, Plymouth magistrates admonished one Joseph Ramsden for locating his house "remotely in the woods from his neighbors" and ordered him "to bring his wife and family with all convenient speed, near unto some neighborhood."

A settler in a typical town in Plymouth Colony in the 1650s received a house lot that ranged from just a single acre to as much as twenty, depending on his social standing. Instead of the tiny wattle-and-daub cottages constructed by the original Pilgrims, the subsequent generation built post-and-beam structures covered with clapboards and shingles and anchored by mammoth brick chimneys.

It took a tremendous amount of lumber to build one of these houses—even a modest house required at least twelve tons of wood. Just as daunting were the heating requirements of the home's open hearth. It's been estimated that the average seventeenth-century New England house consumed fifteen cords, or 1,920 cubic feet, of wood per year, meaning that a town of two hundred homes depended on the deforestation of as many as seventy-five acres per year.

As the number of towns grew, the character of the colony inevitably began to change, and from Governor Bradford's perspective, it was not for the good. The influx of newcomers made it increasingly difficult to ensure the colony's moral purity. Even worse than the cases of premarital sex and adultery were, according to Bradford, those of "sodomy and buggery." In 1642, seventeen-year-old Thomas Granger, a servant to "an honest man of Duxbury," was convicted of having sexual relations with "a mare, a cow, two goats, five sheep, two calves and a turkey." Taking their lead from Leviticus, Bradford and his fellow magistrates executed Granger on September 8, 1642, but not until the boy had witnessed the killing of his animal paramours, which were all buried in a pit. Bradford speculated that "Satan hath more power in these heathen lands," but he also feared that a pernicious complacency had infected the colony.

In 1655, Governor Bradford delivered an ultimatum. If his subordinates did not do something to improve the spiritual state of the colony, he must resign his office. Promises were made, and Bradford continued on as governor, but that did not prevent a profound despair from overtaking him in his final years. Late in life Bradford looked back on the manuscript pages of his history of the colony. Beside a copy of a letter written by Pastor Robinson and Elder Brewster back in 1617, in which they referred to their congregation's "most strict and sacred bond," Bradford wrote, "I have been happy in my first times, to see, and with much comfort to enjoy, the blessed fruits of this sweet communion, but it is now a part of my misery in old age, to find and feel the decay, and . . . with grief and sorrow of heart to lament and bewail the same."

There may have been another dimension to Bradford's sadness—a sadness that reached back to his decision in 1620 to leave his son John in Holland. After his second marriage in 1623, Bradford and his wife Alice had been blessed with three children: William junior, born in 1624; Mercy in 1627; and Joseph in 1630. Bradford adopted Alice's two sons, Constant and Thomas Southworth, as well as eighteen-year-old Thomas Cushman when his father, Robert, died at about the same time as Robinson's death in 1625. Other members of Bradford's extended family included the boys Nathaniel Morton, Joseph Rogers, and William Latham. But as late as 1627 there was one missing member. John, Bradford's son from his first marriage with Dorothy, was still in Europe. By the time he finally did join his father, John was eleven years old; he had been just three when he had last seen his parents, and he must have had little memory of his father.

Bradford's stepson Nathaniel Morton was almost precisely John's age. But while Morton became the governor's right-hand man in the years ahead, John, his firstborn, drifted, eventually moving to Norwich, Connecticut—about as far away from the home of his famous father as it was possible for a New Englander to get.

No one knew what the future held, but Bradford had his suspicions. If New England continued its "degenerate" ways, God would surely wreak his vengeance. In Bradford's view, the seeds for this terrible apocalypse had been sown more than thirty years before, when Thomas

Morton of Merrymount had begun selling guns to the Indians. Almost immediately, the Natives had become more effective huntsmen than the English "by reason of their swiftness of foot and nimbleness of body, being also quick-sighted and by continual exercise well knowing the haunts of all sorts of game." They were also quick to master the mechanical aspects of operating a musket and were soon able to perform their own repairs and manufacture their own lead bullets.

The conservatism of the English made it difficult for them to abandon their old and cumbersome matchlock muskets for the newer flintlocks. The Indians, on the other hand, knew from the start that they wanted only flintlocks. "[T]hey became mad (as it were) after them," Bradford wrote, "and would not stick to give any price they could attain to for them; accounting their bows and arrows but baubles in comparison of them." Suddenly the English were no longer the technological superiors of the Native Americans, and when they happened on "the Indians in the woods armed with guns in this sort, it was a terror unto them."

Over time, however, the English became accustomed to the sight of an Indian with a gun. Indians armed with flintlocks brought in more game and furs to English trading posts. And besides, if the Indians did not get their weapons from the English, they could easily buy them from the French and the Dutch. Selling guns and ammunition was a highly profitable business, and Plymouth magistrates eventually came to sanction the exchange.

From Governor Bradford's perspective, the arming of the Indians was just another symptom of the alarming complacency that had gripped his colony. New England was headed for a fall. And it was the gun-toting Indians who would be "the rod" with which the Lord punished his people:

> For these fierce natives, they are now so fill'd
> With guns and muskets, and in them so skill'd
> As that they may keep the English in awe,
> And when they please, give unto them the law.

* * *

The last days of Bradford's life were spent in what might seem a strange pursuit for the governor of a New England colony: studying Hebrew. He yearned to have as direct a connection as possible with the word of God, and to do that, he must learn the language in which the Bible was originally written. The initial pages of his Plymouth history are filled with a doodlelike scrawl of Hebrew words and phrases. "Though I am grown aged," he wrote, "yet I have had a longing desire to see with my own eyes, something of that most ancient language and holy tongue, in which the law and oracles of God were written. . . . And though I cannot attain to much herein, yet I am refreshed, to have seen some glimpse hereof; (as Moses saw the Land of Canaan afar off)." The community of Saints he had hoped to create in New England had never come to be, but Bradford had earned at least a glimpse of another kind of Promised Land.

In the winter of 1657, Bradford began to feel unwell. His health continued to decline until early May, when a sudden and marvelous change came upon him. All God-fearing Puritans were in search of evidence that they were among the elect. On the morning of May 8, Bradford's doubts and worries were answered with a startling certitude: "[T]he God of heaven so filled his mind with ineffable consolations," Cotton Mather wrote, "that he seemed little short of Paul, rapt up unto the unutterable entertainments of Paradise." Here at long last was proof that his journey through life was to be crowned by redemption. That morning he told those gathered around his sickbed that "the good spirit of God had given him a pledge of happiness in another world, and the first-fruits of his eternal glory." He died the next day, "lamented by all the colonies of New England, as a common blessing and father to them all."

In 1913, a gravel-mining operation in Warren, Rhode Island, uncovered an Indian burial ground. Known as Burr's Hill, the site was in the vicinity of the Pokanokets' ancestral village at Sowams and contained forty-two graves, many of which dated back to the middle of the seventeenth century. The artifacts collected from the graves provide fascinating evidence of the degree to which Western goods had become a part of the Indians' lives. Accompanying the dead, who were buried on their sides with their heads pointed to the southwest, was a stunning array of objects: in addition to traditional Native artifacts such as arrowheads, amulets, and steatite pipes were wine bottles, muskets, spoons, iron axes, kettles, bells, wool blankets, combs, scissors, hammers, horseshoes, locks, keys, hinges, knives, pewter bowls, swords, leather shoes, and a Jew's harp.

One of the graves at Burr's Hill contained a noticeably richer assortment of objects than the others. Included among the grave goods was a necklace made of copper. In the summer of 1621, Edward Winslow had traveled to Sowams and presented Massasoit with a "copper chain." Although no one will ever know who was actually buried in the grave, archaeologists have speculated that this might be the Pilgrim necklace.

When the Indians had first come in contact with the English, they had been, by all accounts, awed and amazed by the *things* the Europeans had brought with them. "They do much extol and wonder at the English for their strange inventions," William Wood wrote. Whether it was an iron plow, a musket, or a windmill, the Indians ascribed to these "strange inventions" a spiritual power known as manit. "[T]here is a general custom amongst them," Roger Williams wrote, "at the apprehension of any excellency in men, women, birds, fish, etc., to cry out *manitoo*, that is, 'It is a God.' . . . [W]hen they talk amongst themselves of the English ships, and great buildings, of the plowing of their fields, and especially of books and letters, they will end thus: *Mannitowock:* 'They are Gods.' "

Massasoit had come to know the English too well to regard them as anything but men and women, but as the objects collected at Burr's Hill attest, the sachem and his people continued to value the remarkable wealth of material goods the English had brought to America. In the forty years since the voyage of the *Mayflower,* the Native Americans had experienced wrenching change, but they had also managed to create a new, richly adaptive culture that continued to draw strength from traditional ways. The Pokanokets still hunted much as their fathers had done, but instead of bows and arrows they now used the latest flintlock muskets; inside their wigwams made of reed mats and tree bark were English-manufactured chests in which they kept bracelets, signet rings, and strings of wampum beads. Attached to their buckskin breeches were brass bells that tinkled as they walked; and when they died, their loved ones made sure that the mysterious power of these objects went with them to the afterlife.

Given the spirituality of the Native Americans, it was perhaps inevitable that many of them also showed an interest in the Englishmen's religion. The Pilgrims had done little to convert the Indians to Christianity, but for the Puritans of Massachusetts it was, or so they told themselves, a priority from the start. The colony's seal, created even before their arrival in the New World, depicted a Native American saying, "Come over and help us." The Puritans believed a Christian must be able to read God's word in the Bible, and early on, efforts were made to teach the Indians how to read and write. A handful of Native Americans even attended the newly founded Harvard College. In the 1650s, the missionary John Eliot undertook the momentous task of translating the entire Old and New Testaments into a phonetic version of the Massachusetts language, titled *Mamusse Wanneetupanatamwe Up-Biblum God.*

Eliot created a series of self-contained Native communities known as Praying Towns. In addition to indoctrinating the Indians in Christianity, Eliot hoped to wean them from their traditional ways. But as was true with their use of Western farm utensils and jewelry, the Indians never wholly abandoned their former identities. Instead, they did as all spiritual people do—they created their own personal relationship with God.

For years to come, Praying Indians on Nantucket Island concluded each Sunday's meeting with a ritual that dated back to long before the *Mayflower:* "And when the meeting was done, they would take their tinder-box and strike fire and light their pipes, and, may be, would draw three or four whiffs and swallow the smoke, and then blow it out of their noses, and so hand their pipes to their next neighbor. . . . And they would say 'tawpoot,' which is, 'I thank ye.' It seemed to be done in a way of kindness to each other." Instead of replacing the old ways, Christianity became, for many Indians, the means by which traditional Native culture found a way to endure.

For a sachem in the seventeenth century, however, Christianity was a tremendously destabilizing influence that threatened the very under-pinnings of his tribe's traditions and his own power and prosperity. As increasing numbers of Indians turned to God, there were fewer left to supply the sachem with the steady stream of tribute on which he had come to depend. At one point, Massasoit ventured out to Martha's Vineyard and spoke with some of the new converts. According to John Eliot, "he inquired what earthly good things came along with [their conversion], and . . . one of them replied, 'We serve not God for cloth-ing, nor for any outward thing.' "

It probably came as no surprise to Massasoit that the Indians on Cape Cod and the islands proved particularly receptive to Christianity. Back in 1623, he had implicated them in the plot against the Pilgrims, and in the traumatic aftermath of the raid on Wessagussett just about every sachem on the Cape had died. By declaring their allegiance to the English god, the Indians from this region succeeded in distancing themselves from the supreme sachem who had once betrayed them.

Massasoit's distrust of Christianity was so great that he attempted to attach a stipulation to one of his final land sales: that the missionaries stop converting his people. Not surprisingly, the English refused to agree to his terms, and in the end, the aged sachem decided not to "fur-ther urge it."

When it came to borrowing from the English, the Indians had demon-strated tremendous creativity and enthusiasm. The English, on the other hand, were much more reluctant to borrow from the Indians. The American wilderness, they thought, was inimical to the godly virtues of order and control.

Yet, despite their best efforts to keep the Indians and their culture at arm's length, the English inevitably began to adopt Native ways, par-ticularly when it came to food. Ever since the Pilgrims stumbled across a cache of seed on Cape Cod, maize had become an essential part of every New Englander's diet. It has been estimated that the Indians consumed between 280 and 340 pounds of corn per person per year, and the English were not far behind. Hominy and johnnycakes were adaptations of Native recipes. Over the years, the English pottage that Massasoit had craved on his sickbed had become more like the Indians' own succotash: a soupy mishmash of corn, beans, and whatever fish and meat were available. When it came to harvesting corn, the English adopted the Native husking bee, a communal tradition in which a young man who came across a red ear of corn was allowed to demand a kiss from the girl of his choosing.

Following the lead of the Dutch in New Netherland, the English used the Indians' finely crafted shell beads as a form of currency. Wampum consisted of strings of cylindrical beads made either from white periwinkle shells or the blue portion of quahog shells, with the purple beads being worth approximately twice as much as the white beads. To be accepted in trade, wampum had to meet scrupulous specifications, and both the Indians and the English became expert in identifying whether or not the beads had been properly cut, shaped, polished, drilled, and strung. A fathom of wampum contained about three hundred beads, which were joined to other strands to create belts that varied between one and five inches in width. When credit became difficult to obtain from England during the depression of the 1640s, the colonies eased the financial burden in New England by using wampum as legal tender. In this instance, the Indians had provided the English with a uniquely American way to do business.

When the Pilgrims had first settled at Plymouth, there had been forty miles between them and Massasoit's village at Sowams. By 1655, there were just a few miles between the Pokanokets' headquarters and the closest English homes clustered at Wannamoisett. There was no "frontier," no clear-cut division between civilization and wilderness. Instead, the boundaries were convoluted and blurred—particularly in Plymouth, the smallest of the Puritan colonies, where the towns tended to be more "straggling" than in Massachusetts Bay and Connecticut and where there was a higher concentration of Native Americans. An intimacy existed between the English and Indians that would have been almost unimaginable to subsequent generations of Americans. The English hired their Indian neighbors as farm hands; they traded with them for fish and game. Inevitably, a pidgin of English-Indian languages developed, and it became second nature for an Englishman to greet a Native acquaintance as "netop" or friend.

But Plymouth Colony was, by no means, a utopia of cross-cultural exchange and cooperation. Intermarriage between the two races was virtually nonexistent, and without children to provide them with a genetic and cultural common ground, the Indians and English would always have difficulty understanding each other's point of view. In the end, the two peoples remained enigmas to one another.

In 1638, Arthur Peach, a veteran of the Pequot War, and three indentured servants attacked and robbed an Indian returning from a trading expedition to Boston. Peach stabbed the Indian with his rapier, and after taking his wampum and cloth, he and his friends left their victim for dead. The Indian lived on for a few days, however, and identified his attackers, who were brought to Plymouth for trial.

According to Roger Williams, the murder put the region in a "great hubbub." Many of the Narragansetts feared that the attack heralded the beginning "of a general slaughter of the natives," and one sachem warned "the English [should] be careful on the highway." The Pokanokets, on the other hand, had a different perspective on the murder. Massasoit pointed out that Peach had once worked for his friend Edward Winslow. Even though Massasoit felt that Peach was guilty, he told Roger Williams that the murderer should be reprieved, "for he was Mr. Winslow's man." Massasoit also claimed that since the victim had been a Nipmuck Indian from the interior portion of New England and was therefore less "worthy," it was wrong that "another man should die for him."

When the case came to trial on September 4, 1638, Massasoit and several Narragansett sachems, as well as the Indian friends of the murdered man, were in attendance. Bradford reported that some of the English, who were of "the rude and ignorant sort," grumbled that it was wrong for a white man to die for killing an Indian. But the jury saw otherwise, and Peach and his cohorts were found guilty and hanged, "which gave [the Indians] and all the country good satisfaction," Bradford reported.

The Indians and English might be strangers to one another, but at the midpoint of the seventeenth century they did the best they could to settle their differences. As they all understood, it was the only way to avoid a war.

In the fall of 1657, a few months after the death of William Bradford, Massasoit, now approaching eighty years of age, signed his last Plymouth land deed. At the bottom of the parchment he sketched an intricate pictogram. What looks to be the upper portion of a man floats above what could be his legs with only a wavy line connecting the two. Whatever it actually portrays, the pictogram conveys a sense of distance and removal. With this deed, Massasoit disappears from the records of Plymouth Colony, only to reappear in the records of Massachusetts Bay as leader of the Quabaugs, a subgroup of the Nipmucks based in modern Brookfield, Massachusetts, more than fifty-five miles northwest of Pokanoket.

Massasoit's pictogram from a 1657 land deed

For years, the Pokanokets had maintained a close relationship with the Quabaugs, who lived with other subgroups of the Nipmucks amid the rivers and lakes between the Connecticut River to the west and the English settlements outside Boston to the east. As early as 1637, Massasoit came before officials in Boston as leader of the Quabaugs, and some historians have speculated that twenty years later, in 1657, he took up permanent residence among them. The move not only distanced the old sachem from the unrelenting pressures of Plymouth, it gave his eldest son, Wamsutta, who was approaching forty years of age, a chance to establish himself as the Pokanokets' new leader.

Wamsutta had already begun to show signs of independence. In 1654, he sold Hog Island in Narragansett Bay to the Rhode Islander

Richard Smith without the written approval of either his father or the Plymouth magistrates. Three years later, Smith appeared in Plymouth court claiming that "he knew not any ban . . . prohibiting him purchasing of the lands of the Natives till of late." Begrudgingly, the court allowed Smith to keep his island as long he agreed to "stand bound unto the government and court of New Plymouth." Massasoit's belated endorsement of the sale, signed on September 21, 1657, seems to have signaled the old sachem's departure from the colony.

Just a few months later, his son refused to part with a portion of the land his father had agreed to sell to the town of Taunton. Displaying a contentiousness that came to define his all-too-brief relationship with the Plymouth authorities, Wamsutta proclaimed that he was unwilling to surrender lands that the proprietors "say is granted by the court of Plymouth." Named as a witness to the document is John Sassamon— an Indian who represented everything Massasoit had come to fear and distrust.

John Sassamon had been one of the missionary John Eliot's star pupils. He had learned to read and write English, and in 1653 he attended Harvard College. For years, he had worked in Eliot's mission, and now he was Wamsutta's interpreter and scribe. In the spring of 1660, perhaps at Sassamon's urging, Wamsutta appeared before the Plymouth court—not to ratify a sale of land but to change his name. The record reads:

> At the earnest request of Wamsutta, desiring that in regard his father is lately deceased, and he being desirous, according to the custom of the natives, to change his name, that the Court would confer an English name upon him, which accordingly they did, and therefore ordered, that for the future he shall be called by the name of Alexander of Pokanoket; and desiring the same in the behalf of his brother, they have named him Philip.

From that day forward, Massasoit's sons were known, at their own request, by Christian names. It was a new era.

* * *

Except for his son's mention of his death in the Plymouth records, we know nothing about the circumstances of Massasoit's passing. It is difficult to believe that he could be buried anywhere but Pokanoket. One thing we do know is that late in life he began to share Governor Bradford's concerns about the future. At some point before his death, he took his two sons, still known by their Native names of Wamsutta and Metacom, to the home of John Brown in nearby Wannamoisett. There, in the presence of Brown and his family, Massasoit stated his hope "that there might be love and amity after his death, between his sons and them, as there had been betwixt himself and them in former times."

It was somewhat unusual that Massasoit had chosen to make this pronouncement not in the presence of Bradford's successor as governor, Thomas Prence, but in the home of an English neighbor. But as the sachem undoubtedly realized, if conflicts should one day arise between his people and the English, it was here, in the borderlands between Plymouth and Pokanoket, where the trouble would begin.

CHAPTER TWELVE

The Trial

*T*HE PILGRIMS HAD BEEN DRIVEN by fiercely held spiritual beliefs. They had sailed across a vast and dangerous ocean to a wilderness where, against impossible odds, they had made a home. The purity of the Old Comers' purpose and the magnitude of their accomplishments could never again be repeated.

From the start, the second generation suffered under the assumption that, as their ministers never tired of reminding them, they were "the degenerate plant of a strange vine." Where their mothers and fathers had once stood before their congregations and testified to the working of grace within them, the children of the Saints felt no such fervor.

By 1660, church membership in Massachusetts Bay had so lapsed that a group of ministers instituted the Half-Way Covenant, an easing of the requirements for membership intended to boost the number of communicants. The Plymouth church did not adopt the Half-Way Covenant until the following century (in part because its rules concerning church membership were less stringent than the Puritans' requirements in Massachusetts Bay). The fact remained, however, that as Governor Bradford had complained, the spiritual life of Plymouth, along with all the colonies of New England, had declined to the point that God must one day show his displeasure. For the children of the Saints, it would be impossible not to see the calamities ahead as the judgment of the Lord.

Instead of the afterlife, it was the material rewards of *this* life that increasingly became the focus of the Pilgrims' children and grandchildren. Most Plymouth residents were farmers, but there was much more than agriculture driving the New England economy. The demand for fish, timber, grain, and cattle in Europe, the West Indies, and beyond was insatiable, and by the midpoint of the century, New England merchants had established the pattern of transatlantic trade that existed right up to the American Revolution.

To take full advantage of this lucrative trade, a colony needed a port, and Boston quickly emerged as the economic center of the region. The Pilgrims' decision to remain at their shallow anchorage doomed Plymouth to becoming the poorest of the New England colonies. But there was always the teasing possibility of economic redemption. On the west shore of the Mount Hope Peninsula, just to the south of the Pokanoket village of Sowams, was a large, deep, and well-protected harbor. However, back in 1640, Plymouth officials had set aside the entire Mount Hope Peninsula, along with the territory known as Pocasset on the east shore of Mount Hope Bay, as an Indian reserve. At least for now, the future site of Bristol, Rhode Island, was off-limits to the English.

Throughout the first half of the seventeenth century, New England had been left to do pretty much as it pleased. Unlike Virginia, there had never been a royal governor in the northern colonies, and with the outbreak of the English civil war, Puritan New England had enjoyed the benefit of a sympathetic government back in the mother country.

Then, in 1660, New England's long-standing autonomy suddenly seemed in jeopardy. With the downfall of the Cromwell regime came the restoration of King Charles II. Since his father had been beheaded by Puritan revolutionaries, the new monarch was not inclined to look favorably on New England. But Charles's initial interest in America lay elsewhere. The collapse of the wampum trade in America combined with the recent defeat of the Dutch navy in Europe had left the Dutch colony of New Netherland vulnerable, and Charles dispatched royal commissioners to oversee the conquest of the rival colony in 1664.

Several merchants in Plymouth traded with the Dutch colony but none was more closely linked with New Netherland than Thomas Willett. Willett had served his apprenticeship at the Plymouth trading post in Penobscot, Maine. He had then married the daughter of Massasoit's confidant John Brown and moved with his father-in-law to Wannamoisett. In addition to being experienced in working with the Indians, Willett, who had immigrated to America from Leiden, was fluent in Dutch. By the 1660s he had established a lucrative trade with New Netherland, and one of the king's commissioners may have had him in mind when he referred to the inhabitants of Plymouth Colony as "mongrel Dutch." It was not surprising, then, that once New Netherland became New York in a bloodless takeover in 1664, Willett became Manhattan's first English mayor.

The increasing amount of time Willett spent in Manhattan soon became a problem for Massasoit's son and heir, Alexander. Since he lived so close to the Pokanokets, Willett had no choice but to develop a good relationship with the Indians, and he appears to have become for Alexander what Edward Winslow had been for Massasoit: the Englishman he trusted above all others.

Willett had inherited Miles Standish's role as the colony's chief military officer. But by 1662, he had been replaced by Edward Winslow's thirty-three-year-old son Josiah. Despite his young age, Josiah was well on his way to becoming Plymouth's most distinguished citizen. One of the few Plymouth residents to have attended Harvard College, he had married the beautiful Penelope Pelham, daughter of Harvard treasurer and assistant governor of Massachusetts Herbert Pelham. A portrait painted in 1651 when Josiah was visiting his father in England depicts a young man with a handsome, somewhat supercilious face and a shoulder-length shock of reddish brown hair. By the 1660s, Josiah and Penelope had taken up residence in Careswell, the Winslow family estate in Marshfield that was named for the home of Josiah's great-grandfather back in England.

Winslow had the polish of an English gentleman, but he had been born in America. Being Edward Winslow's son, he had come to know the Indians well. But from the beginning of his public career, Josiah had a very different relationship with the leadership of the Pokanokets.

By the 1660s, the English no longer felt that their survival depended on the support of the Indians; instead, many colonists, particularly the younger ones, saw the Indians as an impediment to their future

Penelope and Josiah Winslow in 1651

prosperity. No longer mindful of the debt they owed the Pokanokets, without whom their parents would never have endured their first year in America, some of the Pilgrims' children were less willing to treat Native leaders with the tolerance and respect their parents had once afforded Massasoit.

For his part, Alexander had demonstrated a combativeness of his own. Even before his father's death, he had ignored Massasoit's agreement with the colony and sold Hog Island to the Rhode Islander Richard Smith. Then, in the spring of 1662, word reached Plymouth that Alexander had done it again. He had illegally sold land to yet another Rhode Islander.

Ever since Master Jones's decision to sail for Cape Cod instead of the Hudson River, Plymouth's patent had been less ironclad than its magistrates would have liked, despite repeated efforts to secure a new charter from the king. But even if Plymouth's paperwork had all been in order, she would still have been subjected to the border disputes that plagued all the colonies. It was true that the United Colonies of New England had been created, in part, to address this problem, but Rhode Island was not part of the confederation. Plymouth could not allow

Alexander to continue selling land to Rhode Islanders and summoned him to appear.

There were also unsettling rumors that the sachem had spoken with the Narragansetts about joining forces against the English. When Alexander failed to appear in court as promised, Governor Thomas Prence instructed Major Josiah Winslow to bring him in.

Winslow headed out in July of 1662 with ten well-armed men, all of them on horseback, trotting along the same old Indian trail that their forefathers had once walked to Pokanoket. They were in the vicinity of Nemasket, fifteen miles inland from Plymouth, when they learned that Alexander happened to be just a few miles away at a hunting and fishing lodge on Monponsett Pond in modern Halifax, Massachusetts.

It was still morning when Winslow and his men arrived at the Indians' camp. They found the sachem and about ten others, including his wife Weetamoo, eating their breakfast inside a wigwam, with their muskets left outside in plain view. Winslow ordered his men to seize the weapons and to surround the wigwam. He then went inside to have it out with Alexander.

The Pokanoket sachem spoke to Winslow through an interpreter, John Sassamon's brother Rowland, and as the exchange became more heated, the major insisted that they move the conversation outside. Alexander was outraged that Plymouth officials had chosen to treat him in such a condescending and peremptory manner. If there had been any truth to the rumor of a conspiracy would he be here, casually fishing at Monponsett Pond?

Winslow reminded the sachem that he had neglected to appear, as promised, before the Plymouth court. Alexander explained that he had been waiting for his friend Thomas Willet to return from Manhattan so that he could speak to him about the matter.

By this point, Alexander had worked himself into a raging fury. Winslow took out his pistol, held the weapon to the sachem's breast, and said, "I have been ordered to bring you to Plymouth, and by the help of God I will do it."

Understandably stunned, Alexander was on the verge of an even more violent outburst, when Sassamon asked that he be given the chance to speak to his sachem alone. After a few minutes of tense conversation, it was announced that Alexander had agreed to go with Winslow, but only as long as "he might go like a sachem"—in the company of his attendants.

It was a hot summer day, and Winslow offered Alexander the use of one of their horses. Since his wife and the others must walk, the sachem said that "he could go on foot as well as they," provided that the English maintained a reasonable pace. In the meantime, Winslow sent a messenger ahead to organize a hasty meeting of the magistrates in Duxbury.

The meeting seems to have done much to calm passions on both sides. What happened next is somewhat unclear, but soon after the conference, Alexander and his entourage spent a night at Winslow's house in Marshfield, where the sachem suddenly fell ill. One contemporary historian claimed that it was Alexander's "choler and indignation that . . . put him into a fever." More recently, a medical doctor has hypothesized that the sachem may have been suffering from appendicitis. Whatever the case, a surgeon was called for and gave Alexander a "working physic," a strong purgative that would only have exacerbated his condition if he was indeed suffering from an irritated appendix. The sachem's attendants asked that they be allowed to take him back to Mount Hope. Permission was granted, and Alexander's men carried him on their shoulders till they reached the Taunton River in Middleborough. From there he was transported by canoe back to Mount Hope, where he died a few days later.

It was an astonishing and disturbing sequence of events that put into bold relief just where matters stood between the English and Indians in Plymouth Colony. In 1623, Edward Winslow had earned Massasoit's undying love by doing everything in his power—even scraping the sachem's furred mouth—to save his life. Thirty-nine years later, Winslow's son had burst into Alexander's wigwam, brandishing a pistol. Within a week, the Pokanoket leader was dead.

In years to come, the rumors would abound: that Alexander had been marched unmercifully under the burning summer sun until he had sickened and died; that he had been thrown in jail and starved to death. In an effort to counter such hearsay, one of the men who'd accompanied Winslow—William Bradford's son William junior— provided an account of the incident in which he insisted that Alexander had accompanied Winslow "freely and readily."

Alexander's younger brother Philip, on the other hand, became convinced that Winslow had poisoned the sachem. Indeed, Philip's hatred of the Plymouth military officer became so notorious that once war did erupt, Winslow felt compelled to send his wife and children to Salem while he transformed his home at Marshfield into an armed fortress. Intentionally or not, Winslow had lit the slow-burning fuse that would one day ignite New England.

For days, hundreds, perhaps thousands of Indians gathered at Mount Hope to mourn the passing of Alexander. Then the despair turned to joy as the crowds celebrated Philip's rise to supreme sachem of the Pokanokets.

On the eastern shore of Mount Hope is the huge outcropping of rock from which the peninsula gets its name. More than three hundred

Approaching Mount Hope from the south

feet high, Mount Hope provides panoramic views of Narragansett and Mount Hope bays. It is a towering, majestic chunk of gneiss and quartz that puts the relatively minuscule Plymouth Rock to shame.

There is a legend that Philip once stood upon the summit of Mount Hope and, turning west, hurled a stone all the way across the peninsula to Poppasquash Neck more than two miles away. It is a tradition that reflects the sense of power and strength that many Pokanokets may have projected upon their new leader, who was just twenty-four years old in August 1662. That summer, the "flocking multitudes" at Mount Hope became so uproarious that the Plymouth magistrates feared Philip had convened a council of war. Only a few weeks after hauling his brother into court, Governor Prence made the same demand of Philip.

The young sachem who appeared at Plymouth on August 6, 1662, was not about to cower before the English. As Philip made clear in the years ahead, he considered himself on equal terms with none other than Charles II. All others—including Governor Prence and the deceitful Major Josiah Winslow—were "but subjects" of the king of England and unfit to tell a fellow monarch what to do. Philip's "ambitious and haughty" demeanor at the Plymouth court that day moved one observer to refer to him mockingly as "King Philip"—a nickname he never claimed for himself but that followed the sachem into history.

No matter how self-possessed Philip appeared that day in court, he knew that now was not the time to accuse the English of murdering his brother. Alexander's death had thrust him into a difficult and completely unexpected situation. If Philip truly suspected that his brother had been assassinated, he must have believed that Alexander's boldness had gotten him killed. Philip was young enough to be his late brother's son. He had no choice but to be very careful, particularly in the early days of his sachemship.

Instead of indignantly accusing Winslow of murdering his brother—something he did not say openly to an Englishman until near the outbreak of hostilities thirteen years later—Philip told the members of the court exactly what they wanted to hear. He promised that the "ancient covenant" that had existed between his father and Plymouth remained inviolate. He even offered his younger brother as a hostage if it might ease the magistrates' concerns, but it was decided that this was not necessary. As far as Governor Prence was concerned, relations with the Indians were once again back to normal.

Over the next few years, as Philip settled into his new role as leader of the Pokanokets, New England grew more and more crowded. Both the English and the Indians depended on agriculture, and only about 20 percent of the land was suitable for farming. Adding to the pressure for land was the rapid rise of the English population. The first genera-tion of settlers had averaged an astonishing seven to eight children per family, and by the 1660s those children wanted farms of their own.

The English were not the only ones whose world was changing. The Indians of Philip's generation had grown up amid the boom times of the fur trade and had come to regard expensive Western goods as an es-sential part of their lives. But now, with the virtual extinction of the beaver, the devaluation of wampum, and the loss of so much land, this new generation of Native Americans was beginning to confront a future of radically diminished opportunities.

The pressure was particularly intense in Plymouth. Unlike Massa-chusetts Bay and Connecticut, which had large hinterlands, the Indi-ans and English in Plymouth had almost nowhere left to go. Pushed south to the neck of Mount Hope, Philip and his people were hemmed in from almost every side. Looking out from the summit of Mount Hope, Philip could see chimney smoke from the houses of the English to the north in Wannamoisett; to the south, just a half mile from the tip of Mount Hope was Rhode Island (known today as Aquidneck Island), home to the thriving English settlements of Portsmouth and Newport. Off in the distance to the west were the Narragansetts; closer to home was Hog Island, which, thanks to his brother Alexander, had become a part of Portsmouth, Rhode Island, back in 1654. Philip's only relief came when he looked east across Mount Hope Bay to Pocasset in modern Tiverton, Rhode Island, the homeland of Weetamoo, Alexan-der's widow and the "Squaw Sachem" of Pocasset.

Adding to the Pokanokets' growing sense of claustrophobia were the Englishmen's livestock. Domesticated creatures such as cattle, horses, sheep, goats, and pigs were constantly straying off English farms and feasting on the Indians' corn. Despite attempts to address the Indians' complaints (a fence was built across the northern edge of Mount Hope), livestock remained a major irritant in English-Native relations.

But if Philip had inherited a diminished and pressure-filled world, he proved remarkably resourceful in making the most of what was available to him. Yes, the Englishmen's livestock were a nuisance. Well, then Philip would get cattle of his own. In 1665 he acquired a horse; in 1669, his large herd of hogs got him in trouble with the proprietors of Portsmouth, Rhode Island. Philip had the audacity to ferry his pigs out to Hog Island. His brother had sold the island fifteen years ago, but to Philip's mind it was just the place for his swine to forage.

As Philip knew, losing land had the most direct impact on the well-being of his people. If the Pokanokets were to survive as an independent entity, they must hold on to what land his father and brother had not yet sold. Soon after becoming sachem, he and Governor Prence agreed to a seven-year embargo on the sale of Indian land. It was an extraordinary agreement that marked a bold and high-minded departure from the practices of the past, and Philip instructed John Sassamon to write the governor a letter. "Last summer [Philip] made that promise with you," Sassamon wrote, "that he would not sell no land in seven years time. . . . [H]e would have no English trouble him before that time."

But Philip's idealistic resolve soon wavered. The following year, in April 1664, Philip agreed to sell a piece of land bordering the towns of Bridgewater, Taunton, and Rehoboth for a record £66 (roughly $12,000 today)—almost twice the amount his father had received for the Pokanoket homeland of Sowams. If the embargo had proven fleeting, Philip had at least succeeded in getting the English to pay a decent price for his land. Philip was doing just what his father had done forty years before—adapting to the inevitable forces of change.

* * *

PHILLIP alias METACOMET of Pokanoket.
Engraved from the original as Published by Church.

Paul Revere's engraving of King Philip

Because Philip was the supreme sachem of the Pokanokets, his power over his people was, according to Roger Williams, that of "an absolute monarchy." In reality, however, there were practical limits to his authority. If he should do something to lose the trust and respect of his people, the sachem might find himself without anyone to lead. "[V]ery frequently their men will leave them upon distaste or harsh dealing," wrote Daniel Gookin, Massachusetts Bay's superintendent of the Praying Indians, "and go and live under other sachems that can protect them; so that their princes endeavor to carry it obligingly and lovingly unto their people, lest they should desert them, and thereby their strength, power, and tribute would be diminished."

Philip was also expected to conduct himself with the dignity befitting a supreme sachem. In addition to dressing more elaborately than the common people, he possessed a larger wigwam than most and traveled with an entourage of warriors and wives. When a person of lesser

An elm bowl attributed to King Philip

status greeted him, that person must say, "Cowaúnckamish," meaning, "My service to you," as he stroked both of the sachem's shoulders.

By all accounts, Philip *looked* the part. One admiring Englishman who saw the sachem on the streets of Boston estimated his clothing and large belts of wampum to be worth at least £20, approximately $4,000 today. But if Philip was to maintain himself as sachem of the Pokanoket without continuing to rely on the sale of Indian land, he needed to find an alternative to the fur trade that had once supported his father.

Ever since the Pilgrims had watched the gambols of whales around the anchored *Mayflower*, the English had sought to exploit these large sea mammals as a source of oil and baleen. Nowhere were there more whales than in the waters surrounding Nantucket Island—a fifty-square-mile sandbank twenty-four miles off the south shore of Cape Cod. Massasoit had long since determined the rules by which the Nantucket Indians divided up the whales that washed up on the island's shore. As whale oil became an increasingly sought-after commodity in New England, it was crucial that Philip reassert his father's claims over the Indian whalers of Nantucket.

In 1665, Philip received word that a Nantucket Indian named John Gibbs had broken a Native taboo: he had spoken the name of Philip's dead father. Philip decided he must personally oversee Gibbs's punishment, and he set out on an expedition that might also help to strengthen his influence on the island.

In 1665, the Indian population on Nantucket was huge—somewhere in the neighborhood of 1,500 at a time when the total number of Pokanokets and their allies, including those on Nantucket, is estimated to have been about 5,000. The island's English population, on the other hand, barely reached one hundred. On Nantucket, Philip would experience what it had been like in 1621 when the Indians had still been the overwhelmingly dominant force in New England.

By canoe, it was about sixty-five miles from Mount Hope to Nantucket. Philip landed on the west end of the island and then used the sand cliffs along the south shore to conceal his progress east to Gibbs's home near a pond that still bears his name. Soon the Indian was in Philip's custody. But as the sachem prepared to execute the transgressor, some members of the English community offered to pay for his release. Gibbs was a special favorite of the island's interpreter, Peter Folger, and would soon become a minister to Nantucket's Christian Indians. Philip named a price, but the English were unable to meet it. A standoff ensued as Philip refused to lessen his offer, using "threatening language," the island historian Obed Macy later reported, "pronounced with an emphasis which foreboded no good."

Philip appeared to be in control of the situation, especially given that the English were outnumbered by more than ten to one. But as may have become increasingly clear to Peter Folger (whose daughter Abiah would have a son named Benjamin Franklin), Philip did not have the support of the local Indians in this matter. The English "concluded," Macy wrote, "to put all to risk. [T]hey told [Philip], that, if he did not immediately leave the island, they would rally the inhabitants, and fall upon him and cut him off to a man."

Both sides knew it was an empty threat, but it was Philip who backed down. With £11 in hand, he "happily took the alarm, and left the island as soon as possible."

Instead of Philip, it had been the English who had proved their loyalty to the local Indians, and in the years ahead more and more of those Indians would turn to Christianity. With the outbreak of war a decade later, the Indians of Nantucket became one of the first Native groups in New England to "disown" Philip. For a young sachem seeking to assert his authority over one of the most populous and potentially lucrative portions of his territory, the voyage to Nantucket had been a disaster.

By 1667, Philip was five years into his reign as sachem of Mount Hope. Almost thirty years old, he and his wife Wootonekanuske had just had a son, and the birth of the boy appears to have prompted Philip to draft a will. When Philip's interpreter, John Sassamon, read the will back to him, all seemed as the sachem had intended. But, as it turned out, Sassamon had written something else entirely. Instead of leaving his lands to his intended heirs, Philip had, according to the will as written by Sassamon, left his lands to his interpreter. As had happened forty years before with Squanto, a cultural go-between had surrendered to the temptations of using his special powers to his own advantage. When Philip discovered what his trusted interpreter had done, Sassamon, it was reported, "ran away from him." Soon Sassamon was back with his former mentor, John Eliot, working as a teacher and minister to the Praying Indians.

Philip came to blame the interpreter's disloyalty on the influence of Christianity. He later claimed that the Praying Indians were "only dissemblers" and intended "by their lying to wrong their [Indian] kings." John Eliot reported that Philip told him he cared less for Christianity than he cared for the button of his coat. The sachem was talking metaphorically, but his newfound bitterness toward the religion flowed from one man: his former confidant, John Sassamon.

Sassamon's betrayal was just one setback in what proved to be a difficult year for the Pokanoket sachem. That spring Plymouth governor

Prence heard a disturbing rumor. Informants from Rehoboth reported that Philip had been talking about joining forces with the French and Dutch against the English. Not only would this allow the Indians to get back their lands, Philip had claimed; it would enable them to "enrich themselves with [English] goods." Once again, it was time to send Major Josiah Winslow to Mount Hope.

After confiscating the Pokanokets' guns, Winslow found an Indian who asserted that Philip had indeed been talking about a possible conspiracy against the English. Described as "one of Philip's sachem's men," the witness described the circumstances of Philip's boast with so many specific details that Winslow felt the accusation was "very probably true."

Philip, on the other hand, claimed a Narragansett sachem named Ninigret had put the Indian up to it. When that did not prove to be the case, Philip continued to insist that he had been set up, "pleading how irrational a thing it was that he should desert his long experienced friends, the English, and comply with the French and Dutch." As he stood before the Plymouth magistrates, more than a hint of desperation began to creep into Philip's increasingly urgent plea for forgiveness. Should the English decide to withdraw "their wonted favor," he asserted, it would be "little less than a death to him, gladding his enemies, grieving and weakening his friends."

In the end, the Plymouth magistrates decided that even if Philip's "tongue had been running out," he was not about to attack anybody. Quite the contrary, they were now concerned that this most recent debacle had so weakened Philip's stature that he was in danger of being spurned by his own people. From the colony's perspective, it was better to have a vacillating and ineffective leader in place among the Pokanokets than a sachem who might rally his people against them. "[N]ot willing to desert [Philip] and let him sink," the court decided to continue its official backing of Philip and return the confiscated weapons. This did not prevent the magistrates from charging the sachem £40 to help defray the cost of Winslow's fact-gathering mission.

* * *

Reputed to be Ninigret II, son of the Niantic sachem who sided with the English during King Philip's War

More than matching Philip's growing need for money was the English need for land. "[M]any in our colony are in want of land . . . ," the record reads; "all such lands as the Indians can well spare shall be purchased." In 1667 Thomas Willett, who was completing his last year as mayor of Manhattan, was given permission to purchase additional lands in the neighborhood of his longtime home in Wannamoisett and create the township of Swansea contiguous with the Pokanoket lands at Mount Hope.

Philip had begun with the best of intentions, but by the end of the 1660s he was on his way to a prodigious sell-off of Native land, aided and abetted by his brother's former friend Thomas Willett. From 1650 to 1659, there had been a total of fourteen Indian deeds registered in Plymouth court; between 1665 and 1675, there would be *seventy-six* deeds.

Governor Prence and Major Winslow prided themselves on the strategy they had developed to deal with the Indians in the colony. With the help of Willett, the governor served as Philip's primary contact, while Winslow devoted most of his energies to cultivating a relationship with the sachem of the Massachusetts to the north. It was a division of alliances that the two officials modeled on how Governor Bradford and Captain Standish had handled Squanto and Hobbamock in 1622. But as William Hubbard observed, while Bradford and Standish's strategy appears to have worked reasonably well, Prence and Winslow's approach proved far less effective when Prence died in 1673 and Winslow became governor. With Prence gone, Philip was now forced to deal with the one official he detested above all others. Not only was Winslow linked to his brother's death, he had proven himself to be one of Plymouth's most aggressive and unethical purchasers of Indian real estate.

In 1671, Winslow sued William, the son of Philip's sister Amie, for the money he owed on a horse. Without any means to pay, William took out a mortgage on a parcel of his own land in Nemasket. It was not long before Winslow had used the mortgage to acquire an even larger tract of William's land. The dubious practice of mortgaging property to pay off debt, which one historian has called "tantamount to confiscating land," was not legal in Plymouth, and so Winslow revised the law. By the time he became governor in 1673, Winslow had come to embody Plymouth's policy of increasingly arrogant opportunism toward the colony's Native Americans.

It may have been true that from a strictly legal standpoint there was nothing wrong with how Winslow and the other Plymouth officials acquired large amounts of Pokanoket land. And yet, from a practical and moral standpoint, the process removed the Indians from their territory as effectively—and as cheaply—as driving them off at gunpoint. Philip had to do something to stanch the long series of reversals that had come to typify his tenure as leader.

In the beginning, when the English had been, according to Philip, "as a little child" and his father had been "a great man," Massasoit had offered the Pilgrims his protection. Now that the roles were reversed, it was time, Philip insisted, that the English "do . . . as [the Pokanokets] did when they were too strong for the English." Instead of pressing every advantage until they had completely overwhelmed the Indians, Plymouth officials should honor their colony's obligation to the Pokanokets and allow them to exist as an autonomous people.

But as was becoming increasingly apparent, the children of the Pilgrims had very short memories. Now that their daily lives no longer involved an arduous and terrifying struggle for survival, they had begun to take the Indians for granted. In what is the great and terrible irony of the coming conflict—King Philip's War—by choosing to pursue economic prosperity at the expense of the Indians, the English put at risk everything their mothers and fathers had striven so heroically to create. By pushing the Pokanokets until they had no choice but to push back, the colonists were unintentionally preparing the way for a return to the old, horrifying days of death and despair.

In March of 1671, Hugh Cole of Swansea reported that Indians from all over the region were flocking to Mount Hope. At one point, Philip led a group of sixty armed warriors on a march up the peninsula to the edge of the English settlement. Josiah Winslow reported the rumor that in addition to winning the support of the Narragansetts, Philip had hatched a plot to abduct the Plymouth governor and (as the sachem had done with John Gibbs on Nantucket) use him to secure a large ransom. Though not a shot had yet been fired, many in Plymouth believed that after years of rumors, war had finally come to the colony.

It's unclear what triggered Philip to begin preparing for war. The Puritan historian William Hubbard claimed he took up arms "pretend-

*The "Seat of Philip" at the eastern shore
of Mount Hope*

ing some petite injuries done him in planting land." Whatever the specific cause, it was a momentous decision for a leader who had, prior to this, consistently backed away from the threat of any genuine conflict.

Some New Englanders dared to suggest that the Indians were not entirely to blame for the threatened insurrection and that Plymouth was guilty of treating the Pokanokets in an unnecessarily high-handed manner. In an attempt to prove otherwise, Plymouth magistrates invited a delegation from Massachusetts to attend a meeting with Philip at the town of Taunton on April 10, 1671.

Philip and a large group of warriors—all of them armed and with their faces painted—cautiously approached the Taunton town green, where an equally sizable number of Plymouth militiamen, bristling with muskets and swords, marched back and forth. Fearful that he was leading his men into a trap, Philip insisted that they be given several English hostages before he ventured into town. Tensions were so high that many of the colony's soldiers shouted out that it was time for them to attack. Only at the angry insistence of Massachusetts Bay officials were the Plymouth men made to stand down. Finally, after the exchange of several more messages, Philip and his warriors agreed to meet inside the Taunton meetinghouse—the Indians on one side of the aisle, the colonists on the other.

It was a scene that said much about the current state of Plymouth Colony. Forty-four years before, the Dutchman Isaack de Rasiere had described how the Pilgrims assembled in their fort for worship, each man with his gun. Now the children of the Pilgrims had gathered with the Pokanokets in a proper meetinghouse, not to worship but to settle their growing differences—the English on one side of the aisle in their woolen clothes and leather shoes, the Indians on the other with their faces painted and their bodies greased, and all of them, Puritans and Pokanokets alike, with muskets in their hands.

It did not go well for Philip. Once again, the Plymouth magistrates bullied him into submission, insisting that he sign a document in which he acknowledged the "naughtiness of my heart." He also agreed to surrender all his warriors' weapons to the English. According to William Hubbard, one of Philip's own men was so ashamed by the outcome that he flung down his musket, accused his sachem of being "a white-livered cur," and vowed that "he would never [follow Philip] again or fight under him." The son of a Nipmuck sachem left Taunton in such a rage that he was moved to kill an Englishman on his way back to his home in central Massachusetts. He was eventually tried and hanged on Boston Common, where his severed head was placed upon the gallows, only to be joined by the skull of his father five years later.

In the months that followed, the colony required that the Indians from Cape Cod to Nemasket sign documents reaffirming their loyalty to Plymouth. The magistrates also insisted that Philip and his warriors turn over all their remaining weapons. When Philip balked, it seemed once again as if war might be imminent. Fearful that Plymouth was about to drive the Pokanokets and, with them, all of New England into war, the missionary John Eliot suggested that Philip come to Boston to speak directly with Massachusetts Bay officials.

Philip appears to have been thankful for the missionary's intervention. However, Eliot made the mistake of suggesting that his two Indian envoys bring John Sassamon, who was now living in Nemasket, to their meeting with Philip. The sight of his former interpreter appears to have ignited a fresh outburst of anguished rage in the already beleaguered sachem. In early September, when a messenger from Plymouth arrived at Mount Hope, he found "Philip and most of his chief men much in drink." Philip angrily knocked the messenger's hat off his head and "exclaimed much against Sassamon." According to Philip, the hated Praying Indian had told Plymouth officials that the Pokanokets had been secretly meeting with some Narragansett sachems.

Eventually Philip did as Eliot suggested and went to Boston. As the missionary had said might happen, the sachem received a much more sympathetic hearing than he had ever been given in Plymouth. Philip agreed to meet with Plymouth officials on September 24, 1671, as long as a delegation from Massachusetts was also in attendance.

But by the time Philip appeared in Plymouth, the officials from Massachusetts had changed their position. Plymouth was right, and the Pokanokets were wrong. The treaty he was subsequently forced to sign amounted to a total and mortifying capitulation. He must turn over all his weapons, and he must pay a fine of £100. Even worse, he was now a subject of Plymouth and must pay the colony an annual tribute of five wolves' heads. Plymouth had given Philip no options: if he was to survive as sachem of the Pokanokets, he must now go to war.

Philip was disarmed but hardly defeated. He immediately began to make plans for obtaining more muskets—but to pay for the new weapons, he was going to need money—and lots of it.

In August of 1672, Philip took out a mortgage on some land along the Taunton River to pay off a debt of £83; soon after, he sold a four-mile-square piece of land in the same vicinity for £143 (approximately $32,000 today)—the largest price ever paid for a piece of Indian real estate in Plymouth. Of interest are the Indians whom Philip chose to sign this particular deed, two of whom, Annawon and Nimrod, were his principal "captains" or warriors. Philip, it appears, had launched into a calculated strategy of selling land for weapons. That he was about to sell almost every parcel of land he owned was, in the end, irrelevant, since it was all to fund a war to win those lands back. By 1673, with the sale of a neck of land to the west of Mount Hope, Philip had succeeded in selling every scrap of land surrounding his territory.

Playing into Philip's stratagem was English greed. Rather than wonder how he and his people could possibly survive once they'd been confined to a reservation at Mount Hope, or speculate where all this money was going, the English went ahead and bought more land—even agreeing to pay for the rights to fish in the waters surrounding Mount Hope when it meant that the Pokanokets might no longer be able to feed themselves.

The Pokanokets represented just 5 percent of the total Indian population of New England. If Philip was to have any hope of surviving a conflict, he must convince a significant number of the other tribes to join him. He knew he could probably count on the Pocassets and the Nemaskets, which were both led by his near relations, but it was questionable whether the Indians on Cape Cod and the islands would follow him into war. The Indians in this region had looked increasingly to Christianity—a trend that had only accelerated since Philip's voyage to Nantucket in 1665. Closer to home, the Massachusetts, who were so cozy with Winslow, would never join him. Uncas and the Mohegans, along with the remnants of the Pequots, also had strong ties to the English. The Nipmucks, on the other hand, were the Pokanokets' ancient and trustworthy friends, a relationship strengthened by Massasoit's final years with the Quabaugs.

There were two important unknowns. To the south of Pocasset, on a rolling plain that swept down to the sea at a rocky point, were the Sakonnets led by the female sachem Awashonks. The Sakonnets' loyalties were difficult to determine. Even more inscrutable were the Narragansetts, the Pokanokets' traditional foes. Significant inroads had been made in establishing a common ground between the two tribes, but the Narragansetts were too large and diverse to speak with a single voice. Their young warriors were anxious to enlist, but the tribe's older, more cautious sachems were reluctant to go to war. If subsequent English claims are to be believed, a tentative agreement was reached between the two tribes that come the spring of 1676, the fighting would begin.

In cobbling together a pan-Indian force to oppose the English, Philip was attempting to accomplish what not even the great Narragansett sachem Miantonomi had been able to pull off in the 1640s. And while Miantonomi had been known for his bravery in battle, Philip had no such reputation. But if he lacked his predecessor's physical courage, Philip appears to have had a different sort of charisma. His mounting desperation combined with a healthy dose of righteous indignation made him a lightning rod for Indians across the region, all of whom had experienced some version of the Pokanokets' plight. If they did not band together now and stand up to the English, the opportunity might never come again.

For their part, the English remained confident that Philip had committed himself to peace. Instead of being concerned by the Pokanokets' growing desire for guns and ammunition, they saw it as a financial opportunity. Incredibly, in the fall of 1674, Plymouth magistrates voted to annul a law prohibiting the sale of powder and shot to the Indians.

Then, in January of 1675, John Sassamon paid a visit to Josiah Winslow.

In 1675, Sassamon was approaching sixty years of age. Abhorred by Philip as conniving and dishonest, he was nonetheless the son-in-law of Philip's sister Amie. In fact, he lived on land given him by Amie's husband, Tuspaquin, known as the Black Sachem of Nemasket. Despite his intimate connection to Native royalty, Sassamon was working once again for the missionary John Eliot and was minister to a group of Praying Indians in Nemasket.

There is no way of knowing how long John Sassamon had known about Philip's plans for war. There is also no way of knowing how long he wrestled with what he should do with that information. But in mid-January of 1675, he informed Josiah Winslow that Philip was on the verge of war. This was not what the governor of Plymouth wanted to hear. Even when Sassamon warned that his life would be in danger if anyone learned that he had spoken with the governor, Winslow's reaction was to dismiss the claim as yet another Indian overstatement—even if the Indian had attended his alma mater, Harvard College.

At forty-three, Winslow was no longer the brazen young man who had shoved a pistol in Alexander's chest. His health had become a concern (he may have been stricken by tuberculosis), and the prospect of a major Indian war was simply not part of the future he had envisioned for Plymouth.

Sassamon's state of mind after his meeting with the governor can only be imagined. What we do know is that not long afterward, his dead body was discovered beneath the ice of Assawompsett Pond in modern Lakeville. Left lying on the ice were his hat, his musket, and a brace of ducks. It certainly appeared as if Sassamon had accidentally fallen through the ice and drowned. But when the Indian who found the body pulled it from the pond, no water issued from the mouth—an indication that Sassamon had been dead before he went through the ice. The body was also bruised and swollen around the neck and head. When word of Sassamon's death reached Careswell, the governor of Plymouth finally began to believe that the Pokanokets might be up to something.

An investigation was launched, and in March Philip voluntarily appeared in court to answer any questions the officials might have. Strenuously denying his involvement in Sassamon's death, the sachem insisted that this was an internal Indian matter and not the purview of the Plymouth government. The court, however, continued its investigation and soon found an Indian who claimed to have witnessed the murder. Conveniently hidden on a hill overlooking the pond, he had seen three Indians—Tobias, one of Philip's senior counselors; Tobias's son; and one other—seize Sassamon and violently twist his neck before shoving his lifeless body beneath the ice. On the strength of this testimony, a trial date was set for June 1.

As the date of the trial approached, Philip's brother-in-law, the Black Sachem of Nemasket, posted a £100 bond, secured with real estate, as bail for Tobias. This enabled Tobias to speak with Philip, who was justifiably concerned that he would be the next one on trial. To no one's surprise, Philip chose not to attend the hearing. Instead, he remained at Mount Hope, where he surrounded himself with warriors and marched menacingly to within sight of the Swansea border. Reports began to filter in to Plymouth that large numbers of "strange Indians" were making their way to the Pokanoket homeland.

The last thing Philip wanted was to go to war before all was ready. They did not have enough muskets, bullets, and especially gunpowder. But events were quickly acquiring a momentum that was beyond any single person's control. If the English insisted on putting Tobias and the others on trial, he might have no choice.

A panel of eight judges, headed by Winslow, presided over the trial. There were twelve English jurors assisted by six Praying Indians. Winslow later claimed they were the "most indifferentest, gravest, and sage Indians," but this did little to alter Philip's belief that the verdict had already been determined.

According to English law in the seventeenth century, two witnesses were required to convict someone of murder. But the English had only a single witness, and as came out in the trial, he had had prior dealings with one of the accused. Before supposedly witnessing the murder, he had been forced to give up his coat to Tobias to pay off a gambling debt. Even though there was only one witness, and a dubious witness at that, all eighteen members of the jury found Tobias and his accomplices guilty. It was a shocking miscarriage of justice. But what began as an affront to legal process quickly degenerated into an unconscionable display of cruelty.

The executions were scheduled for June 8. Plymouth minister John

Cotton, who had spent several years preaching to the Indians on Martha's Vineyard, took the opportunity to deliver a sermon to the Indians gathered to witness the hangings. As the condemned were brought to the gallows, all three Indians continued to maintain their innocence. Tobias was hanged first, followed by his friend. But when it came time to execute Tobias's son, the rope broke. Whether this was by accident or by design, it had what the English considered to be the desired effect. As the young Indian struggled to his feet, with the still-twitching bodies of his father and family friend suspended in the air above him, he was presented with the chance to save his life. So he changed his story, claiming that the other two had indeed killed Sassamon while he looked on helplessly. With the boy's confession, the authorities now had the number of witnesses the law required.

Traditionally, a condemned man was granted a reprieve after a failed execution. But a month later, with war raging across the colony, Tobias's son was taken from his cell and shot to death with a musket.

By the time Philip received word of the executions, Mount Hope stood at the vortex of a gathering storm of rage and indignation. The trial had been a travesty of justice—and an insulting challenge to the authority of the Pokanoket leader. Now, it seemed, was the time for Philip to take the opportunity given him by the English and lead his people triumphantly into battle.

His warriors were surely for it. Young, with little to lose and everything to gain, the fighting men of the Pokanokets now had the chance to win back what their fathers and grandfathers had so shortsightedly given away. It was a year ahead of Philip's original schedule, but the timing was, for the most part, fortuitous. The trees and underbrush were thick with new leaves, providing the cover the warriors needed when attacking the English. The swamps, which the Indians traditionally used as sanctuaries in times of war, were still mucky with spring rain and were impenetrable to the English soldiers. If they waited until midsummer, when the mire of the swamps started to congeal, it would be too late. They might not have the stores of gunpowder they had hoped to have amassed in a year's time, nor have the firm commitments they had planned to get from the other tribes, but there was nothing they could do about that now. They must strike soon and furiously. Philip, however, had never been one to rush into anything. Since his foray out to Nantucket a decade before, he had developed a talent for inviting conflict, then finding creative, if often humiliating, ways to avoid the final, potentially catastrophic confrontation. But by June 1675, his own warriors were about to call his bluff and demand that they go to war.

Despite all the evidence to the contrary, Governor Winslow remained hopeful that the present troubles would blow over. Except for writing a single letter to Philip in the weeks after the trial for Sassamon's murder, he failed to take an active role in thwarting a possible outbreak of violence. By the end of the month, both Winslow and Philip had become victims of their own rhetoric and posturing. Paralyzed by worry and wishful thinking, they were powerless to restrain what years of reckless greed, arrogance, opportunism, and ineptitude had unleashed among the young warriors of the Pokanokets.

Puritan historians later insisted that Philip maliciously pushed his people into the conflict. The English residents of Swansea told a different story. According to an account recorded in the early part of the following century, Philip and his counselors "were utterly averse to the war" in June 1675. Swansea resident Hugh Cole later told how Philip sent him word that "he could not control his young warriors" and that Cole must abandon his home and seek refuge on Aquidneck Island. Another tradition claimed that when Philip first heard that one of his warriors had killed an Englishman, he "wept at the news."

He had reason to weep. Even with recent recruits from neighboring tribes, his fighting force amounted to no more than a few hundred poorly equipped warriors. Even worse, they were situated on a peninsula. If they were unable to fight their way north into the underbelly of Plymouth Colony, their only means of escape from Mount Hope was by water.

The English had vulnerabilities of their own. Unlike the Indians, who traveled across the countryside on a seasonal basis, the English lived in houses that were fixed permanently to the ground. As a consequence, all their possessions—including clothing, furniture, food, and livestock—were there for the taking. As they were about to discover, an Indian war was the worst fate imaginable for the English of Plymouth Colony.

Philip had been forced to prepare for war out of political necessity. After the disastrous summer of 1671, his survival as sachem had depended on it. But Armageddon had always been in the distant future. Thanks to the murder trial of Tobias and the others, Armageddon had arrived.

PART IV

War

CHAPTER THIRTEEN

Kindling the Flame

*B*Y THE MIDDLE of June 1675, the Pokanokets' war dance had entered its third week. There were hundreds of warriors, their faces painted, their hair "trimmed up in comb fashion," according to a witness, "with their powder horns and shot bags at their backs," and with muskets in their hands. They danced to the beat of drums, the sweat pouring from their already greased bodies, and with each day, the call for action grew fiercer. Philip knew he could not hold them back much longer.

The powwows had predicted that if the Indians were to be successful in a war, the English must draw the first blood. Philip promised his warriors that come Sunday, June 20, when the English would all be away from their homes at meeting, they could begin pillaging houses and killing livestock, thus beginning a ritualistic game of cat and mouse that would gradually goad the English into war.

On Mount Hope Neck, just a few miles north of Philip's village, was a cluster of eighteen English houses at a place known as Kickemuit. As June 20 approached and the belligerence of the nearby Indian warriors increased, several residents of this most remote portion of Swansea decided it was time to abandon their homes and seek shelter elsewhere. To the north, on the other side of a bridge across the Palmer River, was the home of the minister John Miles. Dispossessed residents began to flock to this large structure, which after being reinforced against possible Indian attack became known as the Miles garrison. A few miles to the east in Mattapoisett, there was also the Bourne garrison, a large stone structure that soon contained sixteen men and fifty-four women and children.

The Miles garrison in the early twentieth century

On the morning of Sunday, June 20, seven or eight Indians approached an inhabitant of Kickemuit who had not yet abandoned his home. The Indians asked if they could use his grinding stone to sharpen one of their hatchets. The man told them that since it was the Sabbath, "his God would be very angry if he should let them do it." Soon after, the Indians came across an Englishman walking up the road. They stopped him and said "he should not work on his God's Day, and that he should tell no lies." Unnerved and intimidated, the last residents of Kickemuit left for the shelter of the garrisons. By day's end, two houses had been burned to the ground.

Governor Winslow received word of the vandalism that night, and by the morning of Monday, June 21, he had ordered towns across the colony to muster their militia for a rendezvous at Taunton, where they would be dispatched to Swansea. He also sent a message to officials in Boston, requesting their colony's assistance. There was no reason to assume that Massachusetts Bay would rush to Plymouth's defense. As the flare-up with Philip in 1671 had shown, there were many in that colony who were critical of Plymouth's treatment of the Pokanokets. And for those with long memories, Plymouth had been so slow to come to the Bay Colony's aid during the Pequot War that the Plymouth militia had missed the fighting. In the end, however, Massachusetts Bay decided that it was in its own best interests to support Plymouth. Not only was the uprising a possible threat to its inhabitants, but the conflict might make available large portions of choice Indian land.

In the middle of all this, Governor Winslow decided he needed to put his colony's religious house in order. The latest troubles with the Indians were a sign that God was unhappy with Plymouth. It was time, therefore, that "we humble ourselves before the Lord for all those sins whereby we have provoked our good God sadly to interrupt our peace and comfort." Winslow proclaimed that Thursday, June 24, be designated a day of fasting and humiliation.

Plymouth Colony was rife with sin, but apparently none of those sins involved the treatment of the Indians. Winslow later insisted that "we stand as innocent as it is possible for any person or people towards their neighbor." Even the trial for Sassamon's murder was, in Winslow's view, an example of English justice and mag-nanimity. In a letter to the governor of Connecticut, he claimed that Tobias and

Solid maple war club, inlaid with white and purple wampum, reputed to have been King Philip's

the other condemned men had "give[n] us thanks for our fair trial of them."

The result of this stubborn insistence on rectitude was to dehuman-ize the Indians so that they seemed the wanton and senseless instru-ments of God's will. This meant that there was nothing to be achieved through diplomacy; if the English were to make any progress in their difficulties with the Indians, they must do it through prayer and the sword.

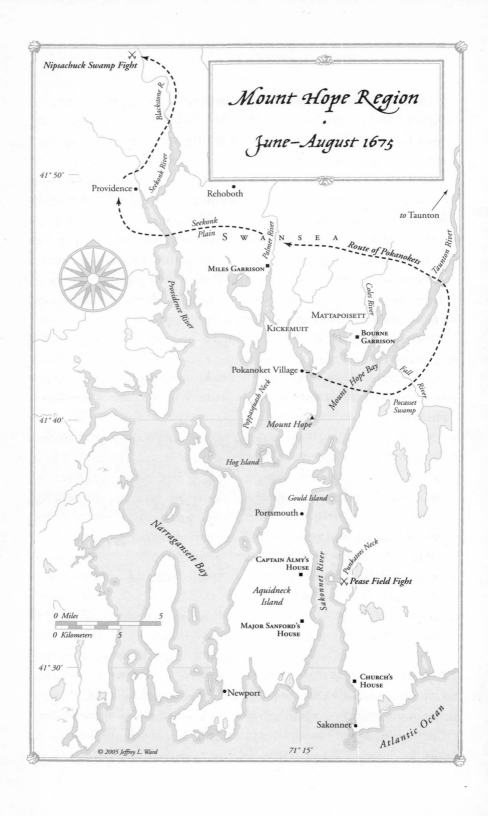

Nipsachuck Swamp Fight

Mount Hope Region
·
June–August 1675

41° 50' —

Providence

Rehoboth

to Taunton

Seekonk
Plain   S W A N S E A   *Route of Pokanokets*

MILES GARRISON

MATTAPOISETT

KICKEMUIT

BOURNE
GARRISON

Pokanoket Village

Mount Hope Bay

Pocasset
Swamp

41° 40' —

Mount Hope

Hog Island

Gould Island

Portsmouth

CAPTAIN ALMY'S
HOUSE

X *Pease Field Fight*

Aquidneck
Island

MAJOR SANFORD'S
HOUSE

41° 30' —

CHURCH'S
HOUSE

Newport

Sakonnet

Atlantic Ocean

0 Miles   5
0 Kilometers   5

© 2005 Jeffrey L. Ward

71° 15'

Narragansett Bay

Providence River

Seekonk River

Blackstone R.

Palmer River

Coles River

Taunton River

Fall River

Poppasquash Neck

Sakonnet River

Punkatees Neck

* * *

By Monday night, companies of militiamen had begun to arrive at Taunton. The elderly James Cudworth of Scituate was designated the army's commander with Major William Bradford, the fifty-five-year-old son of the former governor, as his immediate subordinate.

Since they'd just arrived on the scene, Cudworth and Bradford were as ignorant as everyone else as to the movements of the Pokanokets. There was one man, however, who had firsthand knowledge of the territory to the south and the Indians surrounding Mount Hope Bay. Just the year before, Benjamin Church, a thirty-three-year-old carpenter, had become the first Englishman to settle in the southeastern tip of Narragansett Bay at a place called Sakonnet, home to the female sachem Awashonks and several hundred of her people.

Instead of being intimidated by the fact that he was the only Englishman in Sakonnet (known today as Little Compton, Rhode Island), Church relished the chance to start from scratch. "My head and hands were full about settling a new plantation," he later remembered, "where nothing was brought to: no preparation of dwelling house, or outhousing or fencing made. Horses and cattle were to be provided, ground to be cleared and broken up; and the uttermost caution to be used, to keep myself free from offending my Indian neighbors all round me." Church was a throwback to his maternal grandfather, *Mayflower* passenger Richard Warren. By moving to Sakonnet, he was leaving his past behind and beginning anew in Indian country.

But as became increasingly clear in the traumatic months ahead, Church had moved well beyond his Pilgrim forebears. The early days of Plymouth Colony had been devoted to establishing a community of fellow worshippers. Within the shelter of their wooden wall, the Pilgrims had done their best to separate themselves from both the wilderness and the ungodly. Church, on the other hand, was quite content to be living among the heathen—both red and white. In addition to Awashonks and the Sakonnets, with whom he developed "a good acquaintance . . . and was in a little time in great esteem among them," there were the residents of Aquidneck Island, just across the Sakonnet River to the west. Mostly Baptists and Quakers, these were not the

An engraving of Benjamin Church that
appeared in a nineteenth-century edition
of his narrative

sorts with whom a proper Puritan socialized. Church, on the other hand, "found the gentlemen of the island very civil and obliging." While his wife, Alice, and their two-year-old son, Thomas, stayed with relatives in Duxbury, he labored to prepare a new home for them.

Church had taken up where the former "Lord of Misrule," Thomas Morton of Merrymount, had left off fifty years before. But where Morton had been an outsider from the start, Church was as closely connected by blood and by marriage (his wife was the daughter of Constant Southworth, William Bradford's stepson) to the aristocracy of Plymouth Colony as it was possible to be.

He was also ambitious. Possessed "of uncommon activity and industry," he had already constructed two buildings by the spring of 1675 when he heard a disturbing rumor. Philip, sachem of Mount Hope—just five miles to the north—was "plotting a bloody design."

From the start, Church had known that his future at Sakonnet depended on a strong relationship with sachem Awashonks, and over the course of the last year the two had become good friends. In early June, she sent him an urgent message. Philip was about to go to war, and he demanded that the Sakonnets join him. Before she made her decision, Awashonks wanted to speak with Church.

Church quickly discovered that six of Philip's warriors had come to Sakonnet. Awashonks explained that they had threatened to incite the wrath of the Plymouth authorities against her by attacking the English houses and livestock on her side of the river. She would then have no alternative but to join Philip. Church turned to the Pokanokets and accused them of being "bloody wretches [who] thirsted after the blood of their English neighbors, who had never injured them." For his part, he hoped for peace, but if war should erupt, he vowed to be "a sharp thorn in their sides." He recommended that Awashonks look to the colony for protection from the Pokanokets. He promised to leave immediately for Plymouth and return as soon as possible with instructions from the governor.

Just to the north of the Sakonnets in modern Tiverton, Rhode Island, were the Pocassets, led by another female sachem, Weetamoo. Even though she was Philip's sister-in-law, the relationship did not necessarily guarantee that she was inclined to join forces with him. Church decided to stop at Pocasset on his way to Winslow's home in Duxbury.

He found her, alone and despondent, on a hill overlooking Mount Hope Bay. She had just returned by canoe from Philip's village. War, Weetamoo feared, was inevitable. Her own warriors "were all gone, against her will, to the dances" at Mount Hope. Church advised her to

The site of King Philip's village on the eastern shore of the
Mount Hope Peninsula in the early 1900s

go immediately to Aquidneck Island, just a short canoe ride away, for her safety. As he had told Awashonks, he promised to return in just a few days with word from Governor Winslow.

But Church never got the chance to make good on his promise. Before he could return to Weetamoo and Awashonks, the fighting had begun.

Church had been in Plymouth speaking with Governor Bradford when the call for the militia had gone out, and he had immediately reported to Taunton. As the army prepared to march to Swansea, Major Bradford requested that Church lead the way with a small vanguard of soldiers. Church and his company, which included several "friend Indians," moved so quickly over the path to Swansea that they were able to kill, roast, and eat a deer before the main body of troops caught up with them. Church was already discovering that he enjoyed the life of a soldier. As he later wrote in a book about his experiences during the war, "I was spirited for that work."

But the impetuous Church still had much to learn about military tactics. His mission had been to provide protection to the soldiers behind him. By sprinting to Swansea, he had left the army vulnerable to an Indian ambush. While Church crowed about the speed of his march south, his commanding officers may have begun to realize that this was a soldier whose ambition and zeal verged on recklessness.

Over the next few days, more and more soldiers arrived at Swansea. In addition to fortifying the Miles garrison, a temporary barricade was constructed to provide the growing number of soldiers with protection from possible attack. But no direct action was taken against the Indians. Given that hundreds of Native warriors were said to have rallied around Philip, Cudworth felt that his own force must more than match the Indians' before they marched on Mount Hope.

With each passing day, the outrages committed by the Indians increased. Church and his compatriots could hear their whoops and the crackle of gunfire as the Native warriors slaughtered cattle and pilfered houses. But so far, no English men or women had been injured. By the morning of Wednesday, June 23, some residents had grown bold enough to return to their houses to retrieve goods and provisions.

That morning, a father and son ventured from the garrison and came upon a group of Indians ransacking several houses. The boy had a musket, and his father urged him to fire on the looters. One of the Indians fell, then picked himself up and ran away. Later in the day, some Indians approached the garrison and asked why the boy had shot at one of their men. The English responded by asking whether the Indian was dead. When the Indians replied in the affirmative, the boy snidely said "it was no matter." The soldiers tried to calm the now infuriated Indians by saying it was "but an idle lad's word." But the truth of the matter was that the boy had given the warriors exactly what they wanted: the go-ahead to kill.

Thursday, June 24, the day of fasting and humiliation throughout the colony, proved momentous in the history of Plymouth, but not in the way the governor had intended. Reports differ, but all agree that it was a day of horror and death in Swansea. At least ten people, including the boy and his father, were killed by the Indians. Some were killed on their way back from prayers at the meetinghouse. One couple and their twenty-year-old son stopped at their home to secure some provisions. The father told his wife and son to return to the garrison while he finished collecting corn. But as the father left the house, he was beset by Indians and killed. Hearing gunshots, the son and his mother returned to the house. Both were attacked and in what became a common fate in the months ahead, scalped; and as also happened with terrifying frequency, both survived their scalpings only to die from loss of blood.

For Church and the other soldiers cooped up at the garrison, the days ahead proved an exasperating and humiliating ordeal as they were forced to wait for the reinforcements from Massachusetts Bay to arrive. In a clear attempt to mock the soldiers' impotence, the Indians had the audacity to approach the garrison itself. Two soldiers sent to draw a bucket of water from a nearby well were shot and carried away. They were later discovered with "their fingers and feet cut off, and the skin of their heads flayed off." Even worse, the Indians succeeded in killing two of the garrison's own sentries "under the very noses of most of our forces." On the night of June 26, a total eclipse of the moon was witnessed all across New England. Several soldiers claimed they saw a black spot in the moon's center resembling "the scalp of an Indian." All agreed that an "eclipse falling out at that instant of time was ominous."

Finally on Monday, June 28, with the arrival of several Massachusetts companies from Boston, the number of soldiers had reached the point that Cudworth was willing to venture from the garrison. In addition to a troop of horse under Captain Thomas Prentice and a company of foot soldiers under Captain Daniel Henchman, there was a rowdy bunch of volunteers under the command of Captain Samuel Moseley. The English had not yet fought a single battle, but Moseley, a sea captain, was already something of a hero. In April, Moseley had led a successful assault on some Dutch privateers off the coast of Maine. In

June, several of the captured sailors were put on trial and condemned to death, but with the outbreak of war, they were granted a reprieve as long as they were willing to fight the Indians under Moseley. In addition to this multinational group of pirates, which included a huge Dutchman named Cornelius Anderson, Moseley secured the services of a wild gang of servants and apprentices from Boston. Decidedly lacking in Puritan restraint and with a seaman's love of profanity, Moseley's company proved adept at transferring their talent for murder and mayhem from the wilderness of the high seas to the swamps and forests of New England.

To a pious group of farm boys and merchants, Moseley's men seemed as savage as the Indians themselves. To Benjamin Church, who had suddenly been superseded as one of the army's more colorful and audacious figures, Moseley was destined to become both a rival and a nemesis.

With the arrival of more than three hundred new soldiers, the Miles garrison quickly became charged with a crude and volatile energy. The assault was scheduled for the following day, but some of the new arrivals, led by Quartermasters John Gill and Andrew Belcher, requested liberty to go out immediately and "seek the enemy in their own quarters." Some Indians on the opposite side of the river were taking great delight in firing on the garrison. It was time to put these heathens in their place.

Permission was granted, and twelve troopers prepared to take it to the enemy. In addition to William Hammond of nearby Rehoboth, who was to act as their "pilot" or scout, the troopers requested the services of Benjamin Church. They quickly set out across the bridge, all of them knowing that an audience of several hundred English soldiers was watching their every move.

Almost as soon as they crossed the bridge, about a dozen Indians concealed in some nearby bushes let loose a killing volley of shot. In an instant, Hammond, the scout, was, if not dead, nearly so; Belcher was hit in the knee and his horse was shot out from under him, while Gill was slammed in the gut. Fortunately, he'd worn a protective coat of quarter-inch-thick ox hide, known as a "buff coat," which he had lined with several pieces of well-placed parchment, and had suffered only a severe bruise.

The troopers were so terrified by the attack that they turned their horses around and galloped back for the garrison, leaving Hammond dazed and dying in the saddle and Belcher pinned beneath his horse. As the troopers clattered across the bridge, Church "stormed and stamped, and told them 'twas a shame to run and leave a wounded man there to become a prey to the barbarous enemy." By this time, Hammond had fallen down dead off his horse, and with the assistance of Gill and only one other man, Church attempted to save Belcher's life. Church jumped off his horse and loaded both Belcher and Hammond onto the horses of the other two. As they retreated to the garrison, Church went after Hammond's horse, which was wandering off toward the Indians. All the while, he shouted out to those at the garrison "to come over and fight the enemy." But no one appeared willing to join him.

Massachusetts governor John Leverett wearing an ox-hide buff coat

The Indians had had a chance to reload and were now blasting away at Church as he continued to bawl indignantly at the army on the other side of the river. Every one of the Indians' bullets missed its mark, although one ball did strike the foot of a soldier watching from the safety of the garrison. Church decided he had better join his cowardly compatriots before the Indians had a chance to reload and fire once again. He started back across the bridge but not without proclaiming, "The Lord have mercy on us if such a handful of Indians shall thus dare such an army!"

* * *

It was a grim and awful night. The weather had deteriorated dramatically since they'd seen the lunar eclipse several nights before, and as a cold wind lashed the Miles garrison with rain and Moseley's roughneck crew mocked the troopers with "many profane oaths," a soldier from Watertown lost control of himself. Screaming "God is against the English!" he ran crazily around the garrison until he was finally subdued, "a lamentable spectacle."

The vast majority of the soldiers gathered that night had grown up on stories of the military might of the Puritans during the English civil war. One of the most efficient fighting forces of the age, Cromwell's New Model Army had subdued England, Scotland, Wales, and Ireland. The navy, under the command of Robert Blake, had won so many victories against Holland and Spain that the crews of British ships proudly lashed brooms to their mastheads in recognition of having swept the Channel clean of enemy vessels. Now that Charles II was back on the throne, it was left to them, the militiamen of Puritan New England, to maintain the twin traditions of spiritual purity and martial prowess in the face of an ungodly foe.

There was yet another legacy for these soldiers to consider that night at the Miles garrison. Thirty-eight years before, many of their fathers had served in the Pequot War. The Indians' bows and arrows had proven ludicrously ineffective in the face of English matchlocks, and victory had come in what seemed a single, God-ordained stroke at the massacre at Mystic. It was true that the Indians had since armed themselves with flintlocks, but the assumption remained that a single Englishman was worth at least ten Indians in battle—the previous day's outcome notwithstanding.

The combined Plymouth and Massachusetts Bay forces assembled at the Miles garrison possessed the same equipment and training then current in Europe, where orderly lines of soldiers gathered on open battlefields and fired at one another, often with as little as fifty yards between them. In this kind of fighting, an old matchlock, which was so heavy that a wooden stand was required to prop up the muzzle, was perfectly suitable. The soldier was not expected to aim his weapon at anyone or anything in particular; in fact, the matchlock possessed no sight. Instead, the musketeer was trained to fire in the general direction of the enemy in a coordinated volley. Just as important in European warfare as the musketeer was the pikeman, a soldier who wielded a fourteen-foot-long spear. Pikemen led charges against an enemy line; they also provided a form of defense against a cavalry charge. By driving the butts of their pikes into the ground, the pikemen created a temporary fortress behind which the musketeers could reload their weapons.

Already, New England's militia had begun to alter their equipment and tactics in ways that were well ahead of Europe. Flintlocks were more popular in America than in Europe, where matchlocks were used in battle as late as 1700. The example of the Indians, who used their flintlocks to such good effect in hunting deer, bear, and other game, was impossible to ignore. But old habits died hard, and on the morning of Tuesday, June 29, many of the soldiers still possessed matchlocks and pikes—weapons that soon proved completely ineffective in fighting an enemy that refused to meet them in the open field.

That morning, Moseley and his privateers led the way across the bridge. Schooled in the brutal, haphazard world of hand-to-hand combat on a ship's deck, these sailors were, it turned out, much better adapted than the militiamen to fighting Indians. Ten of the enemy could be seen on the opposite side of the river, about a half mile away, shouting insults at the English. "[N]ot at all daunted by such kind of alarms," Moseley and his men "ran violently down upon them over the bridge, pursuing them a mile and a quarter on the other side."

As Moseley's volunteers chased the Indians until they had disappeared into a swamp—killing, it was later reported, about a half dozen of them—Church was forced to participate in a more traditional military operation. Fanning out in two wings, the troopers created a long line intended to sweep the area of Indians while protecting the foot soldiers in the middle. Unfortunately, the center of the line was, in Church's judgment, "not well headed." With visibility diminished in the rain, some of the soldiers mistook their comrades for the enemy, and one of the troopers, a twenty-year-old ensign named Perez Savage, who "boldly held up his colors in the front of his company," was shot not once but twice, one ball harmlessly piercing the brim of his hat and the other hitting him in the thigh. With the weather getting worse by the moment and no Indians in sight (although several officers insisted that Savage had been hit by Native fire), it was decided to return to the garrison for the night.

The next day, the English forces were in no hurry to march on Mount Hope, where as many as five hundred Native warriors were said to be waiting for them. Not until noon did the English head out once again across the bridge. The previous day they had ventured only a mile and a half into enemy territory; this time they continued on to the English settlement at Kickemuit. Tensions were already high among the militiamen. What they saw at Kickemuit made them only more apprehensive of what lay ahead.

The abandoned houses had been all burned. But even more disturbing than the blackened and smoking remnants of a once thriving community were the pieces of paper seen fluttering in the air, paper that soon proved to be the torn pages of a Bible. For this overwhelmingly Puritan force, it was a shocking outrage to know that the Indians had ripped apart this most sacred of books and scattered God's words to the winds "in hatred of our religion." Then, three miles later, they discovered the remains of eight Englishmen, killed five days earlier at the nearby settlement of Mattapoisett. The Indians had mounted the men's heads, scalps, and hands on poles and planted them beside the roadside in what one commentator described as a "barbarous and inhuman manner bidding us defiance." The body parts were quickly buried, and the soldiers continued on.

Two miles later, they reached the Pokanokets' village. One of the first on the scene was the giant Dutch pirate Cornelius Anderson. It was apparent that the Indians had left in a hurry. Cooking utensils had been left scattered on the ground, and at Philip's own wigwam, the Dutchman found what several local residents recognized as the sachem's hat—a hat that Anderson placed triumphantly on his own huge head. The Pokanokets had also left their drums behind, but not before carefully staving in each one. Spreading out almost as far as the eye could see was an estimated thousand acres of Indian corn. Soon the soldiers began uprooting every stalk. If they could not defeat the Indians in battle, they would do their best to starve them to death. Some of Philip's pigs were found rooting in the mud. There were also a large number of newly masterless Native dogs. Philip's horse, identifiable by its distinctive saddle, was found wandering the fields of Mount Hope. But nowhere was there a single Indian.

Church knew immediately what had happened. So as not to become trapped on the peninsula, Philip and his people had transported themselves by canoes across the sound to Pocasset—not an easy feat given that the waters surrounding Mount Hope were supposedly being guarded by vessels from Rhode Island. Once in Pocasset, Philip had met up with Weetamoo, who now had no choice but to join her brother-in-law. Church recognized it as a brilliant tactical move. Not only did Philip now have "a more advantageous post," he was stronger than he'd ever been. Church's commanders, however, chose to see Philip's flight from Mount Hope as "a mighty conquest" on their part. They had driven the Pokanokets from their homeland.

Church urged his superiors to pursue Philip immediately. If the sachem should break out of Pocasset, all of New England might soon be at war. But the Plymouth commander James Cudworth insisted that they must first comb every inch of the Mount Hope Peninsula for Indians. Then it was decided that the army should build a fort on the site of Philip's village to make sure the Pokanokets did not return to Mount Hope. From Church's perspective, it was nothing but busywork designed to postpone the time when the English must finally face the Indians in battle. " 'Twas rather their fear than their courage," Church wrote, "that obliged them to set up the marks of their conquest."

While the Plymouth forces built a useless fort, the Massachusetts authorities committed an even larger tactical blunder. Instead of sending Moseley and the others after Philip, they decided it was time to turn their attention to the Narragansetts. There were legitimate concerns that the tribe might be preparing to join Philip in the war. Some of the Pokanokets' women and children, it was rumored, had sought shelter with the Narragansetts. In truth, however, there was no clear evidence that the tribe had any hostile intentions toward the English.

The Narragansetts, like all the other tribes in New England, were watching Philip's rebellion very closely. In the beginning, they assumed the conflict was a local affair between Philip and Plymouth. But with the arrival of soldiers from Massachusetts Bay, the Narragansetts began to realize that the English regarded the rebellion in broader terms. Even though Massachusetts Bay had no complaints against Philip, the Puritans had quickly come to their neighbor's defense. Even Rhode Island, which both Plymouth and Massachusetts normally scorned, had offered to help. "[The Narragansetts] demanded why the Massachusetts and Rhode Island rose and joined with Plymouth against Philip," Roger Williams wrote on June 25, "and left not Philip and Plymouth to fight it out. We answered that all the colonies were subject to one King Charles, and it was his pleasure and our duty and engagement for one Englishman to stand to the death by each other in all parts of the world."

By immediately assuming the conflict was a racial rather than a political struggle, the English were, in effect, creating a self-fulfilling prophecy. As the magnitude of the English response increased, Indians across New England discovered that instead of considering them valued allies, the English had suddenly begun to regard them all as potential foes. Perhaps Philip was right: their only option was war.

But there were other factors besides racial fear and national loyalty influencing the Massachusetts Bay officials' decision to send the militia to Rhode Island. Both Massachusetts and Connecticut had designs on obtaining large tracts of land in the western portion of Rhode Island. The Massachusetts Bay leaders decided that they must seize the opportunity to make their military presence known in Rhode Island. And so, under the pretext of securing a treaty with the Narragansetts, the Massachusetts forces left Mount Hope for the western shore of the bay, where they did their best to intimidate both the Indians and the English, whose lands the Puritans coveted. The end result of this misbegotten strategy was to turn what had most probably been a neutral tribe into an increasingly hostile one.

For his part, Church had not given up on his original hope of winning both Weetamoo and Awashonks over to the English side. He was convinced that if he'd been able to speak to the sachems before the outbreak of hostilities, they would have spurned Philip. Even if it was too late to keep the Pocassets and Sakonnets out of the war, there was nothing to be accomplished by remaining at Mount Hope. The Plymouth authorities, however, seemed intent on keeping him on the west side of Mount Hope Bay. His elderly father-in-law, Constant Southworth, requested that Church assume his duties as commissary general of the Plymouth militia. Instead of doing something that might bring an end to the war—whether it was through diplomacy or fighting Philip—he was now forced to attend to the mundane tasks of feeding an army of several hundred men.

There was one officer, however, who agreed with Church that it was time to move into Pocasset. Matthew Fuller was the army's surgeon general. Although he was, in his own words, too "ancient and heavy" to be chasing Indians, he asked Church if he'd go with him to Pocasset. Church responded that "he had rather do anything in the world than stay there to build the fort." So on the night of Thursday, July 8, after taking the ferry that ran from the southern tip of Mount Hope to Aquidneck Island, Fuller, Church, and just thirty-six men were transported by boat to the shores of Pocasset.

After a night spent sleeping in the countryside, they were off in search of Indians. While Fuller went north with half the men, Church took the other half south toward his home in Sakonnet. With luck, he might make contact with Awashonks. Several hours later, his men began to complain that they had not yet found any of the Indians he had promised them. As they made their way along the shore of the Sakonnet River, Church assured them "that if it was their desire to see Indians, he believed he should now soon show them what they should say was enough."

Fifty-five years earlier, Miles Standish had led a similar patrol along the south shore of Cape Cod. The Pilgrims' search for Indians had been part of a voyage of discovery to a new and unknown land. Church was conducting his search just a few miles from his own farm—a land made just as new and strange by the transformative power of war.

They could see signs of recent Indian activity all around them—a network of sinuous trails that crisscrossed the woods and fields. They came upon a wigwam loaded with cooking utensils and clothing. A few of the men asked if they could take some of the goods with them, but Church forbade it, "telling them they might expect soon to have their hands full" with Indians instead of plunder.

On Punkatees Neck, between a ridge of dense forest and the stony shore of the Sakonnet River, they found a newly cultivated field of peas. They also saw two Indians walking through the field toward them. When the Indians turned and started to run, Church called out that he only wanted to talk and would not hurt them. But the Indians continued to run, with Church and his men in pursuit. There was a fence between the field and the woods, and as the Indians scrambled over it, one of them turned and fired his musket. A soldier fired back, and even though the Indians quickly disappeared into the woods, the English heard a strangled cry of pain suggesting that one of them had been hit.

They followed the Indians into the woods. Suddenly the sun-dappled darkness erupted with the roar of dozens of muskets firing simultaneously. Like many other English officers would do in the months ahead, Church had led his men into an ambush. He glanced back, "expecting to have seen half of them dead." But all were still standing and firing blindly into the thick cloud of gray smoke that billowed toward them from the trees. Church ordered them to stop firing. If they discharged their muskets all at once, the Indians might charge them with their hatchets. It was time to retreat to the field.

As soon as they reached the fence, Church ordered those who had not yet fired their muskets to hide themselves behind the fence while the others moved well into the field and reloaded. If the Indians should pursue them to the fence, there would be a trap waiting for them. Church was quickly learning how to use the Indians' own tactics of concealment and surprise against them.

But when Church glanced back to the heavily wooded rise of land from which they'd just come, he immediately began to reevaluate his strategy. From where he stood, the wooded hill appeared to be moving. He soon realized that the rise of land was completely covered with Indians, "their bright guns glittering in the sun" as they poured out of the woods and onto the field. The field bordered the Sakonnet River, and the Indians were attempting to surround the Englishmen before they reached the water's edge.

Church quickly scanned the river. There were supposed to be several boats waiting to take them back to Aquidneck Island. On the other side of the river, less than a mile away, were some boats on the Aquidneck shore. They were too far away to be of much help now.

Near the water were the remnants of a stone wall. He ordered his men to run across the field and take the wall before the Indians reached it. He also told them to strip down to their white shirts so that the men across the river would know that they were Englishmen. In order to get their attention, he ordered three of his men to fire their guns one after the other. Soon they were all dashing across the field, the Indians' bullets cutting through the leaves of the pea plants and sending up spurts of dust as the Englishmen threw themselves over an old hedge and tumbled down the bank to the wall beside the shore.

Unfortunately, it was not much of a wall. As the Indians took up positions around them, using the ruins of an old stone house and any available stumps, rocks, trees, and fence posts for protection, Church and his men were left wide open to shots from the north and south. They grabbed whatever rocks they could find and began widening the wall.

But their biggest problem was not a lack of protection; it was their lack of gunpowder. Church estimated that they were up against several hundred Indians, and there were only twenty of them. Once they ran out of powder, the Indians would be on them in a moment, and they would all be massacred.

Church marveled at how his men "bravely and wonderfully defended themselves" in the face of such an overwhelming force. But there was reason for hope. A sloop had started to sail toward them from

Aquidneck Island. But as soon as the vessel came to within hailing distance, the Indians turned their guns upon it. The wind was blowing onshore from the northwest, and Church asked the boat's master if he might send them the canoe that was tied to his stern so that they could use it to paddle back to his boat. But the sailor refused. One of Church's men cried out, "For God's sake, take us off. Our ammunition is spent!" This was not the kind of information Church wanted the Indians to know. It was time to end the conversation. Marshaling the same kind of fury he had displayed at the Miles garrison, he ordered the boat's master to "either send his canoe ashore or else be gone presently, or he would fire upon him." The vessel promptly headed back for Aquidneck, and the Indians, "reanimated" by the boat's departure, "fired thicker and faster than ever."

Some of Church's men began to talk about making a run for it. Church insisted that their best chance at survival was to stay together. It was already a miracle that they were still alive. God, in his "wonderful providence," had chosen to preserve them. Church was confident that no matter how bad it looked now, "not a hair of their head[s] should fall to the ground" if they continued to be "patient, courageous, and prudently sparing of their ammunition." It was a soldier's version of predestination: God was in control, and he was on their side.

One of the men had become so frightened that he was unable to fire his musket. Church ordered him to devote his energies to reinforcing the wall. As Church delivered his speech, the soldier was in the midst of laying a flat rock down in front of him when a bullet ricocheted off the stone's face. It was exactly the example Church needed. "Observe," he cried out to his men, "how God directed the bullets [to] . . . hit the stone" and not the man. Whether through Providence or not, from that moment forward, everyone "in his little army, again resolved one and all to stay with and stick by him."

All afternoon, beneath a hot sun, Church and his men held their ground as the Indians made the surrounding woods echo with their whoops and shouts. With night approaching, one of Church's soldiers said he could see a sloop sailing toward them from a tiny island several miles up the river. "Succor is now coming!" Church shouted.

He recognized the vessel as belonging to Captain Roger Goulding, "a man," he assured them, "for business."

The sloop glided with the diminishing northwesterly breeze down to the besieged soldiers. Captain Goulding proved as trustworthy as Church had claimed. He anchored his vessel to windward of them and floated a buoy with his canoe tied to it to Church and his men. The sails and hull of his sloop were soon riddled with bullet holes, but Goulding stayed put.

The canoe was so tiny that only two men could fit in it at a time. It took ten agonizingly slow trips back and forth, but at least there was a growing number of soldiers in the sloop to provide cover for those in the canoe. Finally, only Church was left ashore. As he prepared to climb into the canoe, he realized that he had left his hat and cutlass at a nearby well, where he had stopped to get a drink of water at the beginning of the siege. When he informed his men that he was going back to collect his possessions, they pleaded with him to get into the canoe. But Church was adamant; he was not about to leave without his hat and sword. He loaded all the gunpowder he had left in his musket and started for the well.

Since he was the only remaining Englishman, all the Indians' guns were trained on him as he made his way to the stone-encircled spring that today bears his name. A ceaseless stream of bullets flew through the air and drove into the ground at his feet, but none hit Church. On returning to the canoe, with the hat on his head and the cutlass at his side, he fired his musket one last time, but there was barely enough of a charge to push the bullet out of the barrel. Just as he settled into the canoe, a bullet grazed his hair while another splintered the wooden brace against which he'd nestled his chest, but he reached the sloop unscathed.

It had been a remarkable day. For six hours, twenty men had held off three hundred Indians (a number that was later confirmed by the Indians themselves) without suffering a single casualty. It was a deliverance that Church looked to for the rest of his life as indisputable proof of "the glory of God and His protecting providence." William Bradford had learned of it in a dream, but for Benjamin Church it had been revealed in battle: he was one of the elect.

He'd also learned something else during what came to be known as the Pease Field Fight. When it came to Awashonks and the Sakonnets, the time for diplomacy had passed.

Even if the Sakonnets had joined Philip, Church still held out hope that many other Indians in the region might be convinced to stay out of the conflict. As the Puritan historian William Hubbard observed, most Indians in southern New England were unsure of what to do next. It was in the colony's best interests, Church maintained, to welcome all potentially neutral Indians with open and beneficent arms.

But by July 1675, the hysteria of war had taken hold of New England. Shocked by the atrocities at Swansea, most English inhabitants had begun to view all Indians with racist contempt and fear. As a result, many Indians who would gladly have remained at peace were given no choice but to go to war.

Weetamoo was Philip's sister-in-law, but she did everything she could to avoid the conflict. Church had advised her to seek refuge on Aquidneck Island, and that was exactly what she had done. But when she fled to Aquidneck by canoe with six of her men, some of the English inhabitants, who were "in fury against all Indians," insisted that she leave the island. When Philip and his warriors stormed into Pocasset, Weetamoo was left with no option but to join him.

Other Indians attempting to remain neutral were told to flock to the shoreline of their territory, where, if they "did not meddle" with the English in any way, they would be safe. Unfortunately, soldiers such as Anderson the Dutchman made no effort to distinguish between friendly and hostile Natives. At one point during his depredations on Mount Hope, Anderson and twelve men came upon sixty Indians who were hauling their canoes ashore. Anderson and his privateers immediately killed thirteen of them, took eight alive, and once the rest had fled into the swamps, proceeded to burn all forty canoes.

Pocasset Swamp as it appeared in the early twentieth century

Just prior to the outbreak of violence, some Quakers from Aquidneck Island had taken the ferry to Mount Hope and attempted to convince Philip and his advisers that they should submit to some form of arbitration rather than go to war. For a sachem supposedly bent on violence, he had proven surprisingly open to the Quakers' suggestion and admitted that "fighting was the worst way." The Quakers, however, were in no position to speak for Plymouth Colony, and nothing ever came of the overture.

Now, while fighting was still very much a local affair, was the time for Governor Winslow to attempt a diplomatic resolution to the conflict. At the very least, some coordinated effort could have been made to assure nonhostile Indians that they were safe from attack. But none of these measures were taken. In fact, when several hundred Indians surrendered to authorities in Plymouth and Dartmouth after being assured that they'd be granted amnesty, Winslow and his cronies on the Council of War refused to honor the promise. On August 4, the council determined that since some of the Indians had participated in the attacks, *all* of them were guilty. That fall they were shipped as slaves to the Spanish port of Cádiz.

From the perspective of the Plymouth magistrates, there was nothing unusual about enslaving a rebellious Native population. The English had been doing this in Ireland for decades; most recently Cromwell had sent large numbers of Irish, Welsh, and Scottish slaves to the West Indies. After the conclusion of the Pequot War in 1637, Massachusetts Bay officials had sent a shipload of Indian slaves, including fifteen boys and two women, to the Puritan settlement on Providence Island off the east coast of Central America. Selling Indian captives served two functions: it provided income to help pay for the war, and it removed a dangerous and disruptive people from the colony—not to mention the fact that it made the rebels' lands available for later settlement by the English.

But if the policy made perfect sense to Winslow and the Council of War at Plymouth, Benjamin Church regarded it as a shocking abomination of justice that would only prolong the war. Church was no paragon of vitue. In the years ahead he, like many Englishmen in the Narragansett Bay region, would own African slaves. But he would also work diligently to ensure that the Indians he'd come to know in Sakonnet continued to live freely and peacefully in the region. To Church's mind, the enslavement of the Indians from Plymouth and Dartmouth in the summer of 1675 was "an action so hateful . . . that [I] opposed it to the loss of the good will and respect of some that before were [my] good friends."

By Monday, July 19, most of the Massachusetts companies that had been diverted to Narragansett country had returned to Mount Hope, and a combined Plymouth-Massachusetts force crossed the bay for Pocasset. Running along the eastern shore of the bay was a seven-mile-long cedar swamp, beside which Weetamoo and Philip had reportedly camped. For the English it would be a day of disorientation and fear as they pursued the Pokanokets and Pocassets into the depths of what Major William Bradford described as a "hideous swamp." In his memoir of the war, Church says almost nothing about this particular battle, most probably because he was required to fight with the Plymouth companies, which were, according to William Hubbard, the last to enter and the first to retreat.

Instead of Church, it was Samuel Moseley who once again led the
charge. Moseley and his privateers were assisted by a pack of dogs, but
even they proved of limited effectiveness in the Pocasset Swamp. As far
as the English were concerned, the Indians, who camouflaged themselves with tree branches and ferns, were virtually invisible in this dark,
wet, and densely overgrown environment. While the leather shoes of
the English succumbed to the sucking mud, the Indians danced
weightlessly across the mire, their flintlocks cradled in their arms.
Needless to say, the English matchlocks and pikes proved ineffective in
these conditions, so ineffective, in fact, that it would soon become illegal for a militiaman to equip himself with anything but a flintlock and
a sword.

Almost as soon as Moseley's men entered the swamp, five of them
were dead, the bullets flying, it seemed, from the vegetation itself.
The Indians quickly retreated deeper into the gloom, deserting close
to a hundred wigwams made of bark so green that they proved impossible to burn. The English came upon an old man, who was unable
to keep up with the others, and who told them that Philip had just
been there.

For the next few hours, they ranged about the swamp, but soon discovered, in Hubbard's words, "how dangerous it is to fight in such
dismal woods, when their eyes were muffled with the leaves, and their
arms pinioned with the thick boughs of the trees, as their feet were
continually shackled with the roots spreading every way in those boggy
woods." Several soldiers found themselves firing on their own men,
and as darkness came on, all of them gladly gave up the chase and retreated to more solid ground.

That night, Major Cudworth, the leader of the Plymouth forces,
decided that he had had his fill of swamps. They would do as they had
done on Mount Hope: instead of pursuing the enemy, they'd build a
fort. Cudworth and his fellow officers preferred to think that they now
had Philip and Weetamoo trapped. If they carefully guarded the

swamp and prevented the Indians from escaping, they hoped to starve them out. In addition to the soldiers stationed at forts on Mount Hope and in Pocasset, Cudworth proposed that there be a small "flying army," whose purpose was to prevent the Indians from "destroying cattle and fetching in supply of food, which being attended, will bring them to great straits." If this strategy worked—and he had every reason to believe it would—the war was effectively over. Since there was now no need for a large army, most of the companies from Massachusetts Bay, including Moseley's, were sent back to Boston.

There was unsettling evidence, however, that Philip was not the only Indian sachem at war. A week earlier, on July 14, what appeared to have been Nipmucks from the interior of Massachusetts had fallen on the town of Mendon, twenty miles to the west of Boston, and killed six people. Closer to home, Philip's brother-in-law Tuspaquin, the Black Sachem, had laid waste to Middleborough, while Totoson from the Buzzards Bay region, just to the west of Cape Cod, had attacked the town of Dartmouth, burning houses and killing several inhabitants. While yet another "losing fort" was being constructed at Pocasset, Church accompanied the 112 Plymouth soldiers sent to aid Dartmouth.

Unlike the towns to the east on Cape Cod and the islands, where many of the local Indians were Christian and remained faithful to the English throughout the war, Dartmouth was surrounded by hostile Natives. Every English house, except for three garrisons, had been destroyed, and the decision was quickly made to evacuate all the town's inhabitants to Plymouth.

What seems never to have occurred to Major Cudworth, who led the expedition to Dartmouth, and to Captain Henchman, who was left to build the Pocasset fort, was that Totoson's attack might have been a diversion. On July 30, word reached Henchman that the Indians he was supposedly guarding in the Pocasset Swamp were no longer there. Several hundred Pokanokets and Pocassets had been sighted almost twenty miles to the west of the Taunton River, and they were headed north toward Nipmuck country.

* * *

After fleeing across Mount Hope Bay to the Pocasset Swamp, Philip realized that he must escape from Plymouth Colony. Otherwise the Pokanokets would, as Cudworth had predicted, begin to starve to death. He must find a way to reach his father's old haunts among the Nipmucks, approximately sixty miles to the northwest.

They must somehow cross the Taunton River just above Mount Hope Bay and move with lightning speed past the settlements of Taunton and Rehoboth before crossing a stretch of flat, open country known as the Seekonk Plain to the Seekonk River. Once they'd forded the river, they would head north to the Nipmucks. About a hundred women, children, and elderly were judged to be too weak to complete the journey, and as the night of the escape approached, there were undoubtedly many tearful good-byes.

The English had built their fort at the southern end of the Pocasset Swamp, near where the Taunton River flows into Mount Hope Bay. Philip and Weetamoo headed north, working their way up the full seven-mile length of the swamp over ground the English considered impassable. Since the Taunton River was between them and potential freedom to the west, and they no longer had any canoes, this strategy had the benefit of taking them to where the river was fordable. On a night at the end of July, at dead low tide, probably in the vicinity of modern Dighton, where the river is less than an eighth of a mile wide, 250 of Philip's and Weetamoo's warriors, accompanied by a large number of women and children (including Philip's wife and their eight-year-old son), prepared to cross the Taunton River. They constructed crude rafts of driftwood, and after wading out to the center of the stream, they swam and floated their way to the western bank. As dawn approached, they clambered onto shore and disappeared into the woods.

On July 30, some residents of Taunton were astonished to see several hundred Indians making their way west. A messenger was sent to Rehoboth, a village situated some ten miles west of the modern town of that name, where the minister, Noah Newman, began to organize a party of volunteers to pursue Philip. Also in Rehoboth was a group of approximately fifty newly arrived Mohegan Indians under the command of Uncas's son Oneco. Many in New England had wondered

how the Mohegans would respond to word of the Pokanoket revolt, especially since Philip was known to have sought Uncas's support that
spring. The Mohegans' decision to remain loyal to the English was one
of the few pieces of good news the colonies received in the summer of
1675, and Uncas's son eagerly joined the chase.

By sunset of July 31, the English and Mohegans had pursued Philip
across the Seekonk River into the vicinity of modern North Providence. The trail headed northwest for another ten or so miles, and with
it now almost totally dark, several Mohegan scouts were sent up ahead.
They reported hearing the sounds of wood being chopped as Philip's
men made camp. Leaving their horses behind with some attendants,
the English and Mohegans continued on foot another three miles until
they reached a region known as Nipsachuck, in modern Smithfield,
Rhode Island.

It had been hoped that Captain Henchman and his men, who had
sailed from Pocasset to Providence, would have joined them by now.
But even without reinforcements, they decided they must engage the
enemy. As they prepared to attack in the predawn twilight, five Pocassets from Weetamoo's camp, apparently out foraging for food, stumbled upon them. Shots were fired, and the battle began.

The fighting lasted until nine in the morning, when Philip's and
Weetamoo's men were forced to retreat into a nearby swamp. They had
suffered catastrophic casualties—losing twenty-three men, including
Nimrod, one of Philip's bravest warriors, while the English had lost
only two.

Philip had lost even more men to desertion, and he and his sixty or
so remaining warriors were on the verge of surrender as they huddled at
the edge of the Nipsachuck Swamp. They were starving, exhausted,
and almost out of gunpowder, with several hundred women and children depending on them for protection. But instead of pursuing the
enemy, Captain Henchman, who did not arrive from Providence until
after the fighting was over, decided to wait until the Mohegans had finished stripping the bodies of the dead. Not until the next morning did
he order his men to break camp and pursue Philip.

By then it was too late. Both Weetamoo and Philip had managed to escape. They hadn't gone far when Weetamoo, who had been a reluctant ally of Philip's since the very beginning of the war, decided she must leave her brother-in-law. Many of the women and children were unable to go on much farther. Even if it might mean capture and certain death, the Pocasset sachem resolved that she and two hundred women and children, along with a handful of their husbands and fathers, must seek sanctuary among the nearby Narragansetts to the south. Philip's forces, now down to just forty warriors and a hundred or so women and children, continued north until they were met by several Nipmuck warriors, who escorted them to a remote, well-guarded village at Menameset in modern New Braintree, Massachusetts.

Three times Philip had avoided what seemed like certain capture, but he had been driven from his homeland. His original fighting force of approximately 250 warriors was down to 40, only 30 of whom had guns. The Pokanokets were, for all practical purposes, defeated. Yet, by fighting his way out of Plymouth Colony, Philip was poised to transform a local squabble into a regionwide conflagration.

The Pokanokets were devastated, but the Nipmucks were ready to take up the fight. Just a few days before, they had laid waste to the frontier town of Brookfield, Massachusetts. On Friday, August 6, Philip was greeted by three of the Nipmucks' most powerful sachems. Philip possessed a coat made of wampum, and he used it to good effect. Unstringing the valuable white and purple shell beads, he gave "about a peck" to each of the sachems, "which," according to an eyewitness, "they accepted."

Philip had been the beneficiary of his father's foresight and planning. By moving to Nipmuck country in 1657, Massasoit had given his son both an exit strategy from Mount Hope and an army to take up his cause.

In the months ahead, Philip continued to cut "his coat to pieces" as he ritualistically secured the cooperation of sachems from Connecticut to modern Maine. "[B]y this means," William Hubbard wrote, "Philip . . . kindl[ed] the flame of war . . . wherever he [went]."

CHAPTER FOURTEEN

The God of Armies

*U*PON THE RETURN of her husband in August to her family's home in Duxbury, Alice Church did as many a soldier's wife had done before and has done since: she almost instantly became pregnant. In the months ahead, as a son grew in the womb of Alice Church, the war that had begun in New England's oldest colony spread with terrifying speed to the newest and most distant settlements in the region. The frontier of Massachusetts, which included the Connecticut River valley and modern New Hampshire and Maine, erupted into violence, while a sudden and eerie placidity came to Plymouth. As they all knew, it was yet another calm before yet another storm.

The war in Massachusetts had begun in earnest on August 2 with the Nipmucks' attack on the town of Brookfield, one of the most isolated settlements in the colony. Set in the midst of the wilderness between the towns outside Boston and those along the Connecticut River, Brookfield possessed just twenty houses and was a day's journey from its nearest neighbor, Springfield. As happened with frightening frequency in the months ahead, the fighting began with an ambush. A diplomatic delegation from Boston, hoping to establish peace with the Nipmucks, was suddenly attacked from a hillside overlooking the forest path. Eight English, including three residents of Brookfield, were killed, with just a handful of survivors managing to ride back to town. Soon after their arrival, several hundred Nipmucks descended on Brookfield, and one of the most legendary sieges in the history of New England was under way.

For two days, eighty people, most of them women and children, gathered in the home of Sergeant John Ayres, one of those killed in the

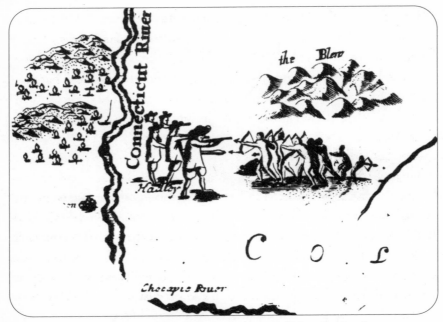

Detail from John Seller's 1675 map of New England

ambush. When the Indians were not burning the rest of the town to the ground, they were firing on the house with guns and flaming arrows, forcing the English to chop holes through the roof and walls so that they could douse the fires. At one point the Nipmucks loaded a cart full of flaming rags and pushed it up against the side of the house. If not for a sudden shower of rain, the garrison would surely have become an inferno. Finally, on the night of August 3, fifty troopers under the command of Major Simon Willard came to the rescue, and the Nipmucks dispersed.

With the attack on Brookfield, inhabitants throughout the western portion of the colony began to fear that they would be next, especially when the Nipmucks moved on Lancaster on August 22 and killed eight English. On August 24, a council of war was held at the town of Hatfield on the Connecticut River, where concerns were voiced about the loyalty of the neighboring Indians. A force of one hundred English was sent out, and the Indians, many of whom did not want to go to war, had no choice but to join the fight against the English. What became known as the battle of South Deerfield resulted in the deaths of nine English and twenty-six Indians as the war quickly spread up and down the river valley. When, four days later, a tremendous hurricane battered the New England coast, the Indians' powwows predicted that the number of English dead would equal the number of trees "blown down in the woods."

On September 3, Richard Beers was sent with thirty-six men to evacuate the town of Northfield. Unaware of the Indians' use of concealment as a tactical weapon, Beers led his men into an ambush and twenty-one were killed. On September 17, a day of public humiliation was declared in Boston. Colonists were told to refrain from "intolerable pride in clothes and hair [and] the toleration of so many taverns." But the Lord remained unmoved. The following day proved to be, according to Hubbard, "that most fatal day, the saddest that ever befell New England."

Captain Thomas Lathrop, sixty-five, was escorting seventy-nine evacuees from the town of Deerfield. They were about to ford a small stream when several of the soldiers laid their guns aside to gather some ripe autumn grapes. At that moment, hundreds of Indians burst out of the undergrowth. Fifty-seven English were killed, turning the brown waters of what was known as Muddy Brook bright red with gore. From then on, the stream was called Bloody Brook. For the Indians, it was an astonishingly easy triumph. "[T]he heathen were wonderfully animated," Increase Mather wrote, "some of them triumphing and saying, that so great a slaughter was never known, and indeed in their wars one with another, the like hath rarely been heard of." But the fighting was not over yet.

Captain Samuel Moseley and his men happened to be nearby, and they heard gunshots. By this time, Moseley was widely known as Massachusetts Bay's most ferocious Indian fighter. An early proponent of the doctrine that the only good Indian is a dead Indian, Moseley refused to trust Native scouts and had nothing but contempt for the colony's Praying Indians. In August he countermanded orders and burned the wigwams of the friendly Penacooks in New Hampshire;

soon after, he seized a group of Praying Indians on a trumped-up charge, strung them together by the neck, and marched them into Boston for punishment. Since Moseley was related to the governor and was now a popular hero, he felt free to do anything he wanted. He also enjoyed shocking the authorities back in Boston. That fall he blithely related in official correspondence that he had ordered a captive Indian woman "be torn in pieces by dogs."

There was no Englishman the Indians hated more, and when Moseley took the field at Bloody Brook, the Nipmuck warriors shouted, "Come on, Moseley, come on. You want Indians. Here are enough Indians for you." For the next six hours Moseley and his men put up a tremendous fight. Scorning the Natives' scattered style of warfare, Moseley ordered his vastly outnumbered men to remain together as a unit as they marched back and forth through the Natives' ranks, firing relentlessly. After hours of fighting, Moseley was forced to ask his two lieutenants to take the lead while he, according to Hubbard, "took a little breath, who was almost melted with laboring, commanding, and leading his men through the midst of the enemy." If not for the arrival of Major Robert Treat and some friendly Mohegans at dusk, Moseley and his men might have been annihilated. The next day, sixty-four Englishmen were buried in a single mass grave.

Less than a month later, on October 5, the Indians fell on Springfield. By day's end, thirty-two houses and twenty-five barns had been burned; several mills had been destroyed and tons of provisions. In all of Springfield, only thirteen of more than seventy-five houses and barns were left standing. "I believe forty families are utterly destitute of subsistence," John Pynchon, son of the town's founder, wrote; "the Lord show mercy to us. I see not how it is possible for us to live here this winter . . . , the sooner we [are] helped off, the better." Pynchon, who had been named the region's military commander, was so shaken by the devastation that he asked to be relieved of his duties.

Prior to the attack, Springfield had enjoyed a long history of good relations with the local Indians. For many Puritans, the burning of Springfield proved once and for all that all Indians—friend and foe alike—were, in Hubbard's words, "the children of the devil, full of all subtlety and malice."

In this climate of mounting paranoia and racial bigotry, the presence of the Praying Indians, situated in their own self-contained villages within a thirty-mile radius of Boston, became intolerable to most New Englanders. When the minister John Eliot and Captain Daniel Gookin, superintendent to the Praying Indians, dared to defend the Indians against unsubstantiated charges of deceit, they received death threats. Finally, Massachusetts authorities determined that the Praying Indians must be relocated to an internment camp on Deer Island in Boston Harbor. On the night of October 30, hundreds of Praying Indians were gathered at a dock on the Charles River. As they prepared to board the three awaiting ships, a scene startlingly reminiscent of the Pilgrims' departure from Delfshaven was enacted. Gookin related "how submissively and Christianly and affectionately those poor souls carried it, seeking encouragement, and encouraging and exhorting one another with prayers and tears at the time of the embarkment, being, as they told some, in fear that they should never return more to their habitations." The ships left at midnight, and in the months ahead, hundreds of Indians died of starvation and exposure on the bleak shores of Deer Island.

By the end of October, New Englanders were desperate for even the most meager scrap of positive news. So many refugees from the towns to the west had flooded Boston that Pynchon's replacement as military commander, Major Samuel Appleton, was instructed to forbid any more inhabitants from leaving their settlements without official permission. Massachusetts Bay and Connecticut were already beginning to run low on food, and in October both colonies embargoed trade in provisions. Some of the bloodiest scenes of the war had occurred in coastal Maine, where the scattered settlement pattern made the inhabitants particularly susceptible to Indian attack. In the months ahead, conditions became so desperate that some Massachusetts authorities considered the possibility of building a palisade wall from the Concord to the Charles rivers and abandoning all the territory to the north, west, and south to the Indians. Since this would effectively have cut off all the settlements in Maine, New Hampshire, and the Connecticut River valley, the wall was never built.

Adding to the fears and frustrations of the English was the elusiveness of the man who had started the conflict. By November, Philip had become an almost mythic figure in the imagination of the Puritans, who saw his hand in every burning house and lifeless English body. In the years to come, traditions sprang up in the river valley of how Philip moved from cave to cave and mountaintop to mountaintop, where he watched with satisfaction as fire and smoke arose from the towns along the blue necklace of the Connecticut.

The truth, however, is less romantic. Instead of being everywhere, Philip appears to have spent much of the summer and fall holed up near the modern Massachusetts-Vermont state border. While he and his handful of poorly equipped warriors may have participated in some of the victories that season, Philip was certainly not the mastermind behind a coordinated plan of Native attack. Indeed, there are no documented instances of his having been present at a single battle in the fall of 1675. Instead of being heralded as a hero, Philip appears to have been resented by more than a few Indians in the Connecticut River valley. One well-known warrior in the Hadley region even attempted to kill the Pokanoket sachem, "alleging," an Indian later recounted, "that Philip had begun a war with the English that had brought great trouble upon them." Although unsuccessful, the assassination attempt indicated that Philip was hardly the dominant and controlling force the English claimed him to be. Rather than looking to the Pokanoket sachem for direction, the Nipmucks and the river valley Indians, as well as the Abenakis in New Hampshire and Maine, were fighting this war on their own.

With Philip having vanished like smoke into the western wilderness, and with unrest and fear growing by the day among the English, colonial authorities needed a foe they could see and fight. To the south, occupying a large and fertile territory claimed by both Massachusetts and Connecticut but presently a part of the infidel colony of Rhode Island, was the largest tribe in the region: the Narragansetts. To date, their sachems had signed two different treaties pledging their loyalty to the English. However, many New Englanders believed that the Narragansetts were simply biding their time. Come spring, when the leaves had returned to the trees, they would surely attack. "[T]his false peace hath undone this country," Mary Pray wrote from Providence on October 20.

The colonial forces determined that as proof of their loyalty the Narragansetts must turn over any and all Pokanokets and Pocassets who were in their midst—especially the female sachem Weetamoo. When an October 28 deadline came and went and no Indians had been surrendered, the decision was made. "The sword having marched eastward and westward and northward," Increase Mather wrote, "now beginneth to face toward the south."

Some Englishmen privately admitted that if the Narragansetts had chosen to join Philip in July, all would have been lost. As the Nipmucks assailed them from the west, the far more powerful Narragansetts might have stormed up from the south, and Boston would have been overrun by a massive pan-Indian army. But instead of acknowledging the debt they owed the Narragansetts, the Puritans resolved to wipe them out.

The United Colonies of Massachusetts, Connecticut, and Plymouth determined to mount the largest army New England had ever seen. From now on, all hope for negotiation was lost. In December, one thousand soldiers, representing close to 5 percent of the region's male English population, would invade the colony of Rhode Island, which refused to participate in the attack. The leader of this mammoth force was to be Plymouth's own Josiah Winslow. Serving as General Winslow's trusted aide was none other than Benjamin Church.

Winslow had originally requested that Church command a company of Plymouth soldiers. But he had declined. In his narrative, he gives no reason for the refusal, saying only he "crave[d] excuse from taking commission." Church was still angry over the enslavement of the Indians the previous summer. In addition, it's probable that he had his doubts about the efficacy of attacking a huge and so far neutral Indian tribe. But there may have been other, more personal reasons for turning down the commission.

As his decision to settle in the wilderness of Sakonnet might indicate, Church preferred to do things his own way. And as the Pease Field Fight had shown, he enjoyed being in charge. Being part of a vast English army was not something that appealed to him. But when General Winslow proposed that he serve as his aide, Church was unable to resist the opportunity to advise the most powerful person in Plymouth Colony.

Church and Winslow rode together to Boston. After meeting with Massachusetts officials, they headed to Dedham Plain, where more than 450 soldiers and troopers were assembling as similar groups gathered in Taunton, Plymouth, and New London. Quotas had been assigned to each colony, with 527 soldiers coming from Massachusetts, 158 from Plymouth, and 325 from Connecticut.

The Massachusetts forces were under the command of Major Appleton, a veteran of the war in the western frontier, with the companies under his command headed by Captains Moseley, Issac Johnson, Joseph Gardner, Nathaniel Davenport, and James Oliver, and a troop of horse under Captain Prentice. The Connecticut forces were under Major Treat, another veteran commander, with Captains Nathaniel Seeley, John Gallop, John Mason, and Thomas Watts heading up the companies. Plymouth's two companies were under Captains William Bradford and John Gorham.

December 2 was declared a day of prayer throughout New England. According to Increase Mather, "the churches were all upon their knees before the Lord, the God of Armies, entreating his favor and gracious success in the undertaking." On December 8, Winslow and his soldiers departed from Dedham. After a night at Woodcock's garrison in modern North Attleboro, the army arrived at Seekonk along the Seekonk River. Winslow ordered Church to sail directly for their next destination, Smith's garrison in Wickford, Rhode Island, while he led the troops on the land route through Providence. That way Church could prepare for his arrival; it also provided Church with the opportunity to share a boat ride with the redoubtable Samuel Moseley.

By this time in the war, Moseley was almost as mythic a figure as Philip himself, while Church, with the exception of the Pease Field Fight, had accomplished almost nothing. If word of Church's righteous indignation over the enslavement of the Indians at Dartmouth and Plymouth had reached Moseley, the former privateer would undoubtedly have viewed the Plymouth carpenter as misguided and weak. It could only be hoped that General Winslow would not rely too heavily on the advice of his softhearted aide.

For his part, Church resolved to prove that he was as skilled at capturing Indians as anyone in New England. Church had been ordered to prepare for Winslow's arrival. But instead of remaining at Smith's garrison in Wickford, Church teamed up with some "brisk blades" from Rhode Island and set out that night in search of Indians. It was a cold December night, but they had the benefit of a nearly full moon. By sunrise the next day, Church and his men had returned to the garrison with eighteen captive Indians. As it turned out, Moseley had also been out that night, and he, too, had captured eighteen Indians.

Winslow and his army had already arrived by the time Church and Moseley returned to Wickford. "The general, pleased with the exploit," Church wrote, "gave them thanks, particularly Mr. Church, the mover and chief actor of the business." There were two Indian children in Church's group, and Winslow decided to make a present of these "likely boys" and send them to friends in Boston. The general grinned at Church and said that "his faculty would supply them with Indians boys enough before the war was ended." As Winslow had made clear last August, slaves were one of the spoils of war.

Moseley had captured an Indian named Peter, who because of a falling-out with one of the Narragansett sachems was willing to talk. Peter claimed the tribe possessed a total of three thousand "fighting men," most of them gathered together with their women and children in the depths of a giant swamp to the southwest. As the English had learned in pursuing Philip, under normal conditions it was almost

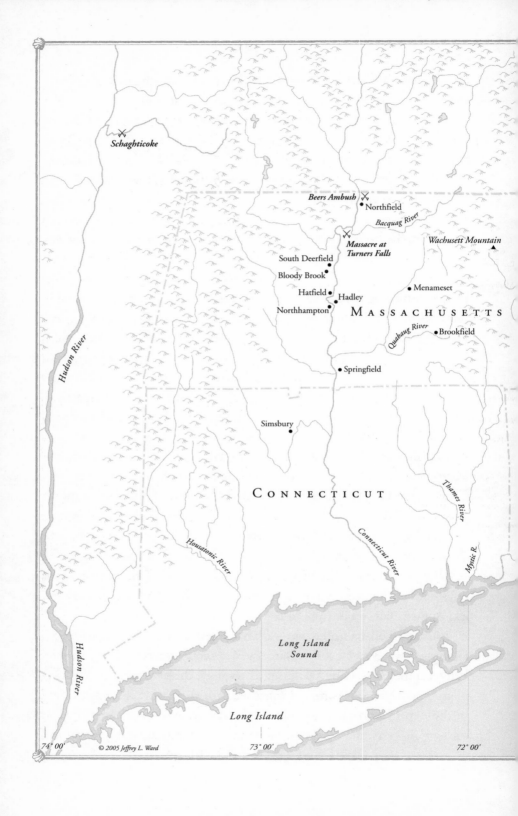

Schaghticoke

Beers Ambush
Northfield

Bacquag River

Massacre at
Turners Falls

Wachusett Mountain

South Deerfield

Bloody Brook

Hatfield
Hadley

Menameset

Northhampton

M A S S A C H U S E T T S

Quabaug River
Brookfield

Springfield

Hudson River

Simsbury

C O N N E C T I C U T

Thames River

Housatonic River

Connecticut River

Mystic R.

Hudson River

Long Island
Sound

Long Island

74° 00'   © 2005 Jeffrey L. Ward   73° 00'   72° 00'

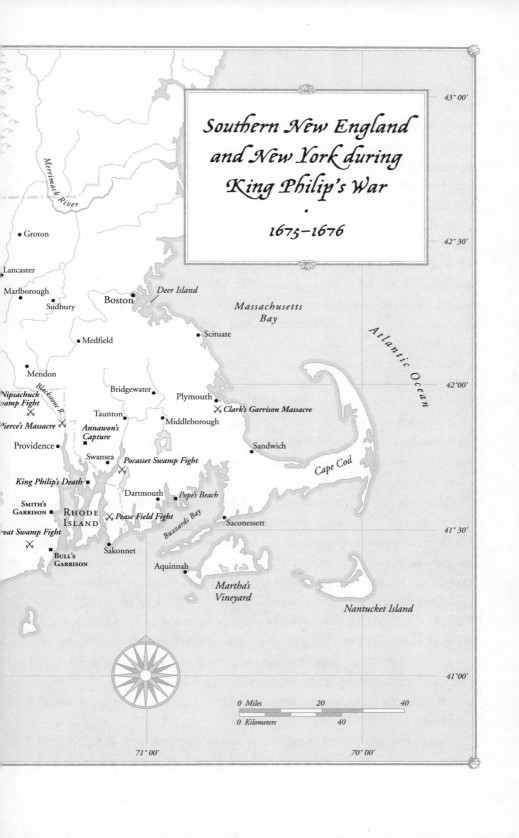

Southern New England and New York during King Philip's War

1675–1676

43° 00'

42° 30'

42° 00'

41° 30'

41° 00'

71° 00'

70° 00'

Merrimack River

Blackstone R.

Groton

Lancaster

Marlborough

Sudbury

Mendon

Nipsachuck
Swamp Fight

Pierce's Massacre

Providence

Bridgewater

Taunton

Annawon's
Capture

Swansea

Pocasset Swamp Fight

King Philip's Death

SMITH'S
GARRISON

RHODE
ISLAND

Great Swamp Fight

BULL'S
GARRISON

Sakonnet

Dartmouth

Pease Field Fight

Pope's Beach

Buzzards Bay

Saconessett

Aquinnah

Martha's
Vineyard

Boston

Deer Island

Medfield

Plymouth

Middleborough

Clark's Garrison Massacre

Scituate

Massachusetts
Bay

Sandwich

Cape Cod

Atlantic Ocean

Nantucket Island

0 Miles   20   40

0 Kilometers   40

impossible to fight the Indians in a swamp. But these were not normal conditions. It had been a bitterly cold December, so cold that the wetlands had frozen solid. As a consequence, Winslow could now take his army just about anywhere. The real problem was how to find the Narragansetts. It was true that there were no leaves on the trees, but the swamplands around modern Kingston, Rhode Island, were still so dense with undergrowth that even the most experienced guide would have difficulty navigating them to the Indians' lair. Peter, however, claimed he could find it.

For them to move on the Narragansetts, Winslow had to march his army south to Jireh Bull's garrison in modern Narragansett, Rhode Island. From there it should be a six- to seven-mile march to the swamp. But on December 15, Winslow received disturbing news. The Indians had attacked the garrison, killing fifteen people and burning it to the ground, effectively robbing him of a location from which to launch the attack. Even more troubling was that the Connecticut soldiers under the command of Major Treat had not yet arrived. Two days later, Winslow learned that Treat and 300 English and 150 friendly Mohegan and Pequot Indians had arrived at the burned-out shell of Bull's garrison. The next day, Winslow's force set out to the south, arriving at the garrison around five in the evening.

The next day was a Sunday, but Winslow decided he had no choice but to attack. Otherwise his entire army might freeze and starve to death. The frigid temperatures had frozen in the supply ships that were to provide his soldiers with food. Most of his men had only enough provisions to last them a single day. With the garrison in ruins, his army had no shelter during one of the coldest nights in New England's history. The temperature was not only bitterly cold, it had begun to snow. "That night was very snowy," Captain Oliver wrote, "We lay a thousand in the open field that long night." By morning, the snow was two to three feet deep. Even before the men headed out at 5 a.m., the hands of many were so frostbitten that they were unable to work their muskets.

For eight hours they marched without stop through the drifting snow, with Moseley's company in the lead and with the soldiers from

Connecticut taking up the rear. What was to have been just a seven-mile trek proved more than double that as the army was forced to follow a circuitous route along the high ground to the north. Finally, around 1 p.m., they came to the edge of a dense swamp. Indians began to fire from the trees and bushes, and Peter announced that they had arrived at their destination. Winslow appears to have had no particular plan of what to do next. Two Massachusetts companies, led by Captains Johnson and Davenport, pursued the Indians into the swamp "without," Hubbard wrote, "staying for word of command, as if everyone were ambitious who should go first."

They had not gone far when they were presented with a truly awe-inspiring sight. Ahead of them, looming above the frozen, snow-covered swamp, was a huge wooden fort. No one had ever seen anything quite like it. Set on a five-acre island and containing approximately five hundred wigwams and thousands of Indians, the fort combined elements of Native and European design. In addition to a palisade wall of vertically planted tree trunks, the fort was surrounded by a sixteen-foot-thick "hedge" of clay and brushwork. At the fort's corners and exposed points were flankers and what the English described as blockhouses—structures made of tree branches from which the Indians could fire at anyone attempting to scale the wall. The fort had a single point of entry, where a massive tree trunk spanned a moatlike sheet of frozen water. Any Englishman who attempted to cross the tree trunk would be picked off by the Indians long before he made it into the fort. If they had any hope of breaching the wall, they must find another way in.

Peter, their Indian guide, was not sure whether there was, in fact, an alternative entrance. Hubbard later insisted that it was God who led the English to the one place where there was a possibility of piercing the Indians' defenses. In a remote corner of the fort there was a section that appeared to be unfinished. Instead of vertical logs and a thick clay barrier, there was a section of horizontally laid tree trunks that was just four feet high and wide enough for several men to scramble into the fort at a time. But what soon became known as the "trees of death" was probably not, as the English assumed, an unfinished portion of the fort. Rather than an Achilles' heel, it may have been an intentional feature designed to direct the English to a single, defensible point. On either side of the gap were flankers, where Indians equipped with muskets could rake any soldiers who dared to storm the opening; there was also a blockhouse directly across from the opening to dispose of anyone who managed to enter the fort. If the Narragansetts' supplies of gunpowder had held out throughout that long afternoon, the English would have come to realize just how ingenious the design of this fort really was.

In the end, the fort provided eloquent proof of who were the true aggressors in this conflict. Instead of joining the Pokanokets and Nipmucks, the Narragansetts had spent the fall and winter doing everything in their power to defend themselves against an unprovoked Puritan attack. If ever there was a defensive structure, it was this fort, and now a thousand English soldiers were about to do their best to annihilate a community of more than three thousand Indian men, women, and children, who asked only to be left alone.

As soldiers spread themselves along the perimeter and poured shot at the fort, the companies led by Captains Johnson and Davenport prepared to go in. With the officers leading the way, they charged the four-foot-high section of the fort. As soon as Johnson reached the logs, he was shot dead. Captain Davenport was wearing "a very good buff suit," and it was believed the Indians mistook him for General Winslow himself. He was hit three times, and after handing his musket to his lieutenant, died of his wounds. The fire from the flankers and blockhouse was so fierce that those soldiers who were not already dead fell on their faces and waited for reinforcements.

It was now time for Captains Moseley and Gardner to give it a try. Moseley later bragged that once inside the fort he saw the muskets of fifty different Indians all trained on him. Moseley survived the onslaught, but his men were unable to make any significant progress into the fort.

Next came Major Appleton and Captain Oliver. Instead of a helter-skelter rush, they organized their men into "a storming column." Crying out, "[T]he Indians are running!" Appleton's and Oliver's men were able to push past their comrades from Massachusetts Bay and take the flanker on the left side of the entrance. In addition to reducing the deadliness of the Indians' fire by approximately a third, the capture of the flanker provided the soldiers with some much-needed protection.

Holding his own Plymouth companies in reserve, Winslow sent in the soldiers from Connecticut. Although one of the flankers had been taken, no one had informed the Connecticut officers of the danger posed by the blockhouse directly opposite the entrance. Major Treat and his men ran headlong into fire so deadly that four of five Connecticut captains were killed. The soldiers were, in Hubbard's words, "enraged rather than discouraged by the loss of their commanders," and pushed on into the fort.

As the fighting raged on, Benjamin Church began to regret his decision not to lead a company of his own. "[I]mpatient of being out of the heat of the action, he importunately begged leave of the general that he might run down to the assistance of his friends." Winslow reluctantly yielded to his request, provided that Church take some soldiers with him. Thirty Plymouth men instantly volunteered, and Church and his makeshift company were on their way into battle.

Church had no sooner entered the fort than he saw "many men and several valiant captains lie slain." There were also many Indian bodies, with more than fifty corpses piled high in a corner of the fort. To his left, fighting amid the wigwams, was a friend of Church's, Captain Gardner of Salem. Church called out to Gardner, and the two men exchanged glances when the captain suddenly slumped to the ground. Church ran up to him and, seeing blood trickle down Gardner's cheek, lifted up his cap. Gardner looked up at Church but "spoke not a word." A bullet had passed through his skull, and before Church could say anything, Gardner was dead.

Studying the wound, Church realized that the bullet had come from the upland side of the swamp and therefore must have come from an English musket. As soldiers pulled Gardner's body from the fort, Church sent word back to Winslow that English soldiers were being killed by their comrades behind them. Now that the tide had turned in the direction of the English, it was time for General Winslow to apply some method to his army's advance. With between three hundred and four hundred soldiers inside this extremely confined space, the English posed as much a threat to themselves as did the Narragansetts, who after several hours of fighting were beginning to run out of gunpowder.

Church could see that many of the warriors had started to abandon the fort, leaving large numbers of Native women, children, and elderly trapped in their wigwams. Instead of running away, the warriors had taken up positions amid the bushes and trees of the swamp and were firing on the English soldiers inside the fort. It was clear to Church that the fort had been effectively taken. It was time for him to take care of the Indians in the swamp. Church led his men out of the fort, and they soon found "a broad bloody track," where the Indians had dragged away their dead and dying men. They came upon an Indian who, instead of firing on them, pulled his gun across his chest in a sign of peace. Hoping to acquire some useful information, Church ordered his men not to hurt the Indian, but to Church's "great grief and disappointment," a soldier coming up from the rear killed the Indian before he had a chance to speak with him.

A shout erupted from the swamp, somewhere between them and the fort. It was a group of Narragansetts "running from tree to tree" as they fired on the English. Now the trick was to attack the Indians without being killed by the soldiers inside the fort. After alerting a sergeant to their presence, Church led his men to a dense clump of bushes just a few yards behind the Indians, who were preparing to fire a coordinated volley at the fort. Church and his men were about to attack them when the sergeant cried out to hold their fire; they were about to kill "friend Indians."

But as Church soon realized, these were not Mohegans and Pequots; these were Narragansetts, and there was now, in Church's words, "a formidable black heap of them" preparing to fire on the unwitting sergeant and anyone else unlucky enough to be near him. "Now brave boys," Church whispered to his men, "if we mind our hits, we may have a brave shot. [L]et our sign for firing on them be their rising up to fire into the fort." Soon after, the Indians stood up in a group to fire, but not before Church and his men gave them such an "unexpected clap on their backs" that those who were not dead were soon running in confusion. About a dozen of them even ran back *into* the fort and took refuge in the blockhouse.

Church and his men quickly followed and approached the blockhouse. The structure appeared to be quite rickety—Church described it as "a sort of hovel that was built with poles, after the manner of a corn crib"—and he decided that the best strategy was simply to topple it over with the Indians still inside. They were running toward the blockhouse when Church realized that one of the Narragansetts had pushed his musket through a gap in the poles and that the gun was pointed not just in his direction but at his groin.

The next thing Church knew, he had been hit by three pieces of lead. The first bullet buried itself harmlessly into a pair of mittens rolled up inside his pocket; the second cut through his breeches and drawers but only nicked him in the side; it was the third bullet that almost killed him—slicing into his thigh before glancing off his hipbone. As Church fell to the ground, he made sure to discharge his gun and wound the Indian who had wounded him.

His men rushed to his side and began to carry him out of the fort, but Church insisted that they first complete their mission, especially since the Indians had no charges left in their muskets. But as they prepared for another assault on the blockhouse, the Indians started to shoot at them with arrows, one of which cut into the arm of the soldier whom Church was clutching for support. Without their commander to lead them, the Plymouth soldiers became, in Church's words, "discouraged" and abandoned their attempt to upset the blockhouse. But by this time Church's attention was elsewhere.

It was approaching five in the evening, and with darkness coming on, some of the soldiers had begun to set fire to the wigwams inside the fort. This was a needless, potentially disastrous act. Not only did the wigwams contain hundreds of Native women and children; they possessed tons of provisions. In fact, there were so many baskets and tubs of corn and meat lining the interiors of the wigwams that Church claimed they had been rendered "musket-proof." A former commissary general, he quickly assessed the situation. The colonial army was on the verge of starvation; it was already close to sundown, and there were at least sixteen snow-covered miles between them and the Smith garrison at Wickford. Dozens, if not hundreds, of men (himself included) were wounded, and a march of this length in subfreezing temperatures was tantamount to collective suicide. Instead of burning the Narragansett fort and the valuable food it held, they should take up residence in it for the night. After helping themselves to the Indians' corn and meat and keeping themselves warm within the snug confines of the wigwams, they could set out the next day for Wickford. Someone must stop these men from torching the fort.

The orders to destroy the fort had just come from the general himself. Church pleaded with the soldiers to desist from firing the wigwams until he had a chance to speak with Winslow. With the assistance of at least one of his men, Church hobbled out of the fort to the low hill where the general surveyed the action from the saddle of his horse.

Winslow listened to Church's impassioned appeal and, after conferring with some of the officers gathered around him, decided that the proposal had much merit. The army would do as Church had suggested and move into the fort for the night. Winslow had begun to ride toward the fort, when Captain Moseley suddenly appeared from the edge of the swamp and asked "[W]hither he was going."

Winslow replied that he was about to enter the fort. Moseley grabbed the reins of the general's horse and exclaimed, "His life was worth a hundred of theirs, and he should not expose himself." Winslow said that "Mr. Church had informed him that the fort was taken . . . [and] that it was most practicable for him, and his army to shelter themselves in the fort."

"Church lies!" Moseley thundered. The fort was not yet secure. If the general moved another inch, he would shoot his horse out from under him.

Had Church not been injured, he might have countered Moseley's insubordination with a threat of his own, but as it was he was barely conscious from loss of blood. It was then that a doctor in the group joined the fray, insisting that Church's proposal would "kill more men than the enemy had killed, for by tomorrow the wounded men will be so stiff that there will be no moving them." Noticing that Church had a serious wound of his own, the doctor threatened to deny him medical attention if the general decided to follow his aide's advice, claiming Church "should bleed to death like a dog before they would endeavor to stench his blood."

It was almost laughably ironic. Throughout the weeks and months of the first phase of the war, the English had been obsessed with *building* forts. Now that they had a perfectly serviceable and well-stocked fort at their disposal, all they wanted to do was destroy it. The difference, of course, was that this was a Native-built structure. For Indian haters like Moseley, the idea of sleeping in a wigwam and eating the Indians' food was abhorrent. It was far better to consume this wretched fortress in purifying fire than spend a single night living like the heathen enemy.

There was also a more justifiable fear of ambush. They had sixteen miles to cover before they reached the safety of the Smith garrison in Wickford. An Indian captive claimed that in addition to the Narragansett warriors who had survived the attack, there were another 1,500 waiting just a mile and a half away. If they did not leave immediately, before the Narragansetts had the chance to regroup, their battered and exhausted soldiers would be virtually defenseless against a well-executed Native ambush. Best to depart while the enemy was still reeling from the attack.

The Plymouth governor might have been named commander of this army, but Massachusetts Bay was apparently in charge. Winslow once again reversed himself, and the fort, along with all its provisions and perhaps hundreds of Native women, children, and elderly, was consigned to the fire. Contemporary accounts of the battle focus on the bravery of the English officers and soldiers but make little mention of the slaughter that followed the taking of the fort. It must have been a horrendous and terrifying scene as Narragansett women and children screamed and cried amid the gunshots and the flames. Thirty-eight years before, Narragansett warriors had been sickened by the burning of the Pequot fort at Mystic, Connecticut. On this day, December 19, 1675, Pequot warriors were there to watch the Narragansetts meet a similar fate. The English later claimed that the Pequots and Mohegans had been faithless allies that day, firing their muskets up into the air rather than at the enemy. One can hardly blame them, if the claim was true.

Sometime after five o'clock, the order was given to begin the long march to Wickford. According to one account, the flames rising up from the burning fort lit the army's way for as many as three miles through the wilderness.

It was the worst night of the soldiers' lives. They had spent the previous night attempting to sleep on an open field in the midst of a snowstorm; that morning they had marched for eight hours and then fought for another three, and now they were slogging their way through the snow—eight hundred men lugging the bodies of more than two hundred of the dead and wounded. "And I suppose," Church wrote, "everyone that is acquainted with the circumstances of that night's march, deeply laments the miseries that attended them, especially the wounded and dying men." The first ones reached the Smith garrison at 2 a.m. Winslow and his entourage became lost and did not arrive at Wickford until seven in the morning.

Twenty-two of the army's wounded died during the march. The next afternoon, thirty-four English corpses were buried in a mass grave; six more died over the next two days. Those wounded who survived the march, including Church and Captain Bradford (who had been injured in the eye), were shipped to Newport on Aquidneck Island for medical treatment. The Puritan historian William Hubbard had an undeniable Massachusetts Bay bias. But after interviewing many of the participants, even he had to admit that Church had been correct: "Many of our wounded men perished, which might otherwise have been preserved, if they had not been forced to march so many miles in a cold and snowy night, before they could be dressed."

The battle became known as the Great Swamp Fight, and more than 20 percent of the English soldiers had been either killed or wounded—double the casualty rate of the American forces at D-day. Of all the colonies, Connecticut had suffered the most. Major Treat (who was the last one out of the fort) reported that four of his five captains had been killed and that eighty of his three hundred soldiers were either dead or wounded. This makes for a casualty rate of almost 30 percent—roughly equivalent to the Confederate losses at Antietam on the bloodiest day of the Civil War. Major Treat insisted that his men return to Connecticut, and despite the outraged objections of Winslow and his staff, who were already contemplating another strike against the Narragansetts, the Connecticut forces marched for Stonington on December 28.

But as Winslow knew all too well, his army was not about to go anywhere. One supply vessel had managed to make it to Wickford, but the rest of the ships were trapped in the ice of Boston Harbor. The severity of the weather meant that it took five anxious days before Bostonians heard the news of the army's hard-fought victory.

As late as 1906 the historian George Bodge insisted that the Great Swamp Fight "was one of the most glorious victories ever achieved in our history, and considering the conditions, as displaying heroism, both in stubborn patience and dashing intrepidity, never excelled in American warfare." It cannot be denied that the assault struck a merciless blow at the Narragansetts. Estimates varied wildly, but somewhere between 350 and 600 Native men, women, and children were either shot or incinerated that day. And yet there were still thousands of Narragansetts left alive. If they could make their way north to Nipmuck country, the number of hostile Indian warriors would be more than doubled. Instead of saving New England, Winslow's army had only increased the danger.

Two young sachems were left to head up the remnants of the tribe: Canonchet, who had traveled to Boston that fall to carry on negotiations with Puritan officials, and Quinnapin, who had brazenly announced his defiance of the English by marrying the Pocasset sachem Weetamoo.

Before he had abandoned the fort, Canonchet had been careful to leave a message for the English. In the final minutes of the battle, as the soldiers moved from wigwam to wigwam with firebrands in their hands, one of them had found it: the treaty Canonchet had signed in Boston. The Puritans looked to the document as proof that the Narragansetts had been fully aware of their treaty violations, but as

Canonchet now knew for a certainty, it was a piece of parchment that had been worthless from the start.

In the weeks ahead, Church lay in a bed in Newport, racked with fever, as his body fought off the infections associated with his wounds. The weather outside remained brutally cold—so cold that eleven of the replacement soldiers sent from Boston during the first week of January died of exposure before they reached Winslow's army at Wickford.

On January 14, some soldiers captured a man who they at first thought was an Indian but who proved to be an Englishman. His name was Joshua Tefft, and he claimed that he had been captured by Canonchet prior to the Great Swamp Fight and forced to become his slave. He had been present at the battle but had not fired a gun. But many soldiers said they had seen him taking part in the fighting.

What made Tefft's guilt a certainty, in many men's minds, was his appearance. Without English clothes and with a weather-beaten face, he *looked* like an Indian to the English. Tefft was a troubling example of what happened to a man when the Puritan's god and culture were stripped away and Native savagery was allowed to take over. Two days after his capture, Tefft was hanged and, as was befitting a traitor, drawn and quartered. Hubbard claimed there were few tears at his execution, "standers by being unwilling to lavish pity upon him that had divested himself of nature itself, as well as religion, in a time when so much pity was needed elsewhere."

In the middle of January, the temperature began to rise. A thaw unlike anything seen in New England since the arrival of the Pilgrims melted the snow and ice. It was just what the Narragansetts had been waiting for. The English could no longer track them in the snow. To augment their scanty provisions, the Indians could now dig for groundnuts. The time had come for the Narragansetts to make a run for it and join Philip and the Nipmucks to the north.

On January 21, Winslow received word that the Indians were "in full flight." Not until almost a week later, on January 27, did the army—swelled to 1,400 with the arrival of Major Treat's Connecticut forces—begin its pursuit.

By this time, Benjamin Church had returned. He was not yet fully recovered, but he agreed to join in what was hoped to be the final knockout punch against the Indians. Reports claimed that there were 4,000 of them, including 1,800 warriors, marching north. If they should reach the wilderness of Nipmuck country, New England was in for a winter and spring of violence and suffering.

About ten miles north of Providence, Winslow's soldiers came upon a pile of sixty horse heads. The Narragansetts were scouring the land for anything that was edible. Unfortunately, this left little for the English, who were almost as poorly provisioned as the Indians. On a few occasions, the soldiers leading the English army were able to catch a glimpse of the rear of the Narragansett exodus only to watch the Indians disappear into the forest as soon as they came under attack.

Without sufficient supplies of food and with no way to engage the enemy, the morale of the English soldiers deteriorated with each day, and desertions became endemic. The temperature started to plummet once again, and illness swept through the English ranks; even General Winslow was reported to be suffering from the flux. Several days into what became known as the Hungry March, they came upon some wigwams beside an icy swamp. After exchanging gunfire, the Indians fled, although a friendly Mohegan managed to capture a Narragansett warrior who had been wounded in the leg.

That night, the Indian captive was brought before General Winslow for interrogation. It appeared to Church that the Narragansett was surprisingly forthcoming, but some of Winslow's advisers suggested that they torture him until he offered "a more ample confession." Church, who doubted that the Indian had anything more to divulge, insisted that he be allowed to live. Once again, Church's advice was ignored. It was pointed out that the captive was injured, and they were in the midst of a strenuous march. To prevent the Narragansett from slowing them down the next day, it was decided that he must be executed.

The Indian was taken over to a large bonfire, where the Mohegan who had captured him prepared to cut off his head. "[T]aking no de-light in the sport," Church limped over to where the army's supply horses were standing in the cold, jets of steam flowing from their nos-trils. Church was about fifty yards from the fire, when the Mohegan raised his hatchet. Just as the weapon was about to slice through his neck, the Narragansett jerked his head to the side and broke free of the Mohegan's grasp. Despite his injury, he began to run—directly, it turned out, for Benjamin Church, who was concealed in the darkness beyond the glow of the fire.

Church was still so lame that he needed the help of at least two peo-ple to mount his horse. He had tents in his wounds—plugs of gauze used to promote the drainage of pus and blood. This did not prevent him from tackling the Narragansett, who was stark naked and slippery with bear grease. After rolling around together on the ground, the In-dian broke free of Church's grasp and was running once again, this time with Church in close pursuit.

Since they were both wounded, there were, in Church's words, "no great odds in the race." They were lumbering over a frozen swamp, and the ice crackled so loudly with each of their steps that Church hoped his English friends back at the fire would "follow the noise and come to his assistance" even though it was impossible to see much of anything in the starless night. The Indian might have escaped if he had not blun-dered into a tree and nearly knocked himself out.

Soon the two of them were once again rolling around on the ground. This time the Indian grabbed Church by the hair and was at-tempting to twist his head and break his neck. Church's wounds had "somewhat weakened him," but he did his best to fight back by apply-ing several "notorious bunts in the [Indian's] face with his head." As they mauled each another, Church could hear the welcome sound of cracking ice approaching from the fire. It proved to be the Mohegan. Feeling for them in the dark, he determined who was the naked Indian and who was the clothed Englishman, and "with one blow settled his hatchet in between them, and ended the strife." The Mohegan gave Church a thankful hug and then "cut off the head of his victim, and carried it to the camp."

* * *

By February 5, the Hungry March had reached the town of Marlborough at the eastern fringes of Nipmuck country. Winslow decided that he had no choice but to disband his army. Church returned to his pregnant wife, Alice, and their son, Thomas, who had been staying with family and friends in Duxbury.

The march had been an unmitigated catastrophe. Back in December, colonial officials had hoped to wipe the Narragansetts off the face of the earth. Instead, they had flushed thousands of them into the arms of the enemy.

The Puritans had claimed it was common knowledge among the Indians that the Narragansetts were planning to join the war in the spring. However, no one seems to have informed the Nipmucks of this plan. When the first Narragansett warriors began to arrive in January, they were shot at. As far as the Nipmucks knew, they were still traitors to the cause and had, in all likelihood, joined the English. Only after the Narragansetts had presented them with English scalps as proof of their loyalty did the Nipmuck sachems begin to realize that they had a new and powerful ally. Thanks to the intervention of the English in Rhode Island, there was yet another tribe eager to take up the fight.

But where were Philip and the Pokanokets?

CHAPTER FIFTEEN

In a Strange Way

SICK, DESPERATE, and fast becoming irrelevant to the war he had started, Philip and his small band of warriors headed more than fifty miles west to the Hudson River valley. In late December they made camp at Schaghticoke on the Hoosic River, an eastern tributary of the Hudson. It was here in the colony of New York, where a remnant of the original Dutch settlers still actively traded with the Indians and where the Hudson River provided access to the French to the north, that Philip hoped to stage his triumphant return to the war.

That fall, Philip had met with a French official on his way back to Canada after a visit to Boston. The Frenchman had presented the sachem with an ornate brass gun and pledged his country's support in his war against the English. Specifically, he had promised Philip three hundred Indian warriors from Canada and all the powder and shot he needed. He even claimed the French navy would set up a blockade along the coast of New England to stop the flow of English supplies from Europe. But the Frenchman also had some requests of Philip. He asked that he and his warriors not burn the meetinghouses, mills, and "best houses." "[F]or we intend to be with you in the spring before planting season . . . ," he said, "and possess ourselves of [the] Connecticut River and other English plantations."

Philip was, once again, following in his father's footsteps. He, too, was attempting to strengthen his decimated tribe through an alliance with a European power. There was no guarantee that the French would be any more trustworthy than the English in the long run, but at least for now Philip would have the warriors and ammunition he desperately needed. So he and his men, led by his principal captain, Annawon, established winter quarters at Schaghticoke and waited for the French and their Native allies.

In early January, New York governor Edmund Andros worriedly wrote to officials in New England that Philip had been joined by "3 or 400 North Indians, fighting men" at Schaghticoke. By February, Philip's forces had reportedly grown to 2,100 and included 600 "French Indians with straws in their noses." Although this figure was undoubtedly exaggerated, Philip had succeeded beyond all expectations in assembling one of the largest forces of Indian warriors in the region.

But there was another Native group to consider. The Mohawks, a powerful subset of the Iroquois, lived in the vicinity of Albany and were the most feared warriors in the Northeast. In addition to being the traditional enemies of the Indians of southern New England, they had a special hatred of the French and their Indian allies to the north. Yet if Philip could somehow succeed in bringing the Mohawks into the war on his side, he would be in a position to bring the New England colonies to their knees.

But Philip was not the only one seeking an alliance with the Mohawks. Governor Andros also hoped to enlist their aid. Unlike the Puritan magistrates, who viewed all Indians as potential enemies, Andros saw the Mohawks and the rest of the Iroquois as powerful independent entities that must be dealt with diplomatically rather than through force and intimidation. Andros and the Iroquois were in the midst of creating what became known as the Covenant Chain, a mutually beneficial partnership between the colony and the Iroquois that would stand for generations. It became Andros's mission to persuade the Mohawks that Philip and the tribes to the east were a threat to that alliance. But it may have been Philip, instead of Andros, who ultimately brought the Mohawks over to the English side.

According to the Puritan historian Increase Mather, the Pokanoket sachem decided he must resort to a deception if he was going to create an alliance with the Mohawks. So he and his warriors killed a "scattering" group of Mohawks and blamed the murders on the English. Unknown to Philip, one of the Mohawks had escaped and reported that the Pokanoket sachem was behind the attack. Whether or not Philip was, as Mather maintained, the cause of his own downfall, sometime in late February, the Mohawks attacked his forces in Schaghticoke. By all accounts, it was a rout. On March 4, Governor Andros witnessed the triumphant return of the Mohawks to Albany. In addition to plenty of prisoners, they proudly displayed the scalps of the many Indians they had killed.

Once again, Philip's forces were on the run, this time headed east, back to the Connecticut River. Instead of leading an invincible Native army, Philip was back to being a mere sachem with a reputation for grandstanding and defeat. The future of the war was in others' hands.

His name was Job Kattenanit. He was a Praying Indian being held on Deer Island. Before he had been transported to the island, his village had been attacked by the Nipmucks, who'd taken his three children captive. By December, Job, who was a widower, was desperate to find his children, and he and another Praying Indian named James volunteered to become spies for the English. They were to infiltrate the Nipmucks at Menameset, the village near Brookfield to which Philip had fled after escaping from Plymouth, and learn anything they could about the Indians' plans for the winter. If Job was lucky, he might also make contact with his three children. It was dangerous duty to be sure, but James and Job could truthfully tell the Nipmucks that they had been so abused and reviled by the English that they had been given no choice but to leave them.

James was the first to return, on January 24. He reported that the Nipmucks had at first threatened to kill them, but a sachem who had fought with James against the Mohawks several years earlier spoke in his defense, and they had been allowed to live. Job had located his children, who were all still alive, and he had decided to remain with them at Menameset for as long as possible. James reported to Daniel Gookin that the Nipmucks had "rejoiced much" when they learned that the Narragansetts had been forced to join their struggle. Now that most of the English towns along the Massachusetts portion of the Connecticut

River had been abandoned, the Indians planned to attack the settlements to the east, including Medfield, Marlborough, Sudbury, Groton, and Concord, but it would begin with Lancaster. James even knew the details of how the Nipmucks planned to do it. First they would destroy the bridge that provided the only access point to the settlement from the east. Knowing that there was no way for English reinforcements to reach it, the Indians could burn the town with impunity.

Much of what James said was corroborated by other reports. But the Massachusetts authorities chose to dismiss his warnings as the untrustworthy testimony of just another Indian. General Winslow and his army were then doing their best to eliminate the Nipmuck-Narragansett menace, and it was hoped the Indians would be unable to resume their attacks. But by early February, Winslow's army had been disbanded, leaving the western portion of the colony more vulnerable than ever before. Then, at ten o'clock on the night of February 9, Daniel Gookin was awakened by an urgent pounding on the door of his home in Cambridge. It was Job.

Like James before him, he had traveled with "rackets on his feet" through the drifting snow of the western frontier. He was starving and exhausted; he was already fearful of what might happen to his children, whom he had been forced to leave with the Nipmucks; but he felt a responsibility to tell Gookin that everything James had reported was true. Four hundred Nipmucks and Narragansetts were about to descend on Lancaster, and there was very little time. The attack was scheduled to begin tomorrow, February 10, at daybreak.

Gookin leaped out of bed and sent a dispatch to Marlborough, where Captain Samuel Wadsworth and about forty troops were stationed. The messenger rode all that night, and by morning Wadsworth and his men were riding furiously for Lancaster, about ten miles away. As both James and Job had predicted, the bridge had been burned, but Wadsworth and his troops were able to get their horses across its still-smoldering timbers. Up ahead the English soldiers could see smoke rising into the sky and hear the shouts of the Indians and the firing of muskets. The attack had already begun.

* * *

Mary Rowlandson was thirty-eight years old, and the mother of three children—Joseph, eleven; Mary, ten; and Sarah, six. In a few years' time she would be the author of *The Sovereignty and Goodness of God,* an account of her capture by the Indians that became one of America's first bestsellers. But on February 10, 1676, she was simply the wife of Lancaster's minister, John Rowlandson, who was away in Boston urging the authorities to provide his town with some protection.

As the wife of a minister, Mary was one of Lancaster's foremost citizens. Instead of Goodwife Rowlandson, she was addressed as Mistress Rowlandson. Adding to her stature in the community was the fact that her father, John White, had been one of Lancaster's earliest and wealthiest residents, and Mary had six brothers and sisters, many of whom still lived in town. Mary and John's large home, built beside a hill and with a barn nearby, served as the town's social center. Mary especially enjoyed the nights before and after the Sabbath, "when my family was about me, and relations and neighbors with us, we could pray and sing, and then refresh our bodies with [food from] the good creatures of God."

On the morning of February 10, the residents of Lancaster had taken the precaution of gathering in five different garrisons, one of which included the Rowlandson home. When the Indians attacked at daybreak, there were between forty and fifty men, women, and children assembled in the Rowlandson garrison.

First they heard the musket fire in the distance. When they looked cautiously out the windows, they could see that several houses were already burning. They could hear shouts and screams as the Indians worked their way from house to house until suddenly they too were under attack.

Dozens of Indians took up positions on the barn roof and on the hill behind the house and began firing on the garrison "so that the bullets seemed to fly like hail." In no time at all, three of the men stationed at the windows had been hit, one of them quite badly in the jaw. The Indians found large quantities of flax and hemp in the barn, and jamming the combustibles up against the sides of the house, they attempted to set the clapboards on fire. One of the men was able to douse the flames with a bucket of water, but the Indians "quickly fired it again," Rowlandson wrote, "and that took." Soon the roof of the house was a roaring maelstrom of flame. "Now is the dreadful hour come," she remembered. "Some in our house were fighting for their lives, others wallowing in their blood, the house on fire over our heads, and the bloody heathen ready to knock us on the head if we stirred out." Mothers and children were "crying out for themselves and one another, 'Lord, what shall we do?' "

With six-year-old Sarah in her arms and her other two children and a niece clustered around her, she resolved "to go forth and leave the house." But as they approached the doorway, the Indians unleashed a volley of "shot so thick that the bullets rattled against the house as if one had taken a handful of stones and threw them." Mary and the children paused, but with the flames roaring behind them, they had no choice but to push ahead, even though they could see the Indians waiting for them with their muskets, hatchets, and spears. Her brother-in-law John, already wounded, was the first to die. The Indians shouted and began to strip his body of clothes as they continued firing at anyone who dared leave the house. Rowlandson was hit in the side, the bullet passing through her and into the abdomen of the child she clutched protectively in her arms. Her nephew William's leg was broken by a bullet, and he was soon killed with a hatchet. "Thus were we butchered by those merciless heathen," she wrote,

A 1771 woodcut depicting the attack on Mary Rowlandson's house

"standing amazed, with the blood running down to our heels." Rowlandson's oldest sister, who had not yet left the house and had just seen her son and brother-in-law killed, cried out, "Lord let me die with them!" Almost immediately, she was struck by a bullet and fell down dead across the threshold of the house.

An Indian grabbed Rowlandson and told her to come with him. Indians had also seized her children Joseph and Mary and were pulling them in the opposite direction. Unbeknownst to Rowlandson, Wadsworth and his troopers had just arrived, and the Indians had decided it was time to leave. She cried out for her children but was assured that if she went along quietly, they would not be harmed. Rowlandson had anticipated this moment and, like many New Englanders, had vowed that "if the Indians should come, I should choose rather to be killed by them than be taken alive." But now, in the presence of the Natives' "glittering weapons" and with Sarah in her arms, she thought differently. She and twenty-three others were taken that day and so began what she later described as "that grievous captivity."

They spent the first night on a hill overlooking the smoldering wreck of Lancaster. A vacant house stood on the hill, and Rowlandson asked if she and her injured daughter might sleep inside. "What, will you love Englishmen still?" mocked the Indians, who exultantly feasted on roasted cattle while Rowlandson and the others were given nothing to eat. "Oh the roaring and singing and dancing and yelling of those black creatures in the night," she remembered, "which made the place a lively resemblance of hell."

They left early the next morning. Rowlandson's wounds had begun to fester, making it impossible for her to carry her daughter. One of the Indians had a horse, and he offered to hold Sarah, who whimpered, "I shall die, I shall die" as Rowlandson staggered behind "with [a] sorrow that cannot be expressed." That night she sat in the snow with her fever-racked daughter in her lap. "[T]he Lord upheld me with His gracious and merciful spirit," she remembered, "and we were both alive to see the light of the next morning."

That afternoon they arrived at the great Nipmuck gathering spot of Menameset. There Rowlandson met Robert Pepper, a captive now for more than five months. Pepper told her to lay oak leaves on her wound, a Native remedy that had helped his injured leg and would also cure Rowlandson. But there was nothing to be done for little Sarah. "I sat much alone with a poor wounded child in my lap," she wrote, "which moaned night and day, having nothing to revive the body or cheer the spirits." Finally on February 18, nine days after being shot, Sarah died.

Before this, Rowlandson had been horrified even to be in the same room with a corpse. Now her daughter's dead body was the only source of comfort she possessed, and that night she slept in the snow with Sarah cradled to her breast. The next morning, the Indians buried her child on the top of a nearby hill. "I have thought since of the wonderful goodness of God to me," Rowlandson wrote, "in preserving me in the use of my reason and sense, in that distressed time, that I did not use wicked and violent means to end my own miserable life." Instead, she went in search of her other two children.

There were more than two thousand Indians gathered at Menameset. Rowlandson had learned that her ten-year-old daughter Mary was living somewhere nearby. That day as she wandered from wigwam to wigwam, she found her. But when her daughter began to sob uncontrollably, the girl's master told Rowlandson that she must leave—"a heart-cutting word to me." "I could not sit still in this condition," she remembered, "but kept walking from one place to another." She prayed to the Lord that he would show her "some sign, and hope of some relief." Soon after, she heard her son's voice.

Joseph had been taken to a village about six miles away. His master's wife had agreed to bring him to his mother, and "with tears in his eyes, he asked me whether his sister Sarah was dead . . . and prayed . . . that I would not be troubled in reference to himself." It was too brief a visit, but Rowlandson could not help but interpret her son's appearance as God's "gracious answer to my earnest and unfeigned desire."

The next day, February 22, several hundred warriors returned from a raid on the town of Medfield, twenty miles southwest of Boston. There had been about two hundred soldiers quartered in the town, but even this sizable force was not enough to prevent the Indians from burning close to fifty houses and killing more than a dozen inhabitants. Even worse, the Indians had the audacity to leave a note. One of the Indians had been formerly employed as a typesetter in Cambridge. Known as James the Printer, he undoubtedly penned the letter that was found stuffed into a gap in a nearby bridge: "Know by this paper, that the Indians that thou hast provoked to wrath and anger, will war this twenty-one years if you will; there are many Indians yet, we come three hundred at this time. You must consider the Indians lost nothing but their life; you must lose your fair houses and cattle."

When the war party returned to Menameset, the warriors shouted a total of twenty-three times to indicate how many English had been killed. "Oh! The outrageous roaring and hooping that there was . . . ," Rowlandson wrote. "Oh, the hideous insulting and triumphing that there was over some Englishmen's scalps that they had taken." One of the Indians had brought back a Bible from the raid, and he offered it to Rowlandson. She immediately turned to chapter 30 of Deuteronomy and read, "though we were scattered from one end of the earth to the other, yet the Lord would gather us together, and turn all those curses upon our enemies." It was a wonderful balm for the grieving and godly Englishwoman. "I do not desire to live to forget this Scripture," she remembered, "and what comfort it was to me."

Rowlandson's master was the Narragansett sachem Quinnapin. Her mistress was Quinnapin's new wife, Weetamoo, the sachem from Pocasset. Much had transpired since Weetamoo had spoken with Benjamin Church about her unwillingness to go to war. After being forced to join her brother-in-law Philip, she had fled to the then neutral Narragansetts. There is evidence that she once again attempted to surrender to colonial authorities, but as had happened before at Aquidneck Island she was once again rebuffed. By marrying Quinnapin, who already had two wives but none as noteworthy as the Pocasset sachem, Weetamoo formally aligned herself with the Pocassets' ancestral foe. After the Great Swamp Fight, all of them were in this together.

By the middle of February word had reached Menameset of the Mohawk attack on Philip. The Pokanoket sachem and what was left of his forces were bound for a village site well to the north on the Connecticut River. It was time for the Nipmucks and Narragansetts to meet with Philip and plan for the spring offensive. When their scouts informed them that a large Puritan army, including six hundred cavalry, was headed for Menameset, the Nipmucks and Narragansetts immediately broke camp and headed north.

So far, Rowlandson had been in close contact with several English captives, including a former neighbor and half a dozen children. But after the departure from Menameset, she saw almost nothing of her fellow captives.

Keeping two thousand Native men, women, and children ahead of a mounted English army might seem out of the question. But as Mary Rowlandson witnessed firsthand, the Indians' knowledge of the land and their talent for working cooperatively under extraordinary duress made them more than a match for the fleetest of English forces.

As a small group of warriors headed south "to hold the English army in play," hundreds upon hundreds of Indians picked up their possessions and began to flee. "I thought to count the number of them," Rowlandson wrote, "but they were so many and being somewhat in motion, it was beyond my skill." It was a scene worthy of Exodus. "[T]hey marched on furiously, with their old and with their young. Some carried their old decrepit mothers, some carried one and some another. Four of them carried a great Indian upon a bier, but going through a thick wood with him, they were hindered and could make no haste; whereupon they took him upon their backs and carried him, one at a time, till they came to Bacquag River."

Known today as Miller's River, the waterway is an eastern tributary of the Connecticut. Swollen with snowmelt, the river was too deep and the current too swift to be forded without some kind of assistance. "They quickly fell to cutting dry trees," Rowlandson wrote, "to make rafts to carry them over the river." Rowlandson and her master and mistress were one of the first ones across the river. The Indians had heaped brush onto the log rafts to protect them from the frigid water, and Rowlandson was thankful that she made it across the river without wetting her feet, "it being a very cold time."

For two days, while the warriors did their best to delay the English, the rafts went back and forth across the river. A temporary city of wigwams sprang up along the northern bank of the Bacquag as the Indians waited for everyone to complete the crossing.

It was the third week of her captivity, and Rowlandson's hunger was such that she greedily ate what she had earlier regarded as "filthy trash," from groundnuts and corn husks to the rancid offal of a long-dead horse. Rowlandson was often on the edge of starvation, but so were her captors, whose ability to extract sustenance from the seemingly barren winter landscape seemed nothing less than a God-ordained miracle. "[S]trangely did the Lord provide for them," she wrote, "that I did not see (all the time that I was among them) one man, woman, or child die with hunger."

Now that she no longer had her daughter to care for, Rowlandson was expected to work. In a finely sewn pouch known as a pocket, she kept her knitting, and she was soon at work on a pair of white cotton stockings for her mistress, Weetamoo. As a sachem, Weetamoo wore both English and Native finery. She also conducted herself with a dignity that Rowlandson, who had formerly been the one to whom deference had been paid, could not help but find offensive: "A severe and proud dame she was, bestowing . . . as much time as any of the gentry of the land [in dressing herself neat]: powdering her hair, and painting her face, going with necklaces, with jewels in her ears, and bracelets upon her hands." In the weeks ahead, as the pressures mounted on both the Indians and their captives, Weetamoo treated Rowlandson with increasing harshness.

By Monday, March 6, everyone had made it across the river. That day they set fire to their wigwams and continued north just as the English army, under the command of Major Thomas Savage, reached the southern bank of the river. But instead of pursuing the Indians, Savage elected to do as so many Puritan commanders had done before him. Even though he had the Indians almost in his grasp, he decided to quit the chase. Over the last few days, hundreds of the old and infirm had somehow managed to ford the river, but Savage claimed it was not safe for his men to attempt a crossing. For Rowlandson, it was a devastating turn of events, but the Lord must have had his reasons. "God did not give them courage or activity to go after us," she wrote; "we were not ready for so great a mercy as victory and deliverance."

The Indians continued north for several days until they reached the Connecticut River near the town of Northfield. Philip, Rowlandson was told, was waiting for them on the opposite bank. "When I was in the canoe," she recalled, "I could not but be amazed at the numerous crew of pagans that were on the . . . other side. When I came ashore, they gathered all about me . . . [and] asked one another questions and laughed and rejoiced over their gains and victories." For the first time of her captivity, Rowlandson started to cry. "Although I had met with so much affliction," she wrote, "and my heart was many times ready to break, yet could I not shed one tear in their sight, but rather had been all this while in a maze, and like one astonished. But now I may say as Psalm 137, 'By the Rivers of Babylon . . . [I] wept.' " One of the Indians asked why she was crying. Not knowing what to say, she blurted out that they would kill her. " 'No,' said he, 'none will hurt you.' " Soon after, she was given two spoonfuls of cornmeal and told that Philip wanted to speak with her.

It was one of several conversations she would have with the Pokanoket sachem. Despite everything she had heard of Philip's malevolence, Rowlandson was treated with kindness and respect by the Native leader. When she entered his wigwam, Philip asked if she would "smoke it." She would gladly have taken up a pipe before her captivity, but by now she had weaned herself from tobacco and had vowed never to smoke again. In the weeks ahead, she would knit a shirt and cap for Philip's son and even be invited to dine with the sachem. "I went," she remembered, "and he gave me a pancake about as big as two fingers; it was made of parched wheat, beaten and fried in bear's grease, but I thought I never tasted pleasanter meat in my life."

Later, while in the midst of yet another extended journey, Rowlandson feared she lacked the strength to continue. As she slogged through the knee-deep mud of a swamp, Philip unexpectedly appeared at her side and offered his hand and some words of encouragement. In her narrative of her captivity, Rowlandson faithfully records these acts of kindness on Philip's part. But nowhere does she suggest that the sachem was unfairly portrayed by her fellow Puritans. Rowlandson had lost her daughter and several other loved ones in the war Philip had started, and nothing—not a pancake or a hand offered in friendship—could ever bring them back.

On March 9, Philip met for the first time with Canonchet, the young leader of the Narragansetts. As they all recognized, the victories they had so far won at Lancaster and Medfield were meaningless if they did not find a way to feed their people. They needed seed corn to plant crops in the spring. Hidden underground in Swansea was a large cache of seed. Canonchet volunteered to lead a group of warriors and women back into the very heart of Plymouth Colony to retrieve the corn. As the women returned with the seed to the Connecticut River valley, Canonchet would remain in Plymouth and bring the war back to where it had begun.

Despite the espionage work of Job and James, distrust of the Praying Indians was at its height. The note left at Medfield by James the Printer was looked at by many as proof that the missionary efforts of John Eliot and Daniel Gookin had only added to the threat posed by the Indians. On February 28, Richard Scott of Boston got very drunk and in the presence of three witnesses began to rail against Gookin, "calling him an Irish dog that was never faithful to his country, the son of a whore, a bitch, a rogue, God confound him and God rot his soul." Scott, a veteran of Moseley's company, claimed that if he should be lucky enough to encounter Gookin on a Boston street at night, "I would pistol him. I wish my knife and scissors were in his heart." There was even talk of leading an assault on the Praying Indians at Deer Island. As Gookin realized, Scott and those like him were merely bullies who, frustrated by the army's lack of success, "would have wreaked their rage upon the poor unarmed Indians our friends."

Plymouth was not immune to such sentiment. In February, the Council of War, headed by Governor Winslow, voted to send the Praying Indians of Nemasket to Clark's Island in Plymouth Harbor and "there to remain and not to depart from there . . . upon pain of death." But even as officials acted to curb the freedoms of the colony's friendly Indians, they were, as Benjamin Church soon found out, reluctant to pay for putting an end to the war.

On February 29, Church attended a meeting of the council at Winslow's home in Marshfield. The raid on Medfield the week before had been followed by an attack on nearby Weymouth, and there were fears that the colony was about to be overrun with hostile Indians from the north. A member of the Council of War proposed that a militia company of sixty be sent to the outlying towns in the colony to defend against a possible Indian attack. The same official proposed that Church be the company's commander. But just as he had done prior to the Great Swamp Fight, Church refused the offer of command. Instead, he had a proposal of his own.

If the Indians returned to Plymouth, it was reasonable to assume that, in Church's words, "they would come very numerous." As Massachusetts had learned, it was a waste of time stationing militias in town garrisons. Although they helped to defend the settlement in the event of an attack, they did nothing to limit the Indians' activities. The only way to conduct the war was to "lie in the woods as the enemy did." And to do that, you not only needed a large force of several hundred men, you needed a large number of friendly Indians. "[I]f they intended to make an end of the war by subduing the enemy," Church insisted, "they must make a business of the war as the enemy did." Instead of worrying about how much money was being spent, Plymouth officials should equip him with an army of three hundred men, a third of them Indians. Give him six weeks, and he and his men would "do good service."

The council turned him down. The colony, it explained, was already woefully in debt, and "as for sending out Indians, they thought it no ways advisable." But Church's words were not without some effect. The man who agreed to serve in his stead, Captain Michael Pierce of

Scituate, was given, in addition to sixty Englishmen, twenty "friend Indians" from Cape Cod.

Church decided his first priority must be to ensure the safety of his
pregnant wife, Alice, and their son, Tom. If the Indians should come in
the numbers he expected, he knew that Duxbury, where they were now
located, was likely to be a prime target. Even though it meant leaving
the colony, he resolved to take Alice and Tom to Aquidneck Island. It
was an unpopular decision both with the authorities, from whom he
needed a permit, and with his wife's relations. Eventually Church was
able to convince Governor Winslow that he could be of some use to
him "on that side of the colony," and he was given permission to relocate to Rhode Island.

Prior to their departure, they stopped in Plymouth to say good-bye
to Alice's parents. The Southworths were adamant: their daughter
should remain in Plymouth safely tucked away with their grandson in
Clark's garrison on the Eel River, just a few miles from the town center.
At the very least, she should remain there until she'd delivered her baby
in May. But Church was just as obstinate, and on March 9, they set out
for Taunton, from which they would proceed by boat down the
Taunton River to Mount Hope Bay and Aquidneck Island.

In Taunton the Churches encountered Captain Pierce and his company. Pierce must have known that Church had spurned the command
that he had chosen to accept, but that did not prevent the captain from
offering to provide Church and his family with an escort to Rhode
Island. Church politely declined Pierce's "respectful offer," and the following day he and his family arrived safely at Captain John Almy's
house in Portsmouth.

A few days later, they heard the shocking news. Clark's garrison in
Plymouth had been attacked by Indians. Eleven people, most of them
women and children, had been killed, and the garrison had been
burned to the ground.

For the English, March of 1676 was a terrible and terrifying month. Indians from across New England banded together for a devastating

series of raids that reached from the Connecticut River valley to Maine and even into Connecticut, a colony that had, up until now, been spared from attack. But it was in Plymouth, on Sunday, March 26, where the English suffered one of the most disheartening defeats of the war.

The previous day, Captain Pierce and his men had skirmished with some Indians fishing for salmon, shad, and alewives at the falls of the Blackstone River. After spending the night at Rehoboth, Pierce set out once again in search of Indians. He suspected that there were an unusually large number of them in the area, and he sent a messenger to Providence to request reinforcements. As it turned out, all of Providence's residents were worshipping in the town's meetinghouse that morning. Reluctant to interrupt, the messenger waited until the service had ended before delivering Pierce's request. By then, it was too late.

Pierce and his force of sixty Englishmen and twenty Indians were marching north along the east bank of the Blackstone River when they spotted some Indians. There were just a few of them, and when the Indians realized they were being followed, they appeared to flee in panic. Pierce's men eagerly pursued, only to discover that they had blundered into an ambush. A force of five hundred Indians, apparently led by Canonchet, emerged from the trees. Pierce and his soldiers ran across the rocks to the west bank of the Blackstone, where another four hundred Indians were waiting for them.

Pierce ordered his company of eighty men to form a single ring, and standing back to back, they fought bravely against close to a thousand Indians, who according to one account "were as thick as they could stand, thirty deep." By the end of the fighting two hours later, fifty-five English, including Pierce, were dead, along with ten of the Praying Indians. Nine English soldiers either temporarily escaped the fighting or were taken alive and marched several miles north, where they were tortured to death at a place still known today as Nine Men's Misery. As Church had warned, the enemy had come in overwhelming numbers, and as he might also have predicted, it was Pierce's small band of friendly Indians who distinguished themselves during the battle.

Given the impossible odds, the Cape Indians would not have been faulted for attempting to escape at the first sign of trouble. But such was not the case. An Indian named Amos stood at Pierce's side almost to the very last. Even after his commander had been shot in the thigh and lay dying at his feet, Amos held his ground and continued to fire on the enemy. Finally, however, it became obvious that, in the words of William Hubbard, "there was no possibility for him to do any further good to Captain Pierce, nor yet to save himself if he stayed any longer." The Narragansetts and Nipmucks had all blackened their faces for battle. Smearing his face with gunpowder and stripping off his English clothes, Amos did his best to impersonate the enemy, and after pretending to search the bodies of the English for plunder, he disappeared into the woods.

There were other instances of remarkable ingenuity on the part of the Cape Indians that day. As the fighting drew to a desperate conclusion, a Praying Indian turned to the English soldier beside him and told him to start to run. Taking up his tomahawk, the Indian pretended to be a Narragansett pursuing his foe, and the two of them did not stop running until they had left the fighting far behind. When word of the heroism of Pierce's Cape Indians began to spread, public opinion regarding the use of friendly Indians in combat started to shift. It still took some time, but New Englanders came to realize that instead of being untrustworthy and dangerous, Indians like Amos, James, and Job might in fact hold the secret to winning the war.

Two days after slaughtering Pierce and his company, Canonchet and as many as 1,500 Indians attacked Rehoboth. As the inhabitants watched from their garrisons, forty houses, thirty barns, and two mills went up in flames. Only one person was killed—a man who believed that as long as he continued to read the Bible, no harm would come to him. Refusing to abandon his home, he was found shot to death in his chair—the Bible still in his hands.

The next day, March 29, the Indians fell on Providence. Most of the town's five hundred inhabitants had left for the safety of Aquidneck

Island, but there remained in Providence a hardy contingent of thirty men, including seventy-seven-year-old Roger Williams. All that day the Indians wandered up and down the streets of the town, firing the houses. Providence was situated on a steep hill overlooking a large salt cove, and when a group of Indians appeared on the opposite shore, Williams, a long staff in his hand, strode out to the end of a point to speak with them. For the next hour, with only a narrow sliver of water between him and the enemy and with Providence burning behind him, Williams conversed with this group of Nipmucks, Pokanokets, Pocassets, Narragansetts, and Connecticut River valley Indians.

"I asked them," he wrote in a letter to his brother in Newport, "why they assaulted us with burning and killing who ever were [kind] neighbors to them, (and looking back) said I, 'This house of mine now burning before mine eyes hath lodged kindly some thousands of you these ten years.'" The Indians replied that even though Rhode Island had remained neutral, it had provided assistance to the other colonies during their assault on the Narragansetts that winter. But Williams would have none of it. "I told them they . . . had forgot they were mankind and ran about the country like wolves tearing and devouring the innocent and peaceable. . . . They confessed they were in a strange way."

Williams warned them that planting time was approaching. A valley sachem said that "they cared not for planting these ten years. They would live upon us, and dear. He said God was with them . . . for [the English] had killed no fighting men but . . . they had killed of us scores." He then invited Williams to go to the site of the Pierce battle and "look upon three score and five now unburied." These words provoked Williams into angrily challenging the Indians to fight the English in the open field instead of "by ambushes and swamps." In the end, however, he offered his services as a peacemaker. The Indians said that after another month spent burning Plymouth Colony, they might speak to him again. "We parted," Williams wrote, "and they were so civil that they called after me and bid me not go near the burned houses for there might be Indians [who] might mischief me, but go by the water side." Williams closed his letter with a word of warning to his brother: "prepare forts for women and children at Newport and on the island or it will be shortly worse with you than us."

By the beginning of April, it looked as if the Indians might do as they had once threatened and drive the English to the very edge of the sea. Adding to the Puritans' troubles was the outbreak of disease. That spring, a lethal influenza claimed the lives of inhabitants in just about every New England town, including several military officers and the governor of Connecticut, John Winthrop Jr. Then, on April 9, an event occurred that changed the course of the war.

Unlike Massachusetts and Plymouth, Connecticut had relied on friendly Indians from the very start of the conflict. In addition to the Mohegans, there were two factions of Pequots, as well as the Niantic Indians, a subset of the Narragansetts, who had remained loyal to the English. In early April a Connecticut force under Captain George Denison was in the vicinity of modern Pawtucket, Rhode Island, when they captured an Indian woman who revealed that Canonchet was nearby. Over the course of the next few days, Denison's eighty or so Mohegans, Pequots, and Niantics competed with one another for the honor of capturing the great Narragansett sachem.

In the last few months, Canonchet had earned the reputation for charismatic leadership that had so far eluded the more famous Philip. Dressed in the silver-trimmed jacket the Puritans had given him during treaty negotiations in Boston, with a large wampum belt around his waist, the young sachem was passionate and decisive and known for his bravery in battle. Even the Puritans, who blamed him for the defection of the Narragansetts, had to admit that Canonchet "was a very proper man, of goodly stature and great courage of mind, as well as strength of body." At considerable risk, he and thirty warriors had succeeded in collecting the seed corn from storage pits just north of Mount Hope. The corn had already been delivered to the Connecticut River valley, where the women would begin planting in May. He was now leading the army of 1,500 Indians that had annihilated Captain Pierce's company and had laid waste to Providence and Rehoboth.

On April 9, Canonchet was resting at the foot of a hill near the Blackstone River with nine of his warriors, trading stories about the attack on Captain Pierce and his company, when he heard "the alarm of the English." He ordered two of his men to go to the top of the hill and report back what they saw, but the men never returned. A third warrior was sent, and he too disappeared. Only after two more men ventured to the top of the hill did Canonchet learn that "the English army was upon him." Taking up his musket and blanket, the Narragansett sachem began to run around the base of the hill, hoping to sneak through the enemy forces and escape behind them. However, one of Denison's Niantic warriors saw the sachem moving swiftly through the woods, and the chase was on.

Canonchet soon realized that Denison's Indians were beginning to catch up to him. Hoping to slow them down, he stripped off his blanket, but the Indians refused to stop for the plunder. Canonchet then shook off his silver-trimmed red coat, followed by his belt of wampum. Now the Indians knew they had, in Hubbard's words, "the right bird, which made them pursue as eagerly as the other fled."

Ahead was the Blackstone River, and Canonchet decided he must attempt to cross it. But as he ran across the slick stones, his foot slipped, and he fell into the water and submerged his gun. Canonchet still had a considerable lead over his pursuers, but he now knew that flight was useless. According to Hubbard, "he confessed soon after that his heart and his bowels turned within him, so as he became like a rotten stick, void of strength." Soon after crossing the river, a Pequot Indian named Monopoide caught up to the sachem, who surrendered without a fight.

The first Englishman on the scene was twenty-two-year-old Robert Stanton. When Stanton started questioning Canonchet, the proud sachem replied, "You much child, no understand matters of war. Let your brother or your chief come, him I will answer."

The English offered Canonchet his life if he helped them convince

Philip and the others to stop the fighting. But he refused, "saying he knew the Indians would not yield." He was then transported to Stonington, where officials blamed him for dragging the Narragansetts into war. He responded that "others were as forward for the war as himself and that he desired to hear no more thereof." When told he'd been sentenced to die, he replied that "he liked it well, that he should die before his heart was soft or had spoken anything unworthy of himself." Just prior to his execution in front of a Pequot firing squad, Canonchet declared that "killing him would not end the war." When Uncas's son responded that he was "a rogue," Canonchet defiantly threw off his jacket and stretched out his arms just as the bullets pierced his chest.

Connecticut officials made sure that all three factions of their friendly Indians shared in the execution. According to one account, "the Pequots shot him, the Mohegans cut off his head and quartered his body, and Ninigret's [Niantics] made the fire and burned his quarters; and as a token of their love and fidelity to the English, presented his head to the council at Hartford."

If the death of Canonchet did not end the war, it was, in Hubbard's words, "a considerable step thereunto." The Indians had lost a leader whose bravery and magnetism had briefly united several groups of Native peoples into a powerful and effective fighting force. In the days and weeks ahead, dissension began to threaten the Indians as the English belatedly came to realize that the Praying Indians were the best ones to drive home the wedge that might break apart the Nipmuck-Narragansett-Pokanoket alliance.

The wedge? A thirty-eight-year-old English captive named Mary Rowlandson.

By late March, a large number of Indians had gathered at Wachusett Mountain to the north of modern Worcester. The steep and rocky terrain provided them with protection from the English yet was far enough east that they could easily attack the towns between them and Boston. On April 5, the Praying Indian Tom Doublet arrived at Wachusett with a letter from colonial officials in Boston. In addition to

An early-twentieth-century view of Wachusett Mountain

the possibility of opening peace negotiations, the letter mentioned the release of English prisoners.

On April 12, Doublet returned to Boston with the Indians' response. They were in no mood, as of yet, to discuss peace: "you know and we know your heart great sorrowful with crying for you lost many many hundred men and all your houses and your land, and women, child and cattle . . . ; [you] on your backside stand." They were willing, however, to discuss the possibility of ransoming hostages. As a minister's wife, Mary Rowlandson was the Indians' most notable captive, and she inevitably became the focus of the negotiations.

In mid-April, Rowlandson, who was still in the vicinity of the Connecticut River with Weetamoo, learned that her presence was required at Wachusett, where Philip and her master, Quinnapin, were already meeting with the Nipmucks. Before receiving this news, she had reached a new nadir. Her son, she had learned, was racked by the flux and was infested with lice; she had heard nothing about her daughter. Without Quinnapin to intervene, Rowlandson's relationship with Weetamoo—difficult from the start—had deteriorated to the point that the sachem had threatened to beat her with a log. "My heart was so heavy . . . that I could scarce speak or [walk along] the path," she remembered. But when she learned that she might soon be ransomed to the English, she felt a sudden resurgence of energy. "My strength seemed to come again," she wrote, "and recruit my feeble knees and aching heart."

Rowlandson arrived at Wachusett Mountain in the midst of preparations to attack the town of Sudbury. With the death of Canonchet having already begun to erode Native confidence, the Indians urgently needed a major victory. They were winning the war, but they were without significant reserves of food. Even if they succeeded in growing a significant amount of corn, they couldn't harvest the crop until late summer. In June, the groundnuts went to seed and became inedible. They must force the English to sue for peace before the beginning of summer. Otherwise, no matter how great their military victories, they would begin to starve to death.

On April 17, Rowlandson became one of the few Westerners to witness a Native war dance. In the center of a large ring of kneeling warriors, who rhythmically struck the ground with their palms and sang, were two men, one of whom held a musket, and a deerskin. As the man with the gun stepped outside the ring, the other made a speech, to which the warriors in the ring enthusiastically responded. Then the man at the center began to call for the one with the gun to return to the deerskin, but the outsider refused. As the warriors in the ring chanted and struck the ground, the armed man slowly began to yield and reentered the ring. Soon after, the drama was repeated, this time with the man holding two guns. Once the leader of the dance had made another speech, and the warriors had "all assented in a rejoicing manner," it was time to leave for Sudbury.

It was a smashing Native victory. Two different companies of English militia fell victim to ambush. The Indians killed as many as seventy-four men and suffered minimal losses. And yet, the Sudbury Fight failed to be the total, overwhelming triumph the Indians had hoped for. "[T]hey came home," Rowlandson remembered, "without that rejoicing and triumphing over their victory, which they were wont to show at other times, but rather like dogs (as they say) which have lost their ears." Even though they had inflicted terrible damage, there were still plenty of English left to fight another day, and for the Indians the days were running out.

The negotiations with the English took on a new urgency. The sachems ordered Rowlandson to appear before them in what they described as their "General Court." They wanted to know what she thought she was worth. It was an impossible question, of course, but Rowlandson named the figure of £20. In the letter accompanying their ransom request, the sachems, led by the Nipmuck known as Sagamore Sam, adopted a far less arrogant tone: "I am sorry that I have done much wrong to you," the note read, "and yet I say the fate is lay upon you, for when we began quarrel at first with Plymouth men I did not think that you should have so much trouble as now is."

In early May, the Praying Indians Tom Doublet and Peter Conway arrived with the Englishman John Hoar from Concord. In addition to the ransom money, Hoar had brought along some provisions to help facilitate the negotiations. It soon emerged that Philip was against the ransoming of English captives, while the Nipmucks were for it. However, since Rowlandson was owned by Quinnapin, it was ultimately up to him.

Traditionally, Native Americans relied on the ritual of the dance to help them arrive at important decisions. The dance that day was led by four sachems and their wives, including Quinnapin and Weetamoo. Even though both of them had been almost constantly on the run for the last few months, the couple still possessed the trappings of nobility. "He was dressed in his Holland shirt," Rowlandson wrote, "with great laces sewed at the tail of it; he had his silver buttons; his white stockings, his garters were hung round with shillings, and he had girdles of wampum upon his head and shoulders. She had a kersey [a twilled woolen fabric] coat and covered with girdles of wampum from the loins upward: her arms from her elbows to her hands were covered with bracelets; there were handfuls of necklaces about her neck and several sorts of jewels in her ears. She had fine red stockings and white shoes, her hair powdered and face painted red that was always before black."

That night, Quinnapin sent a message to John Hoar that he would release Rowlandson the next day if in addition to the ransom of £20, "he should let him have one pint of liquor." Hearing of the Narragansett sachem's offer, Philip ordered Rowlandson to come before him. "[He] asked me what I would give him to . . . speak a good word for me." She asked what it was he wanted. Philip's reply: two coats, twenty shillings, a half bushel of seed corn, and some tobacco. It was the same ploy he had used ten years before on Nantucket Island—an extortion attempt that once again made him appear bullying and opportunistic. As his earlier acts of kindness toward Rowlandson had indicated, Philip was better than this.

As the night wore on, Quinnapin became roaring drunk. "[He] came ranting into the wigwam," Rowlandson remembered, "and called for Mr. Hoar, drinking to him and saying, 'He was a good man,' and then again he would say, 'Hang him, rogue.' " Quinnapin then ordered Rowlandson to come before him, and after drinking to her, but "showing no incivility," he began to chase his young wife around the wigwam, the shillings attached to his pants "jingling at his knees." His wife proved too fast for him and escaped to another wigwam. "But having an old squaw," Rowlandson wrote, "he ran to her and so through the Lord's mercy we were no more troubled that night."

The next morning, the sachems held another meeting—a meeting that Philip, who apparently did not receive his coats and tobacco, refused to attend. To Rowlandson's great joy, it was decided that she should be released. To this day, the place where she gained her freedom, marked by a huge, glacier-scored boulder, is known as Redemption Rock.

By sundown Rowlandson, Hoar, and the two Praying Indians had reached her former home of Lancaster, where they decided to spend the night. "[A]nd a solemn sight it was to me," she wrote. "There had I lived many comfortable years amongst my relations and neighbors, and now not one Christian to be seen, nor one house left standing."

They reached Concord the next day around noon, and by evening they were in Boston, "where I met," Rowlandson recalled, "my dear husband, but the thoughts of our dear children, one being dead and the others we could not tell where, abated our comfort each to other." Over the course of the next few months, both their children were released, and they spent the rest of the war living among friends in Boston.

But Rowlandson found it difficult to leave her captivity behind. "I can remember the time when I used to sleep quietly without workings in my thoughts, whole nights together," she wrote, "but now is other ways with me. . . . [W]hen others are sleeping, mine eyes are weeping."

It was a new era in the war. With the success of Tom Doublet and Peter Conway in negotiating the release of Mary Rowlandson and with increasing numbers of Massachusetts Bay officers using Praying Indians as scouts (even Samuel Moseley came to see the light), New Englanders began to realize that it was both stupid and inhumane to keep hundreds of loyal Indians sequestered against their will. In the middle of May, the Massachusetts General Court ordered that the Praying Indians be removed from Deer Island. "This deliverance . . . ," Daniel Gookin wrote, "was a jubilee to those poor creatures."

On May 18, Captain William Turner with 150 volunteers from Hatfield, Hadley, and Northampton attacked a large Native fishing camp on the Connecticut River. Although Turner and his men were ambushed during their retreat and more than 40 Englishmen, including Turner, were killed, they had succeeded in killing hundreds of Indians. On June 9, the Nipmuck leader Sagamore Sam lost his wife in another English assault. The Nipmucks decided they must sue for peace.

Unwilling to become a Nipmuck bargaining chip, Philip, accompanied by Quinnapin and Weetamoo, left Wachusett Mountain and headed south into familiar territory. With his brother-in-law Tuspaquin, the Black Sachem of Nemasket, leading the charge, Philip's people attacked towns throughout Plymouth and Rhode Island.

From his temporary home on Aquidneck Island, Benjamin Church could see the smoke rising from locations up and down Narragansett Bay. Communication was difficult in these dangerous times, and they were all anxious for any word about their loved ones and friends. On May 12, Alice gave birth to a son named Constant in honor of her father.

A few days later Church took up a knife and stick and began to whittle. He'd been out of the war now for more than three months, and he wasn't sure what he should do now that his son had been born. Perhaps he should take up carpentry. But as he whittled the stick, his hand slipped, and he badly gashed two of his fingers. Church smiled. If he was going to injure himself, he might as well do it in battle.

It was time he returned to the war.

CHAPTER SIXTEEN

The Better Side of the Hedge

ON TUESDAY, JUNE 6, Benjamin Church attended a meeting of the General Court in Plymouth. Travel in the colony was still dangerous, but Church had managed to hitch a ride on a sloop from Newport to Cape Cod. The Cape and islands had remained free of violence throughout the first year of the war. Instead of treating their large Praying Indian population with cruelty and distrust, the English inhabitants had relied on them for their protection. As a result, the Cape had become the colony's one oasis of safety, and Church used it to good effect, securing a horse in modern Falmouth, then known as Saconessett, and riding north along the eastern shore of Buzzards Bay to Sandwich and then on to Plymouth.

More than three months had passed since the Council of War had refused his request to lead a large group of Native Americans against Philip. Over that brief span of time, English attitudes toward the Praying Indians had undergone a fundamental change just as the main theater of the war shifted back to Plymouth Colony. Church sensed that his time had finally arrived.

As it so happened, the Council of War had decided to do almost exactly as Church had proposed back in February. They planned to send out in a few weeks' time a force of three hundred soldiers, a third of them Indians, under the command of Major Bradford. Connecticut and the Bay Colony had also promised to provide companies that included significant numbers of Native scouts.

This was all good news, of course, but Church had no intention of serving under Bradford. Bradford was a trustworthy and loyal officer, but Church had his own ideas about how to fight the war. He must find an army of his own.

Two days later, Church was in a canoe with two Cape Indians headed back to Aquidneck Island. They were approaching the rocky shore of Sakonnet at the southeastern corner of Narragansett Bay. This was the home of Awashonks, the female sachem whom Church had known before the war. He was certain that if given the opportunity, Awashonks would have aligned herself with the English. Instead, she'd taken her people across the bay to the then neutral Narragansetts. After the Great Swamp Fight, the Sakonnets had been forced north along with the Narragansetts and eventually made their way to Wachusett Mountain.

As Church and his two Indian guides approached the jagged rocks and pebble beach of Sakonnet, he saw some of the sachem's Indians fishing in the surf. The Sakonnets, Church realized, had returned home. Perhaps he could convince them to abandon Philip and serve under him.

The Indians began to shout and make signs that Church should come ashore. But when the canoe approached, they retreated and hid amid the clefts of the rocks. Fearful that the Sakonnets might be luring him into a trap, Church ordered the Cape Indians to back away from shore. Over the next few minutes, as the canoe rose up and down with the rhythmic heave of the ocean swell, the Sakonnets and Cape Indians struck up a conversation in their Native language, but it was difficult for them to hear each other above the crashing surf. Church used hand signals to indicate that he was willing to meet with just two of them at the end of a nearby point of sand.

After pulling the canoe up on shore, Church realized that one of the Indians was an old friend named Honest George. George, who spoke English well, said that Church's suspicions were correct; Awashonks "had left Philip and did not intend to return to him any more." Church asked George to deliver a message to his sachem: in two days he would meet her and just two others at a well-known rock near the western shore of Sakonnet.

The next day, Church went to Newport to inform the authorities of his proposed meeting with Awashonks. Since the Sakonnets were re-

Treaty Rock, circa 1900, where the Sakonnet sachem Awashonks agreed to join forces with Benjamin Church

garded as the enemy, he needed official sanction. But the Rhode Island officials refused to grant him a permit, claiming Church "was mad" and would most certainly be killed if he dared meet with the Sakonnets. Church, however, resolved to go ahead with the meeting—with or without the authorities' blessing.

He purchased a bottle of rum and a roll of tobacco to assist with the negotiations, and on the morning of the next day, he and the two Cape Indians prepared to paddle to Sakonnet. But Alice refused to let them go. The Rhode Islanders were right; it was too dangerous. Church did his best to convince "his tender and now brokenhearted wife" that he must go. He assured her that this was nothing compared to the dangers he had already survived; if God looked favorably on his meeting with Awashonks, it might be of "great service" to the colony. Finally, Alice relented. "[C]ommitting her, his babes and himself to heaven's protection," Church set out for Sakonnet.

It was just a three-mile paddle from the Almy house on the east shore of Aquidneck Island to the meeting place. As Church had hoped, he could see some Indians waiting on the bank. One of them was Honest George, who said that Awashonks was nearby and willing to meet with him. When Church asked if she had come with just two others, George did not have time to reply before Awashonks came down to the shore with her son Peter and her principal warrior, Nompash. The sachem shook Church's hand and gestured for him to follow her inland to where a large rock stood at the edge of a meadow of waist-high grass.

Almost as soon as the four of them had assembled around the rock, "a great body" of Indians, all of them armed and with their faces covered in war paint, rose up out of the grass. After a brief pause, Church said that George had indicated Awashonks might be willing to consider peace. She agreed that such was indeed the case. "It is customary," Church replied, "when people meet to treat of peace to lay aside their arms and not to appear in such hostile form as your people do." Only after the warriors had gathered their muskets in a large pile did Church begin the negotiations.

But first they must share in a drink of rum. He had poured the liquor into a calabash made from a large gourd, and after drinking to the sachem's health, he offered the rum to Awashonks. Church could tell by the way she had watched him drink the rum that she suspected the liquor had been poisoned. When the sachem declined to take the calabash, Church poured some rum into his palm, slurped it down, then, raising up the gourd, took yet another "good swig," which he later remembered "was no more than he needed." At last confident that the rum was safe to drink, Awashonks accepted the calabash, and after taking a drink, she and Church began to talk.

The first thing the sachem wanted to know was why he had not returned a year ago, as promised, with a message from the governor. Church explained that the sudden outbreak of the war had made that impossible, and, in fact, he had attempted to contact her when he and a small group of men had come to Sakonnet only to become embroiled in the Pease Field Fight. At the mention of this encounter, the warriors rose up from the grass in a great "hubbub," with one of them shaking his wooden club at Church with an intention that was impossible to misinterpret.

Honest George explained that the warrior had lost his brother at the Pease Field Fight and "therefore he thirsts for your blood." It was then that Nompash, Awashonks's chief warrior, stood up and commanded his men to be silent and "talk no more about old things." Church turned to Awashonks and said that he was confident the Plymouth authorities would spare their lives and allow them to remain at Sakonnet if they disavowed Philip. He cited the example of the Pequots, a tribe that had once warred against the English but was now a trusted ally. He concluded by saying that on a personal level he sincerely looked forward to reclaiming "the former friendship" they had once enjoyed.

This was enough for Nompash. The warrior once again stood, and after expressing the great respect he had for Church, bowed and proclaimed, "Sir, if you'll please to accept of me and my men, and will head us, we'll fight for you, and will help you to Philip's head before Indian corn be ripe." Church had found his warriors. But now he had to secure the permission of Plymouth Colony.

Once the Nipmucks decided they must sue for peace in June, Philip was forced to flee from Wachusett Mountain. Since the Mohawks were now his avowed enemy, he could not head to the west or the north, and the Mohegans were waiting for him in Connecticut to the south. He must return to Plymouth Colony, where there were still considerable supplies of corn hidden in underground storage pits.

Coming south with Philip were the sachems Quinnapin and Weetamoo, and by June, approximately a thousand Pokanokets, Narragansetts, and even some Indians from as far away as the Connecticut River valley had ventured into Plymouth Colony from the north. On June 16, they attacked Swansea and burned all but four garrisons to the ground. On June 26, the Indians returned to that settlement, this time turning their attention to Wannamoisett, the portion of Swansea first settled by the Brown and Willett families in the 1650s. By this time Alexander and Philip's old friend Thomas Willett had been dead almost two years. Willett's twenty-two-year-old son Hezekiah had recently married Anna Brown and was living in a house equipped with a watch-tower. Confident that no hostile Indians were in the vicinity, Hezekiah ventured out with his black servant only to be caught in a vicious cross-fire and killed. The Indians cut off his head and, taking the servant captive, returned to their encampment in triumph.

Hezekiah had been killed by Indians who were unaware of the Willetts' long-standing relationship with Philip and his brother. Before his death, Massasoit had instructed both his sons to be kind to John Brown and his family, and the sight of Hezekiah's dissevered head appears to have had a profound and wrenching effect on Philip. The black servant later told how "the Mount Hope Indians that knew Mr. Willett were sorry for his death, mourned, combed his head and hung peag [wampum] in his hair."

Philip had returned both to the land and to the people he had known all his life. Philip was at war with Plymouth, but a tortured ambivalence had characterized his relationship with the colony from the very beginning. In the weeks ahead, the war that ultimately bore his name acquired the fated quality of Greek tragedy as events drew him, with an eerie remorselessness, home.

Church was having difficulties of his own. Soon after his meeting with Awashonks, he wrote an account of the negotiations and gave it to the sachem's son Peter, who left for Plymouth to speak with the authorities. But on June 27, when Bradford's army arrived at Pocasset, just across the bay from Aquidneck Island, Church had not yet received any word from Peter. Church informed Bradford of the Sakonnets' willingness to serve under him in the fight against Philip, but Bradford would have none of it. He needed to have the official sanction of Governor Winslow before he allowed Church to command a company of Sakonnets. Until he had that, Awashonks and her people must get themselves to Sandwich at the base of Cape Cod, where they would be beyond Philip's influence and reach, and await the governor's decision.

Even though he was not happy with the major's orders, Church urged the Sakonnets to comply. He would go to Plymouth and find out what had happened to Peter. In a week, he promised, he would meet them in Sandwich with a commission from Governor Winslow. And so, with a Cape Indian provided by Bradford leading them with a white flag of truce, the Sakonnets set out for Sandwich.

But Church was fated to suffer a host of additional delays. Given the dangers of traveling overland, he could not simply ride to Plymouth, and he was forced to accompany Bradford's army on an unsuccessful hunt for Philip on Mount Hope. Not until Friday, July 7—several days past the deadline he had promised the Sakonnets—did Church finally reach Plymouth.

To his immense relief, he learned that after a thorough interrogation of Awashonks's son Peter, Governor Winslow had accepted the provisional agreement Church had reached with the Sakonnets. "His honor smilingly told him," Church later remembered, " 'that he should not want commission if he would accept it, nor yet good Englishmen enough to make up a good army.' " It had taken a month to arrange, but it looked as if Church would at last have his own company of Indians.

He decided he needed only half a dozen or so Englishmen, and in just a few hours he had rounded up a group that included thirty-two-year-old Jabez Howland, son of *Mayflower* passenger John Howland, and Church's brother-in-law twenty-eight-year-old Nathaniel Southworth. They mounted their horses and, after riding all that night, arrived in Sandwich just a few hours before daylight. The Sakonnets, they learned, had departed several days before for parts unknown. Church feared that Awashonks had taken offense at yet another broken English promise; adding to his worries was the presence of a considerable number of hostile Indians in the region under the leadership of Totoson, the destroyer of Dartmouth and Clark's garrison in Plymouth. After a few hours' sleep, Church and his men set out to catch up with Awashonks and her people.

He thought it likely that they had headed back for home and were following the western shore of Buzzards Bay toward Sakonnet. After riding more than twenty-six miles, Church and his men came upon a bluff with a panoramic view of a bay that is presently the outer portion of New Bedford Harbor. Ahead, they heard "a great noise"; quickly dismounting from their horses, they began to creep through the underbrush until they had come to the bluff's edge. Below them was modern Pope Beach and a sight that Church never forgot: "[They] saw a vast company of Indians, of all ages and sexes, some on horseback running races, some at football, some catching eels and flatfish in the water, some clamming, etc." Church soon learned that these were indeed the Sakonnets and that Awashonks and her warriors were exceedingly pleased to see him once again.

They found the Sakonnet sachem at an open-sided shelter facing the bay. As Church and his men watched the red sun sink over the hills upon which the city of New Bedford would one day be built, the Sakonnets served them a supper that included "a curious young bass in one dish, eels and flatfish in a second, and shellfish in a third." By the time they'd finished eating, a large pile of firewood had been assembled in front of Awashonks's lean-to, and soon the bonfire was lit, "all the Indians, great and small, gather[ing] in a ring round it."

Many of the Sakonnets had participated in the war dance witnessed by Mary Rowlandson prior to the Sudbury Fight. That night they performed a similar ritual. But instead of preparing to fight *against* the English, they were now preparing to fight *for* the people they had once considered their enemies. After each warrior had danced around the fire with a spear in one hand and a wooden club in the other and vowed to fight against the enemies of the English, Nompash stepped forward and announced to Church that "they were making soldiers for him."

In the weeks ahead, Church's Sakonnet warriors would take him to places that no Englishmen—except perhaps for Joshua Tefft, the renegade from Rhode Island—had been before. With the Sakonnets' help, Church's company would penetrate the hitherto impenetrable swamps of the New England wilderness—the same kind of physical and spiritual landscape in which, fifty-five years before, Massasoit had gathered his people after the arrival of the *Mayflower*.

We will never know what Massasoit's powwows had told him about the future, but we do know that his son Philip took encouragement from his own powwows' insistence that he would never die at the hands of an Englishman. With the Sakonnets' entry into the war on the side of the colony, that prophecy gave the Pokanoket sachem little consolation. Learning of the defection of the Sakonnets was said, according to William Hubbard, to have "broke[n] Philip's heart." From that day forward, he was fighting not just the English; he was fighting his own people.

Church and his new Sakonnet recruits reached Plymouth the next day. Having already acquired a reputation for daring and unconventionality, Church attracted several new English volunteers, including Jabez Howland's brother Isaac, Caleb Cook, Jonathan Delano, and Jonathan Barnes. In their late twenties and early thirties, many of these men were, like Church, either the sons or grandsons of the original Pilgrims. With the help of the Sakonnets, this hardy group of *Mayflower* descendants was about to develop a new way to fight a war.

Church was by no means the first to utilize friendly Indians against the enemy. The Connecticut forces had relied on the Mohegans, Pequots, and Niantics since the beginning of the conflict. Under the leadership of Major John Talcott, Connecticut forces had become known for their relentless pursuit of the enemy—and for massacring almost all those they encountered. In many ways, Talcott had become another Samuel Moseley, but unlike Moseley and his roughneck band of privateers, who enthusiastically butchered Native men, women, and children, Talcott preferred to let his Indians do much of the dirty work. He claimed to be appalled by the brutality of his Mohegan and Pequot scouts, but that did not prevent him from giving them free rein when it came to killing and torturing the Narragansetts.

In early July, Talcott's company surprised several groups of Narragansetts, and in the course of a few days killed more than two hundred of them, including the female sachem known as Queen, whom Talcott described as "that old piece of venom." Talcott decided to keep one of the Narragansetts alive so that his own Native warriors could torture him to death while providing "an ocular demonstration of the savage, barbarous cruelty of these heathen." Ritual torture was a long-standing part of Indian warfare, and Talcott later provided the Puritan historian William Hubbard with a detailed account of how the Mohegans cut the young warrior apart, finger by finger and toe by toe, "the blood sometimes spurting out in streams a yard from his hand," before clubbing him to death.

No matter how shocking such incidents might have seemed in English eyes, they obfuscated an essential truth about King Philip's War. Atrocities were expected in both European and Native conflicts. And yet, the English had to admit that compared to what was typical of European wars, the Indians had conducted themselves with surprising restraint. As Mary Rowlandson could attest, the Native warriors never raped their female captives—a common occurrence in the wars of seventeenth-century Europe.

But that did not prevent the level of violence in King Philip's War from escalating during the summer of 1676. As in the final stages of the English civil war, what has been described as "a kind of victor's justice" began to assert itself. Confident that the Indians were about to go down in defeat, increasing numbers of English commanders followed Talcott's example and refused to grant the enemy any quarter. Since the Indians were in rebellion against the colonial governments to which they had once promised their loyalty, they were, in the English view, guilty of treason and therefore deserving of death. There was another alternative, however, that had the benefit of providing a way to begin paying for the war: slavery.

Some Englishmen preferred to view this as a more humane alternative. But sending large numbers of Native men, women, and children to almost certain death on a Caribbean sugar plantation was hardly an act of mercy. One of the few to object to the policy of enslaving Indians was the missionary John Eliot. "To sell souls for money seems a dangerous merchandise," Eliot wrote. "To sell [the Indians] away from all means of grace . . . is the way for us to be active in destroying . . . their souls." Most New Englanders, however, were so terrified by the prospect of living with the enemy in their midst that they gladly endorsed the policy of shipping Indian captives to the Caribbean and beyond. Onto this dodgy moral ground entered Benjamin Church.

More than anything else, Church wanted the conflict to end. This did not mean that he felt the war was unjustified. From his perspective, Philip and his warriors, some of whom had threatened him personally prior to the war, richly deserved to die, for they had dragged the region into an unnecessary conflict that had resulted in the deaths of thousands of innocent English and Native people. This did not apply, however, to many, if not most, of the other Indians in New England, who had been pushed to become Philip's allies through the ignorance, arrogance, and misplaced zeal of the English. In Church's view, Indians like the Sakonnets, Pocassets, Narragansetts, and many Pokanokets should be given the benefit of the doubt and treated with compassion.

Back in August of the previous year, Church had objected vehemently to Winslow's decision to enslave the Indians taken at Dartmouth. But now, with war raging once again throughout the colony, he had no choice but to adapt to the skewed ethics of a society that still feared it was on the verge of annihilation. The highest priority was to end the fighting, and Church now believed that with the Sakonnets on his side, he could accomplish exactly that.

Unlike the conscripted soldiers under the command of Major Bradford, whose salaries were being paid by the colony, Church's volunteers must, in effect, pay for themselves. Church's agreement with the Plymouth authorities was this: he and his English soldiers received half the money derived from the sale of Indian prisoners and their arms, while the Sakonnets received what Church described as "loose plunder." The arrangement was, in Church's words, "poor encouragement" at best, but it was the only way the government was going to allow him to fight the war on his own terms.

On the evening of July 11, Church's company of approximately two dozen men, more than half of them Indians, left Plymouth for Middleborough, where a mixed group of Pokanokets and Narragansetts had recently been sighted. Church realized he still had much to learn when it came to the subtleties of Indian warfare. As they made their way along the path to Middleborough, he asked the Sakonnets "[h]ow they got such advantage of the English in their marches through the woods." They replied that it was essential to keep the men widely separated or, as Church described, "thin and scattered." According to the Sakonnets, the English "always kept in a heap together"; as a result, it was as "easy to hit [a company of English soldiers] as to hit a house." Church soon discovered that spreading out his men had the added benefit of making his tiny army seem much larger than it actually was.

The Sakonnets also insisted that silence was essential when pursuing the enemy. The English addiction to talking to one another alerted the Indians to their presence. Creaking leather shoes were not to be tolerated; even the swishing sound made by a pair of thick pants could be detected by the Indians. If some form of communication was required, they should use an ever changing vocabulary of wildlife sounds, from birdcalls to the howling of a wolf. They must also learn how to track the enemy. The morning was the best time, since it was possible to trace a man's steps in the dew. But perhaps the most important lesson Church learned from the Sakonnets was never to leave a swamp the same way he had entered it. To do otherwise was to walk into an ambush.

To this markedly Native form of fighting, Church brought influences of his own, many of them derived from living among the mariners of Aquidneck Island. The sword he carried at his side was crudely fashioned compared to the elegant German rapier worn several decades earlier by Miles Standish. Church's sword had a simple maple

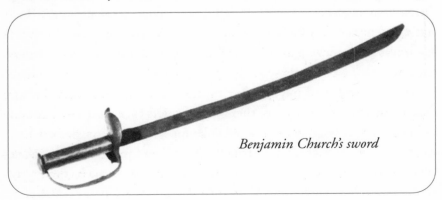

Benjamin Church's sword

handle and a broad, upturned blade typical of the weapons used by Caribbean buccaneers, making it ideally suited to hand-to-hand combat. Church also spoke like a sailor. A Native scout was a "pilot." When someone suddenly veered off in another direction, he "tacked about." And as he soon discovered, exploring the smothering green of a New England swamp in summer had much in common with navigating a treacherous, fogbound coast.

After a few hours' sleep in Middleborough, Church and his men set out after the enemy. Soon one of his Indian scouts reported having found an encampment. Based on the Sakonnets' description of, in Church's words, "their fires and postures," he directed his men to surround the camp, and on his cue, they rushed at the enemy, "surprising them from every side so unexpectedly that they were all taken, not so much as one escaped." Church took an immediate liking to one of the captured Indians, named Jeffrey, who freely told him of the whereabouts of a large number of Indians near Monponsett Pond, where Philip's brother Alexander had been seized back in 1662. Church decided to make Jeffrey a part of their company, promising "that if he continued to be faithful to him, he should not be sold out of the country but should become his waiting man." As it turned out, Jeffrey remained a part of the Church household for the rest of the Indian's life.

After delivering his prisoners to Plymouth, Church and his men were on their way to Monponsett, where they captured several dozen additional Indians. Over the course of the next few weeks, Church's string of successes continued unabated, and he soon became the talk of the colony. On July 24, Winslow broadened Church's powers to allow him to do as he had done with Jeffrey: grant mercy to those Indians who agreed to help him find more of the enemy. Church's recruits were soon convincing other newly captured Indians to do as they had done and come over to what he described as "the better side of the hedge."

It was a deal that was difficult to refuse, but much of its appeal depended on the charisma, daring, and likability of the company's captain. Church prided himself on his ability to bring even the most "treacherous dog" around to his way of thinking. "Come, come," he would say, "you look wild and surly and mutter, but that signifies nothing. These my best soldiers were a little while ago as wild and surly as you are now. By the time you have been but one day . . . with me, you'll love me too." By the end of July, Church's little band of volunteers was routinely bringing in more Indians than all of Plymouth's and Massachusett Bay's companies combined. In his history of the war, Cotton Mather wrote, "[S]ome of [Church's] achievements were truly so magnanimous and extraordinary that my reader will suspect me to be transcribing the silly old romances, where the knights do conquer so many giants."

Church undoubtedly enjoyed the praise, and in his own account of the war he does his best to portray himself as a swashbuckling knight errant of the woods, but as even he admitted, his successes would not have been possible without the presence of Bradford's more traditional army. Based in Taunton, Bradford's men chased Philip throughout the swamps and woods, and in several instances came within minutes of taking the Pokanoket sachem. But, unlike Church's company, morale was a problem among Bradford's conscripted soldiers, and by the end of July many of them had either deserted or found sufficient excuses to return home.

Bradford had been there from the beginning. Back in 1662, he had been present when the young Josiah Winslow took Philip's brother Alexander. Bradford had been injured at the Great Swamp Fight, and when the temperamental Church had gone off in a huff to Aquidneck Island and Captain Pierce and his men had been wiped out in March, he had assumed command of the army no one else wanted to lead. Solid, dutiful, and pious, the fifty-two-year-old major did not share Church's talent for improvisation and risk. Nor did he care to.

In many ways, he was his father's son. In the 1620s, Governor Bradford had objected to Thomas Morton's gambols with the Indians around the maypole at Merrymount. A half century later, Major Bradford had little patience for Church's unorthodox and reckless method of fighting both with and against the Indians. But Bradford was too forthright and humble not to give the man he called "cousin" his due. Church might be prideful and more than a little cavalier with the lives of his men, but he was winning the war. On July 24, Bradford replied to a letter he'd just received from the Reverend John Cotton, who had apparently praised Church's most recent triumphs.

> I am glad of the successes of my cousin Church. The Lord yet continue it, and give him more and more, [but] I shall in no wise emulate any man. The Lord give him and us, or any that have successes on the enemy, to be humble and give God the only praise for his power. . . . I have done my duty and have neglected no opportunity to face upon the enemy, and I am verily persuaded that if we should [have] adventured without the Benjamin Forces, we had been either worsted or also lost many men. He had placed himself in such an advantaged place, and I had rather be accounted a slow person . . . yea, even a coward than to adventure the loss of any of my soldiers. . . . You know the state of things when I came first out. I should have been glad if any would have took in my room, and I know there is many that would have managed it better than myself. But now we have many commanders that are very forward and think themselves the only men. We are going forth this day intending Philip's headquarters. I shall not put myself out of breath to get before Ben Church. I shall be cautious, still I cannot outgo my nature. I will leave the issue with God.

As it turned out, Bradford did not succeed in taking the Pokanoket sachem on July 25. As the major had surely come to suspect, God had, in his infinite and unfathomable wisdom, reserved that honor for Benjamin Church.

On Sunday, July 30, Church took a brief respite from the war to worship at the meetinghouse in Plymouth. But before the conclusion of the service, the Reverend John Cotton was interrupted by a messenger from Josiah Winslow, who had just ridden in from Marshfield. The governor needed to speak with Captain Church.

A "great army of Indians" had been seen massing on the eastern shore of the Taunton River. If they succeeded in crossing the river, the towns of Taunton and Bridgewater would be in danger. Winslow requested that Church "immediately . . . rally what of his company he could." Church leaped into action but, finding no provisions in the town's storehouse, was forced to jog from house to house collecting what bread the goodwives of Plymouth were willing to donate to the cause.

As Church and his company of eighteen Englishmen and twenty-two Indians made their way toward Bridgewater, a handful of the town's militia were already out on a reconnaissance mission of their own. They were approaching the Taunton River when they heard some suspicious noises. They soon discovered that the Indians had felled a huge tree across the river and were at that very moment beginning to cross over toward Bridgewater. There were two Indians on the tree, an old man with the traditional long hair of a Native American and a younger man with his hair cut short in the style of a Praying Indian. One of the militiamen shot and killed the older Indian, and the younger one, who was lugging a container of gunpowder, tossed the powder into the bushes and escaped back into the forest on the eastern shore of the river. The dead Indian turned out to be Akkompoin, Philip's uncle and one of the sachem's most trusted counsellors. They later learned that the other Indian had been Philip himself. In an effort to disguise himself, he had cut off his hair, and for the moment at least, the change in hairstyle had saved his life.

Many of his subjects were not so lucky that day. After more than a year of unrelenting hardship, Philip's people were exhausted, starving, and dispirited. Conditions had become particularly difficult in the last month. With the appearance of Church's company in early July, the swamps that had once provided them with a place of refuge were no longer safe. With no way to protect their children, the Indians had been reduced to the most terrible and desperate extreme a people can ever know. William Hubbard reported that "it is certainly affirmed that several of their young children were killed by themselves, that they might not be betrayed by their crying or be hindered with them in their flight." Another source claimed that the children's parents had resorted to hiring "a cruel woman among them to kill their children; she killed a hundred in one day."

The Bridgewater militiamen reported that the Indians they met on Monday, July 31, were so stunned and terror-struck that many of them were helpless to defend themselves. According to one account, "Some of the Indians acknowledged that their arms shook and trembled so that they could not so readily discharge their guns as they would have done." Ten Indians were shot dead with loaded muskets in their hands, while fifteen others "threw down their guns and submitted themselves to the English." For many of the Indians, there was no reason left to continue.

Early the next morning, Church and his company set out from Bridgewater. They had recruited several men from the local militia, and one of these "brisk lads" guided them to where the Indians had laid the tree across the river. Church and one of his men crept in among the leafy branches of the fallen tree. Looking across the river, they saw an Indian sitting on the tree's stump—an unusual thing for a hostile Indian to be doing the morning after the encounter with the Bridgewater militia. Church took aim, but his Native companion told him to hold his fire; he believed it might be a friendly Indian. But when the Indian, apparently hearing them, glanced in their direction, the Sakonnet immediately realized it was Philip. He fired his musket, but it was too late. The sachem had rolled off the stump and escaped into the woods.

Church and his men ran across the tree and soon came upon a group of women and children that included Philip's wife and nine-year-old son. There was a fresh trail south, and the prisoners informed him that it had been left by sachem Quinnapin and his people, who had resolved to return home to the western shore of Narragansett Bay. But where was Philip? The prisoners claimed that they did not know, "for he fled in a great fright when the first English gun was fired, and they had none of them seen or heard anything of him since."

Leaving some of his men with the prisoners, Church and the rest of the company headed down the trail, hopeful that they might overtake the enemy. It was a muggy summer day, and after several miles of running along the eastern bank of the river, their clothes were drenched in sweat. They came to a shallow portion of the river, where they could tell the Narragansetts had crossed to the other side. The water reached up to their armpits, but they quickly forded the river and continued the pursuit.

But after another mile, Church realized that given the importance of the prisoners he now had in his possession, he must return to the downed tree and get them back to Bridgewater before dark. His Sakonnets, however, were reluctant to give up the chase. They explained that Awashonks's brother had been killed by the Narragansetts, and they wanted revenge. Church designated a Sakonnet named Lightfoot as their captain and "bid them go and quit themselves like men." "[A]way they scampered," Church wrote, "like so many horses."

The next morning Lightfoot and his men returned with thirteen prisoners. They had caught up to the Narrangansetts and killed several of them and "rejoiced much at the opportunity of avenging themselves." Church sent the prisoners on to Bridgewater and, with the Sakonnets leading the way, resumed the search for Philip.

They came upon an abandoned encampment that convinced them the Pokanokets were close at hand. Moving quickly through the woods, they discovered a large number of women and children who were too tired to keep up with the main body of Indians up ahead. The prisoners reported that "Philip with a great number of the enemy were a little before." It was getting late in the day, but Church was loath to give up the chase. He told the Sakonnets to inform their prisoners that "if they would submit to order and be still, no one should hurt them."

As night descended, they could hear the sounds of Philip's men chopping wood and setting up camp. Drawing his men and prisoners in a ring, Church informed them that they were going to spend the night sitting quietly in the swamp. If any prisoner attempted to escape, Church would "immediately kill them all."

Just before daybreak, Church explained to the prisoners that he and his men were about to attack Philip. He had no one he could spare to guard them, but he assured them that it was in their best interests not to escape. Once the fighting was over, they were to follow their trail and once again surrender themselves. Otherwise, he would hunt them down and kill them all.

He sent out two Sakonnet scouts just as, it turned out, Philip sent two scouts of his own. Philip's men spotted the Sakonnets and were soon running back to camp, making "the most hideous noise they could invent." By the time Church and his men arrived, the Pokanokets had fled into a nearby swamp, leaving their kettles boiling and meat roasting on the fire.

Church left some of his men at the place where the Indians had entered the swamp, then led a group of soldiers around one side of the morass while Isaac Howland took another group around the other side. Once they had positioned men at regular intervals around the entire perimeter of the swamp, Church and Howland rendezvoused at the farthest point just as a large number of the enemy emerged from the swamp's interior.

Hopelessly outnumbered, Church and his handful of soldiers could easily have been overrun and massacred by the Pokanokets. Suddenly, a Sakonnet named Matthias shouted out in the Indians' own language, "If you fire one shot, you are all dead men!" Mathias went on to claim that they had a large force and had the swamp completely surrounded.

Many of the Pokanokets did as their brethren had done just a day before: astonished, they stood motionless as Church's men took the loaded muskets from their hands. Not far from the swamp was a depression of land that Church compared to a "punchbowl." He directed the prisoners to jump down into the hollow, and with only a few men standing guard—all of them triple-armed with guns taken from the Indians—he plunged back into the swamp to find Philip.

Almost immediately, Church found himself virtually face-to-face with the Pokanoket leader and several of his warriors. By this point, the sachem's behavior was entirely predictable. When cornered or confronted, Philip invariably ran. As Church and two Sakonnets engaged the Pokanoket warriors, Philip turned and fled back to the entrance of the swamp. This might have been the end of the sachem. But one of the men Church had left waiting in ambush outside the swamp was a notorious drunkard named Thomas Lucas. Whether or not he had just taken a nip, Lucas was, in Church's words, not "as careful as he might have been about his stand." Instead of killing the enemy, Lucas was gunned down by the Pokanokets, and Philip escaped.

In the meantime, Church had his hands full in the swamp. Two enemy warriors surrendered, but the third, whom Church described as "a great stout surly fellow with his two locks tied up with red [cloth] and a great rattlesnake skin hanging to the back part of his head," refused to give up. This, it turned out, was Totoson, the sachem who had attacked Dartmouth and the Clark garrison. While the Sakonnets guarded the others, Church chased Totoson. It looked as if the sachem might escape, so Church stopped to fire his musket. Unfortunately it was a damp morning, and Church's musket refused to go off. Seeing his opportunity, Totoson spun around and aimed *his* musket, but it, too, failed to fire. Once again, the chase was on.

Church momentarily lost him in the undergrowth but was soon back on the trail. They were running through some particularly dense bushes when the Indian tripped on a grapevine and fell flat on his face. Before he could get back up, Church raised the barrel of his musket and killed him with a single blow to the head. But as Church soon discovered, this was not Totoson. The sachem had somehow eluded Church, and filled with rage, Totoson was now coming up from behind and "flying at him like a dragon." Just in the nick of time, the Sakonnets opened fire. The bullets came very close to killing the person they were intended to save (Church claimed "he felt the wind of them"), but they had the desired effect. Totoson abandoned his attempt to kill the English captain and escaped into the swamp.

They had not succeeded in capturing Philip or, for that matter, Totoson, but Church's band of eighteen English soldiers and twenty-two

Sakonnets had nonetheless managed one of the more spectacular feats of the war. Once the fighting had ended, and they had rounded up all their prisoners, they discovered that they had taken a grand total of 173 Indians.

Church asked some of them if they could tell him anything about their sachem. "Sir," one of them replied, "you have now made Philip ready to die, for you have made him as poor and miserable as he used to make the English, for you have now killed or taken all his relations."

When they reached Bridgewater that night, the only place that could accommodate all the prisoners was the pound, a fenced-in area used to collect the town's herds of sheep and cattle. The Sakonnets were assigned guard duty, and Church made sure to provide both the guards and their prisoners with food and drink. "[T]hey had a merry night," Church remembered, "and the prisoners laughed as loud as the soldiers, not [having been] so [well] treated [in] a long time."

On Sunday, August 6, two days after Church delivered his prisoners to Plymouth, Weetamoo and what remained of her Pocasset followers were in the vicinity of Taunton when a group of local militiamen attacked. The English took twenty-six prisoners, but Weetamoo escaped.

Soon after, she attempted to cross the Taunton River, but before she reached Pocasset on the eastern shore, her rickety raft broke apart, and she drowned. A day or two later her naked body was discovered on the shore of Gardner's Neck, once the village site of her father, Corbitant. Not knowing who it was, an Englishman cut off the woman's head and sent it on to Taunton. Upon its arrival, the nameless head was placed upon a pole within sight of the Indians taken prisoner just a few days before. Soon enough, the residents of Taunton knew whose head it was. According to Increase Mather, the Pocassets "made a most horrid and diabolical lamentation, crying out that it was their Queen's head."

A few days later Weetamoo's husband, Quinnapin, was taken captive, and on August 25 he was executed in Newport. To the north in Boston, the Nipmuck Sagamore John won a pardon when he brought in his former ally Matoonas. On July 27 the English looked on as

Sagamore John and his men tied Matoonas to a tree on Boston Common and shot him to death. A month later Sagamore Sam and several other Nipmuck sachems who had been tricked into surrendering were also executed on the Common.

By that time, Totoson, the destroyer of Dartmouth and Clark's garrison, was dead. An old Indian woman later reported that after the sachem's eight-year-old son succumbed to disease, Totoson's "heart became as a stone within him, and he died." The woman threw some brush and leaves over Totoson's body and surrendered herself to the authorities in Sandwich, where she, too, became ill and followed her sachem to the grave.

In terms of the percentage of population killed, the English had suffered casualties that are difficult for us to comprehend today. During the forty-five months of World War II, the United States lost just under 1 percent of its adult male population; during the Civil War the casualty rate was somewhere between 4 and 5 percent; during the fourteen months of King Philip's War, Plymouth Colony lost close to 8 percent of its men.

But the English losses appear almost inconsequential when compared to those of the Indians. Of a total Native population of approximately 20,000, at least 2,000 had been killed in battle or died of their injuries; 3,000 had died of sickness and starvation, 1,000 had been shipped out of the country as slaves, while an estimated 2,000 eventually fled to either the Iroquois to the west or the Abenakis to the north. Overall, the Native American population of southern New England had sustained a loss of somewhere between 60 and 80 percent. Philip's local squabble with Plymouth Colony had mutated into a regionwide war that, on a percentage basis, had done nearly as much as the plagues of 1616–19 to decimate New England's Native population.

In the end, the winner of the conflict was determined not by military prowess but by one side's ability to outlast the other. The colonies had suffered a series of terrible defeats, but they had England to provide them with food, muskets, and ammunition. The Indians had only themselves, and by summer they were without the stores of food and gunpowder required to conduct a war. If Philip had managed to secure the support of the French, it might all have turned out differently. But the sachem's dream of a French-Pokanoket alliance was destroyed when, at New York governor Andros's urging, the Mohawks attacked him in late February. The Puritans never admitted it, but it had been Andros and the Mohawks who had determined the ultimate outcome of King Philip's War.

By August it had become apparent that the fighting was drawing to a close. But as everyone knew, the war would not be over until its instigator, Philip of Mount Hope, had been taken.

By Friday, August 11, most of the English forces that had once been roaming across Plymouth Colony had been disbanded. Only Benjamin Church and his loyal Sakonnets were still out on patrol. They had just spent the day in Pocasset but had come up with nothing. Church decided that he did not care what the authorities back in Plymouth said; he was going to visit Alice.

Church and his men took the ferry to Aquidneck Island. Alice and the boys were now staying at the home of the noted merchant Peleg Sanford in Newport, and Church and half a dozen of his company rode their horses the eight miles to Sanford's house. When she first glimpsed her husband, Alice was so overcome with surprise that she fainted dead away. By the time she had begun to revive, Church noticed that two horsemen were approaching at great speed. He turned to the members of his company and said, "Those men come with tidings."

They proved to be Sanford and Church's old friend, Captain Roger Goulding, the mariner who had saved him more than a year ago during the Pease Field Fight, and sure enough, they had news. An Indian had appeared earlier that day at the southern tip of the Mount Hope Peninsula. He reported that he had just fled from Philip, who had killed his brother for proposing that they sue for peace. The Indian was now on Aquidneck Island and willing to lead Church to Philip's camp.

Church turned to Alice and smiled ruefully. He and his men had not yet had the chance to unsaddle their horses. "[H]is wife," he later wrote, "must content herself with a short visit, when such game was ahead." Church asked Sanford and Goulding whether they wanted to come along. They readily agreed, and soon they were back on their horses and riding north toward Mount Hope.

The deserter was waiting for them at the ferry. He was, according to Church, "a fellow of good sense, and told his story handsomely." Philip, the Indian reported, was on a little patch of high ground surrounded by a miry swamp at the base of the rocky heights of Mount Hope. The sachem had returned to the symbolic if not literal center of his territory, and the disaffected Indian offered to lead Church to him "and to help kill him, that he might revenge his brother's death."

It was after midnight by the time they approached Philip's camp. In addition to Sanford and Goulding, Church had a few of his Plymouth regulars, including Caleb Cook, grandson of the *Mayflower* passenger Francis Cook, to augment his veteran band of Sakonnets. There was also the Pocasset Indian named Alderman, who had left Weetamoo at the beginning of the war and had offered to lead Church to her headquarters soon after the Pease Field Fight—a battle in which Church had fought against the very same Sakonnets who were now his loyal followers. It was a small company of no more than two dozen men, but it epitomized the tangled loyalties of a biracial community that had been ruptured and reconstituted amid the trauma of war.

Church assigned Goulding, the man to whom he already owed his life, to lead the group that would fall upon Philip's headquarters. With the Pokanoket deserter to guide them, Goulding and his men would creep on their stomachs through the underbrush until they came within sight of the enemy. By that time, Church would have stationed the rest of his men at regular intervals around the periphery of the swamp.

Their experience had taught them that the Indians always constructed their shelters so that they were open to the swamp. They also knew that "it was," in Church's words, "Philip's custom to be foremost in the flight." When Goulding and his men attacked, the sachem would immediately flee into the swamp, and Church and his men would be waiting for him.

It was always difficult to distinguish friend from foe in the early-morning darkness of a swamp, so Church instructed Goulding and his men to shout at the top of their lungs once the fighting began. The rest of them would fire on only those "that should come silently through the swamp."

It had come down to just a handful of Philip's toughest and most loyal men. There was the young warrior who was reputed to have fired the first shot back in June of 1675. He would be one of the first to die that morning. There was also the consummate survivor: Annawon.

No one knew exactly how old he was, but he had fought alongside Philip's father, Massasoit, decades before this. It is likely that he had been one of the warriors to carry the dying Alexander on his shoulders back to Mount Hope. For more than a year now, he had been with Philip every step of the way. In just the last month alone, they had covered hundreds of miles as they crisscrossed their homeland, always on the run. Because never, it seemed, was Philip willing to fight. Even when his wife and child were about to fall into the clutches of the English, the sachem had fled.

When they had fallen asleep that night, their exhaustion had been mixed with more than the usual tension and fear. After the desertion of the brother of the executed warrior, they all knew the English would be coming soon. As day approached, Philip awoke from a dream. They must leave immediately, he told Annawon and the others. In his dream he had been taken by the English. They had been betrayed.

One of the warriors stood up to relieve himself. A musket fired, and the yelling began.

As had become a reflex with him, Philip leaped to his feet, threw his powder horn and petunk (a pouch containing bullets) over his shoulder, and with his musket in hand started to run. It would be left to

Annawon and the others to gather their belongings and hold the English off for as long as possible.

As his sachem disappeared into the murky recesses of the swamp, Annawon shouted after him, "Iootash! Iootash!"—"Fight! Fight!" We will never know whether Philip turned back to look at Annawon. But we do know he continued to run.

The first crack of the musket took Church by surprise. He thought one of his soldier's guns might have gone off by accident. But other shots soon followed, and he knew the ambush had begun.

In the eastern portion of the swamp stood two men: twenty-five-year-old Caleb Cook and the Pocasset named Alderman. They could see an Indian coming toward them. He was running, they later reported, "as fast as he could scamper." He was dressed in only his small breeches and stockings. They waited until he had come within range, and now confident that he was one of the enemy, Cook pulled the trigger of his musket, but his weapon refused to fire. It was left to Alderman.

The Pocasset had an old musket with a large touchhole, which

The musket lock of the gun that reputedly killed King Philip

made the weapon less susceptible to the early-morning dampness. He pulled the trigger, and the lever holding the flint, known as a cock, swung forward against the metal frizzen or battery, and the resulting spark dropped down through the touchhole into the firing pan filled with priming powder. The explosion that followed ignited the charge of gunpowder in the musket barrel, hurling two bullets, one of which pierced Philip's rapidly beating heart.

He fell facedown into the mud with his gun beneath him. The warriors coming up from behind heard the shots and veered off in the opposite direction. Annawon could still be heard shouting, "Iootash! Iootash!"

Alderman and Cook rushed over to Church and told him that they had just killed Philip. He instructed them to keep the news a secret until the engagement was over. The fighting continued for a few more minutes, but finding a gap in the English line on the west end of the swamp, most of the enemy, now led by Annawon, escaped.

Church gathered his men on the rise of land where the Indians' shelter had been built and told them of Philip's death. The army, Indians and English alike, shouted "Huzzah!" three times. Taking hold of his breeches and stockings, the Sakonnets dragged the sachem's body through the mud and deposited him beside the shelter—"a doleful, great, naked, dirty beast," Church remembered.

With his men assembled around him and with Philip's mud-smeared body at his feet, Church pronounced his sentence: "That for as much as he had caused many an Englishman's body to lie unburied and rot above ground, that not one of his bones should be buried." He called forward a Sakonnet who had already executed several of the enemy and ordered him to draw and quarter the body of King Philip.

The Sakonnet took up his hatchet, but paused to deliver a brief speech. Philip had been a "very great man," he said, "and had made many a man afraid of him, but so big as he was he would now chop his ass for him." Soon the body had been divided into four pieces. One of Philip's hands possessed a distinctive scar caused by an exploded pistol. Church awarded the hand to Alderman, who later placed it in a bottle of rum and made "many a penny" in the years to come by exhibiting the hand to curious New Englanders.

* * *

Almost exactly a month earlier, on Thursday, July 18, the congregation at Plymouth had formally renewed the covenant their forefathers had struck with God more than a half century before in Leiden. "[W]e are," they had vowed, "though descended of a noble vine, yet become the degenerate plant of a strange vine unto God; we have been a proud generation, though we are the sons and daughters of Zion."

From that day forward, victory had followed victory, and on Thursday, August 17, Pastor John Cotton led his congregation in a day of Thanksgiving. Soon after the conclusion of public worship that day, Benjamin Church and his men arrived with the preeminent trophy of the war. "[Philip's] head was brought into Plymouth in great triumph," the church record states, "he being slain two or three days before, so that in the day of our praises our eyes saw the salvation of God."

The head was placed on one of the palisades of the town's one-hundred-foot-square fort, built near where, back in 1623, Miles Standish had placed the head of Wituwamat after his victory at Wessa-gussett. Philip's head would remain a fixture in Plymouth for more than two decades, becoming the town's most famous attraction long before anyone took notice of the hunk of granite known as Plymouth Rock.

Philip was dead, but Annawon, the sachem's "chief captain," was still out there. Old as Annawon was, the colony would not be safe, the governor insisted, until he had been taken. There was yet another well-known warrior still at large: Tuspaquin, the famed Black Sachem of Nemasket. Tuspaquin was both a powwow and a sachem and was, according to the Indians, impervious to bullets.

Church was expected to hunt down and kill these two notorious warriors, but he had other ideas. He had recently been contacted by Massachusetts Bay about assisting the colony against the Abenakis in Maine, where fighting still raged. With Tuspaquin and Annawon at his side, Church believed, he might be able to subdue the hitherto uncon-querable Abenakis.

On August 29, he learned that the Black Sachem was in the region known as Lakenham, about six miles west of Plymouth. But after two days of searching, he'd only managed to take Tuspaquin's wife and children. He left a message for the sachem with two old Nemasket women that Tuspaquin "should be his captain over his Indians if he [proved to be] so stout a man as they reported him to be." With luck, Tuspaquin would turn himself in at Plymouth, and Church would have a new Native officer.

About a week later, word came from Taunton that Annawon and his men had been seen at Mount Hope. On Thursday, September 7, Church and just five Englishmen, including his trusted lieutenant Jabez Howland, and twenty Indians left Plymouth in search of Annawon.

They ranged about Mount Hope for several days and took a large number of Indians near the abandoned English fort. When Lightfoot came up with the idea of using the fort as a temporary prison, Church took some consolation in the fact that this misbegotten structure had finally been put to good use.

One of the captive Indians reported that his father and a girl had just come from Annawon's headquarters. The old man and the girl were hidden in a nearby swamp, and the captive offered to take Church to them. Leaving Howland and most of the company with the prisoners, Church and a handful of men went in search of the prisoner's father.

That afternoon they found the old man and the girl, each of whom was carrying a basket of provisions. They reported that Annawon and about fifty to sixty men were lodged in Squannakonk Swamp several miles to the north between Taunton and Rehoboth. If they left immediately, they could be there by sundown.

Church was in a quandary as to what to do next. He had only half a dozen men with him. Annawon had a reputation as one of Philip's fiercest warriors, and the Indians said that he had let it be known "that he would never be taken alive." What's more, his men were "resolute fellows [and] some of Philip's chief soldiers." To take them on with just six men was madness.

But Church might never have this good a chance again. As he knew from experience, Annawon was exceedingly difficult to track down. He changed his camp every night and was, in Church's words, "a very subtle man." If they left immediately, the old man and the girl could take them directly to the warrior. If they waited until tomorrow, he would be gone.

Church asked his men if they were willing to "give Annawon a visit." Most of them assented, but one of the Sakonnets pointed out "that it would be a pity that after all the great things [Church] had done, he should throw away his life at last." In the end, however, Church believed the Lord was on his side. He had "no doubt," he told his men, "that if they would cheerfully go with him the same almighty providence that had hitherto protected and befriended them would do so still." In one voice, the Sakonnets said, "We will go." Church then turned to the only Englishman in the company, Caleb Cook, and asked what he thought. "Sir," Cook replied, "I am never afraid of going anywhere when you are with me." And so, with the elderly Indian captive and the girl leading the way, they left for Annawon's encampment.

The two guides walked so briskly over the swampy ground that Church and the rest of the company had difficulty keeping up. The old man insisted that since Church had given him his life, he had no choice but to serve him, and if Church's plan was to work, they needed to get there as swiftly as possible.

They had been traveling for several hours when their guides suddenly stopped and sat down. The old man explained that Annawon always sent out scouts at sunset "to see if the coast were clear." Only after it was completely dark could they resume their journey. As they waited for night, Church asked the old man if he would take a gun and fight for him. The Indian bowed low and said he was willing to lead Church to Annawon, but he would not take up arms against his "old friend." Church agreed to respect his wishes, and they continued on through the dark.

They had not gone far when they heard a rhythmic beating noise. The Sakonnets instantly recognized it as the pounding of a mortar. Annawon's women were grinding corn in preparation for supper.

The old man explained that Annawon had set up camp at the base

A nineteenth-century engraving depicting Church's capture of Annawon

of a steep rock. A surrounding swamp prevented access from any other point. Church and the old man crept up to the edge of the rock. They could see the flickering fires of Annawon's people. There were three different groups, with "the great Annawon" and his son and several others lodged nearest the rock. Their food was cooking on the fires, and Church noticed that their guns were leaning together against a horizontal branch and that a mat had been placed over the weapons to protect them from the dew. He also noticed that Annawon's feet and his son's head were almost touching the muskets.

Church had become a master at using audacity as a tactical weapon. No one in his right mind would dare enter Annawon's camp down the face of this rock. But if he could hide himself behind his two Indian guides, who were known to Annawon and his warriors, he might be able to secure the Indians' guns before they realized who he was.

With the two guides leading the way, Church and his men climbed down the rock face, sometimes clutching at the bushes to keep from falling down the steep descent and using the beat of the mortar to conceal the sounds of their approach. As soon as he reached the ground, Church strode over to the gun rack with his hatchet in his hand. Seeing who it was, Annawon's son pulled his blanket over his head and "shrunk up in a heap." Annawon leaped to his feet and cried out "Howoh." or "Who?" Seeing that the Englishman could easily bludgeon his son, Annawon fell back in despair as Church secured the muskets. Now that he had captured Annawon, Church sent the Sakonnets to the other campsites to inform the Indians that their leader had been taken and that Church and "his great army" would grant them good quarter if they gave up quietly. As it turned out, many of the enemy were related to the Sakonnets and were more than willing to take them at their word, and Church and his company of half a dozen men had soon secured a complete and bloodless surrender.

Church then turned to Annawon and through an interpreter asked what he had to eat—"for," he said, "I am come to sup with you." In a booming voice, Annawon replied, "Taubut," or "It is good."

Sprinkling some of the salt that he carried with him in his pocket on the meat, Church enjoyed some roasted beef and ground green corn. Once the meal had been completed, he told Annawon that as long as his people cooperated they would all be allowed to live, with the possible exception of Annawon, whose fate must be decided by the Plymouth courts.

As the excitement wore away, Church realized he desperately needed sleep. He'd been awake now for two days straight. He told his men that if they let him sleep for two hours, he would keep watch for the rest of the night. But as soon as he lay down for a nap, he discovered that he was once again wide awake. After an hour or so, he looked up and saw that not only his own men but all of the Indians were fast asleep, with one exception: Annawon.

For another hour, they lay on opposite sides of the fire "looking one upon the other." Since Church did not know the Indians' language, and, he assumed, Annawon did not know English, neither one of them had anything to say. Suddenly the old warrior threw off his blanket and walked off into the darkness. Church assumed he had left to relieve himself, but when he did not return for several minutes, he feared he might be up to no good. Church sidled over to Annawon's son. If his father should attempt to attack him, he would use the young man as a hostage.

A full moon had risen, and in the ghostly silver light he saw Annawon approaching with something in his hands. The Indian came up to

Church and dropped to his knees, and holding up a woven basket, he said in perfect English, "Great Captain, you have killed Philip and conquered his country, for I believe that I and my company are the last that war against the English, so [I] suppose the war is ended by your means and therefore these things belong unto you."

Inside the basket were several belts of wampum. One was nine inches wide and depicted flowers, birds, and animals. Church was now standing, and when Annawon draped the belt over his shoulders, it reached down to his ankles. The next belt was one that Philip had commonly wrapped around his head and possessed flags that had hung at his back; the third had been intended for his chest and contained a star at either end. All of the belts had been edged with red, possibly human hair that Annawon said had been secured in Mohawk country. There were also two glazed powder horns and a rich red blanket. These, Annawon explained, were what Philip "was wont to adorn himself with when he sat in state."

The two warriors talked late into the night. Annawon spoke with particular fondness of his service under Philip's father, Massasoit, and "what mighty success he had formerly in wars against many nations of Indians." They also spoke of Philip. Annawon blamed the outbreak of hostilities on two factors: the duplicity of the Praying Indians, i.e., John Sassamon, and the impetuosity of the young warriors. He compared them to "sticks laid on a heap, till by the multitude of them a great fire came to be kindled." He also spoke of spiritual matters. Annawon said that the course of the war had convinced him that "there was a great god that overruled all; and that he had found that whatever he had done to any of those, whether Indians or English, the same was brought upon himself in after-time."

At daybreak, Church marched his prisoners to Taunton, where he met up with Lieutenant Howland, "who expressed a great deal of joy to see him again and said 'twas more than ever he expected." The next day, Church sent Howland with the majority of the prisoners to Plymouth. In the meantime, he wanted Annawon to meet his friends in Rhode Island. They remained in Newport for several days and then finally left for Plymouth.

In just two months' time, Church had brought in a total of seven hundred Indians. He hoped that the debt the colony owed him might make Governor Winslow listen to his pleas that Annawon and, if he should turn himself in, Tuspaquin be granted clemency. He could use them Down East.

Massachusetts governor John Leverett had requested to meet with him to discuss the possibility of his leading a company in Maine, and Church quickly left for Boston. But when he returned to Plymouth a few days later, he discovered "to his grief" that the heads of both Annawon and Tuspaquin had joined Philip's on the palisades of Fort Hill.

Conscience

*A*S EARLY AS the fall of 1675, they had begun to sail from the coast of New England: the slave ships. It began in September when a Captain Sprague departed from Plymouth with 178 Indians. By July of 1676, Plymouth had formalized the process of removing potentially dangerous Native men and boys by determining that "no male captive above the age of fourteen years should reside in the colony." That fall, the English were not sure what to do with Philip's nine-year-old son. Some ministers argued that the Bible granted the magistrates the power to execute the boy; others insisted on a more moderate course. In the end, Philip's son, like his mother before him, was shipped off as a slave.

It has been estimated that at least a thousand Indians were sold into slavery during King Philip's War, with over half the slaves coming from Plymouth Colony alone. By the end of the war, Mount Hope, once the crowded Native heart of the colony, was virtually empty of inhabitants. Fifty-six years after the sailing of the *Mayflower,* the Pilgrims' children had not only defeated the Pokanokets in a devastating war, they had taken conscious, methodical measures to purge the land of its people.

In the years before the war, Native Americans had constituted almost 30 percent of the population of New England. By 1680, they made up less than 15 percent. But if the English had succeeded in asserting their demographic dominance, the war was, at best, a Pyrrhic victory for the colonists. The crushing tax burden required to pay for the conflict stifled the region's economy. When the Mount Hope Peninsula went up for sale in 1680, there were no Plymouth residents with the resources to purchase it, and the land went to a group of

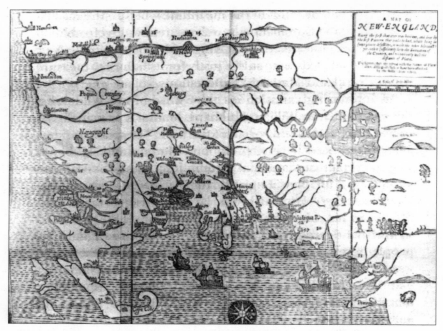

John Foster's 1677 map of New England

investors from Boston. Not for another hundred years would the average per capita income in New England return to what it had been before King Philip's War.

The war that was to have removed forever the threat of Indian attack had achieved exactly the opposite of its original intention. By cutting such a wide and blood-soaked swath between themselves and the Indians, New Englanders had thrown the region out of balance. Without "friend Indians" to buffer them from their enemies, those living in the frontier were left open to attack. Over the course of the following century, New England was ravaged by a series of Indian wars. Unable to defend themselves, the colonies that had once operated as an autonomous enclave of Puritanism were forced to look to the British Crown for assistance. Within a decade of King Philip's War, James II had appointed a royal governor to rule over New England, and in 1692 Plymouth became a part of Massachusetts. By doing their best to destroy the Native people who had welcomed and sustained their forefathers, New Englanders had destroyed their forefathers' way of life.

* * *

The Pilgrims had come to America not to conquer a continent but to re-create their modest communities in Scrooby and in Leiden. When they arrived at Plymouth in December 1620 and found it emptied of people, it seemed as if God had given them exactly what they were looking for. But as they quickly discovered during that first terrifying fall and winter, New England was far from uninhabited. There were still plenty of Native people, and to ignore or anger them was to risk annihilation. The Pilgrims' religious beliefs played a dominant role in the decades ahead, but it was their deepening relationship with the Indians that turned them into Americans.

By forcing the English to improvise, the Indians prevented Plymouth Colony from ossifying into a monolithic cult of religious extremism. For their part, the Indians were profoundly influenced by the English and quickly created a new and dynamic culture full of Native and Western influences. For a nation that has come to recognize that one of its greatest strengths is its diversity, the first fifty years of Plymouth Colony stand as a model of what America might have been from the very beginning.

By the midpoint of the seventeenth century, however, the attitudes of many of the Indians and English had begun to change. With only a fraction of their original homeland remaining, more and more young Pokanokets claimed it was time to rid themselves of the English. The Pilgrims' children, on the other hand, coveted what territory the Pokanokets still possessed and were already anticipating the day when the Indians had, through the continued effects of disease and poverty, ceased to exist. Both sides had begun to envision a future that did not include the other.

For years Philip had used the promise of war as a way to appease his increasingly indignant warriors. Whenever pushed to an actual confrontation, however, he had always backed down, and it appears that as late as June 23, 1675, he held out hope that war might once again be averted. But instead of providing Philip with the support he so desperately needed to control his warriors, Governor Winslow only made matters worse. Indeed, it was his callous prosecution of Tobias and the others, for Sassamon's murder, that triggered the outbreak of violence.

By refusing to acknowledge that Philip's troubles were also *his* troubles, Winslow was as responsible as anyone for King Philip's War.

In the end, both sides wanted what the Pilgrims had been looking for in 1620: a place unfettered by obligations to others. But from the moment Massasoit decided to become the Pilgrims' ally, New England belonged to no single group. For peace and for survival, others must be accommodated. The moment any of them gave up on the difficult work of living with their neighbors—and all of the compromise, frustration, and delay that inevitably entailed—they risked losing everything. It was a lesson that Bradford and Massasoit had learned over the course of more than three long decades. That it could be so quickly forgotten by their children remains a lesson for us today.

King Philip's War officially ended with the sachem's death in 1676, but for Benjamin Church the fighting had just begun. Between 1689 and 1704, Church led five different "eastern expeditions" against the French and Indians in Maine. Joining him on these forays into the wilderness were many of the Sakonnets who had fought at his side against Philip, as well as Church's literal child of war, Constant, who served as one of his captains. By the outbreak of Queen Anne's War in 1702, Church had grown so fat that he required the help of two assistants as he waddled over the forest trails he had once bounded across as a young man.

In 1716, with the help of his son Thomas, he published *Entertaining Passages Relating to Philip's War.* By that time Mary Rowlandson's book about her Indian captivity had gone through multiple editions. But another book, William Bradford's *Of Plymouth Plantation,* still remained in manuscript. After being consulted by a variety of historians working on books about New England, including King Philip's War chroniclers Increase Mather and William Hubbard, the calfskin-bound manuscript was lent by Bradford's grandson Samuel to the Reverend Thomas Prince, who in 1728 placed it in his library in the steeple of the Old South Church in Boston. There it was to remain for the next four decades.

* * *

The Native peoples of southern New England left no known contemporary narrative of what happened to them after the arrival of the *Mayflower*. But that does not mean that no Indian accounts exist. Instead of the written word, the Native Americans relied on oral traditions, and almost as soon as the English came to America they began recording the Indians' stories and legends.

The Indians on Cape Cod and the islands, who came to be known as the Wampanoags, told the legend of Maushop, a mythical giant who had many of the characteristics of a Native leader. In the beginning Maushop was a generous friend to his people, but as the years passed, he underwent a troubling change. He began to extort unreasonable amounts of tribute and created discord where he had once helped make peace. He also began to quarrel with his own family. "He would beat his old woman for nothing," one version of the legend claimed, "and his children for a great deal less."

One day, while his five children were playing on the beach near their home on Aquinnah, on the west end of Martha's Vineyard, Maushop drew his huge toe across the sand. Seawater rushed toward his four sons and one daughter, and as the ocean rose around them, the boys lifted up their sister in a desperate attempt to save her. Just as they were about to drown, Maushop turned them into killer whales and commanded his sons to look after their sister.

Maushop's wife was disconsolate, and her incessant weeping so angered the giant that he picked her up and threw her all the way to the rocky shore of Sakonnet, where she lived out the rest of her life begging for help from those who passed by in their canoes. Eventually she changed into a stone, and when the English arrived, they broke off her head and arms. By that time, Maushop had disappeared, "nobody knew whither." His wife, on the other hand, remains in Sakonnet to this day—a disfigured rock at the edge of the sea.

By the time this legend was first recorded in the eighteenth century, the Indians of Cape Cod and the islands had been reduced to several hundred people, most of them living on reservations in the towns of Mashpee on the Cape and in Aquinnah on Martha's Vineyard. Despite Benjamin Church's efforts to provide for them, the Sakonnets had dwindled from an estimated four hundred in 1700 to just six men and nineteen women by 1774.

In the years ahead, the legend of Maushop, like the legend of the Pilgrim Fathers, would soften into a benign and upbeat version of what had originally been a far more disturbing story. The early versions of the legend, recorded between 1792 and 1829, reflect the anger, fear, dislocation, and loss the Indians of the region felt in the wake of a war that had forced them to fight against their own people.

In the nineteenth century, the Indians of southern New England preferred to remember King Philip's War as a strictly Indian-versus-English conflict. But for those who actually experienced the war or knew those who had, it was not a question of us against them; it was more like being part of a family that had been destroyed by the frightening, inexplicable actions of a once trusted and beloved father.

In 1741, the ninety-five-year-old Thomas Faunce asked to be carried in a litter to the Plymouth waterfront. Faunce had heard that a pier was about to be built over an undistinguished rock at the tide line near Town Brook. With tears in his eyes, Faunce proclaimed that he had been told by his father, who had arrived in Plymouth in 1623, that the boulder was where the Pilgrims had first landed. Thus was born the legend of Plymouth Rock.

In 1769, a group of Plymouth residents formed the Old Colony Club and designated December 22 as Forefathers' Day in celebration of the landing of the Pilgrims on the Rock. Their first meeting was held at Thomas Southworth Howland's tavern on Cole's Hill, but as political differences came to the fore in the years prior to the outbreak of the Revolution, the club's membership, most of whom were Loyalists, decided to disband. It was left to the opposing faction, the Sons of Liberty, to seize upon, literally it turned out, Plymouth Rock.

Despite Faunce's tearful testimony, a solid-fill pier had been built over the Rock. A small portion of the boulder, however, still poked above the sandy surface of the wharf, and on Forefathers' Day in 1774 Colonel Theophilus Cotton arrived with the manpower and equipment

*An 1853 daguerreotype of Hedge's Wharf in
Plymouth, Massachusetts, where a group of
citizens stand behind the exposed portion
of Plymouth Rock*

required to extract the Rock, like a bad tooth, from the pier. But as Cotton and the Sons of Liberty attempted to load the Rock onto an awaiting wagon, disaster struck. The Rock broke in half—a metaphor, some sages insisted, for the looming split between the American colonies and Britain. Cotton and his men left the bottom, and presumably Loyalist, half of the Rock in the ground, and lugged the other piece to the town square, where they deposited it beside a newly raised liberty pole.

The Pilgrims were once again relevant, but so were Benjamin

Church and Mary Rowlandson. Updated editions of their books appeared as their struggle against the Indians came to represent the colonists' fight for independence. As it turned out, Church's grandson, also named Benjamin Church, was found guilty of secretly abetting the British during the siege of Boston. The region's Native Americans, on the other hand, proved more loyal to the cause of American liberty and freedom. An Indian from Rhode Island named Simeon Simon, who was reported to be a direct descendant of Massasoit, fought beside George Washington for all eight years of the Revolution.

In the early days of the war, the Old South Church in Boston was taken over by the British military. After the British evacuation of 1776, several volumes in Prince's church-tower library, including Bradford's manuscript, were discovered missing and assumed lost. But this did nothing to slow the rise of the myth of the Pilgrim Fathers. In 1802, John Quincy Adams, who had been educated in the Dutch city of Leiden while his father served as an ambassador to Holland, gave an address at the annual Forefathers' Day celebration in Plymouth. Instead of the Rock, the intellectual Adams was more interested in the Pilgrims' contribution to American government. In his remarks, he looked to the Mayflower Compact as the document that foreshadowed the flowering of American democracy. "This is perhaps the only instance in human history," Adams intoned, "of that positive, original social compact, which speculative philosophers have imagined as the only legitimate source of government. Here was a unanimous and personal assent by all the individuals of the community, to the association by which they became a nation."

Eighteen years later, Daniel Webster was the keynote speaker at a bicentennial celebration of the Pilgrims' arrival in the New World. Webster's speech, in which he looked to Plymouth Rock as a symbol of the imperishable ideals upon which the new nation had been founded, was widely reprinted and helped give the Pilgrims truly national recognition. In 1834, the piece of the Rock at the town square, which had been significantly reduced in size over the years by hammer-wielding souvenir hunters, was moved to the front of the newly built Pilgrim Hall, a Greek Revival structure that has been called America's first public museum. Once again, disaster struck. After being loaded onto a cart, the Rock was passing by the town's courthouse, when a linchpin jiggled free and the Rock fell to the ground and broke in two. With the help of some cement, the Rock was put back together and mounted in front of Pilgrim Hall.

The proud descendants of the Pilgrims were not the only Americans struggling to create a new and seamless version of a fractured past. The Native inhabitants of southern New England, such as the Mashpee Wampanoags on Cape Cod and the Pequots in Connecticut, had become infused with a renewed sense of identity and purpose. In 1833, the Pequot Methodist minister William Apess traveled to Cape Cod and helped spark a protest against the taking of Indian land by local white inhabitants that became known as the Mashpee Revolt. In 1836, Apess delivered a lecture in Boston titled "Eulogy on King Philip," in which he claimed King Philip's War was "as glorious as the *American* Revolution." Even though both the Pequots and the Mashpees had fought on the side of the English in the conflict, Apess chose to remember differently and portrayed Philip as the leader of a pan-Indian struggle for freedom.

Apess's remarks reflected a nationwide reassessment of King Philip's War. In 1814 Washington Irving had published "Philip of Pokanoket," an essay that probably influenced Apess's sanctification of the Indian leader. In 1829 a play titled *Metamora* (a variant of Metacom, one of Philip's many Native names) premiered in New York City starring America's foremost actor, Edwin Forrest. Metamora was everything the real Philip had struggled to be—forceful, noble, and brave—and the play remained popular for decades. America had come full circle. Instead of a perfidious enemy, Philip and the Pokanokets were patriots whose war against the Puritans prefigured the American Revolution.

In 1855, a Bostonian browsing in an antique-book store in London's Cornhill found an obscure ecclesiastical history that quoted a passage from a manuscript that appeared to be Bradford's *Of Plymouth Plantation*. It was soon established that Bradford's book had somehow made its way to the bishop of London's library in Fulham Palace. No one claimed to know how it had gotten there, but it was not long before a complete transcript of the manuscript was published in 1856. For a country beset by the challenges of western expansion and the approaching storm of the Civil War, the publication was, in the words of Samuel Eliot Morison, "a literary sensation."

Two years later, Henry Wadsworth Longfellow published the best-selling poem "The Courtship of Miles Standish," a florid account of how Priscilla Mullins asked John Alden to speak for himself when Alden attempted to deliver a marriage proposal from his friend Miles Standish. Loosely based on Alden family tradition, Longfellow's poem was extraordinarily popular, selling a reported ten thousand copies in London in a single day. Inevitably, the Pilgrims came to be known not as they had truly been but as those of the Victorian era wished them to have been. With the outbreak of the Civil War a few years later, the public need for a restorative myth of national origins became even more ardent, and in 1863 Abraham Lincoln established the holiday of Thanksgiving—a cathartic celebration of nationhood that would have baffled and probably appalled the godly Pilgrims.

Just prior to the Civil War, the Pilgrim Society, the organization that had built Pilgrim Hall, purchased the wharf containing the *other* half of Plymouth Rock. The society determined to enshrine this portion of the boulder in an appropriate edifice. But to have two Plymouth Rocks was an obvious absurdity, so in 1880, the broken half in front of Pilgrim Hall was transported down to the waterfront and after a more than century-long hiatus was reunited with the portion beside the sea.

But still, Bradford's great book remained in the library of an English bishop. Finally, in 1896, George Frisbie Hoar, a U.S. senator from Massachusetts, decided it was time to repatriate this famous document. Hoar was a descendant of John Hoar of Concord, the man who had brought back Mary Rowlandson from captivity, and it was only appropriate that he be the one who returned Bradford's book from its exile in England. Hoar voyaged to London and began the process that finally brought the manuscript home to New England in 1897.

* * *

In 1891, the body of Miles Standish was exhumed by a group that included the Duxbury Episcopal minister, a medical doctor, and several Standish descendants. It was perhaps appropriate that the man who had overseen the pilfering of Native graves during the winter of 1620 was subjected to a similar indignity 271 years later. His skull and bones were carefully measured, and the doctor claimed that "the bones indicated a man of tremendous physique and strength." The skull was surprisingly large and "of a peculiar formation," and the minister tactfully pointed out that several of the Standish descendants standing beside the grave that day had similarly shaped heads. There was only one tooth left in Standish's lower jaw, and what hair remained on the skull was reddish brown and mixed with gray. But what surprised all of them was the length of the skeleton—five feet seven inches, an average height for a man in the seventeenth century. Had Standish been taller than was previously thought?

Not so, insisted the doctor, who described how "when a human body disintegrates in the grave, the bones fall apart and are crushed apart by the decayed coffin lid and the crushing earth, so that the skeleton in the grave is generally longer than the living man would be." Like all the Pilgrims, Standish was taller in death than he had ever been in life.

With the Civil War a memory and the Indian wars of the Wild West drawing to a close, U.S. citizens at the turn of the century could look with romantic nostalgia toward America's Native population. Instead of the Rock and the compact, Thanksgiving and its reassuring image of Indian-English cooperation became the predominant myth of the Pilgrims. Despite strong regional interest in King Philip's War throughout the first half of the twentieth century, the conflict attracted little attention beyond New England. In the American popular imagination, the nation's history began with the Pilgrims and then leapfrogged more than 150 years to Lexington and Concord and the Revolution.

Out of the tumult of the 1960s a new sense of Native identity emerged that challenged the nation's veneration of Thanksgiving. In

1970, Native activists declared Thanksgiving a National Day of Mourning, and Plymouth was selected as the natural place for it to be observed. In recent decades, Native New Englanders—once regarded as a "vanished people"—have undergone a resurgence. Many of the tribes that participated in King Philip's War have been granted federal recognition, with the Pequots and Mohegans making the most highly visible comebacks thanks to extraordinarily profitable gambling casinos.

The Pilgrims' descendants have proven to be, if nothing else, fruitful. In 2002 it was estimated that there were approximately 35 million descendants of the *Mayflower* passengers in the United States, which represents roughly 10 percent of the total U.S. population.

Today Plymouth is a mixture of the sacred and the kitsch, a place of period houses and tourist traps, where the *Mayflower II* sits quietly beside the ornate granite edifice that now encloses the mangled remains of Plymouth Rock. A few miles from downtown Plymouth on the north bank of the Eel River is Plimoth Plantation, a re-creation of the Pilgrim settlement as it looked in 1627, the last year the original settlers all lived within the confines of the palisade wall. The design and construction of the buildings have been painstakingly researched; the interpreters have been immersed in the language and customs of early seventeenth-century England, as well as everything that is known about the historical characters they are depicting. After the honky-tonk tackiness of the Plymouth waterfront, Plimoth Plantation is a wonderfully satisfying and self-contained evocation of a distant time.

Outside the palisade wall is the re-creation of a small Native settlement known as the Wampanoag Homesite. The interpreters make no attempt to pretend they are anything but people living in the here and now of twenty-first-century America. But even here, beyond the gates of 1627, ghosts from the past intrude.

Archaeological research has revealed that Clark's garrison, where Benjamin Church almost lost his wife and son, was situated on the grounds of Plimoth Plantation between the Wampanoag Homesite and the re-created Pilgrim settlement. On Sunday, March 12, 1676, the building was the scene of a brutal massacre that claimed the lives of eleven

Plymouth residents, most of them women and children. In retaliation, Plymouth authorities executed four Indians accused of participating in the attack. Today the site is a parking lot, with no historic marker.

But no matter how desperately our nation's mythologizers might wish it had never happened, King Philip's War will not go away. The fourteen bloody months between June 1675 and August 1676 had a vast, disturbing impact on the development of New England and, with it, all of America.

It is easy to mock past attempts to venerate and sanctify the Pilgrims, especially given what their sons and grandsons did to the Native Americans. And yet, we must look with something more than cynicism at a people who maintained more than half a century of peace with their Native neighbors. The great mystery of this story is how America emerged from the terrible darkness of King Philip's War to become the United States. A possible answer resides in the character of the man who has been called America's first Indian fighter, Benjamin Church.

In the years after King Philip's War, as the country came to be defined by its relentless push west, a new American type came into being: the frontiersman. As a roughneck intermediary between civilization and savagery, the frontiersman had a natural distrust of authority and relied on his own instincts, bravery, and skill to survive. What makes Church unique is that he was one of the first New Englanders to embrace the wilderness his forefathers had shunned. When war erupted in June 1675, he was the right man in the right place to become a truly archetypal American.

Out of the annealing flame of one of the most horrendous wars ever fought in North America, he forged an identity that was part Pilgrim, part mariner, part Indian, and altogether his own. That so many characters from American history and literature resemble him—from Daniel Boone to Davy Crockett to Natty Bumppo to Rambo—does nothing to diminish the stunning originality of the persona he creates in *Entertaining Passages Relating to Philip's War.* That Church according to Church is too brave, too cunning, and too good to be true is beside the point. America was destined to become a nation of self-fashioned and self-promoting men. What makes his story so special, I believe, is that he shows us how the nightmare of wilderness warfare might one day give rise to a society that promises liberty and justice for all.

There are two possible responses to a world suddenly gripped by terror and contention. There is the Moseley way: get mad and get even. But as the course of King Philip's War proved, unbridled arrogance and fear only feed the flames of violence. Then there is the Church way. Instead of loathing the enemy, try to learn as much as possible from him; instead of killing him, try to bring him around to your way of thinking. First and foremost, treat him like a human being. For Church, success in war was about coercion rather than slaughter, and in this he anticipated the welcoming, transformative beast that eventually became—once the Declaration of Independence and the Constitution were in place—the United States.

Church concludes his account of the war with a vignette. In January 1677, the Plymouth magistrates asked him to lead a few minor mop-up operations. Over the course of the winter he succeeded in capturing several additional Indians. One of the captives was an old man to whom Church took an immediate liking, and he asked the Indian his name.

"Conscience," the old man replied.

"Conscience," Church repeated with a smile; "then the war is over, for that was what they were searching for, it being much wanting."

Church was supposed to deliver the old man to Plymouth, where he would undoubtedly have been shipped off as a slave to the West Indies. Instead, Church asked him where he wanted to live out the rest of his life. The Indian told him the name of an Englishman in Swansea he had known before the war. Church made some inquiries, and soon Conscience had a new home.

It was a small victory to be sure, but in the winter of 1677 it was the best that Benjamin Church could do.

Acknowledgments

THIS BOOK BEGAN on Nantucket Island in 1995 with a Native American symposium sponsored by the Nantucket Historical Association. There I met John Peters, or Slow Turtle, then Wampanoag tribal medicine man and executive director of the Massachusetts Commission of Indian Affairs; Tony Pollard, or Nanepashamet, then curator of Plimoth Planatation's Wampanoag Indian Program; and Russell Gardner, or Great Moose, then Wampanoag tribal historian. Gardner, in particular, was a huge help to me in researching the book I subsequently wrote about Nantucket's Native American legacy, *Abram's Eyes*. Sadly, all three had passed away by the time I began work on this book—a work that draws on many of the insights they provided, both in writing and in person, a decade or more ago. I also owe a debt to Wampanoag tribal members Helen Vanderhoop Manning and June Manning, who guided my earlier researches on Martha's Vineyard, and the late Elizabeth Little, whose knowledge of Nantucket Native Americans was unmatched. Thanks also to the late Albert "Bud" Egan and to his wife Dorothy Egan and their support through the Egan Foundation and the Egan Institute of Maritime Studies.

Over the course of the last three years, I have benefited from the help of many individuals and institutions: James Baker at the Alden House; Ellen Dunlap, John Hench, Nancy Burkett, Georgia Barnhill, Thomas Knoles at the American Antiquarian Society; Jeremy Bangs at the Leiden American Pilgrim Museum; Eleanor Hammond and John York at the Aptucxet Trading Post Museum; Michael Volmar at the Fruitlands Museum; Stuart Frank and Michael Dyer at the Kendall Institute at the New Bedford Whaling Museum; Barbara Hail and Kevin Smith at the

Haffenreffer Natural History Museum; Betsey Lowenstein at the Massachusetts Archives at the State House; William Fowler, Peter Drummey, Anne Bentley, and Kimberly Nusco at the Massachusetts Historical Society; Richard Peuser at the National Archives; Jane Hennedy and her staff at the Old Colony Historical Society; Peg Baker and Jane Port at the Pilgrim Hall Museum; Nancy Brennan, Liz Lodge, Carolyn Freeman Travers, Linda Coombs, Peter Arenstam, Pret Woodburn, and Rick McKee at Plimoth Plantation; and Chuck Turley at the Provincetown Monument and Pilgrim Museum. Thanks also to the staffs of the Jabez Howland House and Isaac Winslow House. Special thanks to the professional staffs of the New England Historic Genealogical Society and the Mayflower Society for their important and ongoing contributions to the scholarshp of seventeenth-century New England.

My research in England was assisted immeasurably by Malcolm Dolby in Scrooby and by Russell Kirby, Mag Kirby, and Tim Connolly in London. Larry Anderson and Fred Bridge showed me the King Philip War sites in Little Compton, Rhode Island. Thanks also to Revell Carr, Alfred Crosby, Jeffrey Crowley, Jud Judson, Jeff Kalin, Frances Karttunen, Dr. Timothy Lepore, Beth Mansfield, Richard and Mary Philbrick, Timothy Philbrick, Andrew Pierce, Michael Tougias, and Charles Soule. Special thanks to Narragansett medicine woman and tribal historian Ella Wilcox Sekatau.

I benefited greatly from the input provided by the following readers: Robert C. Anderson, James Baker, Peggy Baker, Jeremy Bangs, Susan Beegel, Thomas Congdon, Peter Drummey, Peter Gow, Barbara Hail, Michael Hill, Jennie Philbrick, Melissa Philbrick, Marianne Philbrick, Thomas Philbrick, Neal Salisbury, Eric Schultz, Ella Sekatau, Keith Stavely, Carolyn Travers, Len Travers, and Gregory Whitehead. All errors of fact and interpretation are mine alone.

A special thanks to Michael Hill, whose research assistance and wise counsel are greatly appreciated. Thanks also to Celeste Walker and to Timothy Newman.

Many, many thanks to my editor at Viking Penguin, Wendy Wolf, who has once again shown me the way. Thanks to Hilary Redmon and Hal Fessenden for their editorial input and to Cliff Corcoran, Francesca

Belanger, Kate Griggs, Michael Brennan, Gretchen Koss, Greg Mollica, and copyeditor Adam Goldberger. Thanks also to Jeffrey Ward for the maps.

At HarperCollins UK, I am indebted to Richard Johnson for his editorial advice and to Rachel Nicholson for her assistance in planning my research trip to England.

The history of Plymouth Colony is a topic I have been thinking about for a long time, but it was my agent Stuart Krichevsky who first prodded me to turn it into a book. Thanks, Stuart, for all your help. Thanks also to Shana Cohen and Elizabeth Coen Kellermeyer.

Most of all, thanks to my wife, Melissa D. Philbrick, and our two children, Jennie and Ethan, and to my parents, Marianne and Thomas Philbrick, and to my brother, Sam Philbrick, and his family, all of whom were with me every step of the way.

Notes

Abbreviations

AAS   American Antiquarian Society
CCR   Colonial Connecticut Records
EPRPW   *Entertaining Passages Relating to Philip's War* by Benjamin Church, edited by Henry Martyn Dexter
GNNE   *Good News from New England* by Edward Winslow
HIWNE   *History of the Indian Wars in New England* by William Hubbard, edited by Samuel G. Drake
HKPW   *History of King Philip's War* by Increase Mather, edited by Samuel G. Drake
MHS   Massachusetts Historical Society
MR   *Mourt's Relation,* edited by Dwight B. Heath
NEHGR   *New England Historical and Genealogical Register*
NEQ   *New England Quarterly*
OIC   *The Old Indian Chronicle,* edited by Samuel G. Drake
OPP   *Of Plymouth Plantation* by William Bradford, edited by Samuel Eliot Morison
PCR   *Plymouth Colony Records,* edited by David Pulsifer and Nathaniel Shurtleff
PM   *The Plymouth Migration* by Robert Charles Anderson
SGG   *The Sovereignty and Goodness of God* by Mary Rowlandson, edited by Neal Salisbury
WMQ   *William and Mary Quarterly*

PREFACE—*The Two Voyages*

On America's obsessive need for a myth of national origins, see Terence Martin's *Parables of Possibility: The American Need for Beginnings* and Ann Uhry Abrams's *The Pilgrims and Pocahontas: Rival Myths of American Origin.* My brief account of the voyage of the *Seaflower* is indebted to Jill Lepore's *The Name of War: King*

Philip's War and the Origins of American Identity, pp. 150–70. As Lepore points out, in addition to slaves from Plymouth Colony, there was a group from Massachusetts, requiring the *Seaflower's* captain to have certificates from both Plymouth governor Josiah Winslow and Massachusetts governor John Leverett. Winslow's "Certificate to Thomas Smith concerning the transportation of Indian prisoners, August 9, 1676" is in the Stewart Mitchell Papers II at MHS. As Almon Wheeler Lauber makes clear in *Indian Slavery in Colonial Times within the Present Limits of the United States,* the *Seaflower* was one of many New England ships that transported Native American slaves to Bermuda and the Caribbean during and after King Philip's War. See also Margaret Newell's "The Changing Nature of Indian Slavery in New England, 1670–1720" in *Reinterpreting New England Indians and the Colonial Experience,* edited by Colin Calloway and Neal Salisbury, pp. 128–29. In a letter dated November 27, 1683, and cited by Lepore in *The Name of War,* the Puritan missionary John Eliot refers to some Indians who may have been part of the *Seaflower's* cargo: "A vessel carried away a great number of our surprised Indians, in the time of our wars, to sell them for slaves; but the nations, wither they went, would not buy them. Finally, she left them at Tangier; there they be, so many as live, or born there. An Englishman, a mason, came thence to Boston: he told me, they desired I would use some means for their return home. I know not what to do in it," MHS Collections, vol. 3, p. 183. James Drake in *King Philip's War: Civil War in New England, 1675–1676* writes convincingly about the degree to which New England was a bicultural community prior to the war: "By 1675 Indian and English polities had so intermeshed that in killing one another in King Philip's War they destroyed a part of themselves," p. 196; Drake also insists that "it should not be assumed that the English and the Indians had invariably been headed toward a dramatic confrontation," p. 3. William Hubbard in *HIWNE* writes of the region's Indians being "in a kind of maze," p. 59. Douglas Leach in *Flintlock and Tomahawk: New England in King Philip's War* tells of the proposal to build a wall around the core settlements of Massachusetts, pp. 165–66. For statistics on the death toll and carnage from King Philip's War, see Eric Schultz and Michael Tougias's *King Philip's War: The History and Legacy of America's Forgotten Conflict,* pp. 4–5; James Drake's *King Philip's War,* pp. 168–70; and Neal Salisbury's introduction to Mary Rowlandson's *SGG,* p 1.

CHAPTER ONE—*They Knew They Were Pilgrims*

I have adjusted the spelling and punctuation of all quotations to make them more accessible to a modern audience—something that had already been done by the editors of *OPP* and *MR.* When it comes to dates, I have elected to go with the Julian calendar or "Old Style" used by the Pilgrims, with one exception. The Pilgrims' new calendar year began on March 25; to avoid confusion, I have assumed the new year began on January 1. To bring the dates in synch with the calendar we use today, or the "New Style," add ten days to the date listed in the text.

My account of the *Mayflower*'s voyage to America is largely based on *OPP*, pp. 58–60, and *MR*, pp. 4–5. The two dogs are mentioned in *MR*, p. 45. W. Sears Nickerson's *Land Ho!—1620: A Seaman's Story of the* Mayflower, *Her Construction, Her Navigation, and Her First Landfall* is an indispensable analysis of the voyage. Nowhere in *OPP* or *MR* is the name of the ship that brought the Pilgrims to America mentioned. If not for the 1623 land division, in which is listed the land given to those who "came first over in the May-Floure," we might not know it today, although there has been plenty of research that corroborates the name of the Pilgrim ship. Concerning the state of the *Mayflower*'s bottom, Nickerson writes that it "must have been extremely foul with grass and barnacles from being in the water all through the hot months," *Land Ho!*, p. 28. Although Nickerson's experience at sea during the late nineteenth century prompted him to speculate that many, if not most, of the passengers were put up in bunks built in the aft cabins of the ship, *MR* places the Billingtons' cabin in the 'tween decks, p. 31. Also, Edward Winslow advises future voyagers to America to "build your cabins as open as you can," suggesting that they were temporary structures built in the 'tween decks, *MR*, p. 86. On the dimensions of the 'tween decks, see William Baker's *The Mayflower and Other Colonial Vessels*, p. 37. On the importance of beer in seventeenth-century England and America, see James Deetz and Patricia Scott Deetz's *The Times of Their Lives: Life, Love, and Death in Plymouth Colony*, p. 8.

There has been much speculation as to the nature of the "great iron screw" used to repair the *Mayflower*. In his introduction to *The Pilgrim Press*, edited by R. Breugelman, J. Rendel Harris maintained that it was part of a printing press the Pilgrims were bringing over to the New World, pp. 4–5, but as Jeremy Bangs convincingly demonstrates in *Pilgrim Edward Winslow: New England's First International Diplomat*, it was undoubtedly a device "to draw heavy timber to a considerable height"—from Joseph Moxon's *Mechanick Exercises of the Doctrine of Handy-Works*, first published in 1678–80, and cited by Bangs, pp. 9–10.

Bradford discusses the Pilgrims' motives for leaving Holland in *OPP*, pp. 23–27. See also Jeremy Bangs's *Pilgrim Life in Leiden*, pp. 41–45. The statistics concerning the mortality rate in early Virginia are from Karen Ordahl Kupperman's "Apathy and Death in Early Jamestown," *Journal of American History*, June 1979, p. 24. The passage about the brutality of Native Americans is in *OPP*, p. 26. On the Pilgrims' belief in England's leadership role in the coming millennium, see Peter Gay's *A Loss of Mastery: Puritan Historians in Colonial America*, pp. 5–7; William Haller's *The Elect Nation: The Meaning and Relevance of Foxe's Book of Martyrs*, pp. 68–69; and Francis Bremer's *The Puritan Experiment: New*

England Society from Bradford to Edwards, p. 42. On the English disdain for
Spain's treatment of the Indians in America and Richard Hakluyt's insistence
that it was England's destiny to colonize the New World, see Edmund Morgan's
American Slavery, American Freedom: The Ordeal of Colonial Virginia, pp. 15–24.
On the comet of 1618, see Keith Thomas's *Religion and the Decline of Magic,* p.
354. Interestingly, Phineas Pratt's *A Declaration of the Affairs of the English People
That First Inhabited New England* refers to the comet as a prelude to the Pilgrims' settlement in Plymouth: "in the year 1618 there appeared a blazing star
over Germany that made the wise men of Europe astonished there," p. 477.
John Navin's dissertation "Plymouth Plantation: The Search for Community on
the New England Frontier" provides an excellent analysis of social, cultural, and
interpersonal dynamics at work among the Pilgrims during their time in Holland, pp. 141–83. The comments about the Pilgrims' strong spiritual bonds are in
a December 15, 1617, letter by John Robinson and William Brewster in *OPP,*
pp. 32–34. The full passage in which Bradford uses the term "pilgrim" is as follows: "So they left that goodly and pleasant city [Leiden] which had been their
resting place near twelve years; but they knew they were pilgrims, and looked
not much on those things, but lifted up their eyes to the heavens, their dearest
country, and quieted their spirits," *OPP,* p. 47. This passage bears many similarities to the words Robert Cushman had used in "Reasons and considerations
touching the lawfulness of removing out of England into the parts of America,"
which appears at the end of *MR:* "But now we are all in all places strangers and
pilgrims, travelers and sojourners, most properly, having no dwelling but in this
earthen tabernacle; our dwelling is but a wandering, and our abiding but as a
fleeting, and in a word our home is nowhere, but in the heavens," pp. 89–90.

   Almost all the information we have about Bradford's childhood in Auster-
field, short of baptismal records, comes from Cotton Mather's *Magnalia Christi
Americana,* pp. 203–7. See also the biographical sketch of Bradford in Robert
Anderson's *The Pilgrim Migration,* pp. 62–66. I am indebted to local historian
Malcolm Dolby for a tour of both Austerfield and Scrooby and whose mono-
graph *William Bradford of Austerfield* is extremely helpful; see also Bradford
Smith's *Bradford of Plymouth.* On the Geneva Bible, which was in essence the
Puritan Bible, see Adam Nicolson's *God's Secretaries: The Making of the King
James Bible,* pp. 58–59, 68, 229–30. Edmund Haller in *The Elect Nation* writes of
the importance of Foxe's *Book of Martyrs* to England's sense of historical and
spiritual entitlement, pp. 14–15.

   My account of the Pilgrims' spiritual beliefs is drawn from a wide range of
sources, but I found the following works to be especially helpful: Horton
Davies's *Worship and Theology in England: From Cranmer to Hooker, 1534–1603;
The Worship of the American Puritans,* also by Davies; Francis Bremer's *The Puri-
tan Experiment: New England Society from Bradford to Edwards;* Keith Thomas's
Religion and the Decline of Magic; Theodore Bozeman's *To Live Ancient Lives;*

Philip Benedict's *Christ's Churches Purely Reformed: A Social History of Calvinism;* Diarmaid MacCulloch's *The Reformation;* and Patrick Collinson's *The Religion of Protestants.* On covenant theology, the stages by which a Puritan tracked the workings of the Holy Spirit, and Separatism, I have looked to Edmund Morgan's excellent summary of Puritan beliefs in *Roger Williams: The Church and the State,* pp. 11–27, as well as his *Visible Saints: The History of a Puritan Idea,* especially pp. 18–32. I am also indebted to James Baker's invaluable input.

An unattributed pamphlet entitled *St. Helena's Church, Austerfield, Founded 1080* refers to an article by the Reverend Edward Dunnicliffe that claims the date of the stone carving of the snake over the south doorway of St. Helena's "is much earlier than the rest of the church Viz:—Probably the Eighth Century." For information on William Brewster and the manor house at Scrooby, see Henry Martyn Dexter and Morton Dexter's *The England and Holland of the Pilgrims,* pp. 215–330, and Harold Kirk-Smith's *William Brewster: The Father of New England.* Bradford's account of the Pilgrims' escape from England is in *OPP,* pp. 12–15. On the challenges English Separatists experienced in Holland, see Francis Bremer's *The Puritan Experiment,* pp. 30–32. Jeremy Bangs, who provided me with an illuminating tour of Pilgrim sites at Leiden, describes De Groene Poort in "Pilgrim Homes in Leiden," *NEHGR* 154 (2000), pp. 413–45. Bangs tells of the working life in Leiden in *Pilgrim Life in Leiden,* pp. 22–23, 28, 41. Edmund Morgan in *American Slavery, American Freedom* writes, "[T]here were times when the most industrious farmer could find no good way to keep himself and the men he might employ continuously busy. . . . John Law, writing in 1705 . . . took it for granted that the persons engaged in agriculture would be idle, for one reason or another, half the time," p. 64. Francis Dillon in *The Pilgrims: Their Journeys and Their World* provides an insightful analysis of the Pilgrims' attitude toward the rest of the world: "The Pilgrims were never slow in finding little defects in a man's character and would pounce very quickly on minor sins, but were continually being foxed by major rogues. Perhaps they suffered from moral myopia caused by staring too hard at the Whore of Babylon," p. 84.

Bradford provides a moving, heartfelt sketch of Brewster in *OPP,* pp. 325–28. For a documentary history of King James's pursuit of William Brewster, see Edward Arber's *The Story of the Pilgrim Fathers,* pp. 197–228. John Navin in *Plymouth Plantation* argues that had Brewster been allowed to carry forward the negotiations, "the separatist vanguard might not have lost a major portion of its members," p. 201. For information on the Virginia Company and the British colonization of America, I have looked to Viola Barnes's *The Dominion of New England: A Study in British Colonial Policy,* pp. 1–9, and Bernard Bailyn's *The New England Merchants in the Seventeenth Century,* pp. 2–5. Samuel Eliot Morison in "The Plymouth Colony and Virginia" in the *Virginia Magazine,* vol. 62, 1954, provides an excellent account of the procedure by which a patent was procured from the Virginia Company, pp. 149–50. See also Peggy Baker's "The Plymouth Colony Patent" in *Pilgrim Society News*, fall 2005, pp. 7–8. In *England and the Discovery of America, 1481–1620*, David Beers Quinn writes of the Blackwell voyage in the context of the English Separatist scene in Holland, pp. 362–63. Bradford's account of their troubled preparations to leave for America, which include letters from Robert Cushman and others, are in *OPP*, pp. 356–67. The passage about how Bradford interpreted his financial setbacks in spiritual terms is from Mather's *Magnalia*, p. 204. For an account of the Merchant Adventurers and how the deal with the Pilgrims was organized, see Ruth McIntyre's *Debts Hopeful and Desperate*, pp. 17–20. Bradford writes of their moving farewell at Delfshaven in *OPP*, pp. 47–48. In *Hypocrisie Unmasked*, written in 1646, Edward Winslow looks back to that same scene, pp. 88–91; he also mentions the "large offers" of the Dutch concerning a possible settlement in America.

For information about the *Mayflower*, I've relied on Nickerson's *Land Ho!— 1620*, pp. 14–37, and William Baker's *The Mayflower and Other Colonial Vessels*, pp. 1–64. Much of the original historical sleuthing regarding the *Mayflower* and her master and crew is to be found in the following articles: R. G. Marsden's "The *Mayflower*" in *English Historical Review*, October 1904; J. W. Horrocks's "The *Mayflower*" in several volumes of the *Mariner's Mirror*, 1922; and R. C. Anderson's "A *Mayflower* Model," in the 1926 *Mariner's Mirror*. Mary Boast's *The Mayflower and the Pilgrim Story: Chapters from Rotherhithe and Southwark* provides a good overview of the maritime scene from which the ship and her master came. Charles Banks's "The Officers and Crew of the *Mayflower*, 1620–21," *MHS Proceedings*, vol. 60, pp. 210–21, is a useful summary. Concerning Master Christopher Jones and his officers, I've also relied on the information compiled by Carolyn Freeman Travers in 1997 in "The *Mayflower*'s Crew," an unpublished research manuscript at Plimoth Plantation. Important information regarding one of the ship's pilots is contained in Irene Wright's "John Clark of the *Mayflower*" in MHS *Proceedings*, vol. 54, November 1920. For a more general discussion of the maritime culture of the seventeenth century, see David Beers Quinn's *England and the Discovery of America, 1481–1620*, pp. 197–226.

When it comes to the origins of the *Mayflower*'s passengers, there is an incredible wealth of genealogical research on which to draw. Upon its publication in 1986, Eugene Stratton's *Plymouth Colony: Its History and People, 1620–1691*, with biographical sketches written with the research help of Robert Wakefield, became *the* single source for information about the Pilgrims. Since then, the publication of Robert Anderson's *The Great Migration Begins, 1620–1633* has set a new standard—recently surpassed by the updated biographies contained in Anderson's *The Pilgrim Migration*, which incorporates important new research, such as Caleb Johnson's "The True History of Stephen Hopkins of the *Mayflower*" in the *American Genealogist*, which established, almost for a certainty, that Hopkins was the same Stephen Hopkins who had previously been shipwrecked on Bermuda during a passage to Virginia in 1609. Working in the archives in Leiden, Holland, Jeremy Bangs has done much to broaden our understanding of the Dutch origins of the Pilgrims in articles such as "*Mayflower* Passengers Documented in Leiden: A List" in the *Mayflower Quarterly*, May 1985, pp. 57–60, and "The Pilgrims and Other English in Leiden Records: Some New Pilgrim Documents" in the *NEHGR*, July 1989, plus a series of articles in *New England Ancestors*, a publication of the New England Historic Genealogical Society, from 2000 to 2005. See also B. N. Leverland's "Geographic Origins of the Pilgrims" in *The Pilgrims in Netherlands—Recent Research*, edited by Jeremy Bangs, pp. 9–17. Bradford describes the Billingtons as "one of the profanest families amongst them" in *OPP*, p. 234. For an intriguing account of the three More children aboard the *Mayflower*, see David Lindsay's *Mayflower Bastard*, which draws largely on Donald Harris's "The More Children of the *Mayflower*: Their Shropshire Origins and the Reasons Why They Were Sent Away," *Mayflower Descendant*, vols. 43 and 44.

In *Saints and Strangers*, published in 1945, George Willison set forth a new interpretation of the Pilgrim experience based on the claim that more than half the passengers on the *Mayflower* were not part of the original congregation from Leiden. In Willison's view, the Mayflower Compact was an instrument of repression by which the Separatists from Holland were able to assert control over the non-Separatist majority. In the decades since, research by Jeremy Bangs and others has revealed that there were more Leideners aboard the *Mayflower* than was originally thought and that many of those from London and other parts of England had close connections with the congregation. Although the precise number of Saints aboard the *Mayflower* is impossible to determine, Bangs has established that there were at least fifty-two (personal communication), putting the Leideners in the majority. The fact remains, however, that a significant number of the passengers aboard the *Mayflower* were not aligned with the Separatists and that, as Bradford so graphically illustrates, internal conflicts were a problem before, during, and after the voyage to America. As John Navin has shown, the nightmarish preparations for the voyage caused many Leideners to elect to stay in Holland; as a result, "[o]nly a fraction of Robinson's followers remained in the vanguard headed for New England, perhaps less than one-sixth of the whole," *Plymouth Plantation*, p. 264.

Cushman's colorful letter concerning the tyrannical Christopher Martin and the leaking *Speedwell* was written to Cushman's good friend Edward Southworth in London on August 17, 1620; after her husband's death, Southworth's wife, Alice, would marry William Bradford in 1623, and it is presumably through Alice that the Cushman letter came into Bradford's possession. Bradford writes of Reynolds's duplicity in *OPP*, p. 54. Concerning the *Speedwell*, Edward Arber writes in *The Story of the Pilgrim Fathers*, "Imagine for a moment, what might have occurred had not the trim of the *Speedwell* been so unfortunately altered. . . . Most certainly the overmasting of the *Speedwell* . . . is one of the Turning Points of modern history," p. 346. Nathaniel Morton's claims concerning Christopher Jones's complicity in the subterfuge of the Dutch are in his *New England Memorial:* "For [the Pilgrims'] intention . . . was to Hudson's river: but some of the Dutch, having notice of their intentions; and having thoughts, about the same time of erecting a Plantation there likewise, they fraudulently hired the said Jones (by delays while they were in England; and now under the pretence of danger of the shoals, &c.) to disappoint them in their going thither," p. 22. As commentators from Edward Arber to Sears Nickerson have argued, all the evidence points to Jones being a friend to the Pilgrims; it was Reynolds, not Jones, who worked secretly against them. John Robinson's letter to the Pilgrims is in *OPP,* pp. 368–71. Edward Winslow speaks of Robinson's moderating Separatism in *Hypocrisie Umasked,* pp. 92–93. Jeremy Bangs discusses Edward Winslow's account of Robinson's beliefs in *Pilgrim Edward Winslow,* pp. 414–18. Bradford's account of the *Mayflower's* voyage is in *OPP,* pp. 58–60. David Cressy in *Coming Over: Migration and Communication between England and New England in the Seventeenth Century* makes an excellent case for a kind of "bonding" between passengers during a typical transatlantic voyage. Given the discord that erupted between the Leideners and Strangers when the *Mayflower* reached Cape Cod, it's doubtful whether much positive interaction occurred between the two groups during the two-month-long voyage. Both Cressy and I use the phrase "in the same boat," p. 151. Alan Villiers's description of the *Mayflower II* lying ahull is in his "How We Sailed the New *Mayflower* to America" in *National Geographic Magazine,* November 1957, p. 667. Sears Nickerson speaks of the effects of the Gulf Stream on the *Mayflower,* as well as her average speed during the voyage and Jones's use of a cross-staff in *Land Ho!—1620,* pp. 28–33.

CHAPTER TWO—*Dangerous Shoals and Roaring Breakers*

Anyone writing about the *Mayflower's* first few days on the American coast is indebted to Sears Nickerson's *Land-Ho!—1620,* first published in 1931 and recently reissued by the Michigan State University Press and edited by Delores Bird Carpenter. Nickerson brought a lifetime of sailing the waters of Cape Cod to his analysis of the existing evidence. By determining the phases of the moon and tides on November 9–11, 1620, he was able to reconstruct, as only a veteran sailor could, the conditions experienced by Master Jones and the rest of his crew. Even Samuel Eliot Morison in his own extremely useful "Plymouth Colony Beachhead," *U.S. Naval Institute Proceedings,* December 1954, deferred to Nickerson, calling him the "ancient mariner of the Cape who has full knowl-

edge of the winds and currents of those waters," p. 1348. I have relied on Nickerson throughout this chapter.

Bradford describes them as "not a little joyful" to see land in *OPP*, p. 59–60;
the description of the land being "wooded to the brink of the sea" is in *MR*,
p. 15. John Smith's map of New England appears in volume 1 of *The Complete
Works of Captain John Smith*, edited by Philip Barbour, pp. 320–21. My description of how Jones conned the *Mayflower* along the back side of the cape is based
on Nickerson, pp. 32–33, 79, as well as Alan Villiers's account of sailing the
replica *Mayflower II* across the Atlantic in 1957 in "How We Sailed *Mayflower II*
to America," in the *National Geographic*, November 1957, pp. 627–72. Nickerson refers to Pollack Rip as "one of the meanest stretches of shoal water" in
Land Ho!, p. 66. Barbara Chamberlain speaks of the dangers of the back side of
the cape in *These Fragile Outposts:* "The timbers of more than 3000 vessels lie
buried in the offshore sands on the Cape. . . . The shores of Chatham alone—a
few miles of sandy beach—are said to have received half the wrecks of the whole
Atlantic and Gulf coastline of the United States," p. 249. See also John Stilgoe's
"A New England Coastal Wilderness," in which he cites John Smith's famous
dismissal of the accuracy of existing charts as "so much waste paper, though they
cost me more," p. 90. Nickerson describes Champlain's 1606 attempt to penetrate the rip, pp. 43–44. Bradford speaks of the "roaring breakers" in *OPP*, p. 60,
in which he also tells of the "discontented and mutinous speeches," p. 75. William Strachey writes of the "outcries and miseries" of the passengers aboard the
Sea Venture in *A Voyage to Virginia* in 1609, edited by Louis Wright, p. 6. John
Navin in *Plymouth Plantation* writes of the non-Separatists' lack of cohesiveness
and the likelihood that Christopher Martin played a role in standing against the
threatened rebellion, pp. 287, 292, as well as the Separatists' dependence on
Robinson's leadership while in Leiden, where the congregation had "customarily
deferred to the authority of their pastor and church elders in virtually all matters
of discipline and controversy, both inside and outside the church," p. 289. For a
discussion of how the *Mayflower* was rigged, see William Baker's *The Mayflower*,
pp. 44–54.

Edmund Morgan discusses the various views of the relations between church
and state that were possible within the Puritan tradition in *Roger Williams: The
Church and State*, pp. 28–85. The Pilgrims stood somewhere between the ex-
tremes of the theocracy that came to be established in Massachusetts and the total repudiation of this by Roger Williams. Jeremy Bangs makes a strong case for
the importance of Dutch influences on the crafting of the Mayflower Compact
in "Strangers on the *Mayflower*—Part 1" in *New England Ancestors*, vol. 1, 2000,
no. 1, pp. 60–63, and in Part 2, *New England Ancestors*, vol. 1, 2000, no. 2,
pp. 25–27. John Robinson insists on the need for the Pilgrims to become "a
body politic" in his farewell letter in *OPP*, p. 369. In *Hidden History*, Daniel
Boorstin calls the Mayflower Compact "the primeval document of American

self-government" and adds, "The transatlantic distance had given to these transplanted Englishmen their opportunity and their need to govern themselves. The tradition of self-government, which had been established in England by the weight of hundreds of years, was being established in America by the force of hundreds of miles." Boorstin also cites John Quincy Adams's famous claim that the compact was "perhaps the only instance, in human history, of that positive, original social compact, which speculative philosophers have imagined as the only legitimate source of government," pp. 68–69. Robinson's advice about choosing a leader appears in his farewell letter in *OPP*, p. 370. The description of John Carver as "a gentleman of singular piety" is in Hubbard's *History*, cited in Stratton's *Plymouth Colony*, p. 259. The Mayflower Compact appears in *OPP*, p. 75–77, and *MR*, pp. 17–18; Nathaniel Morton was the only one to list the names recorded on the original document, which has not survived, in his *New England's Memorial*, published in 1669. For a discussion of who signed the compact, see Henry Martyn Dexter's edition of *MR*, p. 9, n. 27.

The estimate concerning the number of ships that could be contained within Provincetown Harbor is in *MR*, p.16. Bradford speaks of their voyage "over the vast and furious ocean" and the "hideous and desolate wilderness" in *OPP*, pp. 61–63. The description of the Pilgrims' first wood-cutting expedition to Cape Cod is in *MR*, pp. 18–19. The Pilgrims described the wood they cut as juniper, which was, as Dexter points out (*MR*, p. 11, n. 32), undoubtedly eastern red cedar, the tallest of the junipers.

CHAPTER THREE—*Into the Void*

As Thomas Bicknell points out in *Sowams*, Nathaniel Morton describes the location of Sowams, home of the Pokanokets, as "at the confluence of two rivers in Rehoboth, or Swansea, though occasionally at Mont Haup or Mount Hope, the principal residence of his son, Philip," p. 157. Although Bicknell argues that Sowams is in Barrington, others have maintained that it is in Warren—both in modern Rhode Island. As Ella Sekatau points out in a personal communication, the word Massasoit is a title, not a name. To avoid confusion, I have used it as the Pilgrims used it, as a name. The exact nature of the plague has been the subject of intense speculation and debate. See Dean Snow and Kim Lanphear, "European Contact and Indian Depopulations in the Northeast: The Timing of the First Epidemics," *Ethnohistory*, Winter 1988, pp. 15–33; Alfred Crosby's "Virgin Soil Epidemics as a Factor in the Aboriginal Depopulation in America," *WMQ*, vol. 23, 1976, pp. 289–99, and his " 'God . . . Would Destroy Them, and Give Their Country to Another People,' " *American Heritage*, vol. 6, 1978, pp. 39–42; Arthur Spiess and Bruce Spiess's "New England Pandemic of 1616–1622: Cause and Archaeological Implication," *Man in the Northeast,* Fall 1987, pp. 71–83; and David Jones, "Virgin Soils Revisited," *WMQ* (Oct. 2003), pp. 703–42. On the effects of the disease on population levels, see S. F. Cook's *The Indian Population of New England in the Seventeenth Century,* pp. 35–36. Cook writes about "chronic war" further diminishing the Native population in "Interracial Warfare and Population Decline among the New England Indians," *Ethnohistory,* Winter 1973, pp. 2–3. All evidence points to Pokanoket, not Wampanoag, being the name that Massasoit's people called themselves. According to Kathleen Bragdon in *Native People of Southern New England, 1500–1650,* "*Wampanoag,* as an ethnonym, now used to designate the modern descendants of the Pokanokets, was probably derived from the name *Wapanoos,* first applied by Dutch explorers and map-makers to those Natives near Narragansett Bay. . . . The term means 'easterner' in Delaware, and was probably not an original self-designation," p. 21. Bragdon cites Daniel Gookin's estimates of the preplague populations of the Pokanokets and Narragansetts, p. 25. In 1661, Roger Williams recorded that before founding the settlement that would become known as Providence, Rhode Island, he contacted the Narragansett sachems Canonicus and Miantonomi, who said that Massasoit "was their subject, and had solemnly himself, in person, with ten men, subjected himself and his lands unto them at the Narragansett." Williams then went to Massasoit, who admitted that the Narragansetts were correct but "that he was not subdued by war, which himself and his father had maintained against the Narragansetts, but God, he said, subdued me by a plague, which swept away my people, and forced me to yield." The Narragansetts complained that Massasoit now "seemed to revolt from his loyalties under the shelter of the English at Plymouth," *The Complete Writings of Roger Williams,* vol. 6, pp. 316, 317. Eric Johnson cites Roger Williams's statement that "[a] small bird is called Sachem" in his Ph.D. dissertation, " 'Some by Flatteries and Others by Threatenings': Political Strategies among Native Americans of Seventeenth-Century Southern New England," p. 69.

William Wood's account of the Indians' first sighting of a European ship is included with several other first-contact accounts in William Simmons's *Spirit of the New England Tribes,* p. 66. I have written about the voyages of Verrazano, Gosnold, Champlain, and Harlow to New England in *Abram's Eyes,* pp. 35–51. For an account of Martin Pring's visit to the Cape in 1603 and a convincing argument that he built his fort in Truro rather than, as is often claimed, Plymouth, see David Beers Quinn's *England and the Discovery of America, 1481–1620,* pp. 425–27. On Epenow's experiences in England and his return to Martha's Vineyard, see John Smith's *The General History* in *The Complete Works,* vol. 3, in which Smith states: "[B]eing a man of so great a stature, he was showed up and down London for money as a wonder," p. 403. Also see Carolyn Foreman's *Indians Abroad, 1493–1938* for a more general discussion of Indian abductions.

Phineas Pratt provides an account of the survivors of the 1615 French shipwreck in "A Declaration of the Affairs of the English People That First Inhabited New England" in MHS Collections, vol. 4, 4th ser., pp. 479–80. Thomas Dermer tells of rescuing the French sailors from captivity in a December 27, 1619, letter in *Sir Ferdinando Gorges of Maine,* edited by James Phinney Baxter, pp. 219–22, n. 276. Bradford also speaks of the French shipwreck and the Indians' belief that the *Mayflower* had been sent to revenge the abduction and killing of the sailors in *OPP,* pp. 83–84.

For an account of Squanto's life prior to his meeting the Pilgrims, see Jerome Dunn's "Squanto before He Met the Pilgrims" in *Bulletin of the Massachusetts Archaeological Society,* Spring 1993, pp. 38–42. Thomas Dermer speaks of the Pokanokets' "inveterate malice to the English" in a December 27, 1619, letter in *Sir Ferdinando Gorges of Maine,* edited by James Phinney Baxter, pp. 219–22, n. 276; this letter describes the explorer's visit, with Squanto as his guide, to Pokanoket. On Squanto, I am indebted to Neal Salisbury's "Squanto: Last of the Patuxets" in *Struggle and Survival in Colonial America,* edited by David Sweet and Gary Nash, pp. 228–46. In his December 27, 1619, letter, Thomas Dermer states that he left Squanto with friends in Sawahquatooke, just to the north of Nemasket on the Titicut, now Taunton, River; see the map in *OPP,* p. 306. Concerning Squanto's motivations, Salisbury writes, "[H]e sought . . . a reconstituted Patuxet band under his own leadership, located near its traditional home," p. 243. On Hobbamock/Cheepi/Squanto, I have relied on Kathleen Bragdon's chapter "Cosmology," pp. 184–99, in *Native People of Southern New England,* especially pp. 189–90.

CHAPTER FOUR—*Beaten with Their Own Rod*

It has generally been assumed that the authorship of *MR* was divided between Bradford and Edward Winslow, who clearly wrote some of the later chapters—for example, the description of his journey, along with Stephen Hopkins, to Pokanoket—and whose initials are on the final letter describing the First Thanksgiving. However, the point of view and phrasing of the earlier portions of *MR* seem to point to Bradford being the author. The descriptions of Bradford getting his foot caught in a deer trap, of the First Encounter, and of their desperate boat journey into Plymouth Harbor exemplify the self-deprecating and yet always lively voice of the author of *OPP.* As a result, I have taken the liberty of attributing several of the passages of *MR* to Bradford.

For an account of a typical Puritan Sunday, see Horton Davies's *The Worship of the American Puritans,* pp. 51–59. Henry Martyn Dexter speculates on the location of where the Pilgrim women washed in his edition of *MR,* p. 12, n. 35. For information on blue mussels and shellfish poisoning, I consulted http://

www.ocean.udel.edu/mas/seafood/bluemussel.html and http://vm.cfsan.fda.gov/
~mow/chap37.html. The Pilgrims speak of the whales they saw in Provincetown
Harbor in *MR*, pp. 16, 30; unless otherwise noted, all of the quoted passages
in this chapter are from *MR*. Thomas Morton refers to Miles Standish as "Captain Shrimp" in his *New English Canaan*, p. 143. John Smith refers to Massachusetts as "the paradise of those parts" in *A Description of New England* in
Complete Writings, vol. 1, p. 340. He tells of his frustrations with the Pilgrims in
The True Travels, Adventures, and Observations of Captain John Smith and *Advertisements: or, The Path-way to Experience to Erect a Plantation;* in addition to
complaining about how they insisted that "because they could not be equals,
they would have no superiors," he writes of the way in which their "humorous
ignorances, caused them for more than a year, to endure a wonderful deal of
misery, with infinite patience; saying my books and maps were much better
cheap to teach them, than myself"; he also writes, "such humorists will never
believe well, till they be beaten with their own rod," *Complete Writings*, vol. 3,
pp. 221, 282, 286. Smith attributed much of the Pilgrims' foolhardy arrogance to
their Separatist religious beliefs and the "pride, and singularity, and contempt of
authority" that went with that radicalism. John Canup in *Out of the Wilderness:
The Emergence of an American Identity in Colonial New England* writes insightfully about Smith's opinion of the Pilgrims and their wanderings about Cape
Cod, pp. 92–96. I have also benefited greatly from John Seelye's probing interpretation of the Pilgrims' adventures on the Cape in *Prophetic Waters*, pp. 110–15.
Seelye insists that the Pilgrims did not use John Smith's map and book about
New England; if they had, he argues, "it seems doubtful they would have spent
so much time looking for a river on the Cape—where none appears—and
would instead have headed toward the short but broad waterway which Smith
shows opening into the mainland somewhat to the north," p. 119. But as James
Baker points out in a personal communication, Smith's map and book were part
of William Brewster's library.

Henry Martyn Dexter judges the Pilgrims' first day of marching to be closer
to seven miles rather than the ten they thought it to be in *MR*, p. 16, n. 48. Even
though there is a possibility that at least some of the Pilgrims had seen either references to Indian corn or the actual plant at the University of Leiden's botanical
garden (see Jeremy Bangs's "The Pilgrims' Earball," forthcoming in *New England Ancestors*), Bradford explicitly states that they had "never seen any such before," *OPP*, p. 65. On the strangeness of corn to Europeans, see Darrett
Rutman's *Husbandmen of Plymouth:* "Corn was new and strange, alien and,
therefore, to the English mind, inferior to the more traditional grains," p. 10.
See also Keith Stavely and Kathleen Fitzgerald's *America's Founding Food: The
Story of New England Cooking*, which discusses the discovery of a thousand-year-old cache of maize, p. 8. On the Pilgrims' shallop, see William Baker's *The
Mayflower and Other Colonial Vessels*, pp. 65–74. On the weather conditions of

seventeenth-century New England relative to Europe, see Karen Ordahl Kupperman's "The Puzzle of the American Climate in the Early Colonial Period" in *American Historical Review,* vol. 87, 1982, pp. 1262–89. On the seasonal settlement patterns of Native New Englanders, see Kathleen Bragdon's *Native People of Southern New England,* pp. 55–63. As John Canup comments in *Out of the Wilderness,* it is weirdly ironic that the Pilgrims named the place where they stole the Native seed Corn Hill, then met, only a few months later, Squanto, who had formerly lived in the Corn Hill section of London. Canup, following the lead of John Seelye in *Prophetic Waters,* speaks of the "prophetic meaning" of the Pilgrims' experience on the Cape, p. 95. Seelye refers to the two skeletons unearthed by the Pilgrims as "a male Madonna with child" and sees them as prefiguring what Canup calls "a process of acculturation or intermingling between the Old World and the New," p. 92. In the notes to his edition of *MR,* Henry Martyn Dexter speculates that the elaborately carved board found by the Pilgrims in the Indian grave depicted a trident, "connecting nautical associations with the grave," p. 33.

When it comes to re-creating the sequence of deaths during that first winter, there are several sources: Bradford's "Passengers in the Mayflower" in *OPP,* pp. 441–48, and information taken from Bradford's papers (many of which have since been lost) by Thomas Prince and published in his *Chronological History of New England* in 1736. In his edition of *MR,* Henry Martyn Dexter provides a useful time line, pp. 157–62. Samuel Eliot Morison speculates that the pilot Robert Coppin's Thievish Harbor was really Gloucester Harbor in "Plymouth Colony Beachhead," p. 1352. I am more inclined to agree with John Seelye's assertion in *Prophetic Waters* that it was Boston Harbor instead, especially given Coppin's memory of "a great navigable river," p. 119. On the technology of firearms in the seventeenth century, see Harold Peterson's *Arms and Armor of the Pilgrims,* pp. 13–21. On the technology of the Indians' bows and arrows, see Patrick Malone's *The Skulking Way of War: Technology and Tactics among the New England Indians,* pp.15–17, and Howard Russell's *Indian New England before the Mayflower,* p. 191. My thanks to Dr. Timothy Lepore, who shared with me his personal experience building and using a replica of the famed "Sudbury bow" at Harvard University. On the psychological effect of Indian war cries on the English, see the section "Native American Vocable Sounds" in Richard Rath's *How Early America Sounded,* pp. 150–59. In "The First Encounter" in *Early Encounters: Native Americans and Europeans in New England,* W. Sears Nickerson claims that the site of the First Encounter was at Boat Meadow Creek, about a mile and a half from the historic marker at First Encounter Beach and about eight-tenths of a mile from the Herring River, which Samuel Eliot Morison believed to be the site of the encounter, *OPP,* p. 100–101.

MR does not mention the direction of the wind during the shallop's approach to Plymouth, and the description of how the Pilgrims entered the harbor is open to interpretation. Henry Martyn Dexter and Samuel Eliot Morison, for example, have the wind coming from virtually opposite directions in their accounts of the voyage. One can only wish that Sears Nickerson had also chosen to analyze this part of the Pilgrims' adventures in the New World. Having approached Plymouth Harbor myself in a small boat, I am inclined to agree with Morison's account of the approach in "Plymouth Colony Beachhead," p. 1352; see also his note in *OPP*, p. 71. In a note in his *New England Memorial*, Nathaniel Morton claims it was called Clark's Island "because Mr. Clark, the Master's mate, first stepped on shore thereon," p. 34. It is intriguing to speculate that the traditions associated with the first person to step on Clark's Island, recorded by Morton just forty or so years after the original event, somehow mutated into the more famous traditions concerning who first stepped on Plymouth Rock, originally mentioned by Samuel Davis in "Notes on Plymouth," MHS Collections, vol. 3, 2nd ser., 1815. According to Davis, "There is a tradition, as to the person who first leaped upon this rock, when the families came on shore, December 11, 1620; it is said to have been a young woman, Mary Chilton," p. 174. However, descendants of John Alden, including President John Adams, later claimed that Alden had been the first to the Rock. If not for Elder John Faunce's claim in 1741 that Plymouth Rock was the "place where the forefathers landed," the Rock might have remained buried within a solid-fill pier to this day. For an exhaustive account of the traditions surrounding the Rock, see John Seelye's *Memory's Nation: The Place of Plymouth Rock,* especially p. 384. See also Francis Russell's "Pilgrims and the Rock," *American Heritage,* October 1962, pp. 48–55; Robert Arner's "Plymouth Rock Revisited: The Landing of the Pilgrim Fathers," *Journal of America Culture,* Winter 1983, pp. 25–35; and John McPhee's "Travels of the Rock," *New Yorker,* February 26, 1990, pp. 108–17. Like the skeletons in the Indian graves in Truro, the Rock has become much more important to subsequent generations than it was to the Pilgrims themselves.

Concerning Dorothy Bradford, Cotton Mather writes in his *Magnalia,* "at their first landing, his dearest consort accidentally falling overboard, was drowned in the harbor," p. 205. In 1869, in a story entitled "William Bradford's Love Life" in *Harper's New Monthly Magazine,* Jane Goodwin Austin claimed that she had seen documents proving that Dorothy had committed suicide on learning of her husband's love for Alice Southworth, the woman he would eventually marry in 1623. As George Bowman has shown in "Governor William Bradford's First Wife Dorothy (May) Bradford Did Not Commit Suicide," in the *Mayflower Descendant,* July 1931, Austin's article was a fabrication, pp. 97–103. However, just because Austin misrepresented the facts does not eliminate the possibility that Dorothy Bradford killed herself. Samuel Eliot Morison writes that Bradford's "failure to mention [her death] in the History is consistent with

his modest reticence about his own role of leadership in the colony; but it may
be that he suspected (as do we) that Dorothy Bradford took her own life, after
gazing for six weeks at the barren sand dunes of Cape Cod," *OPP,* p. xxiv. In
"William Bradford's Wife: A Suicide," W. Sears Nickerson claims that according
to family tradition still current on Cape Cod when he was growing up at the
end of the nineteenth century, Dorothy Bradford did, in fact, kill herself. He
also points out that "[i]t is a well-known fact among sailors that acute melan-
cholia frequently results from scurvy," in *Early Encounters: Native Americans and
Europeans in New England,* p. 98. Also to be considered is the psychic trauma of
the immigration experience. As Leon Grinberg and Rebecca Grinberg demonstrate in *Psychoanalytic Perspectives on Migration and Exile,* the stresses associated
with the early stages of immigration can have a crippling effect on a person:
"[I]n the first stage, the predominant feelings are intense pain for all that one
has left behind or lost, fear of the unknown, deep-rooted loneliness, need, and
helplessness. Paranoid, disorienting, and depressive anxieties may alternate with
one another, leaving the person prone to periods of total disorganization," p. 97.
Bradford tells of the settlers' fear of being abandoned on the Cape in *OPP,* p. 92.
Sears Nickerson suggests in *Land Ho!—1620* that she may have fallen from the
poop deck: "I have often wondered if this was the spot from which Dorothy
Bradford dropped overboard to her death in Provincetown Harbor," p. 21. The
four lines of poetry are from a much longer poem Bradford wrote toward
the end of his life that appears in Nathaniel Morton's *New England's Memorial,*
p. 172.

CHAPTER FIVE—*The Heart of Winter*

Unless otherwise noted, all quotations are from *MR,* pp. 38–50, and *OPP,*
pp. 77–87. As noted in the previous chapter, when it comes to re-creating the sequence of deaths during that first winter, there are several sources: Bradford's
"Passengers in the Mayflower" in *OPP,* pp. 441–48, and information taken from
Bradford's papers (many of which have since been lost) by Thomas Prince and
published in his *Chronological History of New England* in 1736. In his edition of
MR, Henry Martyn Dexter provides a useful timeline, pp. 157–62. Both Champlain and John Smith visited Plymouth Harbor and left descriptions of the area
and its people; see introduction to *MR,* pp. xix–xxiii. On the stunning plenti-
tude of fish, lobsters, and clams at this time, see William Cronon's *Changes in
the Land,* pp. 22–23, 30–31. I cite Roger Williams's account of the Narragansetts'
fleeing disease in *Abram's Eyes,* p. 50.

My account of the Pilgrims listening to the cries of Indians owes much to
Richard Rath's *How Early America Sounded,* particularly his chapter entitled

"The Howling Wilderness," pp. 145–72. See Keith Thomas's *Religion and the Decline of Magic* on how the Reformation of the sixteenth and seventeenth centuries increased a sense of "Satan's immediacy": "For Englishmen of the Reformation period the Devil was a greater reality than ever. . . . Influential preachers filled the ears of their hearers with tales of diabolic intervention in daily life. . . . Hugh Latimer assured his audience that the Devil and his company of evil spirits were invisible in the air all around them," p. 561.

On the construction techniques the Pilgrims employed that first winter, I have relied on the James Deetz and Patricia Deetz's *The Times of Their Lives,* pp. 171–84. My thanks to Pret Woodburn and Rick McKee, interpretive artisans at Plimoth Plantation, for their insights into the construction techniques employed by the Pilgrims. On the configuration of the town, see "The Meersteads and Garden Plots of [Those] Which Came First, Laid Out 1620," reproduced in Arber's *The Story of the Pilgrim Fathers,* p. 381. Jeremy Bangs writes of the possible Dutch military influence on the town plan of Plymouth in *Pilgrim Life in Leiden,* p. 36. Robert Wakefield carefully weighs the evidence in determining how the Pilgrims were divided up among the first structures during the first year in "The Seven Houses of Plymouth," *Mayflower Descendant,* January 1994, pp. 21–23.

On English mastiffs see "The History of the Mastiff" at http://www.mastiff web.com/history.htm. On eastern cougars see http://staffweb.lib.jmu.edu/users/bolgiace/ECF/abouteasterncougars.htm. William Cronon's *Changes in the Land: Indians, Colonists, and the Ecology of New England* contains excellent chapters about the Indians' land management; see especially pp. 19–33. On the background of Miles Standish, see Robert Anderson's *The Pilgrim Migration,* pp. 451–57; Standish refers to getting cheated out of his rightful inheritance in his will. John Lyford refers to Standish as a "silly boy" in a letter referred to by William Bradford in *OPP,* p. 156. Bradford's remarks concerning John Billington's "opprobrious speeches" was recorded in Thomas Prince's *A Chronological History of New England,* vol. 3, p. 38. The ages of those orphaned during the first winter (some of which are estimates) are from PM. Concerning the Pilgrims' attempts to create the impression that they were stronger than they actually were, Phineas Pratt in "A Declaration" writes, "[T]hey were so distressed with sickness that they, fearing the savages should know it, had set up their sick men with their muskets upon their rests and their backs leaning against trees," MHS Collections, vol. 4, 4th ser., p. 478. On the demographics of death during the first winter, see John McCullough and Elaine York's "Relatedness and Mortality Risk during a Crisis Year: Plymouth Colony, 1620–1621" in *Ethology and Sociobiology,* vol. 12, pp. 195–209; their findings indicate that those who were part of a family had a slightly better chance of survival and that children with one or more surviving parents had a much greater chance of survival. John Navin also provides a useful analysis of how the deaths of the first winter impacted the makeup of the colony in *Plymouth Plantation,* pp. 392–418. James Thacher in his appendix to *The History of the Town of Plymouth* tells of how a "freshet" revealed the bones of the Pilgrims during the first winter, p. 327. My thanks to James Baker for bringing this reference to my attention.

For information on the Pilgrims' "great guns," see Harold Peterson's *Arms and Armor of the Pilgrims,* pp. 24–27. Richard Rath in *How Early America Sounded* writes suggestively about the importance the colonists placed on thunder and lightning, pp. 10–42. *MR* describes Samoset as simply saying "Welcome" to the Pilgrims, but Prince, whose chronology was apparently based on Bradford's original (now lost) notes, has him saying, "Welcome, Englishmen! Welcome, Englishmen!" in *A Chronological History of New England,* vol. 3, p. 33.

CHAPTER SIX—*In a Dark and Dismal Swamp*

Unless otherwise noted, all quotations are from *MR,* pp. 50–59, and *OPP,* pp. 79–87. Although the Pilgrims did not comment on Samoset's skin color, they later noted that the Indians are "of complexion like our English gypsies," *MR,* p. 53. John Humins in "Squanto and Massasoit: A Struggle for Power" in *NEQ,* vol. 60, no. 1, speculates that Samoset's two arrows symbolized war and peace, p. 56. In *Indians and English: Facing Off in Early America,* Karen Ordahl Kupperman states that "the name [Samoset] gave to the Pilgrims was probably 'Somerset,' given him by the fishermen," p. 185.

Bradford tells of the three-day meeting in "a dark and dismal swamp" in *OPP,* p. 84. Quoting from William Wood, William Cronon writes of swamps: "The Indians referred to such lowlands as 'abodes of owls,' and used them as hiding places during times of war," in *Changes in the Land,* p. 28. According to Kathleen Bragdon in *Native People of Southern New England,* Indians "retreated to deep swampy places in times of war, where they were not only harder to find but had stronger links to their other-than-human protectors," p. 192. On the role of powwows, I have looked to the chapter "Religious Specialists among the Ninnimissinuok" in Bragdon's *Native People of Southern New England,* pp. 200–216 as well as William Simmons's "Southern New England Shamanism: An Ethnographic Reconstruction," *Papers of the Seventh Algonquian Conference, 1975,* edited by William Cowan, pp. 217–56. The description of Passaconaway's ability to "metamorphise himself into a flaming man" and his remarks concerning his inability to injure the English appear in William Simmons's *Spirit of the New England Tribes: Indian History and Folklore, 1620–1984,* pp. 61, 63.

Neal Salisbury in "Squanto: Last of the Patuxets" in *Struggle and Survival in Colonial America,* edited by David Sweet and Gary Nash, states that Squanto's "most potent weapon was the mutual distrust and fear lingering between English and Indians; his most pressing need was for a power base so that he could extricate himself from his position of colonial dependency. Accordingly, he began maneuvering on his own," p. 241; Salisbury also cites Phineas Pratt's claim that Squanto assured Massasoit that if he sided with the English, "enemies that were too strong for him would be constrained to bow to him," p. 238. Bradford in *OPP* speaks of Squanto's insistence that the Pilgrims possessed the plague, as does Thomas Morton in *New England Canaan:* "And that Salvage [Squanto] the more to increase his [Massasoit's] fear, told the Sachem that if he should give offense to the English party, they would let out the plague to destroy them all, which kept him in great awe," p. 104.

In *GNNE,* Edward Winslow writes of the "wicked practice of this Tisquantum [i.e., Squanto]; who, to the end he might possess his countrymen with the greater fear of us, and so consequently of himself, told them we had the plague buried in our store-house; which, at our pleasure, we could send forth to what place or people we would, and destroy them therewith, though we stirred not from home," p. 16. Neal Salisbury in *Manitou and Providence: Indians, Europeans, and the Making of New England, 1500–1643* comments on Quadequina's insistence that the Pilgrims put away their guns, p. 120.

On the *Mayflower's* return to England and her eventual fate, see Sears Nickerson's *Land Ho!—1620,* pp. 34–35. I've also relied on the information compiled by Carolyn Freeman Travers in 1997 and posted on the Plimoth Plantation Web site at http://www.plimoth.org/Library/mayflcre.htm. Although some have argued that Squanto learned to use fish as a fertilizer from English farmers in Newfoundland, this claim has been authoritatively refuted, at least to my mind, by the late Nanepashemet in "It Smells Fishy to Me: An Argument Supporting the Use of Fish Fertilizer by the Native People of Southern New England," *Dublin Seminar for New England Folklife Annual Proceedings,* 1991, pp. 42–50. On Native agriculture, see Kathleen Bragdon's *Native People of Southern New England,* pp. 107–10. The duel between Edward Doty and Edward Leister is mentioned in Thomas Prince's *Chronological History of New England,* vol. 3, p. 40.

CHAPTER SEVEN—*Thanksgiving*

Unless otherwise noted, all quotations are from *MR,* pp. 59–87, and *OPP,* pp. 87–90. According to the genealogist Robert Anderson in a personal communication, "Three months was the average interval between the death of a spouse and remarriage . . . and I have seen a few instances in the six-week range." On marriage in Puritan New England, see Horton Davies's *The Worship of the American Puritans,* pp. 215–28. For an excellent account of the seasonal rhythms of the Indians' lives, see the chapter "Seasons of Want and Plenty" in William Cronon's *Changes in the Land,* pp. 34–53. On the historic importance of the Titicut or Taunton River to the Native Americans and English, see Henry Holt's *Salt Rivers of the Massachusetts Shore,* pp. 14–16, as well as Michael Tougias's *A Taunton River Journey,* pp. 1–19, and Alfred Lima's *The Taunton Heritage River Guide,* pp. 18–30. On Miles Standish's assertion that Sowams was "the garden of the Patent," see John Martin's *Profits in the Wilderness,* p. 80.

Kathleen Bragdon discusses Native games of chance in *Native People of Southern New England,* pp. 222–23. Henry Martyn Dexter surmises that the fish Massasoit caught for Winslow and Hopkins were large striped bass, *MR,* p. 108, n. 354. Francis Billington's discovery of the Billington Sea is described in *MR,* p. 44. Kathleen Bragdon writes of the pniese in *Native People of Southern New England,* pp. 214–15. John Seelye writes of Standish's role as Joshua to Bradford's Moses in *Prophetic Waters,* p. 123. Dexter identifies Corbitant's headquarters as Gardner's Neck in *MR,* p. 54, n. 379. As Neal Salisbury notes in *Manitou and Providence,* the only copy of the September 13, 1621, treaty appears in Nathaniel Morton's *New England's Memorial,* pp. 119–20. On the Pilgrims' parochialism relative to the Puritans, see Seelye, *Prophetic Waters,* pp. 91, 120. On the Pilgrims' First Thanksgiving, I am indebted to James Deetz and Patricia Deetz's *The Times of Their Lives,* pp. 1–9; the Deetzes argue that instead of being what the Puritans would have considered a Thanksgiving, the celebration in 1621 was more in keeping with a secular harvest festival. For a contrasting view, see Jeremy Bangs's "Thanksgiving on the Net: Bull and Cranberry Sauce," www.SAIL1620.org. Bangs argues that even though the Pilgrims did not use the term themselves, the gathering was, in essence, a Thanksgiving. On the history of domesticated turkeys in the New and Old Worlds, I have relied on Keith Stavely and Kathleen Fitzgerald's *America's Founding Food,* pp. 161–62. On winter being the time to hunt turkeys, see William Wood's *New England Prospect:* "Such as love turkey hunting must follow it in winter after a new fallen snow, when he may follow them by their tracks," p. 51. On the changing colors of autumn leaves I have looked to "Fantasy, Facts and Fall Color" at www.agriculture.purdue.edu/fnr/html/faculty/Chaney/FallColor.pdf. In 1675, in the days before the beginning of King Philip's War, Metacom told the Quaker John Easton that "when the English first came their king's father was as a great man and the English as a little child, [and] he constrained other Indians from wronging the English and gave them corn and showed them how to plant and was free to do them any good and had let them have a 100 times more land, than now the king had for his own people," "John Easton's Relation," in *Narratives of the Indian Wars,* edited by Charles Lincoln, p. 10.

CHAPTER EIGHT—*The Wall*

My account of the arrival of the *Fortune* is based on *OPP,* pp. 90–126, and *MR,* pp. 84–96. On how the arrival of the *Fortune* affected the demographics of Plymouth, I have relied on the analysis of John Navin in *Plymouth Plantation,* pp. 397–98. A portion of Robert Cushman's sermon "The Sin of Self-Love" appears in the notes of Ford's edition of *OPP,* vol. 1, pp. 235–36. Unless otherwise indicated, my account of the Narragansett challenge and the other events chronicled in this chapter is based on *OPP,* pp. 96–115, and Edward Winslow's *GNNE,* pp. 7–24. My description of the wall the Pilgrims built around the settlement is based, in part, on Emmanuel Altham's September 1623 letter, reprinted in *Three Visitors to Early Plymouth,* edited by Sydney James Jr., p. 24; in 1624 John Smith wrote, "The town is impaled about half a mile in compass," in notes to Emmanuel Altham's March 1624 letter in *Three Visitors,* p. 37. For information on the differences between English and American felling axes, see volume 3 of *New England Begins,* edited by Jonathan Fairbanks and Robert Trent, p. 543. My account of the impaling of Plymouth is indebted to discussions with Pret Woodburn and Rick McKee, interpretive artisans at Plimoth Plantation, who brought the existence of the Jamestown trenching tool to my attention. In a note in *OPP,* Samuel Eliot Morison speaks of stool ball, p. 97. On the importance of boundaries and enclosures to the Puritans of seventeenth-century New England, see Keith Stavely and Kathleen Fitzgerald's *America's Founding Food,* pp. 148–49.

Karen Ordahl Kupperman makes note of the irony that the Pilgrims found themselves trusting two Indians, Squanto and Hobbamock, who were named for the god that the Pilgrims considered to be the devil, in *Indians and English,* p. 185. Bradford's unwillingness to surrender Squanto to Massasoit may have had something to do with what Leon and Rebecca Grinberg have called in *Migration and Exile* the immigrant's need for "a familiar someone"; this longing for "a trustworthy person who can take over or neutralize the anxieties and fears he feels toward the new and unknown world can be compared to that of a child who is left alone and desperately searches for the familiar face of his mother. . . . One model that comes close to this idea is the ethnologist's notion of 'imprinting,' " pp. 76–77. Eric Johnson talks about Indian assassinations in *"Some by Flatteries and Others by Threatenings":* "How frequent they were is not known; but several assassinations or attempted assassinations were reported, although not all can be proved," p. 194. Whatever the case may be, the similarities between Massasoit's possible assassination of Squanto and his son Philip's reputed assassination of the interpreter Sassamon fifty-three years later are striking. In *Early Encounters: Native Americans and Europeans in New England,* Sears Nickerson claims the Indian skeleton that was "washed out of a hill between Head of the Bay and Crow's Pond" at Monomoyick around 1770 was probably Squanto's, p. 200.

CHAPTER NINE—*A Ruffling Course*

Unless otherwise noted, my account of the Wessagussett attack and the events leading up to it is based on *OPP,* pp. 116–19; *GNNE,* pp. 23–56; and Phineas Pratt's account of his days at Wessagusett, written in 1668 and titled "A Declaration of the Affairs of the English People that First Inhabited New England," MHS Collections, vol. 4, 4th ser., 1858, pp. 474–87. On the lethal malaise that overtook the English settlers at Jamestown, see Karen Kupperman's "Apathy and Death in Early Jamestown," *Journal of American History,* June–September 1979, pp. 24–40. On the use of groundnuts as food, see Howard Russell's *Indian New England before the* Mayflower, p. 156. As Kupperman points out in "Thomas Morton, Historian" in *NEQ,* vol. 50, 1977, pp. 660–64, Morton's *New English Canaan* provides a probing account of the Wessagussett raid that is very different from those of Bradford and Winslow.

The description of typhus comes from Roger Schofield's "An Anatomy of an Epidemic" in *The Plague Reconsidered,* p. 121. My thanks to Carolyn Travers, research manager at Plimoth Plantation, for bringing this reference to my attention. In *New English Canaan,* Morton claims that Standish and his men "pretended to feast the Salvages of those parts, bringing with them pork and things for the purpose, which they set before the Salvages," p. 110. Morton also accuses Standish and company of having no real interest in saving any of Weston's men: "But if the Plimoth Planters had really intended good to Master Weston or those men, why had they not kept the Salvages alive in custody until they had secured the other English? Who, by means of this evil managing of the business, lost their lives," p. 111. Morton makes the claim that after Wessagussett, the Pilgrims were known as "stabbers" or "cutthroats" by the Massachusetts, p. 111. Bradford and Isaac Allerton write of their inability to trade with the Indians after the Wessagussett raid in a September 8, 1623, letter reprinted in the *American Historical Review,* vol. 8, 1903, p. 297. In *Facing East from Indian Country: A Native History of Early America,* Daniel Richter writes, "It is quite possible . . . that there had not, in fact, been anything like a Wampanoag or Pokanoket nation until Massasoit invented it from the surviving remnants who coalesced at Mount Hope Neck and a few other locations such as Mashpee on Cape Cod in the 1620s," p. 99.

In the chapter "Liquidation of Wessagusset" in *Saints and Strangers,* George Willison maintains that the Pilgrims' account of the Indian plot "was fabricated after the event in an effort to justify a series of treacherous actions of which the Pilgrims were always a little ashamed," p. 224. For a withering critique of Willison's account, see Jeremy Bangs's *Indian Deeds,* pp. 13–14. On the other extreme is Charles Francis Adams's version in *Three Episodes of Massachusetts History.* While pointing out that "[h]ad the situation been reversed, and the Indians, after similar fashion, set upon the Europeans in a moment of unsuspecting intercourse, no language would have been found strong enough to describe in the page of history their craft, their stealth and their cruelty," p. 100, Adams maintains that the Pilgrims did what they had to do: "Yet, admitting everything which in harshest language modern philanthropy could assert, there is still no reasonable doubt that, in the practical working of human events, the course approved in advance by the Plymouth magistrates, and ruthlessly put in execution by Standish, was in this case the most merciful, the wisest and, consequently, the most justifiable course," p. 100–101. According to the "moral calculus" of William Vollmann's *Rising Up and Rising Down: Some Thoughts on Violence, Freedom, and Urgent Means,* violent deterrence of the kind the Pilgrims inflicted on the Massachusetts Indians is unjustified "when it is executed proactively as both deterrence and retribution," volume MC, p. 113, which appears to have been the case—at least as far as Standish was concerned—at Wessagusett. John Robinson's letter critical of the Pilgrims' actions at Wessagussett is in *OPP,* pp. 374–75. The festivities surrounding Bradford's marriage to Alice Southworth (including the raising of the blood-soaked flag in tribute to Massasoit) are in Emmanuel Altham's September 1623 letter in *Three Visitors to Early Plymouth,* edited by Sydney James, pp. 29–32.

CHAPTER TEN—*One Small Candle*

Unless otherwise noted, the quotations that appear in this chapter come from *OPP,* pp. 120–347. For information on the great Migration, see David Hackett Fischer's *Albion's Seed: Four British Folkways in America,* pp. 13–17, and Karen Kupperman's *Settling with the Indians,* p. 21. The December 18, 1624, letter from the Merchant Adventurers referring to the Pilgrims as "contentious, cruel and hard hearted" appears in *Governor William Bradford's Letter Book,* reprinted from the *Mayflower Descendant,* p. 4. John Demos in "Demography and Psychology in the Historical Study of Family-Life: A Personal Report," cited in John Navin's *Plymouth Plantation: The Search for Community on the New England Frontier,* claims that Plymouth Colony was typified by "an extraordinary degree of contentiousness among neighbors," p. 660. Navin claims that "the early settlers were far more inclined to become engaged in disputes with newcomers than with each other," p. 660; he also states that in the aftermath of the Reverend John Lyford's expulsion from Plymouth, the colony lost approximately a quarter of its residents, *Plymouth Plantation,* p. 498.

The published material about Thomas Morton and Merrymount is voluminous (see Michael Zuckerman's "Pilgrims in the Wilderness: Community, Modernity, and the Maypole at Merry Mount"; Minor Major's "William Bradford versus Thomas Morton"; and Daniel Shea's "Our Professed Old Adversary: Thomas Morton and the Naming of New England," for just a sampling), but perhaps the most probing words ever written about the future ramifications of the incident come from Nathaniel Hawthorne in his short story "The May-Pole of Merry Mount": "The future complexion of New England was involved in this important quarrel. Should the grizzly saints establish their jurisdiction over the gay sinners, then would their spirits darken all the clime, and make it a land of clouded visages, of hard toil, of sermon and psalm forever," in *The Complete Novels and Selected Tales of Nathaniel Hawthorne* (New York: Modern Library, 1965), pp. 886–87. On the marriage of Elizabeth Warren and Richard Church and their son Benjamin, see Robert Wakefield's "The Children and Purported Children of Richard and Elizabeth (Warren) Church" in the *American Genealogist*, July 1984, pp. 129–39. According to Richard Slotkin in *Regeneration through Violence: The Mythology of the American Frontier, 1600–1860*, "Daniel Boone and Leatherstocking are [Morton's] lineal descendants," p. 63. Morton tells of Standish's attack and the Pilgrims' lack of humanity in *New English Canaan*, pp. 113, 146. William Hubbard writes of Miles Standish in his *General History of New England*, pp. 110–11. Harold Peterson in *Arms and Armor of the Pilgrims* notes that Standish's sword, which is on display at Pilgrim Hall, "is about six inches shorter than the average rapier, which would have made it easier to handle for a small man," p. 9. Isaack de Rasiere's 1627 account of Plymouth on a Sunday is in *Three Visitors to Early Plymouth*, pp. 76–77. John Navin in *Plymouth Plantation* speaks of the militaristic nature of the Plymouth settlement, pp. 576, 631. Bradford writes of his frustrations with Isaac Allerton in *OPP*, pp. 226–34, 237–44. For a view that is more sympathetic to Isaac Allerton, see Cynthia Van Zandt's "The Dutch Connection: Isaac Allerton and the Dynamics of English Cultural Anxiety," in *Connecting Cultures: The Netherlands in Five Centuries of Transatlantic Exchange*, edited by Rosemarijn Hoefte and Johanna Kardux, pp. 51–76. George Langdon provides an excellent summary of Plymouth's financial dealings in *Pilgrim Colony*, pp. 32–33.

Edward Winslow writes of New England being a place "where religion and profit jump together" in *GNNE*, p. 70. For an example of a modern economist who looks to Bradford's decision to abandon a collective approach to farming as the beginning of the capitalist miracle that would become the United States, see Thomas DiLorenzo's *How Capitalism Saved America: The Untold History of Our Country, from the Pilgrims to the Present*, pp. 57–62. Unfortunately in the case of the Pilgrims, their early experimentation with capitalism did not later translate into the financial success they had originally hoped for. For an account of the financial history of Plymouth Colony, see Ruth McIntyre's *Debts Hopeful and Desperate*, especially pp. 47–67.

For transcriptions of the deeds associated with Massasoit's sale of land to Plymouth Colony, see Jeremy Bangs's *Indian Deeds: Land Transactions in Plymouth Colony, 1620–1691*, pp. 260–324. Robert Cushman maintains that it is "lawful now to take a land which none useth" in "Reasons and Considerations touching the lawfulness of removing out of England into the parts of America" in *MR*, p. 92. Bangs makes a strong case for Roger Williams's influence on Plymouth's policy of purchasing Indian land in *Indian Deeds*, pp. 15–18, where he also speaks of the reason behind the insistence on court-approved sale of Indian lands, as does George Langdon in *Pilgrim Colony*, pp. 154–55. Kathleen Bragdon writes insightfully about the Indians' relationship to the land in *Native People of Southern New England:* "In a sense, 'land ownership' was about identity. . . . Technically 'controlled' by the sachem and the corporate groups, access to land was in fact predicated on need and active engagement with it, usually within the context of the household. To make use of land was to be a member of the corporate community, to eat its products was to 'own' the land from which they were gathered," pp. 138–39. Bangs cites the 1639 treaty between Massasoit and the colony in *Indian Deeds*, p. 62. David Bushnell refers to lands bought from the Indians in modern Freetown, Massachusetts, being subsequently sold at a 500 percent profit in "The Treatment of the Indians in Plymouth Colony," *NEQ*, March 1953, pp. 196–97; Bushnell maintains, however, that the Pilgrims "were no more to blame than the Indians themselves for what was a natural consequence of economic laws. Lands effectively brought within the range of world-wide economic forces by the expansion of English settlement were obviously worth more than a native hunting reservation, and the profit was not necessarily speculative when lands were improved before being resold." Soon after the outbreak of King Philip's War in 1675, Josiah Winslow insisted that all the land in Plymouth "was fairly obtained by honest purchase of the Indian proprietors," cited in Bangs's *Indian Deeds*, p. 22. Dennis Connole, on the other hand, in *The Indians of the Nipmuck Country in Southern New England, 1630–1750*, believes that the colonial laws curtailing individuals from purchasing Indian land "were placed on the books with only one purpose in mind: to suppress the fledgling real estate market in the colonies. If a free market had existed, the demand was such that the price of land would have skyrocketed," p. 251.

In an April 12, 1632, entry, of his *Journal*, edited by Richard Dunn et al., John Winthrop describes the Narragansett attack on Massasoit, pp. 64–65; in an August 4, 1634, entry, Winthrop describes the trick the sachem played on Edward Winslow. Samuel Drake in his *Book of the Indians of North America* claims that Massasoit changed his name to Usamequin after the Narragansett attack at Sowams, p. 25.

In "Darlings of Heaven" in *Harvard Magazine*, November 1976, Peter Gomes deftly summarizes the relationship between the Pilgrims and Puritans: "[T]he Atlantic Ocean made them both (Boston and Plymouth) Separatists, and the hegemony of Boston made them both Puritans," p. 33. For more on the distinction between Pilgrim and Puritan, see Gomes's "Pilgrims and Puritans: Heroes and Villains in Creation of the American Past" in MHS *Proceedings*, vol. 45, 1983, pp. 1–16, and Richard Howland Maxwell's "Pilgrim and Puritan: A

Delicate Distinction" in *Pilgrim Society Notes,* series 2, March 2003. On the differences between Puritan and Pilgrim requirements for church membership, see
George Langdon's *Plymouth Colony,* pp. 126–31, as well as Edmund Morgan's
Visible Saints; according to Morgan, "[the New England Puritans'] only radical
difference from the Separatist practice lay in the candidate's demonstration of
the work of grace in his soul," p. 90. Langdon in *Plymouth Colony* provides a
useful summary of the development of governance in Plymouth, pp. 79–99.
William Hubbard speaks of Billington's execution in *General History of New England,* p. 101. Thomas Morton describes how the Puritans burned his house in
New English Canaan, pp. 171–72. On Bradford's 1645 refusal to allow religious
tolerance, and Plymouth and Massachusetts Bay's persecution of the Quakers,
see George Langdon's *Pilgrim Colony,* pp. 63–65, 71–78. Stratton in *Plymouth
Colony* cites the quote from the Quaker sympathizer James Cudworth: "Now
Plymouth-saddle is on the Bay horse," p. 92; Stratton also speaks of the disen-
franchisement of Isaac Robinson, p. 345.

My account of the economic development of New England in the 1630s is
based, in large part, on Bernard Bailyn's *The New England Merchants in the Seventeenth Century,* pp. 16–44. Adam Hirsch discusses how the attack on the Pequot fort changed the attitude toward war in "The Collision of Military
Cultures in Seventeenth-Century New England" in the *Journal of American History,* vol. 74, pp. 1187–1212. William Cronon in *Changes in the Land* looks to
Miantonomi's speech to the Montauks as an exemplary analysis of the ecological
impact the Europeans had on New England, pp. 162–64. Miantonomi's death at
the hands of the Mohegans is discussed in John Sainsbury's "Miantonomo's
Death and New England Politics, 1630–1645" in *Rhode Island History,* vol. 30,
no. 4, pp. 111–23, and Paul Robinson's "Lost Opportunities: Miantonomi and
the English in Seventeenth-Century Narragansett Country" in *Northeastern Indian Lives, 1632–1816,* edited by Robert Grumet, pp. 13–28. Edward Johnson describes Miantonomi's unfortunate use of an English corselet in *Wonder-Working
Providence, 1628–1651,* pp. 220–21. Jeremy Bangs discusses the possible Dutch influences on the formation of the United Colonies of New England in *Pilgrim
Edward Winslow;* he also cites John Quincy Adams's remarks concerning the
confederation, pp. 207–12.

CHAPTER ELEVEN— *The Ancient Mother*

On Edward Winslow's diplomatic career, see Jeremy Bangs's *Pilgrim Edward
Winslow,* pp. 315–400. Samuel Maverick describes Winslow as "a smooth
tongued cunning fellow" in his "Brief Description of New England," written
about 1660, MHS *Proceedings,* vol. 1, 2nd ser., p. 240. In his introduction to
OPP, Samuel Eliot Morison tells of how Bradford might have become "the sole

lord and proprietor of Plymouth Colony," p. xxv. John Demos in "Notes on Plymouth Colony" in *WMQ*, 3rd ser., vol. 22, no. 2, writes of the extraordinary mobility of the Pilgrims and their children and grandchildren, particularly compared to Massachusetts Bay: "The whole process of expansion had as one of its chief effects the scattering of families, to an extent probably inconceivable in the Old World communities from which the colonists had come," p. 266. For an excellent look at those leading the development of towns in Plymouth, including John Brown and Thomas Willett, see John Frederick Martin's *Profits in the Wilderness*, pp. 79–87. Martin also discusses Bradford's fears about the evil influences of growth in the colony, p. III. For information about John Brown, Thomas Prence, and Thomas Willett, see the biographies in Robert Anderson's *The Pilgrim Migration*, pp. 81, 374–81, 497–503. Roger Williams's reference to "God Land" is in his *Complete Writings*, vol. 6, p. 319. John Canup in *Out of the Wilderness: The Emergence of an American Identity in Colonial New England* cites the reference to Joseph Ramsden's living "remotely in the woods" in the Plymouth records, p. 51. George Langdon provides a good summary of what was involved in purchasing a lot and building a house in a typical Plymouth town in *Pilgrim Colony*, pp. 146–47. On the amount of wood required to build a house in the seventeenth century, see Oliver Rackham's "Grundle House: On the Quantities of Timber in Certain East Anglian Buildings in Relation to Local Supplies," p. 3; on the wood consumption of an average seventeenth-century New England home and town, see Robert Tarule's *The Artisan of Ipswich: Craftsmanship and Community in Colonial New England*, p. 36. My thanks to Pret Woodburn and Rick McKee of Plimoth Plantation for bringing these two resources to my attention.

The Granger execution is detailed by Bradford in *OPP*, pp. 320–21. Langdon in *Pilgrim Colony* discusses Bradford's 1655 ultimatum, p. 67. Bradford's mournful note about the congregation's "most strict and sacred bond" begins, "O sacred bond, whilst inviolably preserved! How sweet and precious were the fruits that flowed from the same! But when this fidelity decayed, then their ruin approached," *OPP*, p. 33, n. 6. Bradford Smith in *Bradford of Plymouth* describes Bradford's extended family and the difficulty his son John had being assimilated, pp. 210–12, as does John Navin in *Plymouth Plantation*, pp. 584–86. Bradford writes of the speed with which the Indians took to hunting with muskets in *OPP*, p. 207. In *The Skulking Way of War*, Patrick Malone discusses the "excellent judgment" the Indians possessed when it came to their preference for flintlocks over matchlocks, pp. 31–33; Malone also chronicles colonial attitudes toward selling guns to the Indians, pp. 42–51. Bradford writes of the danger of armed Indians in the poem "In This Wilderness," which can be found in the extremely useful collection *The Complete Works of the* Mayflower *Pilgrims*, edited by Caleb Johnson, pp. 486–95. Isidore Meyer in "The Hebrew Preface to Bradford's History of the Plymouth Plantation" in American Jewish Historical Society

Publications, no. 38, part 4, cites Bradford's own words about learning Hebrew, p. 291. Cotton Mather writes of Bradford's last days in the *Magnalia,* book 2, pp. 207–8.

My account of the Indian burials at Burr's Hill is based on *Burr's Hill: A Seventeenth-Century Wampanoag Burial Ground in Warren, Rhode Island,* edited by Susan Gibson, especially pp. 13–14. Eric Schultz and Michael Tougias in *King Philip's War: The History and Legacy of America's Forgotten Conflict* refer to the existence of "a copper necklace thought to have been presented by Edward Winslow to Massasoit," p. 238. Constance Crosby in "From Myth to History, or Why King Philip's Ghost Walks Abroad" in *The Recovery of Meaning,* edited by Mark Leone and Parker Potter, cites William Wood's reference to the Indians' initial amazement over the "strange inventions" of the English, pp. 194–95; Crosby also cites Roger Williams's discussion of "manitoo" and speaks of the meaning of "manit," pp. 192–94, 198. Virginia DeJohn Anderson writes of "intercultural borrowing" in "King Philip's Herds: Indians, Colonists, and the Problem of Livestock in Early New England" in *WMQ,* 3rd ser., vol. 51, p. 613. On the symbolic importance of Western goods to the Indians, see Elise Brenner's "Sociopolitical Implications of Mortuary Ritual Remains in Seventeenth-Century Native Southern New England" in *The Recovery of Meaning,* edited by Mark Leone and Parker Potter, pp. 173–74.

I have written about the Indians' relationship with Christianity in *Abram's Eyes,* where I cite Zaccheus Macy's account of an Indian church meeting on Nantucket, pp. 123–24. See also David Silverman's "The Church in New England Indian Community Life: A View from the Islands and Cape Cod," in *Reinterpreting New England Indians and the Colonial Experience,* edited by Colin Calloway and Neal Salisbury, pp. 264–98. John Eliot's account of Massasoit's remarks concerning Christianity are in *The Glorious Progress of the Gospel amongst the Indians in New England,* MHS Collections, 3rd ser., vol. 4, p. 117. William Hubbard in *The History of the Indian Wars in New England* recounts Massasoit's attempt to include a proscription against missionary activities in the sale of some lands in Swansea, pp. 46–47.

On English attitudes toward the wilderness, see John Canup's *Out of the Wilderness,* pp. 46–51. Peter Thomas in "Contrastive Subsistence Strategies and Land Use as Factors for Understanding Indian-White Relations in New England" cites Merrill Bennett's estimates concerning the amount of corn an Indian consumed each year in *Ethnohistory,* Winter 1976, p. 12. On the manner in which the English adapted Native foods, see Keith Stavely and Kathleen Fitzgerald's *America's Founding Food: The Story of New England Cooking,* pp. 4–48. On the use of wampum, see Howard Russell's *Indian New England before the Mayflower,* p. 185, and Walter McDougall's *Freedom Just Around the Corner,* p. 63. On the concept of the frontier in New England prior to King Philip's War, see Frederick Turner's "The First Official Frontier of the Massachusetts Bay" in *Publications of the Colonial Society of Massachusetts,* vol. 17, pp. 250–71. Darrett Rutman in *Husbandmen of Plymouth: Farms and Villages in the Old Colony, 1620–1692* tells of how "the towns straggled" in Plymouth, p. 24. On the word "netop" and the use of language in seventeenth-century New England, see Ives Goddard's "The Use of Pidgins and Jargons on the East Coast of North America" in *The Language Encounter in the Americas, 1492–1800,* edited by Edward Gray and Norman Fiering, pp. 72–73. Francis Baylies writes revealingly of the intimacy that typified the Indians and English in Plymouth Colony in *Historical Memoir of . . . New Plymouth,* edited by Samuel Drake: "The English and the Indians were so intermixed that they all had personal knowledge of each other. The hospitalities of each race were constantly and cordially reciprocated. Although their dwellings were apart, yet they were near, and the roving habits of the Indians, and frequent visits had familiarized them as much with the houses of the English as with their own wigwams," vol. 2, p. 17.

On the Peach trial, see *OPP,* pp. 299–301, and two letters written by Roger Williams to John Winthrop in August 1638 in *Letters of Roger Williams,* vol. 1, pp. 110–16. Yasuhide Kawashima writes suggestively about the trial in *Igniting King Philip's War,* pp. 117–18. James Drake in *King Philip's War* writes that during the midpoint of the seventeenth century "the Indians and English entered into a period of cultural accommodation and negotiation. If anything, the two groups perceived more similarity between themselves than there really was, in what functioned as a type of mutual misunderstanding," p. 45.

The 1657 deed in which Massasoit traced a pictograph is at the Plymouth County Commissioners Office, Plymouth, Massachusetts; see also Jeremy Bangs's *Indian Deeds,* p. 277. For an account of Usamequin/Massasoit's "other life" as a Nipmuck sachem, see Dennis Connole's *The Indians of Nipmuck Country in Southern New England, 1630–1750,* pp. 65–66, 76, 78. One of the first scholars to be aware of Massasoit/Usamequin's presence among the Nipmucks was Samuel Drake, who in the *Book of the Indians* cites documents referring to Massasoit/Usamequin's 1661 complaint to Massachusetts officials concerning Uncas and the Mohegans, pp. 102–3; in a note, Drake writes, "By this it would seem that Massasoit had, for some time, resided among the Nipmucks. He had, probably, given up Pokanoket to his sons." Interestingly, in a document cited by Drake, John Mason, a Connecticut official sympathetic to Uncas, claims in a letter to Massachusetts officials that "Alexander, alias Wamsutta, sachem of Sowams, being now at Plymouth, he challenged Quabaug Indians to belong to him; and further said that he did war against Uncas this summer on that account," p. 103. On the relationship of the Nipmucks to other tribes in New England, see Bert Swalen's "Indians of Southern New England and Long Island: Early Period" in *Handbook of North American Indians,* vol. 15, edited by Bruce

Trigger, p. 174. According to a letter dated "28 of the 1st [16]61," from John Eliot, Massasoit/Usamequin had by that point changed his name once again to Matchippa, MHS *Proceedings*, vol. 3, pp. 312–13. See also Josiah Temple's *History of North Brookfield*, pp. 42–48, and the April 21, 1638, and March 7, 1644, entries of John Winthrop's *Journal*, edited by James Hosmer, vol. 1, p. 269, and vol. 2, p. 160. The last reference to Massasoit/Usamequin in the Plymouth Court Records is dated May 4, 1658, in which he and his son are suspected of harboring an Indian guilty of murder, *PCR*, vol. 2, p. 133; there is a 1659 deed with Massasoit/Usamequin's name on it, but it is unsigned; see Bangs, *Indian Deeds*, p. 293. Richard Smith's claim that he did not know about the Plymouth ban on purchasing land from the Indians is in Bangs's *Indian Deeds*, pp. 285–86. Bangs refers to Wamsutta's refusal to part with a portion of the land his father had agreed to sell to the English, p. 84. On John Sassamon, see Yasuhide Kawashima's *Igniting King Philip's War*, pp. 76–87; Kawashima suggests that Sassamon may have urged Wamsutta to acquire English names for himself and his brother; the request is dated June 13, 1660, *PCR*, vol. 2, p. 192. William Hubbard in *The History of the Indian Wars in New England* recounts how Massasoit brought his two sons to John Brown's house, pp. 46–47.

CHAPTER TWELVE—*The Trial*

George Langdon in *Pilgrim Colony* writes, "For the people who left England to settle Plymouth, the working out of this relationship with God in a new world offered excitement and the challenge of great adventure. By 1650 the adventure was over, the spontaneity which had fired the hearts of the early settlers gone," p. 140; Langdon also writes of the Half-Way Covenant and its impact on Plymouth, pp. 130–33. Joseph Conforti provides an excellent account of the second generation of English in Plymouth Colony in *Imagining New England*, pp. 36–78. The reference to "a strange vine" comes from the *Plymouth Church Records*, vol. 1, p. 151. On the economic development of New England and the impact of the Restoration, see Bernard Bailyn's *The New England Merchants in Seventeenth Century*, pp. 75–142. Langdon writes of Plymouth's relative poverty and the teasing prospect of a port at Mount Hope in *Pilgrim Colony*, p. 142. Jeremy Bangs in *Indian Deeds* refers to the reserve tracts of 1640, in which Causumpsit Neck, i.e., Mount Hope Neck, "is the chief habitation of the Indians, and reserved for them to dwell upon," p. 63. Russell Shorto writes of the fall of New Netherland to the English in *The Island at the Center of the World*, pp. 284–300. Samuel Maverick, who had been one of the first settlers in Massachusetts, was appointed one of Charles II's commissioners and in a 1660 manuscript account of New England describes Plymouth residents as "mongrel

Dutch" and speaks of their "sweet trade" with New Netherland. On Thomas Willett and his relationship to John Brown, as well as the locations of their homes in Swansea (modern Central Falls, Rhode Island), see Thomas Bicknell's *Sowams,* pp. 134, 141. Langdon discusses Plymouth's lack of a royal charter in *Pilgrim Colony,* pp. 188–200. In March 4, 1662, Thomas Willett was instructed by Plymouth Court to "speak to Wamsutta about his estranging land, and not selling it to our colony," *PCR,* vol. 4, p. 8.

For information on Josiah Winslow and his wife Penelope, see Pene Behrens's *Footnotes: A Biography of Penelope Pelham, 1633–1703,* as well as *The Winslows of Careswell in Marshfield* by Cynthia Hagar Krusell. Samuel Drake's *The Old Indian Chronicle* (*OIC*) provides an excellent account of the events leading up to Alexander's death, pp. 31–43; Drake judiciously draws primarily on William Hubbard's *The History of the Indian Wars in New England* (*HIWNE*) and Increase Mather's *History of King Philip's War* (*HKPW*). Hubbard in *HIWNE* insists that Alexander's "choler and indignation" were what killed him, p. 50. Eric Schultz and Michael Tougias cite Maurice Robbins's reference to a doctor's theory that Alexander died of appendicitis and that the surgeon's "working physic" would only have worsened the sachem's condition, in *King Philip's War,* p. 24. William Bradford's belated account of the incident is related in a letter from John Cotton to Increase Mather, March 19, 1677; Cotton also refers to the "flocking multitudes" that attended the festivities surrounding Philip's rise to sachem, in *The Mather Papers,* MHS Collections, 4th ser., vol. 8 (1868), pp. 233–34. Just prior to the outbreak of war in 1675, Philip and his counselors told John Easton and some others from Rhode Island that they believed Alexander had been "forced to court as they judged poisoned," in *Narratives of the Indian Wars,* edited by Charles Lincoln, p. 11. George Langdon in *Pilgrim Colony* refers to Winslow's decision to send his family to Salem and to hire twenty men to guard his home, p. 170.

Philip Ranlet provides a detailed look at the events of 1662–1675 in "Another Look at the Causes of King Philip's War," *NEQ,* vol. 61, 1998, pp. 79–100, as does Jenny Pulsipher in *Subjects unto the Same King: Indians, English, and the Contest for Authority in Colonial New England,* pp. 69–100. For a description of the geology of Mount Hope, see Shepard Krech III's "Rudolf F. Haffenreffer and the King Philip Museum" in *Passionate Hobby: Rudolf F. Haffenreffer and the King Philip Museum,* edited by Krech, pp. 56–57. Yasuhide Kawashima in *Igniting King Philip's War* refers to the tradition that Philip threw a stone all the way to Poppasquash Neck, p. 54. In *HIWNE,* Hubbard claims that Philip was nicknamed King Philip for the "ambitious and haughty spirit" he displayed during his 1662 appearance before Plymouth Court, p. 52. In *The Book of the Indians,* Samuel Drake quotes an undated letter of Philip's to a representative of the governor of Massachusetts: "Your governor is but a subject of King Charles of

England. I shall not treat with a subject. I shall treat of peace only with the king, my brother. When he comes, I am ready," book 3, p. 24. Philip's words to the Plymouth Court in 1662 are recorded in *PCR*, vol. 4, p. 25.

Peter Thomas in "Contrastive Subsistence Strategies and Land Use as Factors for Understanding Indian-White Relations in New England" in *Ethnohistory*, Winter 1976, claims that "less than twenty percent of the New England landscape had a high agricultural productiveness," p. 4. John Demos in *A Little Commonwealth: Family Life in Plymouth Colony* includes statistics concerning the size of families in Plymouth Colony, p. 192. S. F. Cook in *The Indian Population of New England in the Seventeenth Century* writes that between 1634 and 1675 the Wampanoags "had enjoyed as stable an existence as was possible for natives during the seventeenth century," p. 37. See Virginia DeJohn Anderson's "King Philip's Herds: Indians, Colonists, and the Problem of Livestock in Early New England," *WMQ*, October 1994, on Philip as a hog farmer, pp. 601–2, as well as her book *Creatures of Empire: How Domestic Animals Transformed Early America*. John Sassamon's undated letter to Governor Prence communicating Philip's desire not to sell any more land for at least seven years is at Pilgrim Hall and reprinted in MHS Collections, vol. 2, p. 40; Jeremy Bangs, who has transcribed the manuscript material at Pilgrim Hall, has assigned the probable date of 1663 to the letter. The deed for Philip's 1664 sale of land to Taunton is in Bangs's *Indian Deeds*, pp. 326–27.

Kathleen Bragdon in " 'Emphatical Speech and Great Action': An Analysis of Seventeenth-Century Native Speech Events Described in Early Sources," in *Man in the Northeast*, vol. 33, 1987, cites Roger Williams's reference to how a person of lesser rank approached a sachem, p. 104; see also Bragdon's *Native People of Southern New England, 1500–1650*, pp. 146–48, where she cites Williams's and Gookin's remarks concerning a sachem's relationship to his followers. John Josselyn reported seeing Philip on the streets of Boston in 1671, when, on the urging of John Eliot, he spoke to Massachusetts authorities, in *John Josselyn, Colonial Traveler*, edited by Paul Lindholdt, p. 101. On Philip's appearance on Nantucket in 1665, see my *Abram's Eyes*, pp. 118–21, in which I rely primarily on accounts by local historians Zaccheus Macy, whose unpublished account is in the Nantucket Historical Association's Collection 96, Folder 44, and Obed Macy, whose account is in his *History of Nantucket*, pp. 54–56. Nantucket's Indians vowed to "disown Philip" at a town meeting in August 1675. S. F. Cook in *The Indian Population of New England in the Seventeenth Century* estimates that there were five thousand Wampanoags in 1675, p. 39.

Since Philip's son was said to be nine years old in 1676, he must have been born in 1667; since the birth of a child often prompts a parent to draft a will, I have postulated that Philip's rift with Sassamon occurred soon after the birth of his son; by September 1667, Philip had a new interpreter named Tom. On the life of John Sassamon, see Yasuhide Kawashima's *Igniting King Philip's War*, pp. 76–87, and Jill Lepore's "Dead Men Tell No Tales: John Sassamon and the Fatal Consequences of Literacy" in *American Quarterly*, December 1994, pp. 493–97. In *A Relation of the Indian War*, John Easton reported the Pokanokets' claim that Sassamon "was a bad man that King Philip got him to write his will and he made the writing for a great part of the land to be his but read as if it had been as Philip would, but it came to be known and then he run away from him," in *Narratives of the Indian Wars*, edited by Charles Lincoln, p. 7; Easton also records Philip's claim that all Christian Indians are "dissemblers," p. 10. I refer to Philip's comparison of Christianity to the button on his coat in *Abram's Eyes*, p. 120. Philip's troubles over a suspected French-Dutch conspiracy in 1667 can be traced in *PCR*, vol. 4, pp. 151, 164–66. Philip's sale of land to Thomas Willett on September 17, 1667, with Tom, the interpreter, listed as a witness, is in Jeremy Bangs's *Indian Deeds*, p. 382; Bangs also discusses the new pressures that the creation of Swansea put on the Pokanokets, pp. 127–28, and quantifies the accelerating pace of Indian land sales, p. 163.

William Hubbard discusses the strategy Prence and Winslow used to handle the sachems of the Wampanoags and Massachusetts and the disastrous consequences that strategy had with respect to King Philip's War in *A General History of New England*, pp. 71–72. Jeremy Bangs points to Josiah Winslow's use of mortgaging Indian property to pay off debt as "tantamount to confiscating land" in *Indian Deeds*, p. 141. When it comes to the subject of Philip's supposed bravery, Samuel Drake writes, "I nowhere find any authentic records to substantiate these statements. On the other hand, I find abundant proof that he was quite destitute of such qualities," in a note to Drake's edition of William Hubbard's *HIWNE*, p. 59. Philip and his counselors spoke of when Massasoit was "a great man" and the English were "as a little child" to John Easton of Rhode Island in June 1675, in *Narratives of the Indian Wars*, edited by Charles Lincoln, p. 10.

Hubbard in *HIWNE* refers to the "petite injuries" that caused Philip to threaten war in 1671, p. 53. Hugh Cole's 1671 report of seeing Narragansett Indians at Mount Hope, where the Indians were "employed in making bows and arrows and half-pikes, and fixing up guns" is in Collections of the MHS, vol. 6, 1799, p. 211, and is cited in Richard Cogley's account of John Eliot's involvement in Philip's negotiations with the colonies of Plymouth and Massachusetts in 1671, in *John Eliot's Mission to the Indians*, pp. 200–203. Francis Baylies's *Historical Memoir of . . . New Plymouth*, vol. 2, edited by Samuel Drake, provides the most detailed account of what happened between the Pokanokets and the English in 1671, particularly at Taunton; Baylies quotes the reproof Massachusetts Bay officials sent Plymouth: "[T]he treatment you have given him, and proceedings towards him, do not render him such a subject [of your colony]," p. 23. I have also looked to Samuel Drake's account of the events of that year in *OIC*, pp. 63–86, and Jenny Pulsipher's *Subjects unto the Same King*, pp. 94–100. Much of the documentary record from this crucial summer is contained in *PCR*, vol. 5, pp. 63–80. Josiah Winslow refers to Philip's supposed scheme to abduct and ransom both himself and Governor Prence in a note on a March 24, 1671, letter from Governor Bellingham to Governor Prence, Winslow Papers II, MHS. William Hubbard in *HIWNE* writes of the unnamed warrior who disavowed Philip after the sachem capitulated at Taunton in April 1671: "[O]ne of his captains, of far better courage and resolution than himself, when he saw [Philip's] cowardly temper and disposition, [did] fling down his arms, calling him a *white-livered cur*, or to that purpose, and saying that he would never own him again, or fight under him, and from that Time hath turned to the English, and hath continued to this day a faithful and resolute soldier in this quarrel," pp. 58–59. Hubbard in *HIWNE* also describes how the son of the Nipmuck sachem Matoonas "being vexed in his mind that the design against the English, intended to begin [in] 1671, did not take place, out of mere malice and spite against them, slew an English man traveling along the road," p. 44. William Harris in *A Rhode Islander Reports on King Philip's War*, edited by Douglas Leach, claimed that Philip's plan to attack the English in 1671 was prevented "twice at least by great rains, which afterward was made known by some Indians," p. 21. The September 1, 1671, letter from James Walker to Governor Prence describing Philip's drunken rant against Sassamon is in MHS Collections, 1st ser., vol. 6, 1799, pp. 196–97.

Concerning the state of the Pokanokets' war plans after 1671 Samuel Drake writes, "Much . . . was to be done, before a war could be undertaken with any prospect of success on their part. The Wampanoags, who were to begin it, were almost without firearms, and it would require much time to obtain a supply," *OIC*, p. 86. Jeremy Bangs describes Philip's final sell-off of his land holdings around Mount Hope in *Indian Deeds*, pp. 162–65. Hubbard in *HIWNE* states that some Narragansett Indians later revealed that their tribe had promised "to rise [with the Pokanokets] with four thousand fighting men in the spring of this present year 1676," p. 58. William Harris in *A Rhode Islander Reports on King Philip's War*, edited by Douglas Leach, wrote that the Pokanokets on Mount Hope had "laid up great quantities of corn, not in the usual manner, but a year ahead of time, as a supply for the war. . . . The intention of the Indians is also revealed by their accumulation of powder, shot, and arrows. The English perceiving this and inquiring about it, the Indians pretended it was a preparation against the Mohawks, but actually it was aimed only at the English," p. 23. Samuel Drake refers to the annulment of the order to prohibit selling powder to the Indians in the fall of 1674 in *OIC*, p. 96.

For information on the murder trial of John Sassamon, I have looked to Yasuhide Kawashima's *Igniting King Philip's War*, pp. 88–111; Jill Lepore's "Dead Men Tell No Tales" in *American Quarterly*, December 1994; James P. Ronda and Jeanne Ronda's "The Death of John Sassamon: An Exploration in Writing New England History" in *American Indian Quarterly*; and James Drake's "Symbol of a

Failed Strategy: The Sassamon Trial, Political Culture, and the Outbreak of King Philip's War" in *American Indian Culture and Research Journal.* In a November 18, 1675, letter to John Cotton, Thomas Whalley refers to Josiah Winslow's "weakness" and "frail body," Curwen Papers, AAS. In addition to hearing the testimony of an Indian witness, the jurors at the Sassamon trial were told that Sassamon's corpse had begun "a bleeding afresh, as if it had newly been slain" when it was approached by Tobias; known as "cruentation," this ancient test of guilt in a murder case was of dubious legal value; see Kawashima's *Igniting King Philip's War,* p. 100.

According to William Hubbard in *HIWNE,* Philip would have lacked the courage to launch the war "if his own life had not now been in jeopardy by the guilt of the foresaid murder of Sassamon," p. 58. In a note to William Harris's reference to the Indians' preference for fighting in the summer and the English preference for winter in *A Rhode Islander Reports on King Philip's War,* Douglas Leach writes, "The English, fearing ambush, disliked fighting against Indians in the months when foliage was thick and when the swamps were miry and difficult to penetrate," p. 63. Samuel Drake cites the traditions concerning Philip's inability to control his warriors in June 1675, as well as his anguished response to the death of the first Englishman in *OIC,* pp. 56–57; see John Callender's *An Historical Discourse on the Civil and Religious Affairs of the Colony of Rhode-Island* for the family traditions about Philip's reluctance to go to war: "He was forced on by the fury of his young men, for against his own judgment and inclination; and that though he foresaw and foretold the English would in time by their industry root out all the Indians, yet he was against making war with them, as what he thought would only hurry on and increase the destruction of his people," p. 73. Francis Baylies in *Historical Memoir of. . . New Plymouth,* vol. 2, edited by Samuel Drake, writes of the Indians' intimate knowledge of both the English and the countryside: "They knew the habits, the temper, the outgoings, the incomings, the power of defense, and even the domiciliary usages of every [English] family in the colony. They were minutely acquainted with every river, brook, creek, bay, harbor, lake, and pond, and with every local peculiarity of the country. They had their friends and their enemies amongst the English; for some they professed a fond attachment; others they disliked and avoided. In short, they seemed as much identified with the English as Greeks with Turks," p. 17.

CHAPTER THIRTEEN—*Kindling the Flame*

In this and subsequent chapters, I have relied on Henry Martyn Dexter's edition of Benjamin Church's *Entertaining Passages Relating to Philip's War (EPRPW);* Dexter's extensive knowledge of New England history and geography makes the edition an invaluable resource. Another excellent edition is that edited by Alan and Mary Simpson and published in 1975; in addition to a solid introduction, their edition includes a wide variety of helpful illustrations. Samuel Drake collected several important contemporary accounts of King Philip's War in the volume *The Old Indian Chronicle (OIC)*, most notably Nathaniel Saltonstall's three extended articles about the war and an account by Richard Hutchinson. Also of importance is the account by John Easton in which Easton describes the unsuccessful attempt by a delegation of Rhode Island Quakers to bring about a peaceful resolution to Philip's difficulties with Plymouth; the account also includes much important information about the early months of the war. Two Puritan ministers wrote histories of the conflict: Increase Mather was the first out with his hastily assembled *History of King Philip's War (HKPW)*, soon followed by William Hubbard's *History of the Indian Wars in New England (HIWNE)*, which received the official blessing of the Massachusetts colonial government. I have used Samuel Drake's editions of the two works; his edition of Mather's history also includes that written by his son Cotton Mather. Another important contemporary source is the letters written by William Harris, which have been collected and edited by William Leach in the volume *A Rhode Islander Reports on King Philip's War*. Daniel Gookin's *Historical Account of the Doings and Sufferings of the Christian Indians in New England in the Years 1675–1677* is unique in that it provides a sympathetic portrayal of the plight of the Praying Indians during the conflict. Neal Salisbury has edited an excellent edition of Mary Rowlandson's account of her capture by the Indians, titled *The Sovereignty and Goodness of God;* Rowlandson's book, published in 1682, became one of America's first bestsellers and invented the genre of the Indian captivity narrative. Richard Slotkin and James Folsom's *So Dreadfull a Judgment: Puritan Responses to King Philip's War* is a useful collection of contemporary accounts from the period. Large and important collections of unpublished letters from the period are located at the Massachusetts Historical Society and the American Antiquarian Society. Although authentic Native voices are tragically lacking in almost all of these sources, there is one notable exception. During the winter of 1676, two Praying Indians, Job Kattenanit and James Quanapohit, volunteered to act as spies for the English. On January 24, 1676, after his return to Boston from the western portion of the colony, where he had lived for weeks with the enemy, James was interrogated by Massachusetts officials. There are two versions of his testimony: a highly edited transcript, published by the MHS, and a much longer, unabridged version reprinted in J. H. Temple's invaluable *History of North Brookfield*, pp. 112–18. James's testimony provides information found nowhere else concerning Philip's movements during the summer, fall, and winter of 1675–76. The testimony of another Praying Indian, George Memicho (also reprinted in Temple's *History of North Brookfield*, pp. 100–101), provides additional information about Philip.

When it comes to secondary accounts of the war, the best place to start is George Ellis and John Morris's *King Philip's War;* published in 1906, this book contains a host of fascinating photographs of war sites. Another book published that same year is George Bodge's *Soldiers in King Philip's War;* in addition to listing the names of the soldiers in each colonial company, Bodge provides an excellent narrative of the war and reprints a large number of contemporary letters. Douglas Leach's *Flintlock and Tomahawk,* first published in 1958, remains an essential resource. More recently, Richard Slotkin has written insightfully about Benjamin Church's place in American literature and culture in *Regeneration through Violence,* pp. 146–79, and in his introduction, "Benjamin Church: King of the Wild Frontier," to Church's narrative reprinted in the collection *So Dreadfull a Judgment,* pp. 370–91. *The Red King's Rebellion: Racial Politics in New England, 1675–1678* by Russell Bourne is an engaging narrative that integrates the findings of recent anthropological and archaeological scholarship. Michael Puglisi's *Puritans Besieged: The Legacies of King Philip's War in the Massachusetts Bay Colony* examines how the effects of the war reached far beyond 1676. Jill Lepore's *The Name of War: King Philip's War and the Origins of American Identity* provides provocative readings of the many written texts created during and after the conflict and demonstrates how the trauma of interracial war was fundamental to forging a uniquely American identity. In addition to providing a readable and richly detailed narrative of the war, Eric Schultz and Michael Tougias's *King Philip's War: The History and Legacy of America's Forgotten Conflict* identifies countless war sites across New England. In *King Philip's War: Civil War in New England,* James Drake persuasively argues that the conflict was much more than a racial war. Jenny Hale Pulsipher's analysis of Indian-English relations throughout the seventeenth century in *Subjects unto the Same King: Indians, English, and the Contest for Authority in Colonial New England* puts King Philip's War in a complex and richly textured historical and cultural context.

There is a wealth of books on the nature of the Indian-English warfare in colonial America. One of the best is Patrick Malone's *The Skulking Way of War: Technology and Tactics among the New England Indians.* Malone demonstrates how the English adopted Native ways of fighting during King Philip's War. In *Conquering the American Wilderness: The Triumph of European Warfare in the Colonial Northeast,* Guy Chet begs to disagree with Malone's thesis, claiming that the Indians had little influence on the way war was ultimately fought in America. To my mind, John Grenier in *The First Way of War: American War Making on the Frontier* convincingly demonstrates that Malone's thesis cannot be so easily dismissed. Armstrong Starkey's *European and Native American Warfare, 1675–1815* is also useful, as is John Ferling's *A Wilderness of Miseries: War and Warriors in Early America.*

All quotations from Church's narrative in this chapter are from *EPRPW,* pp. 1–48; the description of Philip's warriors is from Church, who describes a dance among the Sakonnets in which Awashonks had worked herself into a "foaming sweat." Perhaps not unexpectedly, there is much conflicting information concerning the outbreak of King Philip's War. In November 1675 Governor Josiah Winslow and Thomas Hinckley authored "A Brief Narrative of the Beginning and Progress of the Present Trouble between Us and the Indians," which is in vol. 10 of *PCR,* pp. 362–64; they maintain that "our innocency made us very secure and confident it would not have broke out into a war." They were not the only ones who believed that the threat of war had passed. On June 13, 1675, Roger Williams wrote Connecticut governor John Winthrop Jr., "[P]raise be God the storm is over. Philip is strongly suspected but the honored court at Plymouth (as we hear) not having evidence sufficient, let matters sleep and the country be in quiet, etc," *Correspondence of Roger Williams,* vol. 2, p. 691.

Patrick Malone discusses the typical modifications made to a garrison house in *The Skulking Way of War,* p. 96. Eric Schultz and Michael Tougias provide an excellent description of where the various garrisons were located in Swansea in *King Philip's War,* pp. 98–103. John Callender in the notes to *An Historical Discourse on the Civil and Religious Affairs of the Colony of Rhode-Island,* published in 1739, writes, "I have heard from some old people, who were familiarly acquainted with the Indians, both before and after the war, that the powwows had likewise given out an other ambiguous oracle . . . viz., that they promised the Indians would be successful if the English fired the first gun. It is certain the Indians long delayed and designedly avoided firing on the English, and seemed to use all possible means, to provoke the English to fire first," pp. 73–74. Saltonstall in *OIC* describes the Indians asking an Englishman to grind their hatchet on Sunday, July 20, p. 126. Increase Mather speaks of June 24 being "a day of solemn humiliation through that colony, by fasting and praying, to entreat the Lord to give success to the present expedition," in *HKPW,* p. 54. Josiah Winslow writes of the colony's innocence respecting the Indians and the fairness of the Sassamon trial in a July 29, 1675, letter to Connecticut governor John Winthrop Jr., MHS Collections, 5th ser., vol. 1, pp. 428–29. John Easton writes of the "old man and a lad" shooting at the Indians pilfering a house and killing one of them in "A Relation of the Indian War" in *Narratives of the Indian Wars,* edited by Charles Lincoln, p. 12. Saltonstall in *OIC* writes of the scalping and killing of the father, mother, and son, pp. 128–29. On the history of scalping, see James Axtell and William Sturtevant's "The Unkindest Cut, or Who Invented Scalping?" *WMQ,* 3rd ser., 1980, pp. 451–72. Hubbard in *HIWNE* describes the eclipse of the moon on June 26, pp. 67–68.

Concerning Church's sprint from Taunton to Swansea, Douglas Leach writes in *Flintlock and Tomahawk,* "Perhaps Church would not have thought himself so clever if the enemy had laid an ambush between him and the main force which he was supposed to be shielding," p. 38. Saltonstall in *OIC* describes Samuel Moseley as "an old privateer at Jamaica, an excellent soldier, and an undaunted spirit," pp. 127–28. George Bodge in *Soldiers in King Philip's War* provides a detailed description of Moseley's activities before and during the war and how he put together his company of volunteers, pp. 59–78. Concerning the relationship between Moseley and Church, Bodge writes, "Moseley was the most popular officer of the army, and undoubtedly excited Church's anger and perhaps jealousy by ignoring and opposing him," p. 73. For an example of a buff coat, once owned by Massachusetts governor Leverett, see *New England Begins,* edited by Jonathan Fairbanks and Robert Trent, vol.1, p. 56. Increase Mather in *HKPW* tells of the "many profane oaths of . . . those privateers" and how they prompted a soldier to lose control of himself and proclaim that "God was against the English," p. 58.

On European military tactics in the seventeenth century and how they were adapted to the unique conditions of an Indian war, see Patrick Malone's *The Skulking Way of War,* especially chapter 4, "Proficiency with Firearms: A Cultural Comparison," pp. 52–66; George Bodge in *Soldiers in King Philip's War* writes of how matchlocks quickly gave way to flintlocks in the early days of the war, pp. 45–46. Daniel Gookin in *Doings and Sufferings of the Christian Indians* mentions the belief prior to the war that "one Englishman was sufficient to chase ten Indians," p. 438. Hubbard in *HIWNE* speaks of how Moseley and his men "ran violently down" on the Indians and of the wounding of Perez Savage, p. 70, as well as of the torn Bible pages, p. 76. Saltonstall in *OIC* writes of Cornelius the Dutchman's arrival at Philip's newly abandoned village, and how he placed the sachem's hat upon his head, p. 130; Hubbard in *HIWNE* tells of the many masterless Indian dogs and the fields of corn, p. 72. In a July 6, 1675, letter to Sir John Allin, Benjamin Batten writes of the English taking a horse on Mount Hope "which by the furniture they suppose to be King Philip's," Gay Transcripts, Plymouth Papers, MHS. Roger Williams refers to the Narragansetts' query as to why the other colonies did not leave Plymouth and Philip "to fight it out" in a June 25, 1675, letter to John Winthrop Jr., in *Correspondence,* vol. 2, p. 694.

Hubbard describes the Indians of New England as being "in a kind of maze" in *HIWNE,* p. 59. John Easton tells of Weetamoo's unsuccessful attempts to surrender herself to authorities on Aquidneck Island in "A Relation of the Indian War" in *Narratives of the Indian Wars,* edited by Charles Lincoln, pp. 12–13; he also speaks of the promise made to neutral Indians that "if they kept by the waterside and did not meddle . . . the English would do them no harm," pp. 15–16. Saltonstall describes the assault of Cornelius the Dutchman on the Indians attempting to land their canoes on Mount Hope, p. 130. Easton tells of Philip's statement that "fighting was the worst way," p. 9. On the enslaving of the Indians from Dartmouth and Plymouth, see Almon Lauber's *Indian Slavery in Colonial Times,* pp. 146–47. Lauber also writes of Indian slavery in the Pequot War, pp. 123–24, while James Muldoon in "The Indian as Irishman" in *Essex Institute*

Historical Collections, October 1975, discusses how English policies in the colonization of Ireland anticipated much of what happened in America, pp. 267–89. On Church's efforts to ensure that the Indians of Sakonnet were treated fairly after the war, see Alan and Mary Simpson's introduction to their edition of Church's narrative, p. 39; they also cite his inventory at his death, which includes a "Negro couple" valued at £100, p. 41. William Bradford Jr. writes of the battle in the Pocasset cedar swamp in a July 21, 1675, letter to John Cotton reprinted by the Society of Colonial Wars in 1914. Hubbard in *HIWNE* describes in detail how bewildered the English soldiers were in the swamp, pp. 84–87. Saltonstall in *OIC* relates how the Indians would run over the mucky surface of the swamp "holding their guns across their arms (and if occasion be) discharge in that posture," p. 134. James Cudworth also writes of the engagement and outlines his plan for building a fort at Pocasset and creating a small "flying army" in a July 20, 1675, letter to Josiah Winslow, MHS Collections, 1st ser., vol. 6, pp. 84–85.

Hubbard in *HIWNE* tells of Philip and Weetamoo's escape across the Taunton River and of the hundred women and children left behind at Pocasset; he also details the encounter at Nipsachuck and Philip's eventual escape to Nipmuck country, pp. 87–93; see also Increase Mather's *HKPW,* p. 65. The best source on the encounter at Nipsachuck is Nathaniel Thomas's August 10, 1675, letter reprinted in the appendix of *HKPW,* pp. 227–33. In a July 3, 1675, letter Tobias Sanders informed Major Fitz John Winthrop that Mohegan sachem Uncas had been "in counsel with Philip's messengers three days together in the woods privately and received of them peag [wampum] and coats," MHS Collections, 5th ser., vol. 1, p. 427. The Praying Indian George Memicho recounts the condition of Philip and his people when they arrived at Menameset on August 5, 1675, in testimony reprinted in Temple's *History of North Brookfield;* Memicho reports "that Philip said, if the English had charged upon him and his people at the swamp in his own country one or two days more they had been all taken, for their powder was almost spent; he also said that if the English had pursued him closely [at Nipsachuck], as he traveled up to them, he must needs have been taken," pp. 100–101; Memicho also tells of how the Nipmuck sachems accepted Philip's wampum. Saltonstall in *OIC* speaks of Philip's coat of wampum, p. 154. Hubbard writes of how Philip succeeded in "kindling the flame of war" in *HIWNE,* p. 91.

CHAPTER FOURTEEN—*The God of Armies*

On the attack at Brookfield, see Hubbard in *HIWNE,* pp. 98–104; Increase Mather in *HKPW,* pp. 76–70; and Thomas Wheeler's *Narrative* of the attack in *So Dreadfull a Judgment,* edited by Richard Slotkin and James Folsom, pp. 243–57. Hubbard in *HIWNE* tells of the battle of South Deerfield, pp. 109–110. Saltonstall in *OIC* tells of the powwows' prediction after the hurricane on August 29, 1675, p. 158. A letter quoted in Increase Mather's *HKPW* describes the sins ("intolerable pride in clothes and hair," etc.) of which New England was guilty, p. 83; Hubbard speaks of the "most fatal day" at Bloody Brook in *HIWNE*, pp. 113–17; he also describes Moseley's subsequent battle with the Indians, pp. 117–19. Daniel Gookin was particularly outspoken concerning the outrages Moseley committed against the Indians in *Doings and Sufferings of the Christian Indians*, pp. 455, 464; George Bodge reprints the October 16, 1675, letter in which Moseley adds the postscript: "This aforesaid Indian was ordered to be torn in pieces by dogs" in *Soldiers in King Philip's War*, p. 69. John Pynchon's October 5, 1675, letter describing the attack on Springfield appears in the appendix of *HKPW*, pp. 244–45. Hubbard describes the Indians as "children of the devil" in *HIWNE*, p. 123. Gookin tells how "submissively and Christianly and affectionately" the Praying Indians conducted themselves as they were transported to Deer Island on October 20, 1675, in *Doings and Sufferings of the Christian Indians*, p. 474.

The proposal to build a defensive wall around the core settlements of Massachusetts is mentioned by Douglas Leach in *Flintlock and Tomahawk*, pp. 165–66. Ellis and Morris in *King Philip's War* write of the traditions that sprang up in the Connecticut River valley concerning Philip's activities during the fall of 1675 and add, "but his hand is hard to trace in the warfare of the valley," p. 96. J. R. Temple in the *History of North Brookfield* insists that the Nipmucks were the dominant Native force throughout the war: "There is more reason for calling the conflict of 1675–6 a Quabaug and Nashaway War, than King Philip's War. Philip's power was broken at the outset. The Wampanoags, his own tribe, deserted him. . . . The *Quabaug Alliance* heartily espoused, and never deserted the cause, till it became hopeless," p. 99. James Quanapohit provides the best information we have concerning Philip's activities in the fall and winter of 1675–76; according to James, "a chief captain of [the] Hadley and Northampton Indians who was a valiant man . . . had attempted to kill Philip and intended to do it; alleging that Philip had begun a war with the English that had brought great trouble upon them," reprinted in Temple's *History of North Brookfield*, pp. 114–15. Mary Pray's October 20, 1675, letter to Massachusetts authorities urging that action be taken against the Narragansetts is in MHS Collections, 5th ser., vol. 1, pp. 105–8. Increase Mather in *HKPW* writes of the "sword having marched eastward and westward and northward, now beginneth to face toward the south again," p. 102. William Harris claims that if a pan-Indian force had struck a coordinated blow against the English in the beginning "in an hour or two the Indians might have slain five thousand souls, small and great. And before the English could have been in any good capacity to defend themselves, and begun to fight, the enemy regrettably might have killed another five thousands

souls, so uncertain is our safety here," *A Rhode Islander Reports,* edited by Douglas Leach, p. 65.

In my account of the Great Swamp Fight and the Hungry March, I have re-
lied primarily on Benjamin Church's *EPRPW,* pp. 48–64; Hubbard in *HIWNE,*
pp. 137–65; Increase Mather in *HKPW,* pp. 102–17; Saltonstall in *OIC,* pp.
178–98; Welcome Green's "The Great Battle of the Narragansetts," *Narragansett
Historical Register,* December 1887, pp. 331–43, and George Bodge in *Soldiers in
King Philip's War,* pp. 179–205. Increase Mather speaks of "the God of armies" in
HKPW, p. 104. Hubbard credits Moseley with capturing thirty-six Indians on
December 12, p. 139; however, Church claims to have brought in eighteen that
same night, indicating that Hubbard's number probably included the Indians
brought in by both Moseley and Church. James Oliver's December 26, 1675, letter describing the night spent sleeping "in the open field" the night before the
attack on the Narragansetts is in Bodge, pp. 174–75. Hubbard refers to the companies of Johnson and Davenport charging "without staying for word of command," in *HIWNE,* p. 144; Hubbard claims that God "who as he led Israel
sometime by the pillar of fire . . . through the wilderness; so did he now direct
our forces upon that side of the fort where they might only enter," p. 145. Eric
Schultz and Michael Tougias argue that what the Puritans took to be an unfinished feature of the fort "was intentionally planned by the Narragansett . . . to
ensure that the English would attack at a well-defended point. . . . Had the Narragansett not run out of gunpowder during the fight . . . this contrived entrance
might have been viewed not as a weakness but as a brilliant military tactic . . . in
a smashing Narragansett victory," p. 260. In a note to his edition of Hubbard's
HIWNE, Samuel Drake writes of Captain Davenport: "Being dressed in a full
buff suit, it was supposed the Indians took him for the commander-in-chief,
many aiming at him at once," p. 146. Hubbard in *HIWNE* claims that "the soldiers were rather enraged than discouraged by the loss of their commanders,"
p. 148. Benjamin Church does not mention Samuel Moseley by name, but as
several commentators have noted, there is no mistaking the identity of the Massachusetts captain who arrogantly refused to allow General Winslow to enter the
Narragansett fort. Concerning the decision to burn the fort and march that
night to Wickford, Hubbard writes in *HIWNE,* "[M]any of our wounded men
perished, which might otherwise have been preserved, if they had not been
forced to march so many miles in a cold and snowy night, before they could be
dressed," p. 151. Bodge, on the other hand, feels that "from the standpoint of
military strategy, the immediate retreat to Wickford was best," p. 189. My
thanks to Michael Hill for providing me with the comparative casualty rates at
D-day and Antietam. Hubbard writes of the supply vessels frozen in at Cape
Cod, *HIWNE,* p. 154. Saltonstall in *OIC* talks of the mounting fears back in
Boston when it took five days for word of the fighting to reach the settlement:
"[M]any fears arose amongst us that our men were lost either by the enemy or

the snow, which made many a heartache among us," p. 185. Bodge's reference to the Great Swamp Fight as a "glorious victory" is from *Soldiers of King Philip's War*, p. 189. Hubbard in *HIWNE* tells of how the English soldiers found the treaty in a wigwam of the fort and how it proved that the Indians "could not be ignorant of the articles of agreement," p. 160. Most of what we know about Joshua Tefft comes from a January 14, 1676, letter from Roger Williams to Massachusetts governor John Leverett, in which Williams recounts in great detail Tefft's testimony, *Correspondence*, vol. 2, pp. 711–17. See also Colin Calloway's "Rhode Island Renegade: The Enigma of Joshua Tift," *Rhode Island History*, vol. 43, 1984, pp. 137–45, and Jill Lepore's *The Name of War*, pp. 131–36. Hubbard expresses his disdain for Tefft in *HIWNE*, p. 162. James Quanapohit reported that the first Narragansetts who approached the Nipmucks with two English scalps were "shot at" and told that "they were Englishmen's friends all last summer and would not credit the first messengers; afterward came other messengers from Narragansetts and brought more heads . . . and then these Indians believed the Narragansetts and received the scalps . . . and now they believed that the Narragansetts and English are at war, of which they are glad," in Temple's *History of North Brookfield*, p. 116.

CHAPTER FIFTEEN—*In a Strange Way*

James Quanapohit provides a detailed account of Philip's meeting with the French in his January 24, 1676, testimony; all quotes ascribed to the French diplomat are from that testimony reprinted in Temple's *History of North Brookfield*, pp. 115–16. Increase Mather in *HKPW* writes, "[A] French man that came from Canady had been amongst [the Indians], animating them against the English, promising a supply of ammunition, and that they would come next summer and assist them," p. 177. Before his execution, Joshua Tefft claimed that "Philip hath sent [the Narragansetts] word that he will furnish them [powder] from the French. He saith they have carried New England money to the French for ammunition, but the money he will not take but beaver or wampum. [Tefft] said the French have sent Philip a present viz. a brass gun and bandoliers suitable," *Correspondence of Roger Williams*, vol. 2, p. 712. New York governor Andros writes that "Philip and 3 or 400 North Indians, fighting men, were come within 40 or 50 miles of Albany northerly" in a January 6, 1676, letter in Colonial Connecticut Records (CCR), vol. 2, p. 397. On February 25, 1675, Thomas Warner, a former prisoner with the Indians, testified that "he saw 2,100 Indians, all fighting men, [of] which 5 or 600 [were] French Indians, with straws in their noses," in *A Narrative of . . . King Philip's War*, edited by Franklin Hough, p. 145. According to Neal Salisbury in a personal communication, "Mohawk enmity with the French and their Indian allies dated back to at least 1609 and possibly earlier." Increase Mather's account of Philip's failed attempt to win the Mohawks' support is in *HKPW*, where he writes, "Thus hath he conceived mischief and brought forth falsehood; he made a pit and digged, and is fallen into the ditch which he hath made, his mischief shall return upon his own head," pp. 168–69. On March 4, 1676, Andros wrote from Albany that "about three hundred Mohawk soldiers . . . returned the evening afore from the pursuit of Philip and a party of five hundred with him, whom they had beaten, having some prisoners and the crowns, or hair and skin of the head, of others they had killed," in *Documents Relative to the Colonial History of the State of New York,* edited by John Brodhead, vol. 3, p. 255. Stephen Webb provides an excellent account of Philip's winter in New York in *1676: The End of American Independence,* pp. 367–71.

James Quanapohit's testimony in which he describes his and Job Kattenanit's spy mission is reprinted in J. H. Temple's *History of North Brookfield,* pp. 112–18. Daniel Gookin tells of how Job's arrival at his home in Cambridge on the night of February 9 triggered the attempt to save Lancaster in *Doings and Sufferings of the Christian Indians,* pp. 488–91. All quotations from Mary Rowlandson come from *The Sovereignty and Goodness of God,* edited by Neal Salisbury, pp. 63–112. For information on Rowlandson and her family, I have depended on Salisbury's introduction, pp. 7–20. Hubbard in *HIWNE* quotes the message left by James the Printer at Medfield, p. 171. Francis Jennings in *The Invasion of America: Indians, Colonialism, and the Cant of Conquest* refers to an August 8, 1675, letter from Richard Smith to Connecticut officials in which Smith claims that Weetamoo and a hundred men, women, and children had been delivered to him by a Narragansett sachem, p. 311, n. 36. On a woman's pocket in seventeenth-century New England, see Laurel Ulrich's *Good Wives: Image and Reality in the Lives of Women in Northern New England:* "a woman's pocket was not attached to her clothing, but tied around her waist with a string or tape. . . . A pocket could be a mended and patched pouch of plain homespun or a rich personal ornament boldly embroidered in crewel," p. 34. Ulrich also writes revealingly of Rowlandson's captivity, pp. 226–34. On the meeting between Philip and Canonchet on March 9, 1676, see Temple's *History of North Brookfield,* pp. 127–28. Richard Scott's rant against Daniel Gookin appears in Simon Willard's March 4, 1676, "Deposition of Elizabeth Belcher, Martha Remington, and Mary Mitchell," at MHS. Jenny Pulsipher points out that Scott had served under Captain Moseley in *Subjects unto the Same King,* p. 155. Gookin writes of the threatened attack on the Praying Indians on Deer Island in *Doings and Sufferings of the Christian Indians,* p. 494.

The court order requiring all of Nemasket's Praying Indians to relocate to Clark's Island is in *PCR,* vol. 5, p. 187. All quotations from Benjamin Church are from *EPRPW,* pp. 66–71. My account of the Pierce massacre is based primarily on Hubbard's *HIWNE*, pp. 172–77; Leonard Bliss's *History of Rehoboth*, pp. 88–95; Harris, *A Rhode Islander Reports*, edited by Douglas Leach, pp. 41–43; and Increase Mather in *HKPW*, pp. 125–27. In an April 19, 1676, letter the Rehoboth minister Noah Newman writes, "The burial of the slain [from Pierce's Fight] took us three days," Curwen Papers, AAS. In a letter written in early April 1676, John Kingsley describes the attack on Rehoboth: "They burnt our mills, wreck the stones, yea, our grinding stones; and what was hid in the earth they found, corn and fowls, killed cattle and took the hind quarters and left the rest," CCR, vol. 2, p. 446; he refers to the resident who was killed with the Bible in his hands as a "silly man." Roger Williams describes the attack on Providence and his meeting with the Indians in an April 1, 1676, letter to his brother Robert Williams living on Aquidneck Island in *Correspondence*, vol. 2, pp. 720–24. Increase Mather in *HKPW* writes of the "sore and (doubtless) malignant colds prevailing everywhere. I cannot hear of one family in New England that hath wholly escaped the distemper. . . . We in Boston have seen . . . coffins meeting one another, and three or four put into their graves in one day," pp. 153–54. Most of the quotations describing the capture and execution of Canonchet are from volume 2 of Hubbard's *HIWNE*, pp. 55–60. Saltonstall in *OIC* tells how the Pequots, Mohegans, and Niantics "shared in the glory of destroying so great a prince," p. 232. The Nipmuck sachems' scornful response to possible negotiations on April 12, 1676, is cited by Dennis Connole in *The Indians of the Nipmuck Country in Southern New England*, p. 200. On groundnuts going to seed in early summer, see Howard Russell's *Indian New England before the* Mayflower, p. 156. The much more conciliatory letter from the Nipmuck Sagamore Sam is also cited by Connole, p. 201.

Samuel Moseley's belated request for "fifty or sixty apt or other trusty Indians, to be armed at the country's charge," is in the May 5, 1676, minutes of the Massachusetts General Court in *Records of Massachusetts Bay*, edited by Nathaniel Shurtleff, vol. 5, p. 95. Gookin describes the return of the Praying Indians from Deer Island as "a jubilee" in *Doings and Sufferings*, p. 517. On the battle at Turner's Falls, see Hubbard's *HIWNE*, pp. 229–34. Sagamore Sam refers to how the attacks by Turner and Captain Henchman "destroyed those Indians" and how Philip and Quinnapin "went away to their own country again" in a June letter to Governor Leverett; see *OIC*, p. 272.

CHAPTER SIXTEEN—*The Better Side of the Hedge*

All quotations from Benjamin Church are from *EPRPW*, pp. 71–182. For more information on Awashonks, see Ann Marie Plane's "Putting a Face on Colonization: Factionalism and Gender Politics in the Life History of Awashunkes, the

'Squaw Sachem' of Saconet," in *Northeastern Indian Lives, 1632–1816*, edited by Robert Grumet, pp. 140–65. Increase Mather writes of the attack on Swansea on June 16, 1676, in *HKPW*, p. 162. Hubbard in *HIWNE* details the June 26 killing and beheading of Hezekiah Willett, p. 242. In his diary, Samuel Sewall writes about how the Pokanokets mourned Willett's death, p. 25; Sewall also reports that Willett's black servant "related Philip to be sound and well, about 1,000 Indians (all sorts) with him, but sickly: three died while he was there," p. 25. The June 28, 1676, testimony of Awashonks's son Peter and some other Sakonnet Indians appears in *PCR*, vol. 5, pp. 200–203. In locating the beach where Church and the Sakonnets finally found each other, I am indebted to Maurice Robbins's *The Sandwich Path: Church Searches for Awashonks*, cited in Schultz and Tougias's *King Philip's War*, pp. 119–20. According to John Callender in *An Historical Discourse on . . . Rhode Island*, "The Powwows had foretold Philip, no Englishman should ever kill him, which accordingly proved true; he was shot by an Indian," p. 73. Hubbard in *HIWNE* tells how the defection of the Sakonnets "broke Philip's heart," p. 272. Talcott refers to the Narragansett woman sachem as "that old piece of venom" in a July 4, 1676, letter in *CCR*, vol. 2, pp. 458–59. Hubbard describes the torture of the Narragansett captive in excruciating detail in *HIWNE*, vol. 2, pp. 62–64. William Harris in *A Rhode Islander Reports*, edited by Douglas Leach, writes of Talcott's company: "These Connecticut men capture very many Indians, and kill all they capture except some boys and girls. This so frightens the Indians that they hasten to surrender themselves to Massachusetts, Plymouth, and Rhode Island, where their lives are spared, excepting known notorious murderers," p. 77. James Drake compares the level of violence in the English civil war to that of King Philip's War and how a "victor's justice" began to assert itself at the end of both conflicts in "Restraining Atrocity: The Conduct of King Philip's War," *New England Quarterly*, vol. 70, 1997, pp. 37–38; he also speaks of the lack of rape in King Philip's War, pp. 49–50, and how many Puritans looked to slavery as a humane alternative: "Slavery, in this particular historical context, seemed to many colonists an especially benevolent, and rewarding, alternative to execution," p. 55. Almon Lauber in *Indian Slavery in Colonial Times* cites John Eliot's June 13, 1675, letter to the Massachusetts Bay governor in which he objects to enslaving the Indians, p. 305.

Daniel Gookin in *Doings and Sufferings of the Christian Indians* tells of the Indians' insistence on "a deep silence in their marches and motions" and how they refused to tolerate the sounds made by English shoes and leather pants, p. 442. *New England Begins*, edited by Jonathan Fairbanks and Robert Trent, compares Church's sword (at the MHS) to the weapons of "buccaneers in the Caribbean," pp. 55–56. In his introduction to Church's narrative in *So Dreadfull a Judgment*, Richard Slotkin writes of the nautical aspects of Church's vocabulary: "terms like 'pilot' come more naturally to him then 'guide' or 'scout,' and he speaks of Indians 'tacking about' in battle. Natty Bumppo, who in some ways resembles Church, is wholly a creature of the land and woods; Church still has the smack of salt water," p. 372. Cotton Mather's comparison of Church's accomplishments to "the silly old romances, where the knights do conquer so many giants" is in *HKPW*, p. 197. A transcription of William Bradford's July 24, 1676, letter to John Cotton appears in the January 15, 1876, issue of the *Providence Journal*. Hubbard in *HIWNE* writes of the July 31, 1676, encounter between the Bridgewater militia and the Indians and adds, " '[T]is said that [Philip] had newly cut off his hair, that he might not be known," p. 261. Hubbard also writes of the Indians being forced to kill their own children, p. 276; William Harris in *A Rhode Islander Reports,* edited by Douglas Leach, writes, "The Indians frequently kill their children, partly because they lack food for them. Also the Indians give a reward to a cruel woman among them to kill their children," p. 61. Saltonstall in *OIC* tells of the Indians' arms shaking so badly that they could not fire their weapons, p. 281. In a note to *EPRPW,* Henry Dexter lists Thomas Lucas's long record of public drunkenness, p. 135. Increase Mather in *HKPW* writes of Weetamoo's death and the "diabolical lamentation" of her people when they saw her dissevered head, p. 191. Mather in *HKPW* writes of Sagamore John's execution of Matoonas, p. 185. Samuel Sewall records the hanging deaths of the Nipmuck sachems on Boston Common in his diary, p. 27. The description of Totoson's death is from Church. According to a personal communication from Ella Sekatau, Totoson survived and escaped to Connecticut, and his descendants include Sekatau.

George Langdon in *Pilgrim Colony* compares the percentage casualty rate in World War II to that of Plymouth Colony in King Philip's War, pp. 181–82; my thanks to Michael Hill for providing me with the casualty rate for the Civil War. Sherburne Cook in "Interracial Warfare and Population Decline among the New England Indians," *Ethnohistory,* vol. 20, Winter 1973, provides the statistics concerning the Native American losses during King Philip's War, p. 22. Stephen Webb in *1676: The End of American Independence* writes that "the Anglo-Iroquoian attack on Philip's forces in February 1675/6 had been the decisive action in the war," p. 370. Philip was ahead of his time in recognizing the importance of having a European ally in a war against the English. In *The Dominion of War: Empire and Liberty in North America,* Fred Anderson and Andrew Cayton write, "By the 1720s, nothing could have been clearer than that any [Native] people who wished to defend its autonomy needed a European ally and arms-supplier to do so. In every clash between colonists and natives, from Metacom's War to the destruction of the Yamassees, what weighed decisively in favor of the English colonies was not the martial skill of the militia—which was mostly negligible—but rather that the colonists had the ability to replenish exhausted stocks of arms, ammunition, and food while the Indians—except for those who had a European ally to supply them—did not," p. 88. Increase Mather in *HKPW* claims that during his final night Philip "dreamed that he was fallen into the hands of the English," p. 194. My account of the workings of a flintlock musket are based on the description provided by Patrick Malone in *The Skulking Way of War*, p. 34. The drawing and quartering of notorious rebels was expected in seventeenth-century England; soon after the Restoration, Oliver Cromwell's body was exhumed and then drawn and quartered. The account of how the Plymouth church reaffirmed its covenant on July 18 and Church's arrival with Philip's head on the day of Thanksgiving on August 17 are in *Plymouth Church Records*, vol. 1, pp. 151, 152–53. In his *Magnalia*, Cotton Mather writes of his strange, and telling, response to seeing Philip's head at Plymouth: "[U]pon a certain occasion [I] took off the jaw from the exposed skull of that blasphemous leviathan," p. 197; according to Jill Lepore in *The Name of War*, "By stealing Philip's jawbone, his *mouth*, [Mather] put an end to Philip's blasphemy (literally, his evil utterances)," pp. 174–75. Schultz and Tougias in *King Philip's War* describe the building of the palisade fort at Plymouth during the war and write, "It was on this palisade that Philip's head was set after his death," pp. 125–26. Ebenezer Peirce, who was commissioned by Zerviah Mitchell, a descendant of Massasoit's, to write *Indian History, Biography, and Genealogy*, accuses Benjamin Church of exaggerating his accomplishments in the war, especially when it came to the descent down the rock face prior to capturing Annawon, pp. 207–8. While Annawon's Rock, located in Rehoboth and marked by a plaque (see Schultz and Tougias's *King Philip's War*, p. 131), may not be as steep as Church suggests, an observer only has to imagine the circumstances under which he attempted the descent to appreciate the daring it required. Hubbard in *HIWNE* writes of Annawon's reference to the Praying Indians and the young warriors being the primary causes of the war, as well as his views about "a Great God that overruled all," pp. 277–78. In June 1677, Josiah Winslow sent most of Philip's royalties as a gift to the king of England; in the accompanying letter, he described them as "these few Indian rarities, being the best of the spoils, and best of the ornaments and treasure of sachem Philip the grand rebel, the most of them taken from him by Capt. Benjamin Church (a person of great loyalty and the most successful of our commanders) when he was slain by him; being his crown, his gorge, and two belts of their own making of their gold and silver," in MHS *Proceedings*, 1863–64, p. 481. As Schultz and Tougias relate in *King Philip's War*, the royalties and letter were sent via Winslow's brother-in-law in Essex, England, who appears never to have delivered them to the king. Where the artifacts are now "remains a mystery," p. 140. Hubbard in *HIWNE* claims that Church and his men brought in seven hundred Indians between June and the end of October 1676, and that another three hundred had "come in voluntarily," pp. 272–73.

EPILOGUE—*Conscience*

Almon Lauber in *Indian Slavery in Colonial Times* writes of the departure of Captain Sprague from Plymouth with 178 slaves, as well as the law concerning the removal of all male Indians over fourteen years of age, pp. 125, 145. Jill Lepore in *The Name of War* provides an excellent discussion of slavery in King Philip's War and the controversy surrounding what to do with Philip's son, pp. 150–63. Sherburne Cook in "Interracial Warfare and Population Decline" carefully computes the number of Indians sold into slavery throughout New England and estimates that at least 511 Indians were sold at Plymouth, p. 20. James Drake in *King Philip's War* calculates that while "in 1670 Indians constituted nearly 25 percent of New England's inhabitants, by 1680 they made up only 8–12 percent," p. 169; not only had the Indian population been dramatically reduced by the war, the English population had significantly increased by 1680. Jeremy Bangs in *Indian Deeds* writes of Plymouth's inability to purchase the Mount Hope Peninsula in 1680, p. 184. Stephen Webb in *1676* claims that "Per-capita incomes in New England did not recover their 1675 levels until 1775. They did not exceed this pre-1676 norm until 1815," p. 243. Webb also writes, "[T]he puritan purge of the 'heathen barbarians' from their midst not only externalized but also reinforced the native barrier to New England's growth. A frontier line, between colonists and natives . . . replaced the cellular structure of mixed Indian and colonial villages, and was a far more effective limit on New England expansion. King Philip's War had sapped the physical (and psychic) strength of Puritanism, limited the territorial frontiers of New England, and dramatically reduced the corporate colonies' ability to resist the rising tide of English empire either politically or economically," p. 412. See also T. H. Breen's essay "War, Taxes, and Political Brokers" in *Puritans and Adventurers*. Richard Slotkin in *Regeneration through Violence* writes, "What [the Pilgrims] desired above all was a tabula rasa on which they could inscribe their dream: the outline of an idealized Puritan England," p. 38. Benjamin Church chronicles his five post–King Philip's War expeditions against the French and Indians in the second part of *EPRPW;* see Henry Martyn Dexter's introduction to the second volume, pp. vii–xxxii. Richard Slotkin in his introduction to Church's narrative in *So Dreadfull a Judgment* writes of Church becoming "immensely fat" in old age and needing assistance from two Indian guards, p. 375. In 1718, Church's weight would literally be the death of him when his horse stumbled and threw him over his head; according to an account provided by his descendants, "the colonel being exceeding fat and heavy, fell with such force that a blood vessel was broken, and the blood gushed out of his mouth like a torrent. His wife was soon brought to him; he tried but was unable to speak to her, and died in about twelve hours," quoted in Alan and Mary Simpson's introduction to Church's narrative, pp. 39–41.

For a concise account of the travels of Bradford's manuscript, see Samuel Eliot Morison's introduction in *OPP,* pp. xxvii–xl. On the various editions of Church's narrative, see Dexter's introduction to *EPRPW,* pp. vii–xiv. I have based my account of the legend of Maushop on five different versions collected in William Simmons's *Spirit of the New England Tribes,* pp. 176–91. The earliest, recorded by Benjamin Basset in 1792, was told by the Wampanoag Thomas Cooper, whose Native grandmother had witnessed the arrival of the English on Martha's Vineyard in 1643. The reference to Maushop beating his wife and children comes from an English writer who grew up on Martha's Vineyard in the eighteenth and early nineteenth centuries and heard the legend from his Wampanoag nurse, p. 183. Maushop's disappearance "nobody knew whither" was recorded by James Freeman in 1807, p. 178. I have written about how Native American legends reflect ever-changing historical truths in *Abram's Eyes,* which provides a reading of the Native history of Nantucket through the legends of Maushop, pp. 13–15. On what happened to the Indians of New England after King Philip's War, see Daniel Mandell's *Behind the Frontier: Indians in Eighteenth-Century Eastern Massachusetts* and *After King Philip's War: Presence and Persistence in Indian New England,* edited by Colin Calloway. After 1701, the Sakonnet Indians who had fought with Benjamin Church were granted 190 acres between Sakonnet and Assawompsett, in Mandell, p. 51. The population statistics for the Sakonnets in the eighteenth century come from Benjamin Wilbour's *Notes on Little Compton,* p. 15.

On the travels of Plymouth Rock, see Francis Russell's "The Pilgrims and the Rock," *American Heritage,* October 1962, pp. 48–55. Jill Lepore writes of how the writings of Washington Irving and William Apess and the play *Metamora* reflected changing attitudes toward King Philip's War in *The Name of War,* pp. 186–226. She also cites traditions concerning Massasoit's descendant Simeon Simon during the American Revolution, p. 235. See E. B. Dimock's article about Simon reprinted in the *Narragansett Dawn,* September 1935, pp. 110–11, and cited by Lepore. Records of Simon's service throughout the war are at the National Archives in Washington, D.C. My thanks to Richard Peuser, the supervisory archivist for the Old Military and Civil Records, for bringing these documents to my attention. Ebenezer Peirce, no fan of Benjamin Church, writes gleefully of his traitorous grandson in *Indian History, Biography, and Genealogy* and adds, "Were we a Mather, doubtless we should say, 'thus doth the Lord retaliate,' " p. 162. On the evolution of the myth of the Pilgrims, see James Deetz and Patricia Scott Deetz's *The Times of their Lives,* pp. 10–25; John Seelye's monumental *Memory's Nation: The Place of Plymouth Rock;* and Joseph Conforti's *Imagining New England,* pp. 171–96. James Baker in "Haunted by the Pilgrims" in *The Art and Mystery of Historical Archaeology: Essays in Honor of James Deetz,* edited by Anne Elizabeth Yentsch and Mary C. Beaudry, writes of how it was not until the early twentieth century that the First Thanksgiving "ousted the

Landing and the older patriotic images from the popular consciousness" of the Pilgrims, pp. 350–51. E. J. V. Huiginn in *The Graves of Myles Standish and Other Pilgrims* writes of the 1891 exhumation of Standish's grave, pp. 122–29, 159. My thanks to Carolyn Travers, research manager at Plimoth Plantation, for bringing this source to my attention. The statistics concerning the number of *Mayflower* descendants appear in "Beyond the *Mayflower*" by Cokie Roberts and Steven Roberts in *USA Weekend*, November 22–24, 2002, pp. 8–10. On the influence of Church's narrative on the development of the American literary tradition, see Slotkin's introduction in *So Dreadfull a Judgment*, pp. 386–90, and his *Regeneration through Violence*, pp. 146–79. On the creation and evolution of Plimoth Plantation, see the Deetzes' *The Times of Their Lives*, pp. 273–91. James Deetz claims that the evidence for the Clark garrison being located on the grounds of Plimoth Plantation is "practically conclusive" in "Archaeological Identification of the Site of the Eel River Massacre," an unpublished paper at the Plimoth Plantation Library; my thanks to Carolyn Travers for bringing this document to my attention. In their introduction to Church's narrative, the Simpsons write, "No one was less committed to a war of extermination than Benjamin Church," p. 63. Church writes of Conscience in *EPRPW*, pp. 181–82.

Bibliography

Abbreviations

AAS   American Antiquarian Society. Worcester, Massachusetts
CCR   Colonial Connecticut Records
DSNEF   *The Dublin Seminar for New England Folklife Annual Proceedings,* edited by Peter Benes
MHS   Massachusetts Historical Society
NEHGR   New England Historical Genealogical Register
NEHGS   New England Historic Genealogical Society
NEQ   New England Quarterly
OIC   Old Indian Chronicle, edited by Samuel Drake, 1867.
WMQ   William and Mary Quarterly

Abler, Thomas S. "Scalping, Torture, Cannibalism, and Rape: An Ethnohistorical Analysis of Conflicting Values in War." *Anthropologica* 34 (1992), pp. 3–20.
Abrams, Ann Uhry. *The Pilgrims and Pocahontas: Rival American Myths of American Origins.* Boulder, Col., and Oxford, England: Westview Press, 1999.
Adams, Charles Francis. "Site of the Wessagusset Settlement." MHS Collections, 2nd ser., vol. 7, pp. 22–31.
———. *Three Episodes of Massachusetts History.* 2 vols. Boston: Houghton Mifflin, 1892.
Anderson, Douglas. *William Bradford's Books:* Of Plimmoth Plantation *and the Printed Word.* Baltimore and London: Johns Hopkins University Press, 2003.
Anderson, Fred, and Andrew R. L. Cayton. *The Dominion of War: Empire and Liberty in North America, 1500–2000.* New York: Viking, 2004.
Anderson, R. C. "A 'Mayflower' Model." *Mariners' Mirror* 12 (1926), pp. 260–63.
Anderson, Robert Charles. *The Great Migration Begins: Immigrants to New England, 1620–1633.* Boston: NEHGS, 1995.
———. *The Pilgrim Migration: Immigrants to Plymouth Colony, 1620–1633.* Boston: NEHGS, 2004.
Anderson, Virginia. *Creatures of Empire: How Domestic Animals Transformed Early America.* New York: Oxford University Press, 2004.
———. "King Philip's Herds: Indians, Colonists, and the Problem of Livestock in Early New England." *WMQ.* 3rd ser., 51 (1994), pp. 601–24.
———. *New England's Generation: The Great Migration and the Formation of Society and Culture in the Seventeenth Century.* New York: Cambridge University Press, 1991.
Andrews, K. R., N. P. Canny, and P. E. Hair. *The Westward Enterprise: English Activities in*

Ireland and the Atlantic and America, 1480–1650. Detroit: Wayne State University Press, 1979.

Apess, William. "Eulogy on King Philip, as Pronounced at the Odeon, in Federal Street, Boston (1836)." In *On Our Own Ground: The Complete Writings of William Apess,* edited by Barry O'Connell. Amherst: University of Massachusetts Press, 1992, pp. 275–310.

Appelbaum, Diana K. *Thanksgiving: An American Holiday, an American History.* New York: Facts on File, 1984.

Appleton, William S. "English Ancestry of the Winslow Family." *NEHGR* 21 (July 1867), pp. 209–11.

Arber, Edward, ed. *The Story of the Pilgrim Fathers, 1606–1623.* Boston and New York: Houghton Mifflin, 1897.

Archer, Gabriel, and John Brereton. *The Gosnold Discoveries . . . in the North Part of Virginia, 1602, Now Cape Cod and the Islands, Massachusetts.* Edited by Lincoln A. Dexter. Sturbridge, Mass.: Plaza Printing, 1982.

Arenstam, Peter, John Kemp, and Catherine O'Neill Grace. *Mayflower 1620: A New Look at a Pilgrim Voyage.* Washington, D.C.: National Geographic Society, 2001.

Armitage, David, and Michael J. Braddick, eds. *The British Atlantic World, 1500–1800.* New York: Palgrave Macmillan, 2002.

Armstrong, Starkey. *European and Native American Warfare, 1675–1815.* Norman: University of Oklahoma Press, 1999.

Arner, Robert. "Mythology and the Maypole of Merrymount: Some Notes on Thomas Morton's 'Rise, Oedipus.' " *Early American Literature* 6, no. 2 (1971), pp. 156–64.

———. "Pastoral Celebration and Satire in Thomas Morton's *New English Canaan.*" *Criticism* 16, no. 3 (Summer 1974), pp. 217–31.

———. "Plymouth Rock Revisited: The Landing of the Pilgrim Fathers." *Journal of American Culture* 6, no. 4 (1983), pp. 25–35.

Arnold, Samuel, to John Cotton, September 7, 1676. MHS Collections, 4th ser., vol. 8 (1868), p. 689.

Axtell, James, ed. "The Vengeful Women of Marblehead: Robert Roule's Deposition of 1677." *WMQ,* 3d ser., vol. 31 (1974), pp. 650–52.

———. *The School upon a Hill: Education and Society in Colonial New England.* New Haven: Yale University Press, 1974.

Axtell, James, and William C. Sturtevant. *After Columbus: Essays in the Ethnohistory of Colonial North America.* New York: Oxford University Press, 1988.

———. *Beyond 1492: Encounters in Colonial North America.* Oxford and New York: Oxford University Press, 1992.

———. *The European and the Indian: Essays in the Ethnohistory of Colonial North America.* Oxford and New York: Oxford University Press, 1981.

———. *The Invasion Within: The Contest of Cultures in Colonial North America.* Oxford and New York: Oxford University Press, 1985.

———. "The Unkindest Cut, or Who Invented Scalping?" *WMQ,* 3d ser., vol. 37 (1980), pp. 451–72.

Ayres, Harral. *The Great Trail of New England.* Boston: Meador Publishing, 1940.

Bailyn, Bernard. *The New England Merchants in the Seventeenth Century.* New York: Harper and Row, 1964.

———. *The Peopling of British North America: An Introduction.* New York: Vintage, 1998.

Baker, James W. "As Time Will Serve: The Evolution of Plimoth Plantation's Re-created Architecture." *Old-Time New England* 74, no. 261, pp. 49–74.

————. "Haunted by the Pilgrims." In *The Art and Mystery of Historical Archaeology: Essays in Honor of James Deetz,* edited by Anne Elizabeth Yentsch and Mary C. Beaudry. Boca Raton, Ann Arbor, London, and Tokyo: CRC Press, 1992, pp. 343–58.

————. "Seventeenth Century English Yeoman Foodways at Plimoth Plantation." *DSNEF* 1982, pp. 105–13.

Baker, William A. *The* Mayflower *and Other Colonial Vessels.* London: Conway Maritime Press, 1983.

————. "The *Mayflower* Problem." *American Neptune* 14, no. 1 (January 1954), pp. 5–17.

————. "Some Seventeenth-Century Vessels and the Sparrow-Hawk." *Pilgrim Society Note,* ser. 1, no. 28 (1980).

Bangs, Jeremy Dupertuis. "Commemorating Colonial New England's First Familes: The Triumph of the Pilgrims." In *The Art of Family Genealogical Artifacts in New England,* edited by D. Brenton Simons and Peter Benes. Boston: NEHGS, 2002, pp. 222–44.

————. Foreword in Ralph V. Wood Jr., *Francis Cooke of the* Mayflower. Camden, Maine: Picton Press, 1996.

————. *Indian Deeds: Land Transactions in Plymouth Colony, 1620–1691.* Boston: NEHGS, 2002.

————. Introduction to C. H. Simmons Jr., ed. *Plymouth Colony Records.* Vol 1. Wills and Inventories, 1633–69. Camden, Maine: Picton Press, 1996.

————. "*Mayflower* Passengers Documented in Leiden." *Mayflower Quarterly* 51, no. 2 (May 1985), pp. 57–60.

————. *Pilgrim Edward Winslow: New England's First International Diplomat.* Boston: NEHGS, 2004.

————. *Pilgrim Life in Leiden.* Leiden: Leiden American Pilgrim Museum, 1997.

————. "The Pilgrims and Other English in Leiden Records: Some New Pilgrim Documents." *NEHGR* 143 (July 1989).

————. *The Seventeenth-Century Records of Scituate, Massachusetts.* 3 vols. Boston: NEHGS, 1997, 1999, 2001.

————. "Strangers on the *Mayflower.*" *New England Ancestors* 1 (2000), n. 1, pp. 60–63; no. 2, pp. 35–37.

————. "Towards a Revision of the Pilgrims: Three New Pictures." *NEHGR* 153 (January 1999), pp. 3–28.

————. "William Williamson, the Englishman." *New England Ancestors* 4 (2003), pp. 55–56, 59.

Banks, Charles E. "The Officers and Crew of the *Mayflower,* 1620–21." MHS *Proceedings* 60 (April 1927), pp. 210–21.

————. "William Mullins and Giles Heale." MHS *Proceedings* 60 (1927), pp. 144–50.

Banks, Charles E., and Samuel Eliot Morison. *The English Ancestry and Homes of the Pilgrim Fathers.* Baltimore: Geneological Publishing, 1980.

————. Exchange about Leyden in MHS *Proceedings* 61. (1928).

————. "Thomas Morton." MHS *Proceedings* 58, pp. 147–86.

Barbour, Philip L. "Notes on Anglo-Algonkian Contacts, 1605–1624." In *Papers of the Sixth Algonquian Conference, 1974,* edited by William Cowan. Carleton University, Mercury Series, no. 23 (Ottawa, 1975), pp. 112–127.

Barnes, Viola. *The Dominion of New England: A Study in British Colonial Policy.* New Haven: Yale University Press, 1923.

Basset, Benjamin. "Fabulous Traditions and Customs of the Indians." MHS Collections, vol. 1 (1792).

Batten, Benjamin, to Sir John Allin, June 29, 1675, and July 6, 1675. Gay Transcripts, Plymouth Papers, vol. 1, pp. 39–46, MHS.

Baylies, Francis. *An Historical Memoir of the Colony of New Plymouth. Vol. 1—Part the First. From 1620 to 1641; Volume 2—Parts II, III, IV.* Boston: Hilliard, Gray, Little, and Wilkins. 1830.

Baxter, James Phinney, ed. *Sir Ferdinand Gorges and His Province of Maine.* 3 vols. Boston, 1890.

Beale, David. *The* Mayflower *Pilgrims: Roots of Puritan, Presbyterian, Congregationalist, and Baptist Heritage.* Greenville, S.C., and Belfast, Ireland: Ambassador Emerald International, 2002.

Beck, Horace P. *Gluskap the Liar and Other Indian Tales.* Freeport, Maine: Bond Wheelwright, 1966.

Behrens, Pene. *Footnotes: A Biography of Penelope Pelham.* Montville, Maine: Spentpenny Press, 1998.

Bendremer, Jeffrey C., and Robert E. Dewar. "The Advent of Prehistoric Maize in New England." In *Corn and Culture in the Prehistoric New World,* edited by Sissel Johansessen and Christine A. Hastorf. Boulder, Colo.: Westview Press, 1994, pp. 369–94.

Benedict, Philip. *Christ's Churches Purely Reformed: A Social History of Calvinism.* New Haven and London: Yale University Press, 2002.

Benes, Peter. "Psalmody in Coastal Massachusetts and in the Connecticut River Valley." *DSNEF* 1981, pp. 117–31.

———. "Sleeping Arrangements in Early Massachusetts: The Newbury Household of Henry Lunt, Hatter." *DSNEF* 1987, pp. 140–52.

Bennett, Edmund H. "Historical Address." In *Quarter Millennial Celebration of the City of Taunton.* Taunton, Mass.: City Government, 1889.

Bennett, M. K. "The Food Economy of the New England Indians, 1605–75." *Journal of Political Economy* 63, no. 5 (October 1955), pp. 369–97.

Bercovitch, Sacvan. *The American Jeremiad.* Madison: University of Wisconsin Press, 1978.

———. *The Puritan Origins of the American Self.* New Haven: Yale University Press, 1975.

Bicknell, Thomas Williams. *Sowams, with Ancient Records of Sowams and Parts Adjacent.* New Haven: Associated Publishers of American Records, 1908.

Bierhorst, John. "American Indian Verbal Art and the Role of the Literary Critic." *Journal of American Folklore* 70 (1957), pp. 1–24.

Bliss, Leonard, and George H. Tilton. *The History of Rehoboth.* Boston: Otis, Broaders, 1836.

Boast, Mary. *The* Mayflower *and Pilgrim Story: Chapters from Rotherhithe and Southwark.* London: Council of the London Borough of Southwark, 1973.

Bodge, G. M. *Soldiers of King Philip's War.* 1906; rprt. Baltimore: Genealogical Publishing, 1967.

Boissevain, Ethel. "Whatever Became of the New England Indians Shipped to Bermuda to Be Sold as Slaves?" *Man in the Northeast* 21 (1981).

Bond, C. Lawrence. *Native Names of New England Towns and Villages.* Reading, Mass.: Self-Published, 2000.

Boorstin, Daniel J. *Hidden History.* New York: Harper and Row, 1987.

Borden, John. Remarks on Philip in Theodore Foster, "Materials for a History of Rhode Island." *Collections of the Rhode Island Historical Society* 7 (1885).

Bourne, Russell. *The Red King's Rebellion: Racial Politics in New England, 1675–1678.* New York and Oxford: Oxford University Press, 1991.

Bowden, Henry W., and James P. Ronda, eds. *John Eliot's Indian Dialogues: A Study in Cultural Interaction.* Westport, Conn.: Greenwood Press, 1980.

Bowman, George Ernest. "A Genuine *Mayflower* Relic." *Mayflower Descendant* 34, no. 1 (January 1937), pp. 1–7.

———. "Governor William Bradford's First Wife Dorothy (May) Bradford Did Not Commit Suicide." *Mayflower Descendant* 29, no. 3 (1931), pp. 97–102, 31, no. 3 (1933), p. 105.

———. "Why Did Only Forty-one Passengers Sign the Compact?" *Mayflower Descendant* vol. 22, no. 2 (1920), pp. 58–59.

———. "The Will of William Mullins." *Mayflower Descendant* 1 (1899), pp. 230–31.

Bozeman, Theodore Dwight. "The Puritans' 'Errand into the Wilderness' Reconsidered." *NEQ* 59 (1986), pp. 231–51.

———. *To Live Ancient Lives: The Primitivist Dimension in Puritanism.* Chapel Hill: University of North Carolina Press, 1988.

Brachlow, Stephen. "John Robinson and the Lure of Separatism in Pre-Revolutionary England." *Church History* 50 (1981), pp. 293–301.

———. "More Light on John Robinson and the Separatist Tradition." *Fides et Historia* 13 (1980), pp. 6–22.

Bradford, E. F. "Conscious Art in Bradford's History." *NEQ* 1 (1928), pp. 133–57.

Bradford, William. "A Dialogue or 1st Conference." Plymouth Church Records, 1620–1859. *Publications of the Colonial Society of Massachusetts,* vol. 22, Boston: Colonial Society of Massachusetts, 1920.

———. "A Dialogue or 3rd Conference." Proceedings of the Massachusetts Historical Society, vol. 11. Boston: MHS, 1870, pp. 396–482.

———. *Letter Book.* Bedford, Mass.: Applewood Books, 2001.

———. "A Letter of William Bradford and Isaac Allerton, 1623." *American Historical Review* 8, pp. 294–301.

———. Letters to John Winthrop. MHS Collections, 4th series, vol. 6 (1863), pp. 156–61.

———. Miscellaneous Letters. *Mayflower Descendant* 9 (January 1907), p. 1; MHS Collections, 4th series, vol. 6 (1863), p. 156.

———. *Of Plymouth Plantation.* Edited by Worthington Chauncey Ford. Boston: MHS, 1912.

———. *Of Plymouth Plantation, 1620–1647.* Edited by Samuel Eliot Morison. New York: Knopf, 1970.

———. "Verse History." MHS Collections, ser. 2, vol. 1 (1794), pp. 82–83.

———. "Winslow Letter, 1623." *NEHGR* 109 (October 1955), pp. 242–43.

Bradford, William, Jr., to John Cotton, July 21, 1675. Providence: Society of Colonial Wars, 1914.

——— to John Cotton. July 24, 1676. *Providence Journal,* January 15, 1876.

Bragdon, Kathleen J. " 'Emphaticall Speech and Great Action': An Analysis of Seventeenth-Century Native Speech Events Described in Early Sources." *Man in the Northeast* 33 (1987), p. 101–11.

———. *Native People of Southern New England, 1500–1650.* Norman and London: University of Oklahoma Press, 1996.

Breen, T. H. "Persistent Localism: English Social Change and the Shaping of New England Institutions." *WMQ,* 3d ser., vol. 32 (1975), pp. 3–28.

Breen, T. H., and Stephen Foster. *Puritans and Adventurers: Change and Persistence in Early America.* New York: Oxford University Press, 1980.

Bremer, Francis J. "Endecott and the Red Cross: Puritan Iconoclasm in the New World." Journal of American Studies 24 (1990), pp. 5–22.

———. *The Puritan Experiment: New England Society from Bradford to Edwards.* Hanover, N.H.: University Press of New England, 1995.

Brenner, Elise. "Sociopolitical Implications of Mortuary Remains in 17th-Century Native Southern New England." In *The Recovery of Meaning: Historical Archaeology in the Eastern United States,* edited by Mark P. Leone and Parker B. Potter. Washington, D.C.: Smithsonian Institution Press, 1988, pp. 147–81.

———. "To Pray or to Be Prey: That is the Question; Strategies for Cultural Autonomy of Massachusetts Praying Town Indians." *Ethnohistory* 27 (Spring 1980), p. 135–52.

Breugelman, Ronald, ed. *The Pilgrim Press: A Bibliographical and Historical Memorial.* Nieuwkoop, Netherlands: De Graaf, 1992.

Brewster, Nathaniel, to unknown, July 12, 1675, Winthrop Papers, MHS.

Bridenbaugh, Carl. *Fat Mutton and Liberty of Conscience: Society in Rhode Island, 1636–1690.* Providence: Brown University Press, 1974.

Bridge, John. "Letters of John Bridge and Emmanuel Altham." MHS *Proceedings,* ser. 3, vol. 44 (1910), pp. 178–89.

Briggs, Rose T. *Plymouth Rock: History and Significance.* Boston: Nimrod Press, Pilgrim Society, 1968.

Brown, John, to Josiah Winslow, June 11, 1675, Winslow Papers, MHS.

Bumsted, J. M. *The Pilgrim's Progress: The Ecclesiastical History of the Old Colony, 1620–1775.* New York: Garland, 1989.

Burgess, George Canning. "Thomas Willett." *NEHGR* 61, pp. 157–64.

Burgess, Walter H. *John Robinson, Pastor of the Pilgrim Fathers.* London: Williams and Norgate, 1920.

Bushman, Richard L. *From Puritan to Yankee: Character and the Social Order in Connecticut, 1690–1765.* Cambridge, Mass.: Harvard University Press, 1967.

Butler, Eva M., and Wendell S. Hadlock. "Dogs of the Northeastern Woodland Indians." *Bulletin of the Massachusetts Archaeological Society* 10 (1949), pp. 17–35.

———. "The Treatment of the Indians in Plymouth Colony." *NEQ* 26 (1953), pp. 193–218.

Butler, Jon. *Awash in a Sea of Faith: Christianizing the American People.* Cambridge, Mass.: Harvard University Press, 1990.

———. "Magic, Astrology, and the Early American Religious Heritage, 1600–1760." *American Historical Review* 84 (1979), pp. 317–46.

Caffrey, Kate. *The Mayflower.* New York: Stein and Day, 1974.

Callender, John. *An Historical Discourse, on the Civil and Religious Affairs of the Colony of Rhode Island.* 1739; rev. ed. Providence, 1839.

Calloway, Colin G. "The Abenakis and the Anglo-French Borderlands." *DSNEF* 1989, pp. 18–27.

———, ed. *After King Philip's War: Presence and Persistence in Indian New England.* Hanover, N.H.: University Press of New England, 1997.

———. *Dawnland Encounters: Indians and Europeans in Northern New England.* Hanover, N.H., and London: University Press of New England, 1991.

———. "Rhode Island Renegade: The Enigma of Joshua Tift." *Rhode Island History* 43 (1984), pp. 137–45.

———. "Wanalancet and Kancagamus: Indian Strategy and Leadership on the New Hampshire Frontier." *Historical New Hampshire* 43 (Winter 1988), pp. 264–80.

Calloway, Colin G., and Neal Salisbury, eds. *Reinterpreting New England Indians and the Colonial Experience.* Boston: Colonial Society of Massachusetts, 2004.

Candee, Richard. "A Documentary History of Plymouth Colony Architecture 1620–1700." *Old-Time New England* 59, 3, pp. 59–111.

Canny, Nicholas. *Making Ireland British, 1580–1650.* New York: Oxford University Press, 2001.

Canup, John. *Out of the Wilderness: The Emergence of an American Identity in Colonial New England.* Middletown, Conn.: Wesleyan University Press, 1990.

Carson, Cary, et al. "Impermanent Architecture in the Southern American Colonies." *Winterthur Portfolio* 16, nos. 2/3 (1981), pp. 135–96.

Cave, Alfred A. "Indian Shamans and English Witches in Seventeenth-Century New England." *Essex Institute Historical Collections* 128 (1992), pp. 239–54.

———. *The Pequot War.* Amherst: University of Massachusetts Press, 1996.

Chamberlain, Barbara Blau. *These Fragile Outposts: A Geological Look at Cape Cod, Martha's Vineyard, and Nantucket.* Garden City, N.Y.: Natural History Press, 1964.

Chaplin, Joyce. *Subject Matter: Technology, the Body, and Science on the Anglo-American Frontier, 1500–1676.* Cambridge, Mass.: Harvard University Press, 2001.

Charleton, Warwick. *The Second* Mayflower *Adventure.* Boston: Little, Brown, 1957.

Cheetham, J. Keith. *On the Trail of the Pilgrim Fathers.* Edinburgh: Luath Press, 2001.

Chet, Guy. *Conquering the American Wilderness: The Triumph of European Warfare in the Colonial Northeast.* Amherst: University of Massachusetts Press, 2003.

Church, Benjamin. *Diary of King Philip's War.* Edited by Alan and Mary Simpson. Chester, Conn.: Pequot Press, 1975.

———. *Entertaining Passages Relating to Philip's War.* Edited by Henry Martyn Dexter. Boston: John Kimball Wiggin, 1865.

Clap, Roger. Memoirs. *In Collections of the Dorchester Antiquarian and Historical Society,* vol. 1. Boston, 1844.

Cline, Duane A. "Christopher Jones: Master of the *Mayflower.*" *Mayflower Quarterly* 61 (1995), p. 94.

———. "The *Mayflower.*" *The Mayflower Quarterly* 61 (1995), pp. 92–94.

Cogley, Richard W. "John Eliot and the Millennium." *Religion and American Culture* 1 (1991), pp. 227–50.

———. *John Eliot's Mission to the Indians before King Philip's War.* Cambridge, Mass., and London: Harvard University Press, 1999.

———. "Two Approaches to Indian Conversion in Puritan New England: The Missions of Thomas Mayhew, Jr., and John Eliot." *Historical Journal of Massachusetts* 28 (1995), pp. 44–60.

Cohen, Charles. *God's Caress: The Psychology of Puritan Religious Experience.* New York: Oxford University Press, 1989.

Coldham, Peter Wilson. "Thomas Weston, Ironmonger of London and America, 1609–1647." *Genealogical Society Quarterly* 62, no. 3 (September 1974), pp. 163–72.

Cole, Hugh. Deposition from March 1671. MHS Collections, ser. 1, vol. 6 (1799).

Collinson, Patrick. *Godly People: Essays on English Protestantism and Puritanism.* London: Hambeldon Press, 1983.

———. *The Religion of Protestants: The Church in English Society, 1559–1625.* Oxford: Clarendon Press, 1982.

Conforti, Joseph A. *Imagining New England: Explorations of Regional Identity from the Pilgrims to the Mid-Twentieth Century.* Chapel Hill and London: University of North Carolina Press, 2001.

Connole, Dennis A. *The Indians of the Nipmuck Country in Southern New England, 1630-1750: An Historical Geography.* Jefferson, N.C., and London: McFarland, 2001.

Connors, Donald F. *Thomas Morton.* New York: Twayne, 1969.

Cook, Sherburne F. *The Indian Population of New England in the Seventeenth Century.* Berkeley: University of California Press, 1976.

———. "Interracial Warfare and Population Decline among the New England Indians." *Ethnohistory* 20 (Winter 1973), pp. 1–24.

———. "The Significance of Disease in the Extinction of the New England Indians." *Human Biology* 45 (1973), pp. 485–508.

Cooper, Winifred. *Harwich, the* Mayflower, *and Christopher Jones.* London: Phillimore, 1970.

Cotton, John, Jr., to Increase Mather, March 20, 1676/77. Mather Papers, MHS Collections, 4th ser., vol. 8 (1868), pp. 233–34.

———. Plymouth Church Records. In *Publications of the Colonial Society of Massachusetts* 222 (1920), pp. 152–53.

Cousins, Rodney. *Lincolnshire Buildings in the Mud and Stud Tradition.* Sleaford, Lincolnshire: Heritage, 2000.

Covey, Cyclone. *The Gentle Radical: A Biography of Roger Williams.* New York: Macmillan, 1966.

Cranmer, Leon E. *Cushnoc: The History and Archaeology of Plymouth Colony Traders on the Kennebec.* Augusta: Maine Historical Preservation Commission, 1990.

Cressy, David. *Coming Over: Migration and Communication between England and New England in the Seventeenth Century.* Cambridge, England: Cambridge University Press, 1987.

Cronon, William. *Changes in the Land: Indians, Colonists, and the Ecology of New England.* New York: Hill and Wang, 1983.

Cronon, William, and Richard White. "Indians in the Land." American Heritage 37 (1986), pp. 18-25.

Crosby, Alfred W. *Ecological Imperialism: The Biological Expansion of Europe, 900–1900.* Cambridge, England: Cambridge University Press, 1986.

———. "God . . . Would Destroy Them, and Give Their Country to Another People . . ." *American Heritage* 29, no. 6 (1978), pp. 38–43.

———. "Virgin Soil Epidemics as a Factor in the Aboriginal Depopulation in America." *WMQ* 3d ser., vol. 23 (1976), pp. 289–99.

Crosby, Constance A. "From Myth to History, or Why King Philip's Ghost Walks Abroad." In *The Recovery of Meaning: Historical Archaeology in the Eastern United States,* edited by Mark P. Leone and Parker B. Potter Jr. Washington, D.C.: Smithsonian Institution Press, 1988, pp. 183–209.

Cuckson, John. *The First Church in Plymouth, 1610–1901.* Boston: Beacon Press, 1920.

Cudworth, James, to Josiah Winslow, July 20, 1675, MHS Collections, 1st ser., vol. 6 (1799), p. 84.

Cummings, Abbott Lowell. *The Framed Houses of Masschusetts Bay, 1625–1725.* Cambridge, Mass.: Harvard University Press, 1979.

Cummins, John. *The Hound and the Hawk: The Art of Medieval Hunting.* London: Phoenix Press, 1988.

Curry, Patrick. *Prophecy and Power: Astrology in Early Modern England.* Princeton, N.J.: Princeton University Press, 1989.

Curtin, Ted, and James W. Baker. *Mayflower II: Plimoth Plantation.* Little Compton: Fort Church Publishers, 1993.

Dalton, George. "The Impact of Colonization on Aboriginal Economies in Stateless Societies." *Research in Economic Anthropology* 1 (1978), pp. 131–84.

Daly, Robert. "William Bradford's Vision of History." *American Literature* 44 (1973).

Davies, Horton. *Worship and Theology in England from Andrews to Baxter and Fox, 1603–1690.* Princeton, N.J.: Princeton University Press, 1975.

———. *Worship and Theology in England from Cranmer to Hooker, 1534–1603.* Princeton, N.J.: Princeton University Press, 1970.

———. *The Worship and Theology of the American Puritans.* Morgan, Pa.: Soli Deo Gloria, 1999.

Davis, Jack L. "Roger Williams among the Narragansett Indians." *NEQ* 43 (1970), pp. 593–604.

[Davis, Samuel]. "Notes on Plymouth, Mass." Article 20. MHS Collections, 2d ser., vol. 3 Boston, 1815. Reprinted, Boston, 1846.

Davis, William T. *Ancient Landmarks of Plymouth: Part 1. Historical Sketch and Titles of Estates; Part 2. Genealogical Register of Plymouth Families.* Boston: A. Williams, 1883.

———, ed. *Records of the Town of Plymouth.* Vol. 1, 1636–1705. Plymouth, Mass.: Avery and Doten, 1889.

Days, Gordon M. "English-Indian Contacts in New England." *Ethnohistory* 9 (1962), pp. 24–40.

———. "The Identity of the Sokokis." *Ethnohistory* 12 (1965), pp. 237–49.

———. "The Ouragie War: A Case History in Iroquois–New England Indian Relations." In *Extending the Rafters: Interdisciplinary Approaches to Iroquoian Studies,* edited by Michael K. Foster et al. Albany: State University of New York Press, 1984, pp. 35–50.

Dayton, Cornelia Hughes. *Women before the Bar: Gender, Law, and Society in Connecticut, 1639–1789.* Chapel Hill: University of North Carolina Press, 1995.

Deane, Charles. Letter in MHS *Proceedings 1866–7,* pp. 345–46.

Deane, Samuel. *History of Scituate, Massachusetts.* Boston: James Loring, 1831; reprt. Scituate Historical Society, 1975.

De Costa, B. F. "Stephen Hopkins of the Mayflower." *NEHGR* 133 (July 1879), pp. 300–305.

Deetz, James. *Flowerdew Hundred.* Charlottesville: University Press of Virginia, 1993.

———. *In Small Things Forgotten.* Garden City, N.Y., 1977.

———. "Archaeological Identification of the Site of the Eel River Massacre." Undated 3-page report in archives of Plimoth Plantation.

Deetz, James, and Jay Anderson. "The Ethnogastronomy of Thanksgiving." *Saturday Review of Science* 55 (December 1972), pp. 29–38.

Deetz, James, and Patricia Scott Deetz. *The Times of Their Lives: Life, Love, and Death in Plymouth Colony.* New York: W. H. Freeman, 2000.

DeGering, Etta. *Christopher Jones: Captain of the* Mayflower. New York: David McKay, 1965.

Delabarre, Edmund Burke. *Dighton Rock: A Study of the Written Rocks of New England.* New York: Walter Neale, 1920.

Delbanco, Andrew. *The Puritan Ordeal.* Cambridge, Mass.: Harvard University Press, 1989.

Demos, John. "Demography and Psychology in the Historical Study of Family-Life: A Personal Report." In *Household and Family in Past Time,* edited by Peter Laslett and Richard Wall. Cambridge, England: Cambridge University Press, 1972.

———. *A Little Commonwealth: Family Life in Plymouth Colony.* London, Oxford, and New York: Oxford University Press, 1970.

———. "Notes on Life in Plymouth Colony." *WMQ,* 3d ser., vol. 22 (1965), pp. 264–86.

Denevan, W. M. "The Pristine Myth: The Landscape of the Americas in 1492." Annals of the Association of American Geographers 82 (1992), pp. 369–85.

Derounian-Stodola, Kathryn Zabelle. "The Publication, Promotion, and Distribution of Mary Rowlandson's Indian Captivity Narrative in the Seventeenth Century." *Early American Literature* 23 (1988), pp. 240–43.

———. "Puritan Orthodoxy and the 'Survivor Syndrome' in Mary Rowlandson's Captivity Narrative." *Early American Literature* 22 (1987), pp. 83–84.

———. *Women's Indian Captivity Narratives*. New York: Penguin, 1998.

Dexter, Henry Martyn, and Morton Dexter. *The England and Holland of the Pilgrims*. 1905; reprt. Baltimore: Genealogical Publishing, 1978.

Diamond, Jared. *Collapse: How Societies Choose to Fail or Succeed*. New York: Viking, 2005.

———. *Guns, Germs, and Steel: The Fates of Human Societies*. New York and London: Norton, 1997.

Dillon, Francis. *The Pilgrims: Their Journeys and Their Worlds*. Garden City, N.Y.: Doubleday, 1975.

DiLorenzo, Thomas. *How Capitalism Saved America: The Untold History of Our Country, from the Pilgrims to the Present*. New York: Crown Forum, 2004.

Dimock, E. B. "The Story of Simons from an Old Newspaper." *Narragansett Dawn* 1, no. 5 (September 1935), pp. 110–11.

Dolby, Malcolm. *William Bradford of Austerfield*. Doncaster, Nottinghamshire: Doncaster Library and Information Services, 1991.

Donagan, Barbara. "Atrocity, War Crime, and Treason in the English Civil War." *American Historical Review* 99 (October 1994), pp. 1137–66.

———. "Codes and Conduct in the English Civil War." *Past and Present* 118 (1988), pp. 65–95.

———. "Halcyon Days and the Literature of War: England's Military Education before 1642." *Past and Present* 147 (May 1995), pp. 65–100.

Dow, George Francis. *Everyday Life in the Massachusetts Bay Colony*. New York: Dover, 1988.

Doyle, John. *An Introduction to the History of Plimoth Plantation by Bradford*. Boston: Houghton Mifflin, 1896.

Drake, James. *King Philip's War: Civil War in New England, 1675–1676*. Amherst: University of Massachusetts Press, 1999.

———. "Restraining Atrocity: The Conduct of King Philip's War." *New England Quarterly* 70 (1997), pp. 33–56.

———. "Symbol of a Failed Strategy: The Sassamon Trial, Political Culture, and the Outbreak of King Philip's War." *American Indian Culture and Research Journal* 19 (1995), pp. 111–41.

Drake, Samuel H. G. S. *Biography and History of the Indians of North America*. Boston, 1837.

———, ed. *Early History of New England*. Boston: printed for the editor, 1864.

———, ed. *The History of the Indian Wars in New England*. 2 vols. 1865; rprt. Bowie, Md.: Heritage Books, 1990.

———. *The Old Indian Chronicle*. Boston: Drake, 1867.

Dudley, Joseph. Letter to unknown, December 21, 1675, *NEHGR* 40 (1886), p. 89.

Dunn, Jerome P. "Squanto before He Met the Pilgrims." *Bulletin of the Massachusetts Archaeological Society* (Spring 1993), pp. 38–42.

Durston, Christopher, and Jacqueline Eales. *The Culture of English Puritanism, 1560–1700*. New York: St. Martins, 1996.

Earle, Alice Morse. *The Sabbath in Puritan New England*. London: Hodder and Stoughton, 1982.

Eastman, John. *The Book of Swamp and Bog*. Mechanicsburg, Pa.: Stackpole Books, 1995.

Easton, John. "A Relacion of the Indyan Warre." In *Narratives of the Indian Wars, 1675–1699*, edited by Charles H. Lincoln. New York: Scribner's, 1913.

Egleston, Melville. *The Land System of the New England Colonies*. Baltimore: N. Murray for Johns Hopkins University, 1886.

Eliot, John. "An Account of Indian Churches in New England in 1673." MHS Collections, 1st ser., vol. 10, pp. 124–34.

———. Letter to John Endicott, March 28, 1661, MHS *Proceedings* 3 (1855–58), pp. 312–13.

———. Letter to Robert Boyle, October 23, 1677. MHS Collections, 1st ser., vol. 3 (1794), p. 178.

———. Letter to Robert Boyle, 1683, MHS Collections, 1st ser., vol. 3 (1794), p. 183.

Ellis, George W., and John E. Morris. *King Philip's War.* New York: Grafton Press, 1906.

Erickson, Paul. *Daily Life in the Pilgrim Colony, 1636.* New York: Clarion Books, 2001.

Fairbanks, Jonathan, and Robert Trent, eds. *New England Begins: The Seventeenth Century.* 3 vols. Boston: Boston Museum of Fine Arts, 1982.

Fenn, W. W. "John Robinson's Farewell Address." *Harvard Theological Review* 13 (1920), pp. 236–51.

Ferling, John E. *A Wilderness of Miseries: War and Warriors in Early America.* Westport, Conn.: Greenwood Press, 1980.

Fischer, David Hackett. *Albion's Seed: Four British Folkways in America.* New York and Oxford: Oxford University Press, 1989.

Fleming, Thomas J. *One Small Candle: The Pilgrims' First Year in America.* New York: Norton, 1964.

Ford, W. C. "Captain Wollaston, Humphrey Rasdell, and Thomas Weston." MHS *Proceedings* 51, pp. 219–32.

Foreman, Carolyn. *Indians Abroad, 1493–1938.* Norman: Oklahoma University Press, 1943.

Forman, Charles C. "John Robinson: Exponent of the Middle Way." *Proceedings of the Unitarian Historical Society* 17 (1972–75), pp. 22–29.

Foster, Stephen. *The Long Argument: English Puritanism and the Shaping of New England Culture, 1570–1700.* Chapel Hill: University of North Carolina Press, 1991.

Franklin, Wayne. *Discoverers, Explorers, Settlers: The Diligent Writers of Early America.* Chicago and London: University of Chicago Press, 1979.

Freeman, John. Letter to Josiah Winslow, July 3, 1675, Winslow Papers, MHS.

Freeman, Michael. "Puritans and Pequots: The Question of Genocide." *NEQ* 68 (June 1995), pp. 278–93.

Friederici, Georg. *Scalping and Torture: Warfare Practices among North American Indians.* Ohsweken, Ontario: Irocrafts, 1993.

Gay, Peter. *A Loss of Mastery: Puritan Historians in Colonial New England.* Berkeley: University of California Press, 1966.

George, Timothy. *John Robinson and the English Separatist Tradition.* Macon, Ga.: Mercer University Press, 1982.

Gibson, Susan G., ed. *Burr's Hill.* Providence: Brown University, 1980.

Gill, Crispin. Mayflower *Remembered: A History of the Plymouth Pilgrims.* New York: Taplinger, 1970.

———. *Plymouth: A New History.* Plymouth, Mass.: Newton Abbot, 1966.

Gilpin, W. Clark. *The Millenarian Piety of Roger Williams.* Chicago: University of Chicago Press, 1979.

Godbeer, Richard. *The Devil's Dominion: Magic and Religion in Early New England.* Cambridge, England: Cambridge University Press, 1992.

Goddard, Ives. "The Use of Pidgins and Jargons on the East Coast of North America." In *The Language Encounter in the Americas,* edited by Edward Gray and Norman Fiering. Oxford: Berghahn Books, 2001.

Goddard, Ives, and Kathleen J. Bragdon. *Native Writings in Massachusett.* Philadelphia: American Philosophical Society, 1988.

Gomes, Peter. "Darlings of Heaven: The Pilgrims and their Myths." *Harvard Magazine,* November 1976, pp. 29–36.

———. "Pilgrims and Puritans: 'Heroes' and 'Villains' in the Creation of the American Past." *Proceedings* of the MHS 95 (1983), pp. 1–16.

———. *The Pilgrim Society 1820–1920: An Informal Commemorative Essay.* Plymouth, Mass: Pilgrim Society, 1971.

Gookin, Daniel. *An Historical Account of the Doings and Sufferings of the Christian Indians in New England, in the Years 1675–1677.* 1836; Rprt. New York: Arno Press, 1972.

———. *Historical Collections of the Indians in New England.* Boston: Belknap and Hall, 1792.

———. Letter to Captain Joseph Syll, November 2, 1675, *NEHGR* 41 (1887), p. 403.

Gorges, Sir Fernando. *The Province of Maine.* 3 vols. Edited by James P. Dexter. Boston: Prince Society, 1890.

Gorton, Samuel. Letter to John Winthrop Jr., September 11, 1675, MHS Collections, 4th ser., vol. 7 (1865); p. 627.

Grabo, Norman S. "William Bradford: Of Plymouth Plantation." In *Landmarks of American Writing,* edited by Hennig Cohen. New York: Basic, 1969.

Grace, Catherine O'Neill, and Margaret M. Bruchac. *1621: A New Look at Thanksgiving.* Washington, D.C.: National Geographic Society, 2001.

Grand, W. L., ed. *Voyages of Samuel de Champlain, 1604–1618.* New York: Scribner's, 1907.

Greene, David L. "New Light on Mary Rowlandson." *Early America Literature* 20 (1986), pp. 24–38.

Greene, Welcome Arnold. "The Great Battle of the Narragansetts, Dec. 19, 1675." *Narragansett Historical Register* 5, no. 4 (December 1887), pp. 331–43.

Grenier, John. *The First Way of War: American War Making on the Frontier.* New York: Cambridge University Press, 2005.

Greven, Philip J. "Family Structure in Seventeenth Century Andover, Massachusetts." *WMQ,* 3rd ser., vol. 23 no. 2, pp. 234–56.

———. *Four Generations: Population, Land, and Family in Colonial Andover, Massachusetts.* Ithaca, N.Y.: Cornell Press, 1970.

Grinberg, Leon, and Rebecca Grinberg. *Psychoanalytic Perspectives on Migration and Exile.* New Haven and London: Yale University Press, 1989.

Grumet, Robert S. *Historic Contact: Indian People and Colonists in Today's Northeastern United States in the Sixteenth through Eighteenth Centuries.* Norman and London: University of Oklahoma Press, 1995.

———. ed. *Northeastern Indian Lives, 1632–1816.* Amherst: University of Massachusetts Press, 1996.

Gura, Philip. *A Glimpse of Sion's Glory: Puritan Radicalism in New England, 1620–1660.* Middletown, Conn.: Wesleyan University Press, 1984.

Hadlock, Wendell S. "War among the Northeastern Woodland Indians." *American Anthropologist* 49 (1947), pp. 204–21.

Hagedorn, Nancy L. " 'A Friend to Go between Them': The Interpreter as Cultural Broker during Anglo-Iroquois Councils, 1740–70." *Ethnohistory* 35 (1998), pp. 60–80.

Hakluyt, Richard. *Discourse of Western Planting.* Ed. David B. Quinn and Alison M. Quinn. London: Hakluyt Society, 1993.

———. *The Principal Navigations, Voyages, Traffiques, and Discoveries of the English Nation.* Ed. Irwin R. Blacker. New York: Viking, 1965.

Hall, David D. *Worlds of Wonder, Days of Judgment: Popular Religious Belief in Early New England.* Cambridge, Mass.: Harvard University Press, 1989.

Hall, David D., and David Grayson Allen, eds. *Seventeenth-Century New England.* Boston: Colonial Society of Massachusetts, 1984.

Haller, William. *The Elect Nation: The Meaning and Relevance of Foxe's "Book of Martyrs."* New York: Harper and Row, 1963.

———. *The Rise of Puritanism.* New York: Columbia University Press, 1938.

Hamell, George R. "Strawberries, Floating Islands, and Rabbit Captains: Mythical Realties and European Contact in the Northeast during the Sixteenth and Seventeenth Centuries." *Journal of Canadian Studies* (February 1987), pp. 72–93.

Hannan, Christopher. "Indian Land in Seventeenth-Century Massachusetts." *Historical Journal of Massachusetts* 29, no. 2 (Summer 2001), pp. 115–36.

Harris, Donald F. "The More Children of the *Mayflower:* Their Shropshire Origins and the Reasons Why They Were Sent Away." *Mayflower Descendant* 43, pp. 123–32; 44, pp. 11–20, 109–18.

Harris, William. Letter to Sir Joseph Williamson, August 12, 1676, as edited and transcribed by Douglas Leach. In *A Rhode Islander Reports on King Philip's War: The Second William Harris Letter of August, 1676.* Providence: Rhode Island Historical Society, 1963.

Harrison, William. *The Description of England.* Ed. George Edely. Ithaca, N.Y.: Cornell University Press, 1968.

Haskins, George L. "The Legal Heritage of Plymouth Colony." In *Essays in the History of Early American Law,* edited by David H. Flaherty. Chapel Hill: University of North Carolina Press, 1969, pp. 121–34.

Hauptman, Laurence M. "The Pequot War and Its Legacies." In *The Pequots in Southern New England,* edited by Laurence M. Hauptman and James D. Wherry. Norman and London: University of Oklahoma Press, 1993.

Hauptman, Laurence M., and James D. Wherry. *The Pequots in Southern New England: The Fall and Rise of an American Indian Nation.* Norman and London: University of Oklahoma Press, 1993.

Hayward, Kendall Payne. "The Adventure of Stephen Hopkins." *Mayflower Quarterly* 51, no. 1 (February 1985), pp. 5–9.

Heath, Dwight B., ed. *Mourt's Relation: A Journal of the Pilgrims at Plymouth.* Cambridge and Boston, Mass.: Applewood Books, 1986.

Heaton, Vernon. *The* Mayflower. New York: Mayflower Books, 1980.

Hill, Christopher. *God's Englishman: Oliver Cromwell and the English Revolution.* New York: Harper, 1970.

———. *The World Turned Upside Down: Radical Ideas during the English Revolution.* New York: Viking, 1978.

Hinckley, Thomas. "The Hinckley Papers." MHS Collections, 4th ser., vol. 5 (1861).

Hirsh, Adam J. "The Collision of Military Cultures in Seventeenth-Century New England." *Journal of American History* 74 (1987–88), pp. 1187–1212.

Hodges, Margaret. *Hopkins of the* Mayflower. New York: Farrar, Straus & Giroux, 1972.

Hoffer, Peter Charles. *Sensory Worlds in Early America.* Baltimore: Johns Hopkins University Press, 2004.

Hollingsworth, Harry. "John Alden—Beer Brewer of Windsor?" *American Genealogist* 53, no. 3 (July 1977), pp. 235–40.

Holly, H. Hobart. "Wollaston of Mount Wollaston." *American Neptune* 32, no. 1 (January 1977), pp. 5–25.

Hooker, Samuel. Letter to Increase Mather, MHS Collections, 4th ser., vol. 8 (1868), p. 337.

Horner, George R. "Massasoit and His Sons: Wamsutta and Metacom." *Bulletin of the Massachusetts Archaeological Society* 56 (Spring 1995), pp. 20–22.

Horowitz, David. *The First Frontier: The Indian Wars and America's Origins: 1607–1776.* New York: Simon and Schuster, 1978.

Horrocks, J. W. "The 'Mayflower.' " *Mariner's Mirror* 8 (1922–23), pp. 2–9, 81–88, 140–47, 237–45, 354–62.

Hough, Franklin B., ed. *A Narrative of the Causes Which Led to Philip's Indian War . . . with Other Documents.* Albany, N.Y.: Munsell, 1858.

Howard, Alan B. "Art and History in Bradford's *Of Plymouth Planation.*" *WMQ,* 3rd ser., 28 (1971), pp. 237–66.

Howe, George. *Mount Hope: A New England Chronicle.* New York: Viking, 1959.

———. "The Tragedy of King Philip." *American Heritage* 10, no. 1 (December 1958), pp. 65–80.

Howe, Henry. *Salt Rivers of the Massachusetts Shore.* New York: Rinehart, 1951.

Hubbard, William. *General History of New England.* New York: Arno Press, 1972.

———. *The Present State of New-England Being a Narrative of the Troubles with the Indians.* 1676; rprt. Bainbridge, N.Y.: York Mail, 1972.

Huiginn, E. J. V. *The Graves of Miles Standish and other Pilgrims.* Beverly, Mass.: Huiginn, 1914.

Hull, John. Letter to Philip French, September 2, 1675, John Hull's Letterbook, AAS.

Hume, Ivor Noel. *A Guide to Artifacts of Colonial America.* Philadelphia: University of Pennsylvania Press, 1969.

Humins, John H. "Squanto and Massasoit: A Struggle for Power." *NEQ* 60, no. 1, pp. 54–70.

Hutchinson, J. R. "The 'Mayflower,' Her Identity and Tonnage." *NEHGR* 70 (October 1916), pp. 337–42.

Hutchinson, Thomas. *The History of the Colony and Province of Massachusetts-Bay.* Cambridge, Mass.: Harvard University Press, 1936.

Ingersol, George. Letter to Leif Augur, September 10, 1675, *NEHGR* 8 (1854), p. 239.

Innes, Stephen. *Creating the Commonwealth: The Economic Culture of Puritan New England.* New York, Norton, 1995.

———. *Labor in a New Land: Economy and Society in Seventeenth-Century Springfield.* Princeton, N.J.: Princeton University Press, 1983.

Israel, Jonathan. *The Dutch Republic: Its Rise, Greatness, and Fall, 1477–1806.* Oxford: Clarendon Press, 1998.

Jacob, Richard. Letter to unknown, April 22, 1676, *NEHGR* 40 (1886), pp. 391–92.

James, Sidney V., ed. *Three Visitors to Early Plymouth.* Bedford, Mass.: Applewood Books, 1997.

Jameson, J. Franklin, ed. *Narratives of New Netherland, 1609–1664.* New York: Scribner's, 1909.

Jennings, Francis. *The Invasion of America: Indians, Colonialism, and the Cant of Conquest.* New York: Norton, 1976.

Johnson, Caleb H. "The True Origin of Stephen Hopkins of the *Mayflower.*" *The American Genealogist* 73, no. 3 (July 1998), pp. 161–71.

———, ed. *The Complete Works of the* Mayflower *Pilgrims.* Vancouver, Wash.: Caleb and Anna Johnson, 2003.

Johnson, Edward. *Wonder Working Providence, 1628–1651.* Ed. J. Franklin Jameson. 1910; rprt. New York: Elibron Classics, 2002.

Johnson, Eric S. *"Some by Flatteries and Others by Threatenings": Political Strategies among Native Americans of Seventeenth-Century Southern New England.* Ph.D. diss., University of Massachusetts, 1993.

———. "Uncas and the Politics of Contact." In *Northeastern Indian Lives, 1632–1816,* edited by Robert S. Grumet. Amherst: University of Massachusetts Press, 1996, pp. 29–47.

Johnson, Richard R. "The Search for a Usable Indian: An Aspect of the Defense of Colonial New England." *Journal of American History* 64, no. 4 (1977), pp. 628–31.

Jones, Althea. *A Thousand Years of the English Parish.* London: Windrush Press, 2001.

Jones, David S. "Virgin Soils Revisited." *WMQ,* 3rd ser., 60 (Oct. 2003), pp. 703–42.

Jones, Matt B. "The Early Massachusetts-Bay Colony Seals." AAS *Proceedings* 44 (1935), p. 13.

Jorgensen, Neil. *A Sierra Club Naturalist's Guide to Southern New England.* San Francisco: Sierra Club Books, 1978.

Josselyn, John. *Colonial Traveler: A Critical Edition of Two Voyages to New-England.* Ed. Paul J. Lindholdt. Hanover, N.H.: University Press of New England, 1988.

Jourdain, Silvester. "A Discovery of the Bermudas, Otherwise Called the Isle of Devils." In *A Voyage to Virginia in 1609,* edited by Louis B. Wright. Charlottesville: University of Virginia, 1964.

Kardux, Joke, and Edward van de Bitl. *Newcomers in an Old City: The American Pilgrims in Leiden, 1609–1620.* Leiden: Uitgeverig Burgers dijk and Neirmans, 1998.

Karr, Ronald Dale. " 'Why Should You Be So Furious?': The Violence of the Pequot War." *Journal of American History* 85 (1998), pp. 876–909.

Karttunen, Frances. *Between Two Worlds: Interpreters, Guides, and Survivors.* New Brunswick, N.J.: Rutgers University Press, 1994.

Katz, Steven T. "The Pequot War Reconsidered." *NEQ* 64 (June 1991), pp. 206–24.

Kawashima, Yasuhide. *Igniting King Philip's War: The John Sassamon Murder Trial.* Lawrence: University Press of Kansas, 2001.

———. *Puritan Justice and the Indian: White Man's Law in Massachusetts, 1630–1763.* Middletown, Conn.: Wesleyan University Press, 1986.

Keegan, John. *A History of Warfare.* New York: Knopf, 1993.

Keeley, Lawrence H. *War before Civilization.* New York: Oxford University Press, 1996.

Keith, James. Letter to John Cotton, October 30, 1676, Davis Papers, MHS.

Kellaway, William. *The New England Company, 1649–1776: Missionary Society to the American Indians.* New York: Barnes and Noble, 1961.

Kellogg, Robert. "Oral Literature." *New Literary History* 5 (1973), pp. 55–66.

Kingsley, John. Letter to Connecticut War Council, May 5, 1676, CCR, vol. 2, p. 445.

Kinnicutt, Lincoln. "The Plymouth Settlement and Tisquantum." MHS *Proceedings,* 3rd ser., vol. 48, pp. 103–18.

Kirk-Smith, Harold. *William Brewster: The Father of New England.* Boston and Lincolnshire, England: Richard Kay, 1992.

Knowles, Nathaniel. "The Torture of Captives by the Indians of Eastern North America." *American Philosophical Society Proceedings* 82 (1940), pp. 151–225.

Kolb, Avery. "The Tempest." *American Heritage* 34, no. 3 (April–May 1983), pp. 26–35.

Krech, Shepard, ed. *Indians, Animals, and the Fur Trade: A Critique of 'Keepers of the Game.'* Athens: University of Georgia Press, 1981.

Krim, Arthur J. "Acculturation of the New England Landscape: Native and English Toponymy of Eastern Massachusetts." *DSNEF* 1980, pp. 69–88.

Krusell, Cynthia Hagar, *The Winslows of Careswell.* Marshfield, Mass.: Historical Research Associates, 1992.

Kupperman, Karen Ordahl, ed. *America in European Consciousness, 1493–1750.* Chapel Hill: University of North Carolina Press, 1995.

———. "Apathy and Death in Early Jamestown." *Journal of American History* 66 (June–September 1979), pp. 24–40.

———. "English Perceptions of Treachery, 1583–1640: The Case of the American 'Savages.' " *Historical Journal* 20 (1977), pp. 163–87.

———. "The Founding Years of Virginia—and the United States." *Virginia Magazine of History and Biography* 104 (1996), pp. 103–12.

———. *Indians and English: Facing Off in Early America.* Ithaca, N.Y., and London: Cornell University Press, 2000.

———. *Providence Island, 1630–1641: The Other Puritan Colony.* New York: Cambridge University Press, 1993.

———. "The Puzzle of the American Climate in the Early Colonial Period." *American Historical Review* 87 (1982), pp. 1262–89.

———. *Settling with the Indians: The Meeting of England and Indian Cultures in America, 1580–1640.* Totowa, N.J.: Rowman and Littlefield, 1980.

———. "Thomas Morton, Historian." *NEQ* 50 (1977), pp. 660–64.

Langdon, George D., Jr. "The Franchise and Political Democracy in Plymouth Colony." *WMQ,* 3d ser., vol. 20 (1963), pp. 513–26.

———. *Pilgrim Colony: A History of New Plymouth, 1620–1691.* New Haven, Conn.: Yale University Press, 1966.

Larsen, Clark Spencer, and George R. Milner, eds. *In the Wake of Contact: Biological Responses to Conquest.* New York: Wiley-Liss, 1994.

Lauber, Almon Wheeler. *Indian Slavery in Colonial Times within the Present Limits of the United States.* 1913; rprt. New York: AMS Press, 1969.

Leach, Douglas Edward. "Benjamin Batten and the London Gazette." *NEQ* 36 (1963), pp. 502–17.

———. *Flintlock and Tomahawk: New England in King Philip's War.* 1958. Rprt. East Orleans, Mass.: Parnassus Imprints, 1992.

———. "The Military System of Plymouth Colony." *NEQ* 24 (1951), pp. 342–64.

———, ed. *A Rhode Islander Reports on King Philip's War.* Providence: Rhode Island Historical Society, 1963.

———. "The 'When's' of Mary Rowlandson's Captivity." *NEQ* 34 (1961), pp. 353–63.

Leduc, Michael R. "The Religious Foundation of Democracy." *Pilgrim Society Notes,* ser. 2, September 1996.

Leete, William. Letter to John Winthrop Jr., September 21, 1675, MHS Collections, 4th ser., vol. 7 (1865), pp. 577–78.

Lepore, Jill. "Dead Men Tell No Tales: John Sassamon and the Fatal Consequences of Literacy." *American Quarterly* 46 (1994), p. 494.

———. *The Name of War: King Philip's War and the Origins of American Identity.* New York: Knopf, 1998.

Leverland, B. N. "Geographic Origins of the Pilgrims." In *The Pilgrims in the Netherlands: Recent Research,* edited by Jeremy D. Bangs. Leiden: Pilgrim Documents, Center of the Leiden Municipal Archives, 1985.

Levin, David. "William Bradford: The Value of Puritan Historiography." In *Major Writers in Early American Literature,* edited by Everett Emerson. Madison, Wis., 1972.

Lincoln, Charles H., ed. *Narratives of the Indian Wars, 1675–1699.* New York: Scribner's, 1913.

Lindsay, David. *Mayflower Bastard: A Stranger among the Pilgrims.* New York: St. Martin's Press, 2002.

Linscott, Elisabeth. "The Mayflower Letters, Part 1." *History Today* 20, no. 8 (1970), pp. 543–49.

Lodge, Elizabeth A. " 'Cattle of every kind do fill the land': Historical Recreation of Farm Animals and Animal Husbandry Practices of 1627 New Plymouth." *DSNEF* 1993, pp. 191–204.

Lombard, Percival Hall. *The Aptucxet Trading Post.* Bourne, Mass.: Bourne Historical Society, 1934.

———. "The Seal of the Plymouth Colony." *Mayflower Descendant* 29 (January 1931), pp. 1–9.

Lonkhuyzen, Harold van. "A Reappraisal of the Praying Indians: Acculturation, Conversion, and Identity at Natick, Massachusetts, 1646–1720." *NEQ* 63 (1990), p. 417.

Lovejoy, David S. *Religious Enthusiasm in the New World.* Cambridge, Mass.: Harvard University Press, 1985.

Lowenthal, David. *The Past Is a Foreign Country.* New York: Cambridge University. Press, 1985.

MacCulloch, Diarmaid. *The Reformation: A History.* New York: Viking, 2004.

Main, Gloria L. *Peoples of a Spacious Land: Families and Culture in Colonial New England.* Cambridge, Mass.: Harvard University Press, 2001.

Major, Minor Wallace. *Thomas Morton and His* New English Canaan. Ph.D. diss., University of Colorado, 1957.

———. "William Bradford versus Thomas Morton." *Early American Literature* 5 (Fall 1970), pp. 1–13.

Malone, Patrick M. "Changing Military Technology among the Indians of Southern New England, 1600–1677." *American Quarterly* 25 (1973), pp. 48–63.

———. *The Skulking Way of War: Technology and Tactics among the New England Indians.* Baltimore: Johns Hopkins University Press, 1993.

Mancall, Peter. C *Deadly Medicine: Indians and Alcohol in Early America.* Ithaca, N.Y.: Cornell University Press, 1995.

Marcombe, David. *English Small Town Life: Retford, 1520–1642.* Oxford: Alden Press, 1993.

Markham, Richard. *A Narrative History of King Philip's War and the Indian Troubles in New England.* New York: Dodd, Mead, 1883.

Marsden, R. G. "The 'Mayflower.' " *English Historical Review* 19 (October 1904), pp. 669–80; reprinted in *Mayflower Descendant* 18, pp. 1–13.

Marshall, Joshua Micah. "Melancholy People: Anglo-Indian Relations in Early Warwick, Rhode Island, 1642–1675." *NEQ* (September 1995), pp. 402–28.

Marten, Catherine. "The Wampanoags in the Seventeenth Century: An Ethnohistorical Study." *Occasional Papers in Old Colony Studies* no. 2 (December 1970), pp. 1–40.

Martin, Calvin, ed. *The American Indian and the Problem of History.* Oxford and New York, Oxford University Press, 1987.

———. "Ethnohistory: A Better Way to Write Indian History." *Western Historical Quarterly* 11 (1978), pp. 41–56.

———. "The European Impact on the Culture of a Northeastern Algonquian Tribe: An Ecological Interpretation." *WMQ*, 3d ser., vol. 31 (1974), pp. 17–24.

———. *Keepers of the Game: Indian-Animal Relationships and the Fur Trade.* Berkeley: University of California Press, 1978.

Martin, John Frederick. *Profits in the Wilderness: Entrepreneurship and the Founding of New*

England Towns in the Seventeenth Century. Chapel Hill and London: University of North Carolina Press, 1991.

Martin, Terence. *Parables of Possibility: The American Need for Beginnings.* New York: Columbia University Press, 1995.

Masefield, John, ed. *Chronicles of the Pilgrim Fathers, 1606–1623.* London: Dent, 1910.

Massachusetts Council to Josiah Winslow, April 21, 1676, *NEHGR* 41 (1887), pp. 400–401.

Mather, Cotton. *Magnalia Christi Americana; or, The Ecclesiastical History of New England.* Books 1 and 2. Ed. Kenneth B. Murdock. Cambridge, Mass.: Belknap Press, 1977.

Mather, Cotton. *Magnalia Christi Americana: or, The Ecclesiastical History of New England.* Ed. Thomas Robbins. 2 vols. New York: Russell and Russell, 1967.

Mather, Increase. *The History of King Philip's War.* Ed. Samuel Drake. Boston: Munsell, 1862.

———. Letter to John Cotton, October 20, 1676, MHS Collections, 4th ser., vol. 8 (1868), p. 689.

Matthews, Albert. "The Term Pilgrim Fathers and Early Celebrations of Forefathers' Day." Colonial Society of Massachusetts *Publications* 17, pp. 293–391.

Maverick, Samuel. *A Brief Description of New England and the Several Towns Therein.* MHS *Proceedings,* 2d ser., vol. 1 (1884–85), pp. 231–49.

———. Letter to Earl of Clarendon. 1661. *New York Historical Society Collections* 2, 1869, pp. 40–41.

Maxwell, Richard Howland. "Pilgrim and Puritan: A Delicate Distinction." Pilgrim Society Note, ser. 2, March 2003.

———. "Religious Controversies in Plymouth Colony." Pilgrim Society Note, ser. 2, June 1996.

McCullough, John, and Elaine York. "Relatedness and Mortality in a Crisis Year: Plymouth Colony, 1620–21." *Ethology and Sociobiology,* no. 12 (1991), pp. 195–209.

———. "Relatedness and Kin Structured Migration in a Founding Population: Plymouth Colony, 1620–1633." *Human Biology* 63, no. 3, pp. 355-66.

McDougall, Walter A. *Freedom Just around the Corner.* New York: HarperCollins, 2005.

McGiffert, Michael. "Religion and Profit Do Jump Together: The First American Pilgrim." *Reflections* 87, pp. 15–23.

McIntyre, Ruth A. *Debts Hopeful and Desperate: Financing the Plymouth Colony.* Plymouth, Mass.: Plimoth Plantation, 1963.

McPhee, John. "Travels of the Rock." *New Yorker,* February 26, 1990, pp. 108–17.

McWilliams, John P., Jr. "Fictions of Merrymount." *American Quarterly* 29 (1977), pp. 3–30.

Memicho, George. Testimony. Reprinted in *History of North Brookfield* by J. H. Temple. North Brookfield, Mass., 1887, pp. 100–110.

Merchant, Carolyn. *Ecological Revolutions: Nature, Gender, and Science in New England.* Chapel Hill: University of North Carolina Press, 1980.

Meyer, Isidore S. "The Hebrew Preface to Bradford's History." American Jewish Historical Society *Publications,* no. 38, part 4 (June 1949), pp. 289-303.

Miller, Christopher I., and George R. Hamell. "A New Perspective on Indian-White Contact: Cultural Symbols and Colonial Trade." *Journal of American History* 73 (1986), pp. 311–28.

Miller, David C. *Dark Eden: The Swamp in Nineteenth-Century American Culture.* Cambridge, England: Cambridge University Press, 1989.

Miller, Lee. *Roanoke: Solving the Mystery of the Lost Colony.* New York: Penguin, 2002.

Miller, Perry. *Errand into the Wilderness.* Cambridge, Mass.: Harvard University Press, 1956.

———. *The New England Mind: From Colony to Province.* Cambridge, Mass.: Harvard University Press, 1953.

————. *Orthodoxy in Massachusetts, 1630–1650.* Cambridge, Mass.: Harvard University Press: 1933.

Miner, Kenneth. "John Eliot of Massachusetts and the Beginnings of American Linguistics." *Historiographical Linguistica* 1 (1974).

Moody, Joseph. Letter to John Cotton, May 1, 1676, Curwen Papers, AAS.

Morgan, Edmund S. *American Slavery, American Freedom: The Ordeal of Colonial Virginia.* New York: Norton, 1975.

————. "The Puritans and Sex." *NEQ* 15 (1942), pp. 591–607.

————. *Roger Williams: The Church and the State.* New York: Harcourt Brace, 1967.

————. *Visible Saints: The History of a Puritan Idea.* New York: New York University Press, 1963.

Morison, Samuel Eliot. *Builders of the Bay Colony.* Boston: Northeastern University Press, 1981.

————. *The European Discovery of America: The Northern Voyages A.D. 500 to A.D. 1600.* New York: Oxford University Press, 1971.

————. *Harvard in the Seventeenth Century.* Cambridge, Mass.: Harvard University Press, 1936.

————. "New Light Wanted on the Old Colony." *WMQ,* 3d ser., vol. 15 (July 1958), pp. 359–64.

————. "The Pilgrim Fathers: Their Significance in History; Why Are the Pilgrim Fathers Significant?" *By Land and by Sea: Essays and Addresses by Samuel Eliot Morison.* New York: Knopf, 1953.

————. "The Plymouth Colony and Virginia." *Virginia Magazine of History and Biography* 42 (1954), pp. 147–65.

————. "Plymouth Colony Beachhead." *United States Naval Institute Proceedings* 80 (December 1954), pp. 1344–57.

————. *The Story of the 'Old Colony' of New Plymouth, 1620–1692.* New York: Knopf, 1960.

————. "The Witch and We, the People." *American Heritage* 34 (1983), pp. 6–11.

Morrison, Kenneth M. "Mapping Otherness: Myth and the Study of Cultural Encounter." In *American Beginnings: Exploration, Culture, and Cartography in the Land of Norumbega.* Edited by Emerson Woods Baker II, Edwin A. Churchill, Richard D'Abate, et al. Lincoln: University of Nebraska Press, 1994.

Morton, Nathaniel. *New-England's Memorial.* 1669. Rprt., Boston: Congregational Board of Publication, 1855.

Morton, Thomas. *New English Cannan.* 1637. Reprint edited by Jack Dempsey. Scituate, Mass.: Digital Scanning, 2000.

Moseley, Samuel. Letter to John Leverett, August 16, 1675, *NEHGR* 37 (1883), pp. 177–79.

Moynihan, Ruth Barnes. "The Patent and the Indians: The Problem of Jurisdiction in Seventeenth-Century New England." *American Indian Culture and Research Journal* 2, no. 1 (1977), pp. 8–18.

Muir, Diana. *Reflections in Bullough's Pond: Economy and Ecosystem in New England.* Hanover, N.H., and London: University Press of New England, 2000.

Muldoon, James. "The Indian as Irishman." *Essex Institute Historical Collections* 3 (October 1975), pp. 267–89.

Murdock, Kenneth B. "William Hubbard and the Providential Interpretation of History." *AAS Proceedings,* new ser., vol. 52 (1942), pp. 34–35.

Murrin, John M. "Beneficiaries of Catastrophe: The English Colonies in America." In *The New American History,* edited by Eric Foner. Philadelphia: Temple University Press, 1990, pp. 3–23.

————. "Magistrates, Sinners, and a Precarious Liberty: Trial by Jury in Seventeenth-Century New England." In *Saints and Revolutionaries: Essays on Early American History,* edited by David D. Hall, John M. Murrin, and Thad Tate. New York: Norton, 1984, pp. 152–206.

————. " 'Things Fearful to Name': Beastiality in Early America." In *The Animal Human Boundary,* edited by Angela N. H. Creager and William Chester Jordan. Rochester, N.Y.: University of Rochester Press, 2002, pp. 115–56.

Nabokov, Peter. *Native American Architecture.* New York: Oxford University Press, 1989.

Naeher, Robert. "Dialogue in the Wilderness: John Eliot and the Indian Exploration of Puritanism as a Source of Meaning, Comfort, and Ethnic Survival." *NEQ* (September 1989), pp. 346–68.

Nanepashemet. "It Smells Fishy to Me: An Argument Supporting the Use of Fish Fertilizer by the Native People of Southern New England." *DSNEF* 1991, pp. 42–50.

Nash, Gary. *Red, White, and Black: The Peoples of Early North America.* Englewood Cliffs, N.J.: Prentice-Hall, 1992.

Nash, Roderick. *Wilderness and the American Mind.* New Haven and London: Yale University Press, 1967.

Navin, John. *Plymouth Plantation: The Search for Community on the New England Frontier.* PhD. diss., Brandeis University, 1997.

Nelsen, Anne Kuesner. "King Philip's War and the Hubbard-Mather Rivalry." *WMQ* 27 (1976), pp. 615–29.

Newall, Margaret Ellen. "The Changing Nature of Indian Slavery in New England, 1670–1720." In *Reinterpreting New England Indians and the Colonial Experience,* edited by Colin Calloway and Neal Salisbury, Boston: Colonial Society of Massachusetts, 2004, pp. 106–36.

Newman, Noah. Letters Written during King Philip's War. Curwen Papers, AAS.

Nickerson, W. Sears. *Early Encounters: Native Americans and Europeans in New England.* Ed. Delores Bird Carpenter. East Lansing: Michigan State University Press, 1994.

————. *Land Ho!—1620: A Seaman's Story of the Mayflower, Her Construction, Her Navigation, and Her First Landfall.* Boston: Houghton Mifflin, 1931.

Nicolson, Adam. *God's Secretaries: The Making of the King James Bible.* New York: Harper-Collins, 2003.

Occum, Sampson. "Account of the Montauk Indians, 1761." Collections of the MHS, 1st ser., vol. 10 (1809), pp. 106–11.

Oldale, Robert N. *Cape Cod, Martha's Vineyard, and Nantucket: The Geologic Story.* Yarmouth Port, Mass.: On Cape Publications, 2001.

Oliver, James. Letter to unknown, January 26, 1676, *NEHGR* 39 (1885), p. 380.

Pafford, John M. *How Firm a Foundation: William Bradford and Plymouth.* Bowie, Md.: Heritage Books, 2002.

Pearce, Roy Harvey. *Savagism and Civilization: A Study of the Indian and the American Mind.* Berkeley: University of California Press, 1988.

————. "The Significances of the Captivity Narrative." *American Literature* 19 (1947), pp. 1–20.

Peirce, Ebenezer W. *Indian History, Biography, and Genealogy, Pertaining to the Good Sachem Massasoit of the Wampanoag Tribe and His Descendants.* North Abington, Mass.: Zerviah Gould Mitchel, 1878.

————. *Peirce's Colonial Lists.* 1881; reprt. Baltimore: Genealogical Publishing, 1968.

Penhallow, Samuel. *The History of the Wars of New-England.* Cincinnati: William Dodge, 1859; reprt. New York: Kraus Reprint, 1969.

Peterson, Mark A. "The Plymouth Church." *NEQ* 66 (1993), pp. 570–93.

Peterson, H. L. *Arms and Armor of the Pilgrims.* Plymouth, Mass.: Plimoth Plantation and the Pilgrim Society, 1957.

———. "The Military Equipment of the Plymouth and Bay Colonies: 1620–1690." *NEQ* 20 (1947), pp. 197–208.

Philbrick, Nathaniel. *Abram's Eyes: The Native American Legacy of Nantucket Island.* Nantucket, Mass.: Mill Hill Press, 1998.

———. *Away Off Shore: Nantucket Island and Its People, 1602–1890.* Nantucket, Mass.: Mill Hill Press, 1994.

Philip, King. "A Letter from King Philip to Governour Prince," n.d. MHS Collections, 1st ser., vol. 2 (1793), p. 40.

———. "Sachem Philip, His Answer to the Letter Brought to Him from the Governor of New-Plymouth." MHS Collections, 1st ser., vol. 6 (1799), p. 94.

Plane, Ann Marie. "Putting a Face on Colonization: Factionalism and Gender Politics in the Life History of Awashunkes, the 'Squaw Sachem' of Saconet." In *Northeastern Indian Lives, 1632–1816,* edited by Robert Grumet, Amherst: University of Massachusetts, 1996, pp. 140–65.

Plooij, D., and J. R. Harris, eds. *Leyden Documents Relating to the Pilgrim Fathers.* Leiden: E. J. Brill, 1920.

———. *The Pilgrim Fathers from a Dutch Point of View.* New York: New York University Press, 1932.

Pope, Charles Henry, ed. *The Plymouth Scrap Book.* Boston: C. E. Goodspeed, 1918.

Pope, Robert G. "New England versus the New England Mind: The Myth of Declension." *Journal of Social History* 3 (1969–70), pp. 95–108.

Porter, H. C. *The Inconstant Savage: England and the North American Indian, 1500–1660.* London: Duckworth, 1979.

Powicke, F. J. "John Robinson and the Beginnings of the Pilgrim Movement." *Harvard Theological Review* 13 (1920), pp. 252–89.

Pratt, Phineas. *A Declaration of the Affairs of the English People That First Inhabited New England.* 1662. MHS Collections, 4th ser., vol. 4, 1858, pp. 474–91.

Pray, Mary. Letter to James Oliver, October 20, 1675, MHS Collections, 5th ser., vol. 1, p. 105.

Prince, Thomas. *A Chronological History of New England, in the Form of Annals. Bibliotheca Curiosa.* 1753; rprt. Edinburgh, Scotland: Privately printed, 1887.

Puglisi, Michael J. *Puritans Beseiged: The Legacies of King Philip's War in the Massachusetts Bay Colony.* New York: University Press of America, 1991.

Pulsipher, Jenny Hale. "Massacre at Hurtleberry Hill: Christian Indians and English Authority in Metacom's War." *WMQ,* 3rd ser., vol. 53, no. 3 (July 1996), pp. 459–86.

———. *Subjects unto the Same King: Indians, English, and the Contest for Authority in Colonial New England.* Philadelphia: University of Pennsylvania Press, 2005.

Quanapohit, James. "Testimony, January, 1676." Reprinted in *History of North Brookfield* by J. H. Temple, pp. 112–18.

Quinn, David Beers. *England and the Discovery of America, 1481–1620.* New York: Knopf, 1974.

———. *The English New England Voyages, 1602–1608.* London: Hakluyt Society, 1983.

Rackham, Oliver. "Grundle House: On the Quantities of Timber in Certain East Anglian Buildings in Relation to Local Supplies." *Vernacular Architecture* 3 (1972), pp. 3–8.

Ranlet, Philip. "Another Look at the Causes of King Philip's War." *NEQ* 61 (1988), pp. 79–100.

Rath, Richard Cullen. *How Early America Sounded.* Ithaca, N.Y., and London: Cornell University Press, 2003.

Rawson, Edward. Letter to Josiah Winslow, August 20, 1676, Winslow Papers, MHS.

Richter, Daniel K. *Facing East from Indian Country: A Native History of Early America.* Cambridge, Mass.: Harvard University Press, 2001.

———. "War and Culture: The Iroquois Experience." *WMQ,* 3d ser., vol. 40 (1983), pp. 530–34.

———. "Whose Indian History?" *WMQ,* 3rd ser., vol. 50 (1993), pp. 379–93.

Robinson, Paul A. "Lost Opportunities: Miantonomi and the English in Seventeenth-Century Narragansett Country." In *Northeastern Indian Lives, 1632–1816,* edited by Robert S. Grumet. Amherst: University of Massachusetts Press, 1996, pp. 13–28.

Romani, Daniel A. Jr. " 'Our English Clover-grass sowen thrives very well': The Importance of English Grasses and Forages in Seventeenth-Century New England." *DSNEF* 1995, pp. 25–37.

Ronda, James P. "Red and White at the Bench: Indians and the Law in Plymouth Colony, 1620–91." *Essex Institute Historical Collections* 110 (1974), pp. 200–215.

———. " 'We Are Well as We Are': An Indian Critique of Seventeenth-Century Christian Missions." *WMQ,* 3d ser., vol. 34 (1977), pp. 66–82.

Ronda, James P., and Jeanne Ronda. "The Death of John Sassamon: An Exploration in Writing New England History." *American Indian Quarterly* 1 (1974), pp. 91–102.

Rosenmeier, Jesper. "With My Own Eyes: William Bradford's *Of Plymouth Plantation.*" In *Typology and Early American Literature,* edited by Sacvan Bercovitch. Amherst: University of Massachusetts Press, 1972, pp. 69–105.

Rowlandson, Mary. *The Sovereignty and Goodness of God . . . , Being a Narrative of the Captivity and Restoration of Mrs. Mary Rowlandson.* Edited by Neal Salisbury. Boston: Bedford Books, 1997.

Roy, Ian. "England Turned Germany? The Aftermath of the Civil War in Its European Context." *Transactions of the Royal Historical Society,* 5th ser., vol. 28 (1978), pp. 127–44.

Rubertone, Patricia E. *Grave Undertakings: An Archaeology of Roger Williams and the Narragansett Indians.* Washington and London: Smithsonian Institution Press, 2001.

Russell, Francis. "The Pilgrims and the Rock." *American Heritage* 13, no. 6 (1962), pp. 48–55.

Russell, Howard S. *Indian New England before the* Mayflower. Hanover, N.H., and London: University Press of New England, 1980.

———. *A Long, Deep Furrow: Three Centuries of Farming in New England.* Hanover, N.H., and London: University Press of New England, 1982.

Rutman, Darrett B. *Husbandmen of Plymouth: Farms and Villages in the Old Colony, 1620–1692.* Boston: Beacon Press, 1967.

———. *Winthrop's Boston: Portrait of a Puritan Town, 1630–1649.* Chapel Hill: University of North Carolina Press, 1965.

Sainsbury, John A. "Indian Labor in Early Rhode Island." *NEQ* 48 (September 1975), pp. 378–93.

———. "Miantonomo's Death and New England Politics, 1630–1645." *Rhode Island History* 30, no. 4 (1971), pp. 111–23.

Salisbury, Neal. "Indians and Colonists in Southern New England after the Pequot War: An Uneasy Balance." In *The Pequots in Southern New England,* edited by Laurence M.

Hauptman and James D. Wherry. Norman and London: University of Oklahoma Press, 1993, pp. 81–95.

———. "The Indians' Old World: Native Americans and the Coming of Europeans." *WMQ,* 3d ser., vol. 53 (1996), pp. 435–58.

———. *Manitou and Providence: Indians, Europeans, and the Making of New England, 1500–1643.* New York and Oxford: Oxford University Press, 1982.

———. "Red Puritans: The 'Praying Indians' of Massachusetts Bay and John Eliot." *WMQ,* 3d ser., vol. 31 (1974), pp. 27–54.

———. "Social Relationships on a Moving Frontier: Natives and Settlers in Southern New England, 1638–75." *Man in the Northeast* 33 (1987), pp. 89–99.

———. "Squanto: Last of the Patuxets." In *Struggle and Survival in Colonial America,* edited by David Sweet and Gary Nash. Berkeley: University of California Press, 1981, pp. 228–46.

———. "Toward the Covenant Chain: Iroquois and Southern New England Algonquians, 1637–1684." In *Beyond the Covenant Chain: The Iroquois and Their Neighbors in Indian North America, 1600–1800,* edited by Daniel Richter and James Merrell. Syracuse, N.Y.: Syracuse University Press, 1987, pp. 61–73.

Saltonstall, Nathaniel. "A Continuation of the State of New England." *OIC,* pp. 171–205.

———. "A New and Farther Narrative of the State of New England." *OIC,* pp. 207–46.

———. "The Present State of New England with Respect to the Indian War." 1675. *OIC,* pp. 119–70.

Sanborn, V. C. "Pickering vs. Weston, 1623." MHS *Proceedings* 54, pp. 165–78.

Sanders, Tobias. Letter to Fitz-John Winthrop, July 3, 1675, Winthrop Papers, MHS Collections, 5th ser., vol. 1 (1871), pp. 426–27.

Sargent, Mark L. "William Bradford's 'Dialogue' with History." *NEQ* 65 (September 1992), pp. 389–421.

Schama, Simon. *The Embarrassment of Riches: An Interpretation of Dutch Culture in the Golden Age.* New York: Knopf, 1987.

Schmidt, Gary D. *William Bradford: Plymouth's Faithful Pilgrim.* Grand Rapids, Mich.: Eerdmans, 1999.

Schofield, Roger. *The Plague Reconsidered: A New Look at Its Origins and Effects in Sixteenth- and Seventeenth-Century England.* Cambridge: Local Population Studies in association with SSAC Cambridge Group, 1977.

Schroeder, Betty. "The True Lineage of King Philip (Sachem Metacom)." *NEHGR* 144 (July 1990), pp. 211–14.

Schultz, Eric B., and Michael J. Tougias. *King Philip's War: The History and Legacy of America's Forgotten Conflict.* Woodstock, Vt.: Countryman Press, 1999.

Scull, G. D. "Edward Winslow." *NEHGR* 38 (January 1884), pp. 21–26.

Sears, Clara Endicott. *The Great Powwow: The Story of the Nashaway Valley in King Philip's War.* Boston: Houghton Mifflin, 1934.

Seed, Patricia. *Ceremonies of Possession in Europe's Conquest of the New World, 1492–1640.* New York: Cambridge University Press, 1995.

———. "Taking Possession and Reading Texts: Establishing the Authority of Overseas Empires." *WMQ,* 3d ser., vol. 49 (1992), pp. 183–209.

Seelye, John. *Memory's Nation: The Place of Plymouth Rock.* Chapel Hill and London: University of North Carolina Press, 1998.

———. *Prophetic Waters: The River in Early American Life and Literature.* New York: Oxford University Press, 1977.

Sehr, Timothy J. "John Eliot, Millennialist and Missionary." *Historian* 46 (1983–84), pp. 187–203.

———. "Ninigret's Tactics of Accommodation: Indian Diplomacy in New England, 1637–75." *Rhode Island History* 36, no. 2 (1977), pp. 42–53.

Sewall, Samuel. *The Diary of Samuel Sewall, 1674–1729.* 2 vols. Ed. M. Halsey Thomas. New York: Putnam's, 1973.

Shea, Daniel B. " 'Our Old Professed Adversary': Thomas Morton and the Naming of New England." *Early American Literature* 23, no. 1, (1988), pp. 53–69.

Sheppard, John H. "Genealogy of the Winslow Family." *NEHGR* 17, pp. 159–62.

Sherman, Robert M., and Verle D. Vincent. "James Chilton." *Mayflower Families through Five Generations: Volume Two.* Ed. Robert M. Sherman. Plymouth, Mass.: General Society of *Mayflower* Descendants, 1978.

Sherwood, Mary B. *Pilgrim: A Biography of William Brewster.* Falls Church, Va.: Great Oak Press, 1982.

Shorto, Russell. *The Island at the Center of the World.* New York: Doubleday, 2004.

Shuffelton, Frank. "Indian Devils and Pilgrim Fathers: Squanto, Hobomok, and the English Conception of Indian Religion." *NEQ* 49 (1976), pp. 108–16.

Shurtleff, Nathaniel B., ed. *Records of the Colony of New Plymouth in New England.* Boston, 1855; rprt. New York: AMS Press, 1968.

Silverman, David. "The Church in New England Indian Community Life: A View from the Islands and Cape Cod." In *Reinterpreting New England Indians and the Colonial Experience,* edited by Colin G. Calloway and Neal Salisbury. Boston: Colonial Society of Massachusetts, 2004, pp. 264–98.

Siminoff, Faren R. *Crossing the Sound: The Rise of Atlantic American Communities in Seventeenth-Century Eastern Long Island.* New York: New York University Press, 2004.

Simmons, Charles H., ed. *Plymouth Colony Records: Volume 1—Wills and Inventories, 1633–1669.* Camden, Maine: Picton Press, 1996.

Simmons, William S. *Cautantowitt's House.* Providence: Brown University Press, 1970.

———. "Conversion from Indian to Puritan." *NEQ* 52 (1979), pp. 197–218.

———. "The Earliest Prints and Paintings of New England Indians." *Rhode Island History* 41, no. 3 (1982), pp. 73–85.

———. "Return of the Timid Giant: Algonquian Legends of Southern New England." *Papers of the Thirteenth Algonquian Conference,* edited William Cowan. Ottawa: Carleton University, 1982, pp. 237–42.

———. "Southern New England Shamanism: An Ethnographic Reconstruction." In *Papers of the Seventh Algonquian Conference, 1975,* edited by William Cowan. Ottawa: Carleton University, 1976, pp. 217–56.

———. *Spirit of the New England Tribes: Indian History and Folklore, 1620–1984.* Hanover, N.H., and London: University Press of New England, 1986.

Simpson, Alan, and Mary Simpson. Introduction to *Diary of King Philip's War, 1675–1676.* Chester, Conn.: Pequot Press, 1975, pp. 1–66.

Slotkin, Richard. *Regeneration through Violence: The Mythology of the American Frontier, 1600–1860.* Middletown, Conn.: Wesleyan University Press, 1973.

Slotkin, Richard, and James K. Folsom. *So Dreadfull a Judgment: Puritan Responses to King Philip's War, 1676–1677.* Middletown: Wesleyan University Press, 1978.

Smith, Bradford. *Bradford of Plymouth.* Philadelphia: Lippincott, 1951.

Smith, Bruce R. *The Acoustic World of Early Modern England: Attending to the O-Factor.* Chicago: University of Chicago Press, 1999.

Smith, Henry Justin. *The Master of the* Mayflower. Chicago: Willett, Clark, 1936.

Smith, John. *The Complete Works of Captain John Smith (1580–1631)*. 3 vols. Ed. Philip Barbour. Chapel Hill: University of North Carolina Press, 1986.

Smith, Richard, Jr. et al. *Further Letters on King Philip's War*. Providence: Society of Colonial Wars, 1923.

Snow, Dean R., and Kim M. Lanphear. "European Contact and Indian Depopulation in the Northeast: The Timing of the First Epidemics." *Ethnohistory* 35 (Winter 1988), pp. 15–33.

Snow, Stephen Eddy. *Performing the Pilgrims: A Study of Ethnohistorical Role-Playing at Plimoth Plantation*. Jackson: University Press of Mississippi, 1993.

Spady, James. "As If in a Great Darkness: Native American Refugees of the Middle Connecticut River Valley in the Aftermath of King Philip's War." *Historical Journal of Massachusetts* 23 (Summer 1995), pp. 183–97.

Speck, Frank G. "Territorial Subdivisions and Boundaries of the Wampanoag, Massachusett, and Nauset Indians." *Indian Notes and Monographs* 44. Ed. F. W. Hodge. New York: Museum of the American Indian, Heye Foundation, 1928.

Spiess, Arthur E., and Bruce D. Spiess. "New England Pandemic of 1616–1622: Cause and Archaeological Implication." *Man in the Northeast* 34 (1987), pp. 71–83.

Springer, James Warren. "American Indians and the Law of Real Property in Colonial New England." *American Journal of Legal History* 30 (1986), pp. 45–46.

Sprunger, Keith L. *Dutch Puritanism: A History of English and Scottish Churches of the Netherlands in the Sixteenth and Seventeenth Centuries*. Studies in the History of Christian Thought, vol. 31. Ed. Heiko A. Oberman. Leiden: E. J. Brill, 1982.

———. *Trumpets from the Tower: English Puritan Printing in the Netherlands, 1600–1640*. Leiden: E. J. Brill, 1994.

Starkey, Armstrong. *European and Native American Warfare, 1675–1815*. Norman: University of Oklahoma Press, 1998.

Starna, William A. "The Pequots in the Early Seventeenth Century." In *The Pequots in Southern New England*, edited by Laurence M. Hauptman and James D. Wherry. Norman and London: University of Oklahoma Press, 1993, pp. 33–47.

Stavely, Keith, and Kathleen Fitzgerald. *America's Founding Food: The Story of New England Cooking*. Chapel Hill and London: University of North Carolina Press, 2004.

Steele, Ian K. *Warpaths: Invasions of North America*. New York and Oxford: Oxford University Press, 1994.

Stiles, Ezra. *The Literary Diary of Ezra Stiles*. Vol. 3, *1782–1795*. New York: Scribner's, 1901.

Stilgoe, John R. "A New England Coastal Wilderness." *DSNEF* 1980, pp. 89–105.

Stout, Harry S. *The New England Soul: Preaching and Religious Culture in Colonial New England*. New York: Oxford University Press, 1986.

Strachey, William. "A True Repository of the Wreck and Redemption of Sir Thomas Gates, Knight." In *A Voyage to Virginia in 1609*, edited by Louis B. Wright. Charlottesville: University Press of Virginia, 1964, pp. 3–116.

Stratton, Eugene A. *Plymouth Colony: Its History and People, 1620–1691*. Salt Lake City: Ancestry Publishing, 1986.

Swalen, Bert. "Indians of Southern New England and Long Island: Early Period." In *Northeast*, edited by Bruce Trigger. Vol. 15 of William C. Sturtevant, ed., *Handbook of North American Indians*. Washington, D.C.: Smithsonian Institution Press, 1978.

Sweet, David G., and Gary B. Nash, eds. *Struggle and Survival in Colonial America*. Berkeley: University of California Press, 1981.

Takaki, Ronald. "The *Tempest* in the Wilderness: The Racialization of Savagery." In *The*

Tempest, edited by Gerald Graff and James Phelan. Boston and New York: Bedford/ St. Martin's, 2000, pp. 140–72.

Tarule, Robert. *The Artisan of Ipswich: Craftsmanship and Community in Colonial New England.* Baltimore and London: Johns Hopkins University Press, 2004.

Temple, J. H. *History of North Brookfield.* North Brookfield, Mass.: Town of North Brookfield, 1887.

Thacher, James. *History of the Town of Plymouth: From Its first Settlement in 1620, to the Year 1832.* 1835; reprt. Salem, Mass.: Higginson, 1991.

Thomas, Keith. "History and Anthropology." *Past and Present* 24 (April 1963), pp. 3–24.

———. *Religion and the Decline of Magic.* New York: Scribner's, 1971.

Thomas, Peter A. "Contrastive Subsistence Strategies and Land Use as Factors for Understanding Indian-White Relations in New England." *Ethnohistory* 23 (1976), pp. 1–18.

———. "Cultural Change on the Southern New England Frontier, 1630–1665." In *Cultures in Contact: The Impact of European Contacts on Native American Cultural Institutions, A.D. 1000–1800,* edited by W. W. Fitzhugh. Washington, D.C., and London: Smithsonian Institution Press, 1985, pp. 131–61.

Thrower, W. R. *Life at Sea in the Age of Sail.* London: Phillimore, 1972.

Tipson, Baird. "How Can the Religious Experience of the Past Be Recovered? The Examples of Puritanism and Pietism." *Journal of the American Academy of Religion* 43 (1975), pp. 695–707.

Tougias, Michael J. *A Taunton River Journey.* Bridgewater, Mass.: Taunton River Watershed Alliance, 1996.

———. *Until I Have No Country.* Norfolk, Mass.: Weekender Publishing, 2001.

Tougias, Michael J., and Eric Schultz. *King Philip's War: The History and Legacy of America's Forgotten Conflict.* Woodstock, Vt.: Countryman Press, 1999.

Travers, Len, "Reconstructing an Early-Seventeenth-Century 'American' Dialect." *DSNEF* 1983, pp. 120–31.

———, ed. "The Missionary Journal of John Cotton, Jr., 1666–1678." *Proceedings of the MHS.* Boston: Northeastern Press, 1998, pp. 52–101.

Trigger, Bruce, and Wilcomb Washburn, eds. *The Cambridge History of Native Peoples of the Americas.* Cambridge, England: Cambridge University Press, 1996.

Turner, Frederick Jackson. "The First Official Frontier of the Massachusetts Bay." *Publications of the Colonial Society of Massachusetts* 17 (1915), pp. 250–71.

Ulrich, Laurel Thatcher. *Good Wives: Images and Reality in the Lives of Women in Northern New England, 1650–1750.* New York: Oxford University Press, 1982.

Usher, Roland. *The Pilgrims and Their History.* New York: Macmillan, 1920.

Van Zandt, Cynthia J. "Isaac Allerton and the Dynamics of English Cultural Anxiety." In *Connecting Cultures: The Netherlands in Five Centuries of Transatlantic Exchange,* edited by Rosemarijn Hoefte and Johanna C. Kardux. Amsterdam: VU University Press, 1994, pp. 51–76.

Vaughan, Alden T. *New England Frontier: Puritans and Indians, 1620–1675.* 3d ed. Norman: University of Oklahoma Press, 1995.

Vaughan, Alden T., and Daniel K. Richter. "Crossing the Cultural Divide: Indians and New Englanders, 1605–1763." *AAS Proceedings* 90, no. 1 (1980), pp. 23–99.

Villiers, Alan. *Give Me a Ship to Sail.* New York: Scribner's, 1959.

———. "How We Sailed *Mayflower II* to America." *National Geographic* 112, no. 5 (November 1957), pp. 627–72.

———. *The New* Mayflower. New York: Scribner's, 1958.

———. "The Voyage of *Mayflower II.*" *Mariner's Mirror* 44, no. 2 (1958), pp. 91–93.

———. "We're Coming Over on the *Mayflower.*" *National Geographic* 111, no. 5 (May 1957), pp. 708–28.

Vollmann, William T. *Rising Up and Rising Down: Some Thoughts on Violence, Freedom, and Urgent Means.* 7 vols. San Francisco: McSweeney's Books, 2003.

Wakefield, Robert S. "Little Compton RI Marriages." *American Genealogist* 61 (1985–86), pp. 133–40.

———. "Plymouth Colony Casualties in King Philip's War." *American Genealogist* 60 (1984), pp. 236–42.

———. "Richard Church." *American Genealogist* 60 (1984), pp. 129–39.

———. "The Seven Houses of Plymouth." *Mayflower Descendant* 44, no. 1 (January 1994), pp. 22–23.

Waldron, Richard. Letter to Daniel Denison, September 25, 1675, *NEHGR* 23 (1869), pp. 325–27.

Walker, James. Letter to Governor Prince, September 1, 1671, MHS Collections, 1st ser., vol. 6 (1799), pp. 197–98.

Walker, Philip. "Captan Perse & his coragios Company." Edited and with an introduction by Diane Bornstein. *AAS Proceedings* 83 (1973), pp. 67–102.

Walker, Williston, ed. *The Creeds and Platforms of Congregationalism.* 1893. Philadelphia: Pilgrim Press, 1960.

Walker, Zachariah. Letter to his brother, September 23, 1675, Curwen Papers, AAS.

Wall, Robert Emmet, Jr., *Massachusetts Bay: The Crucial Decade, 1640–1650.* New Haven: Yale University Press, 1972.

Walley, Thomas. Letters written during King Philip's War, Curwen Papers, AAS.

Ward, Harry. *Statism in Plymouth Colony.* Port Washington, N.Y., London: Kennikat Press, 1973.

Washburn, Wilcomb E. "Governor Berkeley and King Philip's War." *NEQ* 30 (1975), pp. 363–77.

———. "Seventeenth-Century Indian Wars." In *Northeast,* edited by Bruce Trigger. Vol. 15 of William C. Sturtevant, ed., *Handbook of North American Indians.* Washington, D.C.: Smithsonian Institution Press, 1978.

Watson, Patty Jo, and Mary C. Kennedy. "The Development of Horticulture in the Eastern Woodlands of North America: Women's Role." In *Engendering Archaeology: Women and Prehistory,* edited by Joan M. Gero and Margaret Conkey. Oxford: Basil Blackwell, 1999, pp. 255–75.

Webb, Stephen Saunders. *1676: The End of American Independence.* New York: Knopf, 1984.

Westbrook, Perry D. *William Bradford.* Boston: Twayne, 1978.

Weston, Thomas. *History of the Town of Middleboro.* Boston and New York: Houghton Mifflin, 1906.

Weinstein, Laurie Lee. "The Dynamics of Seventeenth-Century Wampanoag Land Relations: The Ethnohistorical Evidence for Locational Change." *Bulletin of the Massachusetts Archaeological Society* 46, no. 1 (1985), pp. 19–35.

———, ed. *Enduring Traditions: The Native Peoples of New England.* Westport, Conn.: Bergin and Garvey, 1994.

———. "Land Politics and Power: The Mohegan Indians in the Seventeenth and Eighteenth Centuries." *Man in the Northeast* 42 (1991), pp. 9–16.

Whalley, Thomas. Letter to John Cotton, April 17, 1676, Davis Papers, MHS.

———. Letter to John Cotton, July 18, 1676, Davis Papers, MHS.

———. Letter to John Cotton, October 9, 1676, Curwen Papers, AAS.

White, B. R. *The English Separatist Tradition: From the Marian Martyrs to the Pilgrim Fathers.* London: Oxford University Press, 1971.

White, Richard. "Discovering Nature in North America." *Journal of American History* 79 (1992), pp. 874–91.

———. *The Middle Ground: Indians, Empires, and Republics in the Great Lakes Region, 1650–1815.* Cambridge, England: Cambridge University Press, 1991.

Whitney, Gordon. *From Coastal Wilderness to Fruited Plain: A History of Environmental Change.* Cambridge, England: Cambridge University Press, 1994.

Wilbour, Benjamin Franklin. *Notes on Little Compton.* Ed. Carlton C. Brownell. Little Compton, R.I.: Little Compton Historical Society, 1970.

Willard, Simon. "Deposition of Elizabeth Belcher, Martha Remington, and Mary Mitchell," March 4, 1676, Photostats, MHS.

Williams, Alicia Crane. "John Alden: Theories on English Ancestry." *Mayflower Descendant* 39, no. 2; pp. 111–22; 40, no. 2, pp. 133–36; 41, no. 2, p. 201.

———. "John and Priscilla We Hardly Know Ye." *American History Illustrated* 23, no. 8 (December 1988) pp. 40–7.

Williams, Herbert U. "The Epidemic of the Indians of New England, 1616–1620, with Remarks on Native American Infections." *Bulletin of the Johns Hopkins Hospital* 20 (1909), pp. 340–49.

Williams, Roger. *The Complete Writings of Roger Williams.* New York: Russell and Russell, 1963.

———. *The Correspondence of Roger Williams.* 2 vols. Ed. Glenn W. LaFantasie. Hanover, N.H.: University Press of New England, 1988.

———. *A Key into the Language of America.* Ed. John J. Teunissen and Evelyn J. Hinz. Detroit: Wayne State University Press, 1973.

Willison, George F. *Saints and Strangers.* New York: Reynal and Hitchcock, 1945.

Winslow, Edward. *Good Newes from New England.* 1624; rprt. Bedford, Mass.: Applewood Books, 1996.

———. *Hypocrisie Unmasked: A True Relation of the Proceedings of the Governor and Company of the Massachusetts against Samuel Gorton.* 1646; rprt. New York: Burt Franklin, 1968.

Winslow, Josiah. Letter to All Christian People, August 9, 1676, Stewart Mitchell Papers, MHS.

———. Letter to John Leverett, June 21, 1675, Massachusetts Archives, vol. 67, p. 202.

———. Letter to John Leverett, July 6, 1675, Davis Papers, MHS.

———. Letter to John Winthrop Jr., July 29, 1675, MHS Collections, 5th ser., vol. 1 (1871), p. 429.

———. Letter to the King of England, June 26, 1677, MHS *Proceedings* 7 (1864), pp. 481–82.

———. Letter to Weetamo and her husband, July 15, 1675, Winslow Papers, MHS.

Winsor, Justin. "The Bradford Manuscript." MHS *Proceedings,* 2d ser., vol. 11 (1897), pp. 299–304.

———. *A History of the Town of Duxbury.* Boston: Crosby and Nichols, and Samuel G. Drake, 1849.

Winthrop, John. *The History of New England from 1630 to 1649.* Ed. James Kendall Hosmer. 2 vols. New York: Scribner's, 1908.

———. *The Journal of John Winthrop, 1630–1649.* Ed. Richard S. Dunn, James Savage, and

Laetitia Yeandle. Cambridge, Mass., and London: Belknap Press of Harvard University Press, 1996.

Winthrop, John, Jr. Letter to Fitz-John Winthrop, July 9, 1675, MHS Collections, 5th ser., vol. 8 (1882), p. 170.

Winthrop, Wait. *Some Meditations Concerning our Honorable Gentlemen and Fellow Souldiers, in Pursuit of those Barbarous Natives in the Narragansit Country; and Their Service there. Committed into Plain Verse for the Benefit of those that Read it.* n.p., 1675; New London, 1721.

Witherell, Daniel. Letter to John Winthrop Jr., July 29, 1675 (but misdated as 1677), MHS Collections, 3d ser., vol. 10 (1849), p. 118.

Wogan, Peter. "Perceptions of European Literacy in Early Contact Situations." *Ethnohistory* 41 (1994), pp. 407–30.

Wood, Betty. *The Origins of American Slavery: Freedom and Bondage in the English Colonies.* New York: Hill and Wang, 1997.

Wood, William. *New England's Prospect.* Ed. Alden T. Vaughan. Amherst: University of Massachusetts Press, 1977.

Worrall, Arthur. "Persecution Politics and War: Roger Williams, Quakers, and King Philip's War." *Quaker History* 66 (1977), pp. 73–86.

Wright, Irene A. "John Clark of the *Mayflower.*" MHS *Proceedings* 54 (November 1920), pp. 61–76.

———. "Spanish Policy toward Virginia, 1606–1612: Jamestown, Ecija, and John Clark of the *Mayflower.*" *American Historical Review* 25, no. 3 (April 1920), pp. 448–79.

Young, Alexander. *Chronicles of the Pilgrim Fathers.* Boston: Little and Brown, 1841.

Zakai, Avihu. *Exile and Kingdom: History and Apocalypse in the Puritan Migration to America.* Cambridge, England: Cambridge University Press, 1992.

Zuckerman, Michael. "The Fabrication of Identity in Early America." *WMQ,* 3d ser., vol. 34 (1977), pp. 183–214.

———. "Pilgrims in the Wilderness: Community, Modernity, and the Maypole of Merry Mount." *NEQ* 50 (1977), pp. 255–77.

Index

Note: Page numbers in italics refer to maps and illustrations.

Picture Credits

American Antiquarian Society: pp. 227, 289; Author's Collection: pp. 204, 208, 216, 230, 236, 252, 305; Collection Rijksbureau voor Kunsthistorische Documentatie (RKD), The Hague: p. 22; Fruitlands Museums, Harvard, Massachusetts: p. 231; John Carter Brown Library, Brown University: p. 260; Little Compton Historical Society, photo by Edward Denham: p. 313; Massachusetts Historical Society: pp. 1, 11, 16, 58, 80, 209, 213, 234, 322, 336, 341, 346; Massachusetts State Archives—State House: pp. 121; Photograph courtesy Peabody-Essex Museum: p. 240; Pilgrim Hall Museum: pp. iv–v, 83, 102, 107, 159, 164, 174, 176, 181, 201; Plymouth County Commissioners: p. 195; Society for the Preservation of New England Antiquities (SPNEA): p. 351.